The Circle of Initiates
Past and Present

A Brief Generic Biography and Critical Study of the
Structure of Their Rays and Their Initiation Level

Volume I

By the Tibetan Master
Djwhal Khul

Klaire D. Roy

Printed in Canada in March 2016 by Marquis

©The Circle of Initiates, Past and Present, Klaire D. Roy

ISBN: 978-0-9809694-7-4

Orange Palm Publications©
Copyright Registration: first trimester 2016
National Library of Quebec
National Library of Canada

Translated from the original French version (2011) by Aurore Samman
Additional text translated by Johanne Durocher Norchet (2016)

Cover design: Sylvie Auger, Lucie Robitaille, Lucie Létourneau
Typesetting: Sareyu Honan Roy
Translation Reviewers: Kristiane Roy, Sareyu Honan Roy, Stefan Roy
Proofreaders: Lisa Corbeil, Luc Lemaître

Orange Palm Publications©
1206 Saint-Luc Boulevard, Suite 110
Saint-Jean-sur-Richelieu, Quebec, J2Y 1A5, Canada
info@PalmPublications.com
www.PalmPublications.com

I wish to thank D.K. for his patience
and insistence on seeing me accomplish this work with Him,

Thank you also to my guide and spouse, Simhananda,
for his support and love during this process.

And finally thanks to Djwella and Djetsun, our children,
for so joyfully rooting me in life's "Ray-diation".

Contents

Part II: Ray Structures

The Circle of Initiates – Volume II

Foreword by Simhananda

In superior service to Humanity the greater universal religion of the future will be that of LIGHT.

Both the dark occulted Light usually preceding entry into the various gradated levels of emptiness, silence, or shunyata; and the cold, clear Light which is invariably experienced as variegated states of "emptiness" are more deeply penetrated, are to be scientifically studied... taking into account the psychological, psychic and spiritual level of the humanly Divine Consciousness, which inhabits every man, woman and child whose form, (physical and subtle), abides on this planet.

Right psychological training in the future will be based on a sound scientific study of the 7 Rays, which operate universally in the Cosmos, and whose energies and forces categorically condition man, and clearly make him who and what he is, in any particular incarnated time of human history.

The contemporary science of the 7 Rays will, in effect, become the new evolutionary psychology of the future modern man.

A scientific approach toward occult meditation will promote and inspire a fresh avenue to the study of man's evolutionary consciousness.

A modern spiritual direction is required. Novel revolutionary sets of incisive tools and accurate methods are needed to measure, predict and positively influence world affairs, in the allied fields of economics and politics, religion and sociology, medicine and scientific research, anthropology and global ecology.

Consciousness is supplicating man for a cardinal, perhaps plenary, change of thought, to help usher-in the birth of an informed Aquarian Age of enlightened awareness.

This will most likely happen through a radical reorganization of seed ideas, and a definitive shifting of all human knowledge. A new earth is on a crash course to forming an occult tryst with a new heaven.

Many metamorphic, contemporary ways to the Divine will be tried and duly recognized, and will find their rightful niche within the matrix of the Religion of LIGHT.

Every path and pathway, door and doorway, hall and hallway, dharma wheel and Buddha field, will be inspirationally studied and creatively essayed in a visionary process of spiritual networking with the godly goal of "drawing near to Him and He drawing nearer to us".

The next great world religion will assuredly emanate from the Universal LIGHT of the ONE UNIQUE SOURCE… Sometimes called:

"HE WHO IS the ONE without a Second, About Whom Naught Can Be Said".

The enlightened inspiration for this book comes from the prodigious literary outflow of the Hierarchical Master DJWHAL KHUL, the Tibetan, (which is a nom de plume, and not his real name).

His literary amanuensis for the present epoch, the first quarter of the 21st Century, is a clairvoyant woman whose real name, is Klaire D. Roy.

As a conscious and conscientious scribe for Master Djwhal Khul, she delves into a scientific analysis of the rays and their structural schemes, as brought out into applicatory effect by the Monad, Soul, Personality, Mental, Astral and Physical bodies of those individuals, who are here considered to be upon the distinguished list of the "Circle of Initiates, Past and Present".

The close scrutiny and detailed depth of study of the men and women who have influenced human affairs and left their mark upon Humanity, will prove to be a most interesting and passionate purview of the consciousness of the physical form's impact, whilst in incarnation.

Never before, has there been such a comprehensive probe of the influential and interesting personalities of the world, and never has there been such a scholarly study as to the why, where and wherefore, of their Soul's mission.

Whether the predicated subject is Steven Spielberg, Eckart Tolle, Ken Wilber, Sakyong Jamgon Mipham Rinpoche, or Oprah Winfrey of the present times, or Jane Addams, Shakespeare, Benjamin Franklin, Drukpa Kinley, or Atatürk of past eras… all are treated with the utmost respect, and as purposeful beings functioning within the limitations of their environment, and confines of their time.

Their life task, purpose, or destiny is better comprehended through Master Djwhal Khul's deft and compassionate treatment of their main motivating ray, and functional sub-ray structures, affecting their Monad, Soul and Personality construct, together with their Mental envelope, Astral/emotional configuration, Physical body and brain cast.

The ray structure and character delineation of each interesting individual studied in this revolutionary etude, is elaborated psychologically, psychically and occultly by Master Djwhal Khul, in a surprisingly accurate consideration of historic fact and sociological observation.

Every word not only rings true, but if the reader does his own research and homework, he will most probably come to the percipient conclusion that the amalgamated analysis in its minutiae, is as close to the Truth as truth can be.

Also dealt with synergistically in the addendum, the author, Klaire D. Roy details the psychological significance and psychic influence inherent within the rays themselves. She deftly incorporates in the endeavor, all the salient features and fine points to be looked for within each of the five major levels of Initiation.

Included within the study, of course, are generally what an individual's contribution, service and accomplishment should be at a particular Initiatory level, within the scheme of evolutionary development.

Not only individual, but social institutions and even nations, are governed by the fateful impact of the rays upon them. For instance, as a religious institution, the Roman Catholic Church is manifestly characterized by:

- its SOUL Ray, which is 1 — power and politics.

- its PERSONALITY Ray, which is 3 — temporal power procured via commercial enterprise and financial ventures.

- its MENTAL Ray, which is 6 — an amalgam of religious practice, of belief (in Jesus, heaven and hell), original sin, indoctrination, disciplinary measure, penance, one-pointedness, and narrowness of vision.

- its ASTRAL Ray, which is 6 — a show of sincere emotional warmth, passionate prayer and fierce mysticism; and a kindly love with charitable ideals; and the inspiriting of guilt and sin, sin, sin... with the practice of obligatory confession and compensatory, (or punitive), penance; and also demonstrates an ostensibly aggressive, prejudicial catholicism with emphasis on discernible conversion tactics, such as seen in the infamous Inquisition.

- its PHYSICAL Ray, which is 7 — placing emphasis on organizational skills and the practice of rituals... to the point of saintly crystallization.

In summary, the saving grace of the Catholic Church will come about mainly through the means of its great skill in action, (Ray 3 supported by Ray 7), as well as an abundance of love (Ray 2, the synthetic universal Ray), supported by Ray 6, authentic warmth and considerate compassion given out in willing service to the poor and common people everywhere.

Developing man is found to be at a crucial moment in his Initiatory evolution.

He is now being forced to look back upon his historical shortsightedness and past cruelty, and made to reflect seriously upon the dour amplitude of his ignorance. Except for a few enlightened individuals, man in general has never been able to concretely grasp the portentous Truth, which is succinctly expressed in the occult phrase: "All Power, Love, Intelligence and Wisdom that Is and ever was, is to be found Now, in the ever-Living present".

The general perspective of the mass of men is thoroughly lacking in sensitivity, compassion and foresight. There is much too much preoccupation with the life there is to be found in the lower self. That immature, material self likes to dally, seemingly forever (lost) in the foreground of daily life... with its many moods, emotional dramas, social interactions, sexual pleasures, endless ambitions, financial states, changing politics, constant vicissitudes, and vacation time... and all of the ordinary state of affairs which typically characterize the common man, and surprisingly also, many of the spiritual aspirants of the world.

Contrary to past trends and emphasis, it now seems presently opportune for man to gaze with more concentration upon the apparently formless structure of his Being.

He must inquire earnestly into the arena of the rays, energies and forces, which together, dynamize his consciousness, and which, even in the face of powerful opposition, propel his destiny implacably forward, upon the path of Spiritual Evolution.

It may be true that in some lives, or earthly incarnations, there can be found, at rare times, a discernible Soul retrogression, and therefore, a temporary involutionary phase is reluctantly lived.

Nevertheless, the process of the incarnated Soul's ordained progression towards an evocative evolution is invariably assured... despite all the seeming setbacks that may challenge the expanding consciousness of individual invention, or group growth.

Cooperative states of consciousness for soul groups and spacious sensitivity of perceptive awareness for the individual Soul are important goals indeed for Initiates in progress.

The model mechanism of Ray Structure, Ray Interplay and Ray Influence prove to be a competently ideal measuring tool for our greater comprehension of the Circle of Initiates, whose collective thought, inspiration and action, creatively compose the seeds of our future.

This book, transmitted discriminately and compassionately by Master Djwhal Khul to his amanuensis, Klaire D. Roy, is more scholarly, deeper, wiser and more practical than any literature written beforehand on the subject of the rays, and their living dynamic application.

This sensitive study of each Initiate, within the book of 'The Circle of Initiates', is most discerning and captivating. This charming volume invites all readers to go beyond themselves and touch their high states of consciousness, which some within the elite Circle of Initiates did court while in their earthly incarnation.

These select few Initiates attended to the life of group, state, nation and the whole wide world of Humanity, through their intuitive recognition of Spiritual Hierarchy, and through their enlightened service to all of the known Kingdoms of CREATION.

Understandably, some Initiates did fail… or were found failing, (and flailing), in their Soul purpose and Life plan. However, Master Djwhal Khul's constructive criticism and sagacious comments on these temporarily lost and wayward few, remain respectfully impartial and impersonally just.

May there be a true spiritual community of Knowers, and a spiritual continuity of ever evolutionary, ongoing Occult Knowledge. May it accrue in leaps and bounds far into the New Age.

And may this book mark a milestone in our timely recognition of the emergence of the Science of the Rays.

May Master DJWHAL KHUL's perceptive commentaries on individuals and their point of evolution, help metamorphose the transformative making of the spiritual man, (finally), into that of a world Initiate.

Preamble of Master Djwhal Khul

Those who know me will immediately understand that the purpose of this treatise is not to evoke curiosity, nor to encourage the comparison of those initiates who are found therein. In any case, I do not wish to impress, nor influence, whomsoever at all. I graciously accepted to write this primarily exploratory book, in order that the human consciousness opens itself to new perspectives, which will permit man to better understand and appreciate the complete complexity and intelligible immensity that inhabits us all.

Earlier on, in my prior works written by my former amanuensis Alice A. Bailey, I delineated somewhat the fine points of the rays, as well as the Initiations in quite some detail, tarrying not more on their positive than on their negative aspects.

At that time, Humanity showed little interest in seriously working on itself. As a consequence, I was constrained to temporarily forgo the transmission of my teachings. The waiting period, however, was beneficial, for the winds of change blew favourably over the West, whose vision is now opening up to a new era of spirituality. I am not making allusion here to the 'New Age' groups, but rather, to the individual Consciousness in each man, woman and child, which is presently awakening and expanding toward a greater knowledge, and therefore, coming near and nearer to his or her Divine nature.

To those who so desire, the serious study of the influence of the rays offers, without contest, a whole new look at Man and throws a fresh perspective upon what exactly constitutes a human being and what qualities make him universal.

In this book, I am bringing to light both the accurate Initiatory level as well as the Ray-structure of known contemporary personalities, in order to encourage a better understanding of their influence, or effect, upon the aggregate energy of the planet. Certainly, some among you will be veritably shocked, while others will show an honest-to-goodness surprise and even delight, vis-à-vis the degree of Initiation procured by a known individual in this life or in past ones. You will also discover that there are certain karmic connections that weave through and serve to splice certain lives, some of course, remaining rather kindred, while others solicit considerable changes.

You will be better able to see the vast mosaic of life, which inevitably shows itself to be infinitely more complex than the average 'New Age' books purport everything to be. The simple, magical thought of easy transformation does not exist. The only real parameter that truly exists is the astute and maintained effort to acquire, life after life, a greater mastery of our self through the occult process of Initiation and the potent influence of the rays.

Throughout my writings, I often make allusion to the term 'Initiate', in primary reference to the planetary point of view of the individual having reached the First Initiation. At this major turning point, the Soul itself 'initiates' the incarnated earthly vehicle to a whole new, revolutionary energy.

However, the process of evolution is slow, so very slow, that it habitually takes a multitude of lives before the Soul can effect a serious impact upon the evolving Initiate. Therefore, you will not see within this volume, the study of an individual, male or female, found to be energetically inferior to that of the First Initiation[1].

---

[1] NDE: one exception, Nicolae Andruța Ceausescu.

I wish to make the comment before completion of this preamble, that all the levels of Initiation must remain a self-disciplinary responsibility, which each individual so 'Initiated' must assume consciously. It may be well to reiterate that this work was not written for the dubious purpose of comparison, but rather, for the enlightened goal of the world's greater comprehension.

After a comprehensive reading of this book, it is my earnest wish that you look upon yourself and life in a fresh new way… most especially regarding the esoteric subject of Initiations, which most people in the past have consistently misinterpreted to their own personally-biased advantage. The process of Initiation can now be correctly gauged and interpreted in the interest of the greater well-being and evolutionary benefit of every sentient being.

Part I

Presentation of Initiates

 ADDAMS, JANE

Given Name: Jane Addams
Nationality: American
Place and Date of Birth: Cedarville, Illinois (United States), September 6, 1860
Date of Death: Chicago, Illinois (United States), May 21, 1935
Profession: Sociologist, writer and philosopher

MASTER DJWHAL KHUL'S COMMENTARY

Jane Addams was a remarkable woman for her time, who influenced the end of the 19th century and the beginning of the 20th. Without her fight for human rights and liberties, the United States would face enormous political and social difficulties. Without her, democracy would not be what it is in this country that promotes freedom of expression yet still demonstrates resistance to change, even today.

This country houses enormous fears, fears which did not scare Ms. Addams, who fought them relentlessly in order to eradicate them within the population. These fears stemmed from the ignorance subtly promoted by the political world that opposed women's education as well as the social implication of women and immigrants.

Misunderstood by some and wrongly judged by most, like all those who meet the challenge of changing human consciousness for the better, she never ceased to believe in human nature and to hope that humanity would ease the burden of poverty in every respect. She was deeply touched by the misery she was seeing along the streets of American cities, hardship seeking new victims among the least educated and the least affluent.

She displayed an unshakable faith and was supported in her work by Master Djwhal Khul, disciple of Koot Hoomi, and by the Count of St. Germain, who helped her build and structure her humanitarian work. More or less aware of this help, she always knew that she had a task that she needed to achieve in this life.

In a previous incarnation as Maximilien Robespierre, she enjoyed the same impetuous character, but more measured because of a feminine and fragile physical body. Many slanders were propagated concerning Robespierre; we will only say that his excessive devotion (caused by his ray 6 Personality at the time) sometimes lacked vision but never sincerity. He lacked judgement, but he was also ill-judged and wrongly accused of much harm. In his Addams incarnation, he succeeded in lessening his fits of temper in order to achieve this new task entrusted to him. This Soul is presently working in America for humanitarian organisations and as a diplomat. Her identity will not be revealed, as it would be unwise to divulge it now, her work not having been completed.

Let us return to the Jane Addams incarnation.

Initiation Level: 2.5

This initiation level is very commendable.

Ray Structure

Monad: 2	Soul: 2	Personality: 1-6
Mental: 7-5	Astral: 6-4	Physical: 3-7

Monad and Soul

Her Monad had very little influence on her, contrary to her Soul, which manifested a growing influence and directed her actions in many situations. It allowed her to have a gentle and open heart. The constant sadness on her face came from the suffering she felt in all those who were subjected to many forms of injustice. She wished to save as many people as possible but knew that this task would be almost impossible. Let's not forget that her physical body was weakened, which increased this extreme sensitivity.

Personality

Her Personality, governed by the influence of ray 1, sub-ray 6, provided her with strength which supported her all her life. Ray 1 gave her a broader vision and allowed her to easily see the goal to reach (with the help of Ray 7 in her higher mental body). This ray motivated her not to flinch when facing adversity and to keep her focus on the task at hand. It helped her keep her simplicity and not derive any vanity from her successes. She was simply efficient.

Sub-ray 6 endowed her with warmth that softened the rigidity of ray 1, sometimes, in her wish to reach her goal. However, ray 1 not being resentful, diminished the reactions of sub-ray 6 when confronted with injustices. This sub-ray conferred to her a limitless devotion, although well channeled, thanks to the influence of ray 1.

Mental Body

Her mental body, infused with the energy of ray 7, sub-ray 5, allowed her to succeed in business. Ray 7 conferred a logical order for her to carry out her work, quickly strengthened by the contribution of sub-ray 5. Ray 7 enabled her to remain fair and orderly. It allowed a certain assurance in her actions, because with the help of sub-ray 5, she never acted without doing some research and ensuring the validity of her approach.

Sub-ray 5 qualified her with a logic that gave her a brilliant intelligence. She left nothing to chance and possessed an extraordinary power of concentration (increased by the energy of rays 7 and 1). She was not half-hearted but committed in a disciplined and intelligent fashion. It was difficult to make her lose her cool, which would have pleased her detractors.

Astral Body

Her astral body, shaped by the energy of ray 6, sub-ray 4, made her a loving and confronting woman. Ray 6 granted her the enthusiasm, warmth and the wish to help people in need. Not a romantic, in spite of this ray that should have given her this trait, she used the impersonal dedication aspect more instead of the "need for personal love" aspect. More polarized towards the Soul than her personal needs, she never wished to marry or fall in love, because she knew very well that a family would be detrimental to her work.

Sub-ray 4 endowed her with a sense of fight for human rights, which sustained her all her life. Ray 4 also allowed her to be multitalented in many fields. She was never caught off guard and liked challenges. Sometimes subjected to a mild depression, she would quickly take hold of herself, because her Soul and the Masters threw her off internally to prevent her from falling into lethargy.

Physical Body

Her physical body, filled with the energy of ray 3, sub-ray 7, equipped her with a constitution that favoured the execution of her work. Ray 3 gave her an intelligent and subtle mind. She used it efficiently and knew how to outplay talkers unsympathetic to her comments. She had the gift of gab; this gift came, among others, from ray 3 that was always effervescent in her head. She thought fast and acted fast when necessary. She did not put her foot in her mouth and knew how to act adequately when opportunities arose.

Sub-ray 7 added a very particular touch to her thinking, which was refined and orderly. When she made a decision, following a fruitful introspection brought about by this influence that immediately quieted the ceaseless buzzing of ray 3, she had no doubt as to the task at hand and this in the most minute details. This sub-ray endowed her with strong intuition; she knew everything and could guess everything, which sometimes irritated her entourage. We would rather say that her sub-ray 7 physical brain working together with her ray 7 higher mental created a psychic antenna through which the Masters could efficiently communicate.

This woman, unrecognized by most of us, remains a source of inspiration for many who see in her a female leader who was able to display a loving will and was, undoubtedly, efficient in lifting the veil of injustice and, above all, of the ignorance to which America is still too often subjected.

February 18, 2010

 ASHOKA

Given Name: Ashoka Bindusara Maurya
Nationality: Indian
Place and Date of Birth: Pataliputra (India), 304 B.C.
Date of Death: 232 B.C.
Profession: Emperor of the Maurya Dynasty

MASTER DJWHAL KHUL'S COMMENTARY

Ashoka was a great king, a great man who brought a new vision to the Hindu world. Where dissension and anger reigned, he was able, thanks to his attitude, to restore to order the troubled atmosphere of his time. Because India was still basking in Buddha's energy, he knew how to capture the Buddha essence and transform it into an inner elixir that continuously guided him all his life. The Buddha was his main source of inspiration. Having been close to him as a disciple, he kept in his Soul memory this paramount link created when the Buddha was still alive. The Buddha was his Master and this link followed him from life to life, for several incarnations.

His wish to reincarnate as a monarch, like his Master in a past life, allowed him to achieve a lot for his people whom he loved so much. For him, all that had a beating heart possessed the right to live and deserved respect. Thus, he ruled his empire with a mind and a heart increasingly opened.

Initiation Level: 3.2

He possessed a certain vision that guided him in his task. Often feeling lonely, he took refuge in his Soul and let its energy rock him. His greatest regret was the absence of a successor at the level of his expectations, because the empire after his death returned to colours he disliked (violence, animal sacrifices and cast inequalities). However, thanks to him, India was never again the same.

Ray Structure

Monad: 2	Soul: 2	Personality: 3-1
Mental: 7-5	Astral: 6-2	Physical: 3-7

Monad and Soul

His Monad had not yet carried out a serious work, although its influence was certainly demonstrated. As to his Soul, it was his most faithful companion, even though sometimes it was troubling and hurtful to his Personality. He noticed this dichotomy within himself and knew how to distinguish the Soul's desires, more altruistic, from those of the Personality still attracted by success and beautiful objects.

Personality

His Personality, influenced by the union of ray 3, sub-ray 1, allowed him to act with discernment and firmness. He liked to manipulate, at first for his own pleasure, then for other's pleasure. Ray 3 made him curious and thirsty for knowledge. It gave him a taste for travelling and experimentation, especially on the meditative level, because he strongly practiced meditation at the end of his life. He did not renounce the world because of his love for his country. This ray made him a great scholar; he enjoyed explaining things while leaving to others the possibility of teaching him. He had a great humility which came mainly from the influence of his Soul.

His sub-ray 1 gave him the strength to govern and to attract respect. Sometimes, he could be tough and severe. However, his sense of justice always prevailed and he knew how to communicate his love through his ray 6, sub-ray 2 astral body.

Mental Body

With a ray 7, sub-ray 5 mental body, he had the capacity to rule in a very balanced way. Ritualistic, even superstitious at times, he governed and conducted business as he wished. He could see far and well. His ray 7 gave him the taste for beauty and the respect for all that surrounded him. Always well-groomed, he would never go unnoticed even when he dressed like a pauper to sound out the people.

Sub-ray 5 conferred to him a very intelligent and brilliant mind. He knew how to calculate risks and act accordingly. He never lost a battle, whether at the physical level or with words. He always found the right reply to everything.

Astral Body

His astral body, influenced by ray 6, sub-ray 2, made him a loving, warm and discreet monarch. Ray 6 conferred to him the sense of loyalty and family (even extended). Faithful to his ideas, his beliefs and his family, he could not stand treason; however, forgiveness was easy for him. He would have become a great politician had he lived among us.

Thanks to his sub-ray 2, he was sensitive and empathetic; he could easily put himself in someone's shoes and feel his happiness or his distress. He had to be careful because, at times, he would demonstrate too much sensitivity and show a love that could appear as a weakness to those around him. Luckily, his strong Personality easily masked this so-called weakness in the eyes of those who could have taken advantage to supersede him.

Physical Body

His ray 3, sub-ray 7 physical body gave him a pleasant appearance to look at and endowed him with a remarkable physical resistance. Indefatigable, he did not sleep much. Ray 3 allowed him to be fast and efficient. He enjoyed walking and meditated while walking. During his first years, it was often difficult for him to remain quiet. He was constantly on the move and could not adequately enjoy the moments in life where rest was recommended. However, as he grew older, he succeeded in dominating the constant agitation caused by ray 3 in order to rest in the contemplation and the ritualism at his disposal through the influence of ray 7.

Sub-ray 7 conferred to him an imposing bearing favoring respect and gratitude. He was loved and appreciated by his people. Sometimes misunderstood and misjudged, he always elicited respect even during discordant times.

Ashoka lived a noble life that allowed him to become an ascetic in several following incarnations. He lived in isolation in order to perfect his evolution and live his fourth initiation at the time when Jesus lived. He was one of his Masters when Jesus travelled before reaching age 30. He remained with him approximately a year in a cavern located at the north of what is now known as Calcutta.

He lived several incarnations as a hermit. He does not like to be in the limelight preferring discretion and isolation.

This man was a star in this world, a star still shining today because of the changes he was able to bring into the Hindu mentality. Presently incarnated, he lives in the West. His Head Office is located in Europe, mainly in Istanbul.

October 22, 2010

BACH, JOHANN SEBASTIAN

Given Name: Johann Sebastian Bach
Pseudonym: The Cantor of Leipzig
Nationality: German
Place and Date of Birth: Eisenach, Thuringia (Germany) March 21, 1685
Date of Death: Leipzig (Germany), July 28, 1750
Profession: Composer, organist and Baroque musician

MASTER DJWHAL KHUL'S COMMENTARY

Johann Sebastian Bach was a renowned composer whose legacy is one of extraordinary music, still misunderstood in its most occult aspects. His music allowed the union of the two aspects of the Soul, the ego aspect incarnated by the human soul and the light aspect incarnated by the divine Soul. In this union lives what we call the occult harmony, which vibrates within the world of matter.

This simply means that Bach succeeded in making the material aspect of things less dense and with more light. To listen to his music gives the possibility to create in oneself the desire to grow and evolve towards a more divine aspect of ourselves. However, desire not being action, although it precedes the latter, will not bring changes as long as the human soul listening to Bach's music does not want to evolve towards its own light incarnated by the divine Soul, which proves to be definitely more evolved.

While privileged in many respects, his life was not easy; he constantly suffered from fatigue and found it difficult to make the material and musical aspects of his life coexist. Music allowed him to experience harmony, essential to the creation of his art. He would forget everything, but daily matters would rapidly catch up with Bach forcing him to remain functional, down to earth, a condition he would sometimes find difficult, even painful.

Initiation Level: 2.4

He was very evolved for his time. Because of this, he would often feel alone and misunderstood.

Ray Structure

Monad: 2	Soul: 2	Personality: 2-3
Mental: 7-5	Astral: 6-4	Physical: 3-6

Monad and Soul

His Monad did not really exercise any influence; however, the influence of his Soul was increasingly felt. Internally, he received certain information that he qualified as intuitions and that guided him in the composition of his music. His ray 2 Soul gave him wisdom. He loved life, music, his family and his friends. People appreciated his company thanks to his genius that permeated his music.

Personality

His Personality, influenced by ray 2, sub-ray 3, made him a kind and nice man suffering sometimes from excessive sensitivity. His ray 2 shaped him as a good teacher, someone who taught with passion and love. He liked to see his students work with an energy indicative of this passion that he succeeded in passing on to them. This ray made him a good listener to the needs of others, and he was able to adjust rather easily.

Sub-ray 3 created in him the beat that translated into notes under his fingers. This sub-ray also granted him the leisure to be a good diplomat and to adapt well to situations. It also gave him the capacity to work on several things simultaneously. He never stopped, which caused in him this great fatigue that he forgot most of the time because he was relentlessly active.

Mental Body

His mental body, imbued with energy from ray 7, sub-ray 5, allowed him to be disciplined, and responsive to the subtle world that transmitted certain melodies to him. Ray 7 enticed him to concentrate and to be constantly busy. This ray also enabled him to absorb a lot of tension and to remain balanced. Do not forget that he had many children and needed a lot of focus to compose in this noise.

Sub-ray 5 heavily anchored him in the material world because he had to provide for his family. He actually made certain decisions thanks to this influence. It dictated some rules of conduct for him to follow in order to ensure more stability in his life and, therefore, to be able to provide for the needs of his family. This sub-ray granted him a concrete aspect that forced him to always remain "here and now" when he must.

Astral Body

The influence of his astral body, coloured with ray 6, sub-ray 4, gave him the sense of family life. Ray 6 made him affectionate despite huge inner tensions. It shaped him to be devoted, loving and warm to his family and also towards his music. However, ray 6 induced him to sometimes be stubborn and narrow-minded, as he did not like to change his mind.

Sub-ray 4 conferred an "artistic" aspect that he controlled well. He sometimes experienced emotional ups and downs. However, under the strong influence of his mental body, he managed to maintain a serene balance. He could have easily fallen into depression but by clinging to his mental body and to his ray 6 astral body, he was able to maintain hope and grow internally. This sub-ray 4 equipped him with this courageous aspect that allowed him to never give up.

Physical Body

His physical body, under the influence of ray 3, sub-ray 6, conferred to him a rather sturdy constitution. Ray 3 gave him agility that allowed his brain to quickly compose his musical arrangements. This ray also prepared him to carry on a lot of work in various fields (writing, teaching, music, family life, marital life, etc.). Being idle displeased him, a feeling derived from the influence of this ray 3 that gave him a particular *joie de vivre* he almost always kept.

Sub-ray 6 sparked in him a certain strength that complemented the agility of ray 3. This latter ray gave him the ability to appreciate life's pleasures and made him a passionate individual. Bach was faithful to his ideas and to his loved ones. He was also devoted and devout.

Johann Sebastian Bach was a musical genius who still influences our times. One cannot listen to his music without feeling a deep devotion for everything which moves us internally. He succeeded in capturing the essence of our immortal passion and transforming this feeling into music. He lives today in Tibet, hidden in a monastery. He holds an important position within the Buddhist community. He temporarily withdrew from the world of music in order to deepen his inner being. This is his second consecutive life as a Tibetan monk, the first having been very short.

August 26, 2009

 # BAILEY, ALICE ANN

Given Name: Alice LaTrobe Bateman
Nationality: British
Place and Date of Birth: Manchester (England), June 16, 1880
Date of Death: Vatican, December 15, 1949
Profession: Writer, esotericist and occultist

MASTER DJWHAL KHUL'S COMMENTARY

This remarkable woman was a precious friend for many years. Thanks to her, Eastern wisdom became more occult, more suited to the West. She allowed me to transmit, at my beloved Master's request, important information that has helped the conscious man to better understand himself as well as life, not to say "lives", because man possesses more than one body, having an effect on different aspects of the conscious Universe, but mainly the unconscious.

Ms. Bailey did not live a happy life. An Initiate, whoever he may be, is rarely given the possibility of living a peaceful life, because his duty is to promote and to foster changes at the level of the collective consciousness, which always triggers uncomfortable turbulences for the Initiate as well as for those he is attempting to help.

She worked hard, under my guidance, to offer a more effective teaching to a humanity seeking profound truths. She pursued the work undertaken by Helena Blavatsky. This resulted in making the Masters' faces more accessible and the awakening of man more conscious. Secrets were revealed, secrets which coexist with humanity's occult past. Ms. Bailey was able to become a good instrument for the transmission of information that is still surprising today, and which fosters spiritual progress on Earth. Often criticized and misunderstood, she was determined to continue her task relentlessly.

She knew that her work would be better understood in the decades following her death. The most important aspect was that these teachings gave back to man the responsibility of his life and his evolution in this solar system.

Initiation Level: 3.5

Ray Structure

Monad: 2	Soul: 2	Personality: 2-3
Mental: 1-7	Astral: 6-4	Physical: 3-6

Monad and Soul

Her Monad had little influence because her Soul's influence was more important. However, the Monad knew how to direct her towards a more occult teaching and contributed to reduce her fears, of which she had plenty.

Her Soul exercised a great influence on her writing; thanks to this awakening (the potential of the light of her Soul), I was able to get close enough to transmit to her information on the hidden aspect of man and his evolution. Her Soul was our meeting point and the instrument which allowed her to undertake and complete such a huge task.

Personality

Her ray 2, sub-ray 3 Personality, made her an intelligent and sensitive woman. Ray 2 gave her a sensitivity and an intuition that served her in her work. This ray made her open despite her fears, which often created obstacles that later had to be eliminated by her ray 1 mental body. Because of her ray 2 Personality, she had to suffer an unhappy first marriage; she cultivated certain romantic ideas (the influence of ray 6 in her astral body) and wished to "save the world." Finally, she understood her mistake and put herself at the "service of the world" with love and patience. The influence of the energy of her ray 2's (she had three in her make-up) fostered in her the culture of a great humility, which allowed her the possibility to reach the third initiation at age 30.

Because of her sub-ray 3, she was capable of surviving difficult times, as she was able to accomplish a lot in a short period of time. During the transition period between her two marriages, this sub-ray supported her in taking care of her daughters' well-being. She had the ability to express herself well, thanks to this sub-ray's influence. Her ray 3's, she had two, helped her find solutions and not get discouraged.

Mental Body

Her mental body, equipped with a ray 1, sub-ray 7, proved to be necessary for the writing of her books. Her ray 1 remained focused and determined, because she needed all her capacity of concentration in order to convey what I dictated to her through her Soul. This ray allowed her to weather the storm "energetically" and not believe she was losing her mind. It boosted her character which strengthened her ray 2, as well as giving her "a backbone." Without this ray 1, it would have been impossible for her to complete her task with me.

Her sub-ray 7 allowed her to adjust the energy thus that the teachings were direct, precise and detailed. It gave her the ability to better see the framework of the inner planes and to descend it into matter. It also offered her the possibility to better understand the occult aspect of her writings, particularly those pertaining to white magic.

Astral Body

Her ray 6, sub-ray 4 astral body, endowed her with warmth, which sometimes compensated for the coldness of the ray 1 in the mental body. Ray 6 allowed her to take good care of her daughters, although she was too attached to them, which delayed her work somewhat. She loved them deeply and dedicated her time and warmth to them. In her private life, she proved to be affectionate, charming and always ready to help others. This ray 6 inspired her dedication towards her family, myself and her work. She was not the type to let people down.

Sub-ray 4 was necessary because it gave her fluidity in her emotional life, as well as in her writings. It allowed her to conceive that the impossible did not really exist, that it was simply just a limitation of the human brain. This sub-ray also gave her the taste for beauty and things done well. It also endowed her with a fighting spirit for her family as well as for her task.

Physical Body

She had a pleasant appearance. Ray 3 imparted on her a dynamic gait and the capacity to work rapidly and efficiently. The enormity of the task to be accomplished did not scare her as she enjoyed challenges and knew how to face them. This ray allotted her a body that could bear a lot of tension and work without interruption, although she felt tired.

Sub-ray 6 added determination to her system of thought. When she had a precise idea, she would not easily let it go. One can say that she was sometimes narrow-minded and that good explanations were needed for her to change her mind.

This woman is presently in incarnation in America where she is consciously working for the Masters. We will keep her identity secret.

March 6, 2010

 # BEETHOVEN, LUDWIG VAN

Given Name: Ludwig van Beethoven
Nationality: German
Place and Date of Birth: Bonn (Germany), December 17, 1770
Date of Death: Vienna (Austria), March 26, 1827
Profession: Composer and musician

MASTER DJWHAL KHUL'S COMMENTARY

A remarkable man with a strong and dauntless Personality, Beethoven not only loved music, but was continually inhabited by it. Music was without a doubt his premier passion and he envisioned it as his whole life purpose. His Soul's role was to channel a musical potency that would influence many generations to come, in order that people deepen and sensitize themselves to the reality of their inner self.

By dint of his determination and strength of courage, Beethoven was able to woo from the high heavens a music that would not only deeply delight, but could make the trumpets of angels be heard in every dimension of the Universe.

Had he lived in our modern era, it would have been impossible for him to round out, or complete his mission. The instruments of his era were much more adaptable to a form of musical expression which vibrates with an outpouring of naturally acoustic sounds, rather than electronic ones. His growing deafness allowed his inner ear to greatly refine itself, thereby according him the possibility to capture the mesmerizing beauty and utter harmony of sound from the subtle planes. This infirmity cut him off from the outside world and allowed him to hear what no other human being had perceived previously. Immersed in and riding upon great celestial waves, he often felt unable to transmit them exactly and correctly through his music; he, therefore, endured great hardships of interpretation and great frustration. However, he was a Gandarva, a celestial musician who was sent into incarnation in order to help Humanity grow and evolve more rapidly.

Born into a family that gave him the solid musical foundation needed for his specialized mission, he was consequently, divinely adumbrated, or celestially enveloped, by a Musical Entity which emanated from the higher spheres of this planet; we could even say from the seventh heaven of the seventh astral dimension, which would qualify him as an incarnated *Gandarva* in the eyes of those who can "see" and those who "know".

His life was distressingly difficult, which at that time period, was the common lot shared by most people; misery was ever-present. Thanks to the other-worldly beauty Beethoven transmitted through his music, he was able to alleviate many heavy hearts and infuse them with a just measure of hope.

Initiation Level: 3.2

His initiation level of 3.2 was very rare for that epoch. Beethoven suffered greatly, as a result of the incomprehension of those close to him, the minikin smattering of real culture people had, plus the betrayal of those who claimed to be his friends. Brusque by nature, (we will understand why when we study his rays), he was a frank and direct individual and could seem cruel at times, which was not really the case. Forged in the school of hard knocks, he responded accordingly to those who approached him. Frustration often overwhelmed him and easily transformed itself into anger and fury when he was unduly disturbed, for this inopportuned him and made him lose the very precious thread connecting him to his "inner" music.

Ray Structure

Monad: 2	Soul: 2	Personality: 1-3
Mental: 4-7	Astral: 6-4	Physical: 3-4

Monad and Soul

His Monad and Soul instilled in him a great sensitivity, which at times tortured him. Detesting seeming appearances and finding them deceitful, he revealed little by way of outer refinement. However, he proved to be a highly cultivated and subtly refined individual in his inner being, where the most exquisite and harmonious melodies gave voice from out of the Silence, inspired by his Soul, as well as other celestial sways. He truly heard what no one else could hear.

Personality

His ray 1, sub-ray 3 Personality enabled him to be strong-willed and to pursue his destiny relentlessly. Ray 1 gave him a forceful Personality, which many found abrasive. He was endowed with the will to succeed, which helped persuade the heavenly music haunting him incessantly, to descend to the physical plane. Ray 1 also gave him the required strength and capacity to completely channel the Celestial Entity who was responsible for the transmission of his musical genius. Without the major influence of this ray, Beethoven would not have accomplished as much, nor attained, the true greatness that he did.

His sub-ray 3 Personality accorded him the measure of manipulation he needed, thereby allowing him to obtain what he wanted. However, he rarely made use of this energy, preferring rather the ray 1's honesty and forthrightness. Nevertheless, when his deafness started to bother him and get the better of him, this sub-ray helped him to conceal his weakness, so that it would not unduly hamper his work.

Mental Body

His mental body equipped with a ray 4, sub-ray 7, frequently tormented him. However, it also allowed him to become the ingenious instrument who channelled and transcribed (relatively perfectly) what he heard. Musically, he seemed to be adorned with special antennae springing sensitively from his consciousness, giving him the possibility (and opportunity) to hear what remained inaudible to the common mortal. Ray 4 would grant him no rest. He worked night and day to capture, transcribe, and play the heavenly music he heard. His working methodology sometimes seemed like a slow form of torture. Silence could never reign in his head, as this ray detected (without repose) those sounds which he metamorphosed into music.

The sub-ray 7 proved to be a perfect complement to his ray 4 mental body. This being the ray of ritual and magic, permitted him to transcribe rather accurately what he heard innerly, despite his deafness. Being also the ray of ceremony and order, it proved indispensable to him in the classification and writing of what he heard. Sometimes, he really did not know where this music started, or what denouement it should have. This sub-ray allowed him to discern a logical progression to the musical sounds he was able to apprehend.

Astral Body

His ray 6, sub-ray 4 astral body, bestowed upon him a tempestuous temperament. He was naturally intense as well as hot headed, although contrapuntally, he could be very sensitive, deep and expressively warm in his composition of music, to which he was indisputably devoted. The influence of ray 6 altered his moods according to what he lived momentarily. He could be warm one moment, then several minutes later he would become cold and distant, or even hard and intractable, if he felt that he had been betrayed, misunderstood, or misjudged by his peers. He often isolated himself, fleeing from that which he detested the most: that is, the baseness of human nature, embodied by those who would sell out to the highest bidder, either for fame or fortune. Being wholehearted in almost everything he undertook, forgiveness did not come easily to him... except when he detected sincerity in the eyes of a poor soul entreating him for clemency.

The sub-ray 4 plagued him with emotional ups and downs, which increased the destructive side of his Personality. He rarely took good care of himself. His lifestyle was characterized by a constant self-destruction as he kept himself too busy with work. Washing, eating and dressing nicely were in his eyes, a waste of time, merely affectations of the societal life he detested. If he could have fled to a place far away from everything, including the most basic needs of the human body, he would have done so.

Physical Body

His physical body, which was upon ray 3, sub-ray 4, granted him a fair measure of vigour, as well as a highly useful sensitivity. Ray 3 conferred upon him a powerful mind and a well-honed gift for repartee. He hated indulging in small talk, although he could express himself very well, and easily outmaneuver challengers. He liked having the last word and silencing those who made life difficult for him. It was safer and wiser to stay on his good side, as his skill with words was as sharply honed as his musical talent, nothing short of exceptional.

His sub-ray 4 Physical ensured that he could delicately feel musical vibrations through his skin, through his refined sense of touch. The sound vibrations emitted by his piano transferred the aural waves of what he wanted to produce to his receptive and intuitive physical body. This sub-ray also gifted him with a rugged-like beauty, (almost savage in nature), which pleased women enormously.

This creative giant of a man has yet to be reincarnated. He is presently operating on those higher dimensional planes, carefully planning a strategy for a revolutionary new generation of music, which will come to pass in the near ensuing years, when his next incarnation is destined to occur, circa 2020.

February 28, 2009

Blavatsky, Helena Petrovna

Given Name: Helena Petrovna von Hahn
Nationality: Russian
Place and Date of Birth: Yekaterinoslav (Russia), July 30, 1831
Date of Death: London (England) May 8, 1891
Profession: Adventurer, writer and occultist

Master Djwhal Khul's Commentary

Madame Helena Blavatsky was a remarkable woman in every respect, although difficult to deal with at times. Always devoted to the cause of the Masters, she made her life even as she redeemed it. The unrelenting intensity of her life permitted her to settle an equally intense karmic debt she had contracted with the Ashram of ray 1, a debt which definitely, also affected the Ashram of ray 2. She had certain reparation to pay and she exonerated herself well.

In what possible way could a third-level initiate, whom she was in her previous incarnation as the influential Count of Cagliostro, break faith with or betray the Masters? To put it simply, by according much too much importance to the goal, and ignoring, or neglecting to listen to important basic advice regarding the proper administration of an Ashram. If such a transgression takes place and it is serious, the initiate pays dearly and is obliged to make conscious reparations in a later incarnation.

Initiation Level: 4.5

At the time of her death, her initiation level was 4.5; she is presently working toward her fifth initiation, which she should attain by the year 2025. She currently lives in Russia and inhabits a man's body.

Ray Structure

Monad: 2	Soul: 1	Personality: 3-6
Mental: 1-5	Astral: 6-2	Physical: 3-6

Monad and Soul

Her great strength was derived from her Monad, supported by the strength of her soul. This time, she worked in total devotion to the Masters and her love for the Hierarchy was incontestable. Sometimes, her ray 1 Soul made her too frank and too direct, but it also accorded her a will of iron, which helped in the accomplishment of her life mission, despite hindrances.

Personality

Her Personality, consisting of ray 3, sub-ray 6, inspired a breadth of genuine flexibility into her robust desire to achieve her life's goal. Ray 3 granted her the ability to adapt to any situation. She sometimes liked to provoke people in order to stir a certain questioning in those whom she addressed. Also, she carefully chose her words to produce an energizing effect in them.

Her sub-ray 6 gave her a dedication and stubbornness which clearly defined her, growing out of the intense desire to serve the Masters at any cost. It also allotted her a fugacious warmth which compensated somewhat for the coolness of her ray 1 in both the Soul and mental body. In addition, the sub-ray 6 also gave her the will to never give up, which served her well during her earthly travels and spiritual quests.

Mental Body

Her vivacious intelligence was conjugated by the congruence of her ray 1, sub-ray 5 mental body. Ray 1 gave her the courage and strength to persevere, despite all the difficulties and obstacles she encountered. It also conferred upon her a clarity of vision and allowed her to move and motivate people. She was mentally polarized and sympathized little with mysticism, due, in part, to the particular configuration of her mental body.

Her sub-ray 5 bestowed upon her the singular manner with which she expressed herself, that is, affirmatively and with conviction. It also allowed her to be more occult than mystical. Thanks to this sub-ray she could see all the work to be done in concrete terms without fear of consequences. She could also explicate and extrapolate upon the so-called indescribable. The ray 5, being primarily rational, permitted her to intromit a firm foundation for intuitive understanding into her listeners, even as she forayed forth into an occult exegesis of the divinely mysterious Spiritual Worlds.

Astral Body

Her ray 6, sub-ray 2 astral body, made her human in her arbitrations. Ray 6 allowed her to be attentive and helpful to others. It also garnered her with that single-minded passion and dedication that so characterized her in the realization of her lifework. She was a woman of authentic authority, (due to her ray 6 which dictates and ray 1 which directs). She knew how to claim her rightful place; she could in no uncertain terms be considered lukewarm. In terms of friendship, she was loyal and devoted; we could count on her any time.

Her sub-ray 2 blessed her with a type of sensitivity which enabled her to be genuinely attentive to the needs of others. This sub-ray also bestowed upon her an intuitive acuity that never failed her. She clearly could "feel" and she responded accordingly.

Physical Body

Her physical body, which was upon ray 3 with a sub-ray 6, granted her great resistance and perseverance, as was the case for Ms. David-Neel. Despite pain and discomfort, she perdured and attained her goal. The ray 3 gave her a positive toughness and graced her with an intelligent and quick-thinking brain. Indeed, she was a difficult person to box into a corner, and her gift for repartee was truly formidable.

Her sub-ray 6 provided her with an apparent corpulence necessary to her; otherwise, she would have left her physical body more rapidly. This particular sub-ray prompted her to appreciate fine food, as well as the niceties of life. Paradoxically, the excess weight she carried permitted her to be more efficient, as it obliged her to slow down and focus even more on her work.

Her contacts with the Himalayan Masters were genuine, and They dictated part of their knowledge to her. They provided for an adequate development of her occult side without any distortion. Both her vision and intuition, almost perfect in all respects, were educed from the apt conjunction of her mental body with her Monad.

June 11, 2007

 # BROTHER ANDRÉ

Given Name: Alfred Bessette
Nationality: Canadian
Place and Date of Birth: Saint-Grégoire-le-Grand, Québec (Canada), August 9, 1845
Date of Death: Saint-Laurent, Québec (Canada), January 6, 1937
Profession: Religious leader

MASTER DJWHAL KHUL'S COMMENTARY

A pious and reserved man, Brother André knew how to transmit a particular faith to the French Canadian people of his time. Incredibly influenced by ray 6, this man, devoted to his God or if you prefer his conception of God, could sometimes reveal himself to be very hard and uncompromising, particularly towards the feminine nature of which he did not understand. Limited by his level of consciousness that was relatively little evolved, he could not see beyond certain appearances that sometimes proved to be deceptive.

His compassion for the poor and for human beings derived from the influence of rays 6 and 2. He could give everything wholeheartedly and feel the pain of people suffering. However, influenced by the Christian religion that frequently generated fear more than love and compassion, he at times demonstrated a subtle arrogance and a disdain towards certain behaviours he considered reprehensible. He sees his errors now, from where he is as he has not yet taken a physical body. A time of rest is necessary because he wore out his physical body and exhausted his astral body with his work. This depletion results mainly from the fact that he could not abstain from judging and acting ruthlessly against sins; thus, the energy of love could not flow freely and regenerate him.

His miracles were, in large part real. He drew directly from the cosmic energy produced by prayers, and by the affluence of the faithful and their beliefs within the Catholic Church. He prayed correctly and his prayers touched the conducting fiber of the energy of good that flows within the energy of the ether transported within the ethereal body of the planet. This faculty came from a recent previous life where he learned to concentrate well and heal through earthly medical means. In that life as a doctor, he developed a good intuition that served him throughout his incarnation as "Brother André."

Recently canonized, he is now recognized as a Saint within the Catholic Church, which reasserts the value of the Church and its believers. We can confirm that he was a saint as to reach saintliness does not always require a very high level of evolution. The combined effects produced by rays 6 and 2 can sometimes mirror sainthood without having really reached the state of Sanctity with a capital "S".

Initiation Level: 1.3

He had begun the process of opening his heart, which the majority of the population had not yet attained. He loved better than most people but still with a lot of imperfections. Thoroughly study his life and you will understand.

Ray Structure

Monad: 2	Soul: 6	Personality: 6-2
Mental: 3-7	Astral: 6-4	Physical: 3-2

Monad and Soul

His Monad and his Soul exerted little influence. However, thanks to his Personality, the Soul was able to transmit a special energy to improve his life and its expression.

Personality

His Personality, warm at times, but often distant and cold, was shaped by the influence of ray 6 but mainly by the influence of sub-ray 2. Ray 6 gave him an air of sanctity and kindness when he was active only, because none of his pictures reveal a really loving nature. His severe features expressed more frustration and fatigue than love for his fellow man. However, he mellowed towards the end of his life, his Soul's energy wanting to be more active. He possessed a certain arrogance betrayed by the corners of his mouth, at times martyrical and other times subtly arrogant. He could display charm and warmth when he did not feel threatened by the behaviour of those he would mix with. It is true that the lack of energy at the level of his physical body exhausted his emotional body and largely influenced his Personality. Always tired, he carried the feeling of being constantly burdened.

The sub-ray 2 of his Personality sometimes softened his look and rendered him even angelic for short moments. He would then resume the task he was supposed to carry on, which gave him the impression of forgetting himself and working with devotion for God's glory. He entertained great illusions but who does not have any? His self-styled humility came from the combined influence of rays 6 and 2 that aroused a lack of confidence in himself, often confused with humility.

Mental Body

His ray 3, sub-ray 7 mental body allowed him to survive and not sink into mental illness. Very sensitive (because of his lack of energy), he experienced great difficulty remaining centered and efficient. However, the influence of his ray 2's offered him the possibility to become a great contemplative, which also ensured that he remained somewhat balanced in spite of the difficulties he encountered. The influence of ray 3 was such that despite a slightly reduced intelligence because of his lack of energy, he was able to work in an acceptable way in his community. This ray also urged him to be perseverant in spite of his fatigue and discouragement that sometimes wore him down.

Sub-ray 7 conferred on him a desire for perfection in everything, which increased the effect of his ray 6's that became a little fanatic and judgemental. He had fixed ideas on several thorny issues (women, who he considered inferior to men; children who he found too turbulent and sometimes not too intelligent; childbirth, sexuality, alcohol abuse, etc.). He was fragile and religious life gave him the opportunity to find a particular strength in order not to yield to his desires he believed to be "sins."

Astral Body

His astral body of ray 6 sub-ray 4 made him fragile and very superstitious. He disliked the unpredictable and preferred the comfort of routine to the challenges of the unknown. A lot of fears tormented him, fears created both by the influence of ray 6 (fear of sin, of the devil, of God's punishment) and of ray 2 (fear of death, of being sick, fear of women, etc.) However, his great faith (coming from his ray 6's) incited him to go beyond his fears. It is true he would seek refuge in prayer, which often represented an escape and a real shield against life's bad influences. We also have to say that ray 6 in general conferred to him a stubbornness that served him all his life, sometimes for the good and sometimes for the lesser good.

His sub-ray 4 provided him with a great sensitivity that he hid beneath an austere appearance. He often felt depressed and his behaviour as a martyr regularly bordered self destruction. He lived ups and downs that he hid behind his devotion and deprivations.

Physical Body

Physically fragile, he remained more influenced by sub-ray 2. Ray 3 had to give in to his unconscious desire to be "weak" and "fragile" in order to cultivate the humility he believed to be necessary to his personal life (at the beginning) and spiritual life (later). However ray 3 allowed him to be tenacious and not to easily surrender in spite of the difficulties (sent by God).

Sub-ray 2 coloured all his life for better and for worse. It rendered him sensitive, fragile and empathetic at times. However, when his physical energy diminished, he would become more a victim of the influence of this sub-ray, which created in him fears and behaviours revealing a high level of closure. It then led him to isolate himself in prayer and flee from his entourage who no longer understood him.

This man will reincarnate when the time comes for him to reach another level of evolution. He still has to wait for a while because the energy carried by the adoration of those faithful to him temporarily impedes his own evolution.

November 4, 2010

 # Bruckner, Anton

Given Name: Josef Anton Bruckner
Nationality: Austrian
Place and Date of Birth: Ansfelden (Austria), September 4, 1824
Date of Death: Vienna (Austria), October 11, 1896
Profession: Organist and composer

Master Djwhal Khul's Commentary

Anton Bruckner lived a sad life, though interesting from the standpoint of evolution. We say "sad" because he felt a lot of solitude and never really felt appreciated in several areas of his life. He had a subdued nature and lacked the necessary charisma to create favourable impressions coming from his Personality. Yet, his soul emitted a special light that only Initiates could recognize.

He was one of the greatest composers of his time. In spite of being slighted by many and the frustration that tormented him, he continued to create. This life of solitude was his soul's desire in order to deepen and understand several feelings carried out by human life. He possessed a certain humility, therefore favouring to internalize things. However, he suffered many times from the lack of recognition, or at least the lack of appreciation from critics and his entourage.

The impact of the rays he chose for this incarnation favoured his melancholic aspect. He tended to be regularly carried away by the subdued characteristic of certain rays.

Initiation Level: 1.8

Anton Bruckner was getting closer to his second initiation, which triggered his great sensitivity and his strong wish to be recognized. However, he was missing sufficient inner power to tip the scales in his favour. This deficiency produced the sad and melancholic air of someone who "knows" but who has a lack of power necessary to perfect or start to practice a sincere (and essential) humility allowing him to get to the second initiation, one that so few people succeed in reaching. This results then, in arrogant people, difficult to live with and difficult to correct. We hope that Mr. Bruckner will have learned a lesson that will help him remain a (genuinely) humble man.

Ray Structure

Monad: 2	Soul: 2	Personality: 2-3
Mental: 7-5	Astral: 6-4	Physical: 3-2

Monad and Soul

His Monad had no influence on him. His Soul, on the other hand, started an interesting one that combined with the other ray 2's creating in him a feeling of powerlessness and depreciation that communicated to him a certain humility he had to learn.

Personality

His Personality, influenced by ray 2, sub-ray 3, imparted to him a great kindness and a subtle way to manipulate his partners. Ray 2 injected him with a sensitivity that came out in his work. It also created certain fears in him (including the fear of not succeeding, being poorly judged and misunderstood)… fears he was constantly fighting. This ray, paired with his Soul's influence, allowed him to listen to certain music that he would then transpose on paper, sometimes with difficulty, because what he heard did not always coincide with what he was transcribing.

Sub-ray 3 allowed him to roll up his sleeves in the darkest moments and to carry on his work. Thanks to this sub-ray influence, he sometimes succeeded in attracting people's sympathy. This allowed him to receive a little human warmth. Having little charisma, Anton Bruckner sometimes used, unconsciously, the energy of this sub-ray, thus generating a bit of humour in his life which gave him temporary magnetism. But this humour disappeared rapidly, leaving behind a platonic energy that attracted no one.

Mental Body

His mental body, ruled by ray 7, sub-ray 5, endowed him with an inner pride that never faded. Ray 7 gave Bruckner the taste for perfection that he believed he would reach with difficulty. In other words, he was never entirely satisfied with his work. This ray gave him a sense for details that sometimes exasperated his relatives as well as a certain rhythm he transferred to his music.

Sub-ray 5 bestowed on him a down to earth aspect that he needed to survive. Logically, he knew that he needed to work to house himself, eat and dress. Without this sub-ray that always brought him back to a certain reality, he would have died younger, more alone and isolated; this sub-ray forced him to go out and earn a living.

Astral Body

His astral body, coloured by the energy of ray 6, sub-ray 4, was a real problem in his life. Ray 6 gave him a certain discreet arrogance and a sense of dedication towards the art of music. It often made him pessimistic towards life and increased his despair when this did not turn the way he wanted. This ray, coupled with sub-ray 4, created a certain gloom he had trouble shaking.

The influence of sub-ray 4 generated positive effects on his music but negative ones on his life. This sub-ray created an ambiguous feeling that compelled him to isolate himself to try to find a certain balance; it increased the feeling of loneliness, rejection and lack of understanding. However, it allowed him to see aspects of human life that enriched the experience of his soul. Without this sub-ray, his life would have been easier; however, he would have never become "Bruckner" or, if you prefer, the composer that he was. This sub-ray 4 could not be in the first ranks, because due to the lack of strength (the influence of ray 2's), he would have shortened his life, his discomfort proving to be too painful to bear.

Physical Body

His physical body, conditioned by the energy of ray 3, sub-ray 2, unlike his Personality, was chosen to promote a certain balance that more or less succeeded.

Ray 3 endowed him with an efficient brain, almost tireless. However, sub-ray 2 that increased his sensitivity also generated some ethereal weaknesses that manifested themselves by great fatigue and an almost constant weariness. This provoked in him a dichotomy he had trouble managing; his mind wanted to be clear (ray 3 influence) but at the same time, he experienced great fatigue (sub-ray 2 influence). He would start a project, galvanized by the energy derived by it, but then rapidly feel a fatigue which would slow him down. In other words, his body could not adequately follow his mind.

Bruckner presently lives in New York; he is evolving in the world of the arts and is working hard towards his second initiation. He still feels a great loneliness that will help him cross this second gate. He chose a female body in order to better understand and live this sensitivity that still inhabits him through his soul. He has to discover the power of this sensitivity in order to use it well.

September 9, 2009

 # BUSH, GEORGE W.

Given Name: George Walker Bush
Nationality: American
Place and Date of Birth: New Haven, Connecticut (United States), July 6, 1946
Profession: Businessman and statesman

MASTER DJWHAL KHUL'S COMMENTARY

I am very pleased to present you the ray configuration for this man, George W. Bush, who gave us so much work to do. Driven by an extremely narrow vision, he would have been capable of pushing humanity to the brink of disaster.

We can qualify George W. Bush as a social climber. He was always driven by an ambition, comparable to his immense illusions. We have here a good man, though restricted by an extremely narrow vision. His rise to power could have undoubtedly led to the creation of a tyrant if the American people had not "awakened" following certain monumental errors he committed on the world stage.

The expression "Hell is paved with good intentions" fits him perfectly. He wanted what was good for his people; this desire was, however, tainted with self-centred intentions, subject to his vision (influenced by ray 6) that was incompatible with an expansion of global consciousness. It is true that his initiation level did not serve him well; let us simply say that the American people attracted this kind of "dictator" due to the abuses of power the United States had committed in the past. The American people, intrinsically proud, must now lean towards a less sexist worldview, more open to the world in all its diversity and evolution. Their vision must change in order to save the honour of the American image, now tarnished by policies pursued at the beginning of the second millennium.

Let us return to Mr. Bush who exhibits a level of evolution less than that of his father and an even narrower vision. We must say that leading a country such as the United States of America with this initiation level and ray configuration could have only incited him to act as he did. His behaviour did, however, make the American people think and see the necessity of having better leaders after witnessing the missteps of their president. The American consciousness "sought" the arrival of a more evolved leader, a request that we hope will be fulfilled in future Presidential elections.

Here, then, is Mr. Bush's initiation level, which will illustrate the arduous task he had to accomplish without being equipped with either great wisdom or the tools to execute his task.

Initiation Level: 1.0

He just managed to attain this level of initiation during his last incarnation.

Ray Structure

Monad: 3	Soul: 2	Personality: 6-3
Mental: 5-3	Astral: 6-2	Physical: 3-5

Monad and Soul

If you observe his rays, you will understand to what we can attribute his lack of vision. Since his level of initiation is not very high, the Soul exerts very little influence on his Personality. We can say that he is "led" primarily by his Personality and his astral body, both endowed with a powerful and unbalanced ray 6.

Personality

His ray 6, sub-ray 3 Personality provides him with a limited vision caused by the unstable combination of ray 6 and sub-ray 3, which help maintain his narrowness of vision. An individual influenced by ray 6, who is closer positioned to the bottom of the evolutionary scale, will pursue a goal we cannot necessarily qualify as noble. He will develop a Personality thirsting for fame and recognition, and will act as if he were imbued with power and wisdom, which is rarely the case when the level of initiation is below 2. Ray 6, in its immaturity, is self-centred, focusing on the relentless rule of his needs and fears. This is even more so when the astral body is also guided by this ray. The union of ray 6 in the Personality and the astral body proves explosive.

This type of configuration creates potential dictators, as they rule with an iron fist, guided by the narrowness of their limited vision. Ray 6 creates numerous fears regarding all that is unknown or foreign to it. This ray will grant no concession and will always act out of fear rather than wisdom. Fearful of being deceived, it would seek to crush or profit instead of cooperating. When this ray is immature, everything seems black or white with no middle ground allowed. It leads according to its vision, which it believes is right and just, and destroys anything that gets in its way. It thinks it is the only one who sees and acts correctly; it is very judgemental and egotistic, and always narrow minded.

When ray 6 is assisted by sub-ray 3, Mr. Bush's configuration, it makes for a manipulator who will use any means whatsoever to control the situation. He knows how to play with words in such a way as to confuse his adversaries or those who oppose his ideas. Those who do not share his vision better watch their backs: he proves merciless when opposed and feels clearly superior to anyone else. He shows no leniency, as we noted when he was the Governor of the State of Texas, giving his consent to carry out numerous executions. Ray 3, under the hold of ray 6, will accentuate deficiencies rather than ironing them out.

Mental Body

The ray 5, sub-ray 3 mental body makes him intelligent and calculating, which is again attributable to this famous ray 3 that supports the cold logic of ray 5. He will know what arguments to bring to bear in a given situation, in order to emphasize his point of view. Heartless, he will take action not as a result of what his heart tells him, but according to what his feelings of manipulation and hunger for power force him to do.

A ray 5 mental body proves cold and calculating, and demands proof for everything presented to him. In contrast, if he wants to prove certain points, he demonstrates that he is ready to fabricate evidence to get his point across. He seems logical, direct and devoid of any feeling of kindness.

Again, ray 3 can accentuate this devastating tendency and create a dual challenge for those who try to counter a ray 5 mental body, negatively polarized, as is often the case for initiates before their second initiation. ray 3 will help falsify evidence and manipulate an audience, who will be dazzled by his charm and blend of the "pseudo-scientific ray 5" and "pseudo-intelligent ray 3." You would have to be a skilled observer to see through this masquerade, which manages to blind others. Don't forget that ray 3 can be very charming and magnetic.

Astral Body

The ray 6, sub-ray 2 astral body does not do much to help the cause: Ray 6 dominates, and sub-ray 2 heightens the fears already present at the core of the inadequately polarized astral body of ray 6. Ray 6 proves to be vindictive, cruel and separatist in order to shield itself from the source of fear, especially of the unknown. Keep in mind that Mr. Bush had never travelled outside the U.S. before becoming President. This is proof of the fears that inhabited him and continue to do so. How can a man, limited this way to a single country, develop any form of global vision?

Sub-ray 2 granted him an air of holiness and a desire to save the world, always in his own way however, which, coupled with the mirage of a saviour, revealed itself as the best according to him, and always him, since he thought he was God's gift to mankind. This sub-ray has difficulty seeing beyond its own limited universe, since it was instilled with too many fears obliging it to remain a prisoner of small ideas and, all too often, small spaces.

Physical Body

His ray 3, sub-ray 5 physical proves even to this day problematic and easily manipulated by involutive forces, for we find the same union of rays 3 and 5. His brain (physical) being polarized by ray 3, makes him a man who thinks with the energy of this ray. This means manipulative, deceptive, fast talking and secretive.

Mr. Bush is an interesting prey for involutive forces. On the one hand, sub-ray 5 supports him and, on the other hand, he is linked on the physical plane by virtue of this sub-ray to elementals that can use this kind of initiation for ends we would qualify as rather unorthodox. Thus, intuition which so well designates the energy of ray 5 becomes negatively polarized intuition, and the initiate becomes a conduit for these powers. We will not speak more of this as there would be much to say and we do not want to burden the reader with details that could invite discordant energy.

Mr. Bush must still accomplish a great deal of work on himself. During his next incarnation, we will see if his experiences in this current incarnation bear fruit and if he will manifest more wisdom since at the present time, he is not evolving.

June 6, 2008

 CARREY, JIM

Given Name: James Eugene Redmond Carrey
Double Nationality: Canadian and American
Place and Date of Birth: Newmarket, Ontario (Canada),
January 17, 1962
Profession: Actor and humourist

MASTER DJWHAL KHUL'S COMMENTARY

Jim Carrey is a strange man who seeks his place in this world. He has a ray 7 Soul and is still seeking how to properly feel its influence. He is a born magician and a comedian to the very depths of his being. His rays strongly influence his behaviour, sometimes hindering his communication style.

He comes from another planet, like all of us, but he has not yet succeeded in feeling at home here. He looks like a Soul searching to rest but does it with difficulty. He needs grounding, and his way to do it is through sexuality. He likes beer and certain drugs that he should be more wary about because he becomes more animalistic under their influence.

Sometimes, he does not know how to stop and, in a way, goes too far because he likes to experiment. Due to his ray 7 Soul, he does not feel any real fear, because for him, nothing is really tangible, except human nature which confuses him with its dual opposites that he uses himself, contentedly. He likes to challenge (due to his ray 4 Personality) and does not appreciate stagnation. For him, everything must move, otherwise it means death. He can be trusted if it is in accordance with his plan, otherwise he can betray (for our welfare) because the conscience is there to be adapted and reworked (according to his vision).

He has a big heart but sometimes finds it difficult to give the heart (that he often finds unreasonable) priority over reason.

Initiation Level: 1.8

Because he has reached a fairly high initiation level, he could become somewhat dangerous because of his lack of control. He enjoys to challenge but he is also endowed with a great sensitivity that inhibits sometimes and creates in him a desire to destroy everything. He does not seem to reflect what he really is because as he is too focused on his astral body, he encounters difficulties to properly manage his rays.

Ray Structure

Monad: 2   Soul: 7   Personality: 4-3
Mental: 7-2   Astral: 6-4   Physical: 7-4

Monad and Soul

His Monad has no influence but his Soul has started to exercise a certain control over his body. He does not feel entirely himself, as the Soul sometimes injects energies in him that he tries to understand and analyze. He is a perfectionist, a man who fears few things except the suffering from a lack of love. He has a lot of difficulty to really love, because he confuses love with the magnetism of beauty. When he is trustful, he is a sensitive and a delicate being. He adores his daughter and would give the shirt off his back for her (if she proves to be deserving) because his ray 7 mental body strengthens in him the desire for perfection that has to extend to others close to him. Very sensitive, he would have a fit of anger if things do not go according to his wishes.

Personality

His ray 4, sub-ray 3 Personality makes him a versatile individual who knows how to entertain people. Because he is very sensitive, he feels the energies and feelings of his social partners. He likes to frighten and challenge without malice, for the *feeling* he gets out of it. This behaviour gives him the sensation of holding a certain control over the energy of those looking at him or listening to him. Ray 4 will sometimes make us doubt his mental balance, because he plays with opposing polarities without getting attached to them. He is not made to live alone although he is unbearable to live with. A lot of patience and tolerance is required to live with such a being.

His sub-ray 3 increases the effect of ray 4 and allows him to be a good imitator. He can laugh at himself as well as at others. He thinks and acts fast. In life, he can change his Personality in a few seconds and does the same in his profession. He enjoys playing parts and this helps to keep him alive. He tries not to take himself too seriously while it is quite the opposite. He suffers a lot because he would prefer to feel like he does in his dreams. He is a born dreamer.

Mental Body

His ray 7, sub-ray 2 Mental makes him acutely sensitive. Ray 7 perceives thought waves and translates them into images in his brain. He tries to decode and bring to the surface what he perceives, which is not always possible. To follow his temporary madness is quite an ordeal because he always recovers from it, which is not the case for others. He is tortured by his ray 7 because he loves beauty and women too much. He adores the form and does not know how to cope; he proves to be very sexual, which disturbs him at times.

His sub-ray 2 makes him sensitive and close to the suffering of others (when ray 7 is not too present). This sub-ray equally equips him with antennae that capture the energy of the moment and makes him interfere. The mix of rays 2 and 3 allows him to easily change the atmosphere or attitude. Ray 2 can sometimes prove heartless when he feels he has to do something different from what presently occupies him. The fear of not succeeding, an integral part of ray 2, generally prompts him to act with all his power in order to succeed. He then becomes a warrior who pushes his fears aside (here we are talking of ray 2 in general) in order to accomplish his destiny.

Astral Body

His ray 6, sub-ray 4 astral body makes him a committed individual (most of the time) who can be very frivolous if sub-ray 4 demands it. Ray 6 will grant him some stability and several links with the Earth and his significant others. Without this ray, he would no longer be part of this world for lack of interest in it. In love, he is very stubborn, possessive and jealous. He must be the centre of the universe of the person with whom he shares his life. Otherwise, everything becomes unbearable.

Sub-ray 4 gives him a certain charm that lasts as long as there is levity in a relationship. If it becomes too serious, a malaise and explosion will occur.

Physical Body

His ray 7, sub-ray 4 physical body grants him a grace that does not go unnoticed. His sub-ray 4 provides him with agility and flexibility. He can transform himself at will thanks to the mix of these two rays. Ray 7 provides him this perfection that is transmitted in his films. Like a magician, he can completely transform his image. This ray confers on him a sense for detail that helps him in his roles but often poisons those around him.

Sub-ray 4 gives him access to the magic of opposites, while increasing the magic of ray 7. This sub-ray shaped him into a funny individual, although impulsive at times. It allows him to remain compelling making him charming and mysterious.

This is a strange man who deserves particular interest. He will accomplish huge progress in his next incarnation, thanks to the life experience obtained in this one and because there remains in him an aspect which is beyond convention that wants to see beyond the Hollywood mirage.

November 20, 2008

CASTANEDA, CARLOS

Given Name: Carlos Cesar Salvador Arana Castaneda
Double Nationality: Brazilian and American
Place and Date of Birth: Cajamarca (Peru), December 25, 1925
Date of Death: Los Angeles, California (United States), April 27, 1998
Profession: Writer and Shaman

MASTER DJWHAL KHUL'S COMMENTARY

Carlos Castaneda is a strange being who still fascinates a lot of people on this planet. He could have become a great Master, but he chose to be a Sorcerer on the White Path. He was not working for the dark forces although he often played with them in order to defy them. Frequently, he could have lost his life if he was not endowed with this vital force that characterized him so well. Although of small physical stature, he demonstrated dynamism and tirelessness. His attraction for the weaker sex proved to be a great weakness in his life. He could have lived longer but his vitality had certain limits for which he was unable to compensate.

In terms of energy, he resembled Bernard de Montréal[1]. They could have passed for brothers, in part, because of their rays.

Initiation Level: 3.2

He had succeeded to give up many things, even life (under some of its aspects). However, there remained for him the need to renounce himself and the power he cultivated in this incarnation and in many others. He loved power and played with it in a childish way.

---

[1] Bernard de Montréal (1939-2003) was a non-conformist thinker, lecturer and author. He taught, according to his own definition, "an evolutionary psychology for the new man."

He wasted his life to a certain extent in trying to experience the material and ethereal worlds that fascinated him. He met nature spirits that taught him a lot about their evolution but also about the human unconsciousness.

Ray Structure

Monad: 3	Soul: 4 heading towards 1	Personality: 3-6
Mental: 7-5	Astral: 4-2	Physical: 3-7

Monad and Soul

Unfortunately, his Monad had little influence, because the Soul power took a lot of space. He believed in it and thought nothing was superior to it. This is in part what prevented the Monad from working with him. In his next incarnation, the Monad will be more present and will guide him more. His Soul, influenced by the energy of ray 4, loved to challenge, dominate and play with situations (not with other Souls). It had a lot of fun probably knowing that it won't be able to do the same in the next incarnations. In a way, he was captive of his Soul's influence. It made him destroy some barriers and understand what was on the other side of the mirror.

It is also true that the influence of ray 4 in the astral body also increased the sometimes deceptive effect of ray 4. However, the Soul being wise had, in many instances, tried to bring his body to reason when he became too domineering or flighty (unsuccessfully) because we should not forget that the Soul fosters freedom and the respect of others, what he did not often do.

Personality

His ray 3, sub-ray 6 Personality allowed him the possibility to adapt to different situations without apprehension or remorse. Ray 3 enabled him to enjoy all kinds of experiences. He was an astute manipulator and a nasty liar. Few are those who knew his real face. He was always hiding behind some roles because he was afraid that someone may steal his essence, which was a myth he believed in all his life because he was very vulnerable and sensitive. He feared everything, but his ray 4 conferred on him courage that allowed him to always move ahead of potential obstacles, without apprehension or remorse.

Sub-ray 6 allowed him to demonstrate warmth and be a good salesman. He could convince anybody of his good faith and the truthfulness of his adventures. Thanks to this sub-ray, he gave the illusion of having had a special and extraordinary relationship with everyone, particularly women. When he displayed his charm, they could not resist him. He was, however, loyal to his Master and friends who were voluntarily scarce.

Mental Body

With a mental body governed by the influence of ray 7, sub-ray 5, he was, unquestionably, a very intelligent man and knew it. He knew how to use the energy of ray 7 to increase his magnetism and power. A skilful talker, he could mesmerize anybody at will by his simple choice of words and the modulation of his voice. This ray allowed him to structure his imaginary world and to render it genuine.

Sub-ray 5 put him in contact with the forces of nature with which he could practically converse. While some of his experiences were based on the imaginary, this sub-ray triggered in him a vibration allowing him to start a relationship, thanks to his ethereal connections with entities really living in worlds parallel to ours. He could produce paranormal effects that seemed real, thanks to these links. In reality, these effects resulted from the resonance of the mental body of others, under the influence of the energy produced by the vibrations of his mental body. These effects produced spectacular illusions that were mixed up with the reality produced by the devas dominated by his energy and arrogance. Therefore, his experiences were sometimes coloured by reality but often by illusions.

Astral Body

Endowed with an astral body influenced by the light of ray 4, sub-ray 2, he could become a "saviour" and rapidly change into a "dictator" for the purpose of his cause. Ray 4 allowed him to play with his feelings and those of others. It is true he was often the victim of this influence that made him vulnerable to the beauty of women, which he could not resist. This ray shaped him to become spectacular and miserable, robust and weak, happy and pitiful. It allowed him to hide his real identity so well that at the end of his life, he was unable to find it.

Sub-ray 2 gave him a great sensitivity and a remarkable intuition. He could "sense" things, particularly the feelings of others. The influence of this ray gave him the possibility to get in tune with the sentimental needs of others, to scrutinize them and understand them (while often using them to his own advantage). Conceited, he was easily hurt although he did not hesitate to hurt others. He was not really evil-minded, but simply a manipulator.

Physical Body

His physical body, programmed by the influence of ray 3, sub-ray 7, was not imposing. Ray 3 gave him, however, the agility and sight of an eagle. He could move silently or become noisy depending on the effect he wanted to produce. He liked playing with form and possessed a flexibility that allowed him to act quickly and efficiently. This ray also gave him great resistance, and the combination of these two rays allowed him little sleep while remaining functional.

Sub-ray 7 gave him a mysterious and "magical" air. He exuded mystery, which he enjoyed producing because it increased his potential as a domineering individual and facilitated his vision in the ethereal as well as his imaginary world. We will never know which was the real part lived in his adventures, since he himself was unaware of it. Caught in the web of his own magic, he firmly believed in the adventures he was telling himself.

He was a great magician but also someone who aroused people's curiosity. While his "game" may have harmed certain people, we admit that it allowed a certain awakening within the "ordinary" population imprisoned in its boring day-to-day existence. However, we hope he will know how to use more wisdom in his next incarnation, which will increase his influence in the proper sense of the word.

March 18, 2007

 # Castro, Fidel

Given Name: Fidel Alejandro Castro Ruz
Nationality: Cuban
Place and Date of Birth: Biran (Cuba), August 13, 1926
Profession: Statesman

Master Djwhal Khul's Commentary

An influential politician, Fidel Castro enabled the Republic of Cuba to become somewhat independent, but at a high cost. As a consequence, this resulted in a nation where freedom of speech was banned in order to maintain the status quo within an ever- dissatisfied population.

Loved, notwithstanding, by the majority of his people, Fidel Castro no longer enjoys the same popularity, and his hatred of the American capitalism has only increased over time. He tried to save his people while forgetting to give them something essential: freedom.

The Cuban people are indebted to Fidel Castro, but the time has come for this nation to live with the rest of the world, and particularly to be part of it. This cloistered population suffers various hardships, that have no foundation today.

Initiation Level: 1.8

His initiation level endowed him with a certain vision, which remained however, persistently narrow. He always wanted to keep his country under his control from fear of not being able to live up to what he believes he could be. He feels like a saviour and still tries to preserve this perception.

His initiation level explains his desire to remain the leader and to be recognized as such. Although he seems to have yielded his power to his half brother, the fact remains that he still governs the country with an iron fist. As long as he remains in his present incarnation, the country has little chance to open up and grow. Still considered a dangerous man, it is preferable not to strongly oppose him.

Ray Structure

Monad: 2	Soul: 3	Personality: 1-7
Mental: 7-3	Astral: 6-4	Physical: 3-7

Monad and Soul

His Monad has no influence on him. However, his Soul is starting to exercise some influence but it has to face a strong Personality that is not easily manipulated. Ray 3 likes to experiment, likes to control (manipulate) through word and gesture, and is graced with a bright intelligence. Castro has, in a way, manipulated and taken advantage of ray 3 via his other bodies that are also under the influence of ray 3 (sub-ray of his mental body and major ray of his physical body).

Personality

His ray 1, sub-ray 7 Personality made him a tough man, straightforward and loyal to his cause. Ray 1 graced him with a narrow vision that allowed him to reach his goal despite the human and non-human obstacles he faced. It transmitted strength to his speech and strengthened his physical body, making him more powerful and stronger. He does not go unnoticed even if his ray 3 physical body is betrayed by his age — he sometimes bends his back while walking and talking what a ray 1 never does, even in his old age.

Sub-ray 7 gave him a certain refinement appreciated by women. He had several mistresses and illegitimate children. We can say that he benefitted from his status to enjoy sex, alcohol and good cigars to the maximum. He became tireless because of this sub-ray and was capable of intuitively understanding the intentions of his adversaries. We can even assert that he has a sixth sense to outplay those who hold a grudge against him.

Mental Body

His ray 7, sub-ray 3 mental body made him an intelligent man, very skilled in developing strategy. Ray 7 can sometimes make the mind biting or harsh up to the smallest details, which is true with Castro. He is also a man of action and not a philosopher, resulting from his ray 7, supported by sub-ray 3 that grants him a particular flexibility in the way he conceives facts. He judges a lot and is often right. Some of his fears, aided by ray 7, force him to remain closed and unable to confide in anyone.

Sub-ray 3 helps him make his strategies a reality. He can think and act fast. This sub-ray inspires him with the taste to read because he enjoys exploring other worlds besides his own.

Astral Body

His astral body of ray 6, sub-ray 4 shapes him as a narrow-minded individual albeit warm. He worked hard for his country that he wants to control. Like any unbalanced ray 6, he likes to dominate and hates to be betrayed. Forgiveness is not easy for him. Devoted to his cause, he is still striving for it with determination although his vision is incorrect.

His sub-ray 4 made him unfaithful to his women and to his children who he loves despite everything. It creates in him mood swings and fits of anger unpleasant to watch. He can also become very gloomy. This sub-ray has cast a shadow on his life by creating the fear that he was not up to his expectations.

Physical Body

His ray 3, sub-ray 7 physical body gave him a resilient body. Ray 3 endowed him with an efficient brain and a particular sense of humour.

He is not seen laughing often but can easily smile when his astral body of sub-ray 4 does not display a state qualified as "down." He likes intelligent people and proves it well.

Sub-ray 7 has adequately supported the work of ray 3. It made him physically resistant and gave him the taste for perfection. He likes details in certain projects, details he considers essential most of the time.

His real friendship for Pierre Elliott Trudeau remains a mystery for most. This friendship does not date from this present incarnation and the two men recognized each other without really becoming conscious of it. Trudeau did not always like the way Castro handled his obligations. However, because Trudeau believed that a good education was the beginning of the road to freedom, he admired Castro for having favoured access to education for all Cubans. Being more evolved than Castro, Trudeau was entertaining his secret ambition to change the Cuban leader, while wishing the latter would demonstrate a certain flexibility towards his people.

April 23, 2009

CEAUSESCU, NICOLAE

Given Name: Nicolae Andruta Ceausescu
Nationality: Romanian
Place and Date of Birth: Scornicesti (Romania), January 26, 1918
Date of Death: Târgoviste (Romania), December 25, 1989
Profession: Statesman

MASTER DJWHAL KHUL'S COMMENTARY

An unscrupulous man, Nicolae Ceausescu knew how to demonstrate the thirst for power as a very young Soul. An easy prey for the ego and negative energies, he usurped the right for freedom, equality and independence from his people. He will have to correct these three serious errors in his next incarnation, which will probably not occur in the present century because his re-education will be long and arduous.

From the three errors he committed stem all kinds of hardships: from lack of physical food to psychological and spiritual food. He starved them at all levels, treating them more like animals than humans. He was only thirsty for power and injustice for those he came close to. He liked to dominate and make others suffer in order to keep a constant grip on his people he exploited and ignored as a "free people." True good intentions never surfaced and the dark forces took advantage of his thirst for power to use him for unorthodox ends. He allowed them to destroy hope in human beings: the hope to be free, to be loved and treated fairly, to live comfortably and to live a rewarding and spiritual life.

How did such an unevolved man dominate a whole population? He was simply very intelligent, very magnetic and slightly more evolved that the masses. This weak gap, when added to an appropriate education, sometimes provides the recipe for the creation of a dictator that will spread terror in his country. These are experiences that very young souls live on the planet (the fact of being dominated in this fashion) but which end with the arrival of more evolved beings that will awaken the global consciousness and will allow human suffering to change in terms of quantity and quality. Man will no longer suffer unconsciously, because suffering will become a very important awakening tool and not simply an experience as is the case presently.

Initiation Level: 0.9

The opening of the heart not having yet been achieved, Nicolae Ceausescu was nothing but a perfect tool of degradation and dictatorship.

Ray Structure

Monad: 2	Soul: 3	Personality: 3-7
Mental: 5-4	Astral: 6-2	Physical: 3-6

Nicolae Ceausescu had no ray 1 in his configuration because of his young Soul. His hardness came from his initiation level but mainly from his ray 6 in his astral body. His other rays helped support this ray 6, always more hungry for power and dictatorship.

Monad and Soul

His Monad and Soul had no influence whatsoever on him. In a way, he did not have a Soul because the polarization had not yet occurred, the Soul sending weak inner messages that he was constantly ignoring.

Personality

His ray 3, sub-ray 7 Personality made him an intelligent man, a manipulator refined in his manipulations. Ray 3 gave him much magnetism and helped his verbal expressions. He would rapidly jump to conclusions and would rarely think before acting.

Sub-ray 7 encouraged the expression of a certain aura of elegance. He appeared educated, intelligent but mainly sure of himself. This sub-ray bestowed on him in a way, intuition, which allowed him to act at the right moment, thus increasing his power.

Mental Body

His ray 5, sub-ray 4 mental body gave him a strong intelligence because sub-ray 4 supported ray 5 in his deviated aspect of the manifestation of matter. Ray 5 calculated so that everything would be to his advantage. It allowed him to express himself like a scientist, which pleased his audience. Ray 5 dangerously increased his arrogance because he believed himself to be clearly superior to the masses.

Sub-ray 4 made him believe that he sometimes had strokes of genius while in reality this sub-ray increased his mental superiority deviation. It created in him the illusion that he was receiving privileged intuitions coming from his inner being that he perceived as being indestructible. He imagined himself to be a real genius, strongly cultivated by this sub-ray that boosted him with an inner buoyancy. This enthusiasm removed his fears that should have manifested themselves as a result of what he was doing. He was blind to the outside world and could not conceive the end of his political rule.

Astral Body

His ray 6, sub-ray 2 astral body made him an emotional person, hot-tempered, incapable of perceiving his own wish for power. At first, we could see, behind his ambition, that he was endowed with a certain consciousness since he wanted to rule his people for the good of all. However, he rapidly became blinded by his ambition and turned into a real despot who controlled and manipulated towards purely selfish ends. He believed he was the chosen one, the one through whom everything can happen, the one to be admired and feared.

His sub-ray 2 granted him the semblance of a heart, particularly for his family. However, all could assert that they feared him because of his tough, unstable and sometimes distrustful character. He did not tolerate refusal and only accepted obedience. This sub-ray produced a mirage that he was kind and was acting for the good of his people, while manipulating them for their good. His mind was twisted, which explains the time frame he will have to respect before he is given another chance to reincarnate.

Physical Body

His ray 3, sub-ray 6 physical body gave him a robust body and a manipulative brain (ray 3 influence) as well as a stubborn (ray 6 influence) character. He was not easy to live with and proved untiring. Hard on his body (ray 6 influence) while possessing a certain flexibility of speech (ray 3) in order to better magnetize his audience, he was endowed with rapid thought due to his ray 3 influence.

The human race should not be proud of such individuals; it has to learn and act in such a way that dictators have no place on this planet which will soon become sacred.

May 7, 2009

 CHIA, MANTAK

Given Name: Mantak Chia
Nationality: Thai
Place and Date of Birth: Bangkok (Thailand), April 4, 1944
Profession: Taoist Master, teacher, and author

MASTER DJWHAL KHUL'S COMMENTARY

Mantak Chia is a teacher of *Qigong*, Taoism, and sexual tantrism, who while knowing a lot, knows very little about the real nature of his work. He has a gift to transmit certain energies through his writings. This powerful energy often leads his readers to live certain experiences for which they are not prepared. His teachings instruct the masses while they should be known and experimented within a closed environment where vigilance on the part of the teacher can be carried out.

In a way, he breeds trouble within the etheric body of devotees who have neither the maturity nor the wisdom to work with such an energetic power. While being beneficial from a certain viewpoint, his teaching may cause irreparable harm to those who are unprepared to live such an experience. His exercises lit energetic volcanoes by the stimulation of the chakras — flowing into the *nadi* — thus creating a premature destruction of impurities not yet absorbed by the ether. In other words, he bypasses Karma by preventing it from doing its work, because Karma has a positive aspect ignored by many. Abandoned without the inside checkpoints created by karma, the individual floats in an unknown ocean, not moored to reality and a victim of tidal waves in the raging etheric. This creates an uncomfortable malaise that could lead to madness, suicide or serious physical problems. Without real supervision, this apprenticeship becomes a dangerous element for very young souls on the way to Perfection.

Initiation Level: 2.5

He works well, but remains too unconscious of the effects produced by his writings. We wish he would affix an energetic seal so that only those who can really work with the energy contained in his books may access it.

Ray Structure

Monad: 2	Soul: 2	Personality: 3-4
Mental: 7-5	Astral: 6-4	Physical: 3-6

Monad and Soul

His Monad has very little influence on his life. However, his Soul has started to adequately guide his vehicle, although it is still animated by a lack of discernment. The Soul dictates the teaching to him. It gives him the desire to teach to everybody. He really believes he is a unique individual, capable of helping his fellow humans evolve towards their own inner light.

Personality

His Personality, ruled by ray 3, sub-ray 4, gives him magnetism and fearlessness. He does not fear energy. In fact, he likes to experiment with it endlessly. Ray 3 shapes him like a manipulator on many levels: energy, thought, speech and people. It grants him the taste to experiment everything and see and try everything. It gives him the capacity to easily describe what he sees internally. He loves to try to control the energy, to force it to act and react to the strength of his thought pattern.

His sub-ray 4 activates his lack of fear of experiences. He believes he is invincible because of the influence of the two sub-ray 4's (Personality and Astral). He also likes to challenge the invisible in order to master it. He often has brushes with disaster. His past experience, during his incarnation as Chang Hsueh-ch'eng (1738-1801) allowed him to be stronger and not to fear ridicule. As he died poor at this time, he did not wish to relive such a sacrifice in this present life. Between this life and his life as Chang Hsueh-ch'eng, he lived a life as a monk in a Japanese monastery where he learned some shaolin martial arts techniques. Although the *shaolin* monks were mainly located in China, there is some written evidence of the contribution of certain techniques pertaining to *shaolin* martial arts in Japan.

Mental Body

His mental body, influenced by the energy of ray 7, sub-ray 5, bestows on him a very good concentration and an impeccable memory of what he learns and experiments. Ray 7 inspires magic in his writings, and in his teachings. He knows how to work with energy thanks to the influence of this ray that strongly guides his life and inspires him with rigor, patience and strong intuition. This ray allowed him to rapidly master certain movements, while understanding the energy carried through the performance of this movement.

Sub-ray 5 grants him a serious sense of experimentation. It motivates him to listen to the invisible world and be aware of astral and etheric energies. This sub-ray puts him in direct connection with the world of the *devas* that he knows how to use adequately. He works a great deal with the elements of fire and water, both being subtle forms of energy circulating within the body (*kundalini* and ether). He knows how to manage, observe and be obeyed by them, which is unfortunately not the case for his readers.

Astral Body

Thanks to his astral body coloured by the influence of ray 6, sub-ray 4, he is a man very devoted to his cause. He likes what he does and shines through his teaching. Rarely faithful, in spite of the influence of ray 6, he advocates a sexual freedom that sometimes creates confusion among his students. He cannot conceive of limitations to this fire that, according to him, can destroy everything to better heal and revitalize. Due to this ray, he can sometimes be narrow-minded and stubborn. He sometimes finds it difficult to recognize the benefits of meditation practices other than his own. Hard-headed at times, he has a lot of trouble to forgive.

His sub-ray 4 activates in him different desires with which he strives to properly harmonize. Sexually, he tries everything and fears nothing. However, this conduct tends to occasionally generate strange reactions that he succeeds fairly well to disguise and creates irrational fears that he has to fight. He then withdraws in order to conquer "these demons" that continuously harass him. Feeling sometimes a temporary guilt that he hides behind arrogant traits, he succeeds in maintaining a steady course in his life that seems to display a perfect mastery on all levels.

Physical Body

Since he is rather small in stature, the combined energies of ray 3, sub-ray 6 make him look stronger and taller than he really his. Ray 3 grants him a good stamina and an ability to execute the movements he teaches. This ray also provides him with a special gift to clearly explain the different steps of these exercises. This ray confers on him an appetite for life's experiences. He does not seem to be in a hurry to reach wisdom, because he believes he is already wise, a magical illusion due to ray 3.

Sub-ray 6 ensures him of a suitable basis that allows him to keep a fairly good physical and psychic balance. It helps him to chemically maintain the nerve cells of his brains in a good functioning state and to place certain beacons favouring a solid energetic contribution within matter. Without this well-anchored sub-ray, he would experience great difficulties in keeping his balance in the material world.

This man possesses a real power that he must learn to properly manage and channel. One should not forget the importance and the responsibilities of the writings; the influence carried this way proves as powerful as the influence created by words and actions. He will soon experience an important illness that will help him correct his inner development.

April 14, 2010

CHÖDRÖN, ANI PEMA

Given Name: Deirdre Blomfield-Brown
Nationality: American
Place and Date of Birth: New York, New York (United States),
July 14, 1936
Profession: Teacher of Tibetan Buddhism

MASTER DJWHAL KHUL'S COMMENTARY

Pema Chödrön is a good student. She is learning to become a Master, because this will be her mission in her next incarnation. Currently, she is teaching to people younger than her. She does not yet possess the power to transform people, which she will acquire at the end of her next incarnation if she is well guided.

She is working hard, particularly on her vanity that she knows is still very present. She has difficulty to avoid feeling a certain pride coming from her human soul that is learning from this aspect of the human condition, an aspect that must disappear for her to cross the third door of initiation. Madam Chödrön has not yet crossed it, but this present life in its entirety is preparing her. She will take giant leaps in her next incarnation which will not occur in the East as she wishes but, rather, in the West which will become a hub for evolution.

In a way, Asia is dying because it is becoming too polluted by the onset of technology. It is a fact that in the coming centuries, spirituality will grow stronger in the West because the human souls who are living there would have broken part of the magnetism derived from technological evolution. The reign of ray 7 will trigger an evolving leap at all levels. The human soul will meet interesting challenges that will result in getting it closer to its true nature: definitely divine.

Pema Chödrön will reveal herself to be a precious resource for future researchers. She has searched so extensively that she will become an efficient guide. She must, however, still cross some important steps that will take place in her next incarnations.

Initiation Level: 2.2

Ray Structure

Monad: 3	Soul: 2	Personality: 2-3
Mental: 7-5	Astral: 6-2	Physical: 3-5

Monad and Soul

Her Monad has no influence yet, but her Soul is starting to really have an influence on her vehicle. The more this hold is proven serious and important, the more she will direct herself towards wisdom and reveal herself to be an excellent teacher who will transmit energy allowing her students to take giant leaps during their incarnations. Incidentally, several of her present students will become her disciples when she crosses the stage for her third initiation.

Personality

Her Personality governed by the influence of ray 2, sub-ray 3, makes her a good instructor who listens to the needs of her students. Ray 2 sometimes acts in such a way that she feels limited because she does not always know how to guide her students. However, her Master is watching over her and corrects the mistakes she may commit. This ray also creates fears in her that she will have to get rid of in her next incarnation. It also shapes her as warm and forthcoming.

Sub-ray 3 infuses in her the desire to always learn and experiment on the inner planes. She sometimes feels the need to express herself. This sub-ray makes her flexible while increasing her stubbornness because it likes to maintain its opinions while producing the illusion that it understands other people, that it will consider… and perhaps change!

Mental Body

Her mental body, influenced by ray 7, sub-ray 5, grants her discipline in her writing and makes her very ritualistic. She likes rituals that allow her to feel at ease with herself and safer. Certain beacons are necessary to accomplish her rituals well. Ray 7 transmits the desire to perform and be perfect.

Sub-ray 5 allows her to be well-anchored in spite of the experiences she lives internally. Without this sub-ray that keeps her grounded, she would feel lost and fear experimenting. This sub-ray also allows her to write in a more adapted fashion for the Western world.

Astral Body

Her astral body, directed by the energy of ray 6, sub-ray 2, ensures her this maternal aspect and this magnificent smile, so well known. Ray 6 shapes her as warm and loving, kind and sweet when she acts according to the desire of her emotions which is different when she acts according to her mental body or her Personality. This ray makes her dedicated and faithful. She is a sincere friend that is good to have.

Sub-ray 2 motivates her to be very sensitive, very intuitive. She can understand other people's problems and easily slips into their skin. She loves to love, the same way she loves discipline and meditation.

Physical Body

Her physical body, governed by the influence of ray 3, sub-ray 5, makes her efficient, however, often exhausted. Ray 3, influencing her brain, tries to fight the effect of sub-ray 5, that in turn tries to reduce the effect of ray 3, thus producing a mental fatigue. Harmony between these two rays is non-existent. Ray 3 encourages experimentation while ray 5 fosters caution. Ray 3 produces a flexibility that is weakened by sub-ray 5, because it proves to be stronger and rigid. Ray 3 supports a philosophical way of thinking that sub-ray 5 attempts to render Cartesian. Ray 3 encourages speed in gesture and expression while sub-ray 5 supports restraint.

This lack of harmony between both rays is the result of a rift created at birth, a karmic crack whose origin derives from a previous life where the use of hallucinogenic drugs encouraging inner experience was too strong. She lived then in North America and was part of an Indian culture in the American Southwest. A tribal chief and Shaman, she tried to rule her people to the best of her knowledge by using mushrooms and herbs that stimulated the Vision.

The strength of her meditations will allow her to heal this crack and become endowed with a better-performing etheric body during her next incarnation.

August 13, 2009

CHÖGYAM TRUNGPA RINPOCHE

Given Name: Chögyam Trungpa
Nationality: Tibetan
Place and Date of Birth: Province of Kham, Oriental Tibet, February 1939
Date of Death: Halifax, Nova Scotia (Canada), April 4, 1987
Profession: Buddhist teacher

MASTER DJWHAL KHUL'S COMMENTARY

Chögyam Trungpa, a very honest and interesting man, always wished for the best, but has, unfortunately often personally reaped the worst. He has had drinking and sexual problems but never one of power. He was, in a way, under the spell of the West and Westerners, although he brought a lot of light to this darkness that is America. He sacrificed part of himself to allow men to better understand themselves and to better grasp the illusions of the mental and astral bodies.

Initiation Level: 4.2

He felt no fear, except of himself. Too pure to live in the West, he suffered greatly from this situation. His rays also complicated his existence.

Ray Structure

Monad: 3	Soul: 2	Personality: 4-2
Mental: 3-2	Astral: 6-3	Physical: 6-1

Monad and Soul

Thanks to his Monad, under the influence of ray 3, he began a more direct manipulation of the world of matter, including of the human intellect. He enjoyed experimenting at this level, however, he was often secretly disappointed because this allowed him to perceive human limitation and the little control and evolution of humanity. Discouraged at times, which could partially explain his love for alcohol, he never ceased to hope in man's capacity to improve.

His Soul, influenced by ray 2, conferred to him a great sensitivity. He suffered tremendously when he saw humanity's degree of unconsciousness. His deepest wish was to teach to those willing, the path that would free them from the constraints they inflicted on themselves. He loved everything and everybody without reservation. His ray 2 Soul gave him the capacity to see the "love" aspect in everyone, which helped him not to definitely lose hope in humanity.

Personality

When faced by a Personality governed by the energy of rays 4 and 2, such as Trungpa's, it is certain that we discover an individual who is capable of excesses of all kinds because ray 4 has fun and learns this way, while regularly nearly missing his own destruction. Ray 4 pushes the limits of all experimentations, and Trungpa liked this radical exploration. He gave of himself entirely for all. When he sailed more like a "human", he let himself be carried by the waves of his rays instead of really trying to master them. However, when he endorsed his duty as a Master, no ray had any tangible power over him. He used them to his convenience in order to accomplish the work that had to be done.

Sub-ray 2 made him extremely sensitive. The union of the influence of both rays 4 and 2 pushed him to drink extensively in order to survive in this world whose suffering he constantly felt. Alcohol served as a support in order to get rid of the excess undesirable energy that penetrated his aura. In which way? By allowing him to increase his inner frequency with the help of the *devas* present in these drinks. These *devas*, while getting him closer to the human condition, offered him the possibility to expel from his energy field the psychic pollution carried by his students by distilling the undesirable thought forms (at his request). Thanks to the great sensitivity of ray 2, he proved to be an extraordinary teacher by simply indicating the inexplicable in its complexity.

Mental Body

The influence of ray 3, sub-ray 2 on his mental body increased the sometimes "mysterious" and "magnetic" aspect he displayed. Ray 3 conferred to him the "mystery" aspect; by playing with words, this ray may create thought forms that solicit the creative imagination of the individual in an "active listening" mode. In this way, it creates "infinite possibilities" within the thinker's mind that interacts with the one projecting a transformative energy through the fabulous universe of words. Chogyam Trungpa, a Master in this regard, gave many humans the ability to acknowledge themselves as "divine" and animated with a soul eager to express itself in the world of matter.

Sub-ray 2 vibrated the "magnetic" aspect, rendering him often irresistible to his students (particularly women) who considered him like a living God. He used this magic to communicate, mainly by his speech and gestures, the necessary energy to fabricate in them the sensitive chord allowing them to vibrate their atomic expression. This sub-ray also increased the mysterious effect of his speech. It facilitates the contact with the higher vibratory realms beyond the astral plane. Thus, Trungpa often touched the first levels of the astral plane in his verbal expression.

Astral Body

From the standpoint of human feelings, the influence of rays 6 and 3 Astral gave him the appearance of an extra-terrestrial. Ray 6 provided him with behaviours encouraging family life, dedication and faithfulness in his relationship, while sub-ray 3 jostled all these rules, making them almost ridiculous. He sometimes played with other people's feelings as he played with his own. We agree that he did not have an easy life, particularly with regards to love because he loved everybody and was faithful to them. He did not feel at ease on earth where everything seemed complicated while it should have been simple.

A ray 3 in the astral body proves to be very rare and uncomfortable. It complicates feelings, making them incomprehensible at times. It leads the individual to live several sentimental lives, simultaneously. It, therefore, becomes nearly impossible to be in love with one person at a time. This sub-ray made Trungpa very malleable during his interventions with others. He never used the same strategy and triggered shocks regularly because his behaviour constantly changed. This sub-ray served Trungpa's role as a Master but not as a man because it facilitated his early departure during his incarnation as Chögyam Rinpoche.

Physical Body

The energy released by his ray 6, sub-ray 1 physical allowed him to carry on so long, despite his alcohol and drug consumption. This happened because, in his life, the universe seemed imperfect and uncomfortable, and the lack of depth in his students often discouraged him. He succeeded well with most of them, what he failed to see. He wanted more for them; more light and understanding in their lives, more love on their part towards humanity… which was not the case in his eyes. He found that humanity was still too self-centred and indifferent to the needs of others. Man appeared to him as a selfish being, sometimes heartless, but that he deeply loved regardless.

Ray 6 compelled him to dedicate himself in spite of the physical fatigue caused by the excesses he imposed on his body. It gave him the perseverance and the strength to always carry on.

Sub-ray 1 offered him a greater resistance and a brain that could fight the fog produced by alcohol and drugs. He could, with his will, become very clear in his mind, what ray 6 did not allow him to do. The support of this sub-ray granted an additional pillar to ray 6 that could only bow in the face of the energy transfer necessary during certain interventions. Naturally, this order coming from the Soul demanded clear thought from Trunkgpa, in order to express itself through him. When the work was finished, the energy of sub-ray 1 would withdraw and be replaced by the energy of ray 6, which although more confused, was more dedicated. Sub-ray 1 stirred energy and ray 6 cradled it like a mother cradling her infant.

As you can see, when man has acquired a certain level of wisdom, he can become a virtuoso in the manipulation of his ray energies, which was the case for Trungpa.

This man is not presently incarnated. However, he will be shortly. He needed time to heal his subtle bodies and prepare himself for his next incarnation which will not be restful.

December 17, 2006

 CHOPRA, DEEPAK

Given Name: Deepak Chopra
Double Nationality: Indian and American
Place and Date of Birth: New Delhi (India), October 22, 1946
Profession: Doctor, thinker and writer

MASTER DJWHAL KHUL'S COMMENTARY

Deepak Chopra is an excessively magnetic and intelligent being. He helps the masses to grow and increase their awareness, although it is not in a profound manner as he does not have the initiation level that allows him to do so. He will make great progress in this lifetime because he is guided by a Master of Babaji's lineage. If he listens to his Soul, he will go in retreat at the end of his life and reflect on his actions by perceiving in part, their "pros" and "cons." He is performing a work that was requested by his Master, that of which he is more or less conscious. The energy supporting him in the invisible realm is behind his great popularity. He undertakes a work that would have been impossible to accomplish for a great Initiate, who would become quickly polluted by all the relations he establishes, particularly with the world of artists.

Arrogant, a feature due to his initiation level and his rays, Chopra likes power and money. However, we believe that, if necessary, he would give up everything to pursue his destiny because he is an idealist.

Initiation Level: 2.3

Mr. Chopra has the possibility to reach the initiation level of 2.5 at his death.

Ray Structure

Monad: 3	Soul: 2	Personality: 2-4
Mental: 7-5	Astral: 6-2	Physical: 3-5

He has three ray 2's in his ray configuration, which endow him with a lot of compassion for others. He knows how to listen and loves to help those who suffer. To a certain degree, he has adopted a 'saviour complex' resulting from the mix of his ray 2's and his ray 6 Astral. His ray 2's impart on him a great sensitivity, an intuition that serves him in his writings and a good listening ability that helps him to be "in the right place, at the right moment."

Monad and Soul

His Monad has practically no influence on his life. It patiently waits while he gets closer to his third initiation. Conversely, his Soul guides him fairly well. It sensitizes him to other's miseries and motivates him to give of himself in order to reduce the discomfort of those around him who desire his help.

Personality

As previously mentioned, ray 2 in the Personality produces a beneficial effect on him. It endows him with this "listening" ability that he demonstrates to close relations and his audience. This ray grants him empathy and reveals a sincerity that emanates from him. He sincerely wishes to help his fellow man. This ray makes him a good teacher and a good writer. He succeeds very well in explaining what he wants others to understand.

His sub-ray 4 gives him a charming and magnetic appearance (double ray 2). It brings him an "artistic " aspect that serves him well and a "comfortable" aspect with the public and artists. He sometimes experiences downs that bring him back to his Centre and finally allow him to roll up his sleeves and continue to convey his teachings.

Mental Body

His arrogance comes from his ray 7, sub-ray 5 Mental that renders him conservative, intelligent, ordered in his thoughts, efficient, intellectual (which pleases the highbrows), and magnetic in his speech. Due to this ray 7 and the ray 2's, he is almost irresistible. Women like him and he reciprocates the feeling.

Ray 7 grants him a logic that expresses his thoughts well. Being ordered in his thoughts helps him write so many books. He plans goals that he reaches most of the time.

His sub-ray 5 bestows on him an earthly aspect that pleases his contacts, who feel confident with his statements. He possesses a scientific aspect that allows him to bring logic to what may appear to be illogical. This aspect gives him a good basis in spirituality because he is looking to understand the inexplicable, which gives him, therefore, a lot of credibility.

Astral Body

His ray 6, sub-ray 2 astral body makes him a warm and sensitive man. Ray 6 renders him dedicated to others and increases his desire to serve them well. He believes in Divinity and is happy when he can touch the public with his vision of things. He needs to feel loved. Sensitive, he could be easily hurt. He knows how to pick himself up and pursue his task at top speed. He is not a quitter.

Because of sub-ray 2, he displays a lot of gentleness and softness. However, he can be assertive at times when he is polarized to his mental body because rays 7 and 5 do not always express themselves delicately. This sub-ray grants him the capacity to cultivate a certain intuition that he uses quite appropriately.

Physical Body

His ray 3, sub-ray 5 physical body equips him with impressive strength and endurance as well as a youthful look. His brain, influenced by ray 3, offers him the possibility to think fast and well. His sub-ray 5 inspires a scientific approach.

We believe he accomplishes good work that addresses a certain community of young souls. He gives people the ability to see something different than their dreary daily lives and brings them a little happiness and hope.

June 30, 2007

# CHRISTIE, AGATHA

Given Name: Agatha Mary Clarissa Miller
Nationality: English
Place and Date of Birth: Torquay, Devon (England), September 15, 1890
Date of Death: Wallingford, Oxfordshire (England), January 12, 1976
Profession: Fiction writer (Novelist)

MASTER DJWHAL KHUL'S COMMENTARY

Agatha Christie is a young soul who knew how to socially entertain people. She did not contribute to the evolution of the population, although she was able to activate ray 5, which was dormant.

Her writing style, tinged with a deft, light touch, regardless of the subject covered, entertains by "educating" through the effect of ray 3 (revealing, through humour, that appearances are often misleading) and of ray 5, which testifies to the occult intelligence in motion. This lady really presented herself as an amalgamate of rays 3 and 5.

She housed an inward secret that she was careful never to reveal to others. She liked the occult aspect of things that she was trying to understand, making use of life's mystery and the mystical aspect created by the beliefs commonly held at the time. In spite of the fame that followed the publication of her books, she never took herself seriously.

Very sensitive, her ray 4 Soul drove her to ignore life's most difficult aspects. When she experienced shock, particularly emotional ones, she would isolate herself for a short while then rolled up her sleeves in order to pursue her task. This ray infused her with the fighting instinct that was typical of her.

Christie allowed women to attain a certain status, attesting to feminine intelligence. Remember that in the era of her youth, women were considered of little consequence, some people even doubting that they had souls.

Initiation Level: 2.2

Without this initiation level, she would not have experienced fame. Please note that her writings demonstrate that she still has work to do on the emotional level, where her novels reveal a superficial aspect, even appearing almost simplistic.

Ray Structure

Monad: 2	Soul: 4	Personality: 3-7
Mental: 7-5	Astral: 6-2	Physical: 3-5

Monad and Soul

Her Monad had no real influence. However, her Soul "inclined" towards her more and more. Under the influence of ray 4, she would sometimes experience temporary ups and downs, but her ray 7, sub-ray 5 Mental would bring her stability. This ray 4 gave her the courage to dive into the field of writing and never give up. Thus, we can easily understand that she isolated herself for a while (it was even rumoured that she had disappeared) when her marriage collapsed upon her husband's departure. This ray's energy had propelled her into the depths of despair that demanded time to rest, recover her balance and allow her mental body to overcome the situation.

We already said that she did not feel at ease in this emotional body (ray 6, sub-ray 2), which she was unable to master. Her mind was her refuge; she would isolate herself for the time needed to work out the influence of ray 4, thus restoring her balance and great creativity. Ray 4 communicated inspiration, the ray 7, sub-ray 5 mental body aligned to structure her work in physical terms, whereas the physical brain influenced by ray 3, sub-ray 5, embellished her writing with a sense of humour and intelligence, both in concrete and active terms.

Personality

Her ray 3, sub-ray 7 Personality made her a dynamic and efficient woman. Ray 3 granted her a subtle intelligence coloured with a certain *glow*. She could easily pass unnoticed as she did not appreciate fame. She took pleasure in writing but not in being seen and recognized. This ray conferred on her a certain sense of British humour, very much appreciated by people. She could if desired, with a deadpan sense of humour, put on an act (particularly with ray 4 influence in the Soul).

Her sub-ray 7 bestowed on her the taste for perfection in her writings as well as in various aspects of her life. It predisposed her for simplicity and a certain elegance that sometimes seemed austere. She liked warm and soft textures; she favoured elegant clothes, but placed comfort first. This sub-ray 7 prevented her from becoming too extravagant, which once more offset the eccentricity of her ray 4.

Mental Body

Her ray 7, sub-ray 5 mental body enticed her to write with logic within the framework of a story that could look illogical at times. Ray 7 made her attentive to detail (both to hide and reveal) and submitted her to the discipline of writing. Superstitious (a feature of ray 7) and ritualistic, she applied the following proverb: a place for everything and everything in its place. Thus, a book would call for a certain dexterity requiring flexibility, humour and intelligence, not to mention the element of surprise. This latter trait was very important to her because without it, her books would have been meaningless.

Her sub-ray 5 provided her the latitude to conduct research as well as to delve into experiences so that the facts related in her books would be somewhat realistic in tone. A down-to-earth logic had to reveal itself through the investigative process carried by her heroes. Hercule Poirot manifested her 7-5 aspect, whereas Miss Marple, in addition to enjoying these rays, revealed a bit of rays 4 and 3, much like Christie herself.

Astral Body

Because of her ray 6, sub-ray 2 astral body, she was a sensitive and loving woman. Her ray 6 made her loyal and endowed her with a talent for fiery oratory when she had to defend her ideas at times. This ray imbued her countenance with a touch of warmth, that occasionally pierced the severity of ray 7. It also provided her with the desire to help others and understand them.

Sub-ray 2, with which she felt more or less at ease, conferred on her sensitivity and romanticism, which she sometimes perceived as a weakness to be suppressed. She made sure it would exert little influence, polarizing more towards her mental body so that all would not collapse like a house of cards when circumstances would reveal to be emotionally painful. In her next incarnation, she will have to face the music and demonstrate an increased mastery of her emotional body.

Physical Body

Her ray 3, sub-ray 5 physical body granted her a certain robustness that served her all her life. She would have liked to have been more beautiful; she would then have had to sacrifice all of the support of sub-ray 5.

This ray 3 gave her a productive tool (her brain) that allowed her to write efficiently and rapidly. It equipped her with tools that while writing a novel, helped her come up with ideas for her next novel. This ray granted her flexibility in her writing and a facility to transmit what she received. It also injected into her writings a sense of humour greatly appreciated by her readers.

Sub-ray 5 facilitated the task started at the level of the mental body; it dictated to her what to write so that the facts she described would seem credible. It embellished with intelligence the progress of her novels and communicated to her an intuitive sense she conveyed through her work. She loved nature, which allowed her to maintain her balance. Unfortunately, this sub-ray gave her traits that were not refined enough for her liking. However, it allowed her to cultivate a humility totally void of any glamour or overly feminine magnetism.

Agatha Christie is presently reincarnated in the body of a young man around 12 years of age. She lives in London and is planning to write science-fiction novels that will prove quite plausible.

November 6, 2009

 # CHURCHILL, WINSTON

Given Name: Winston Leonard Spencer Churchill
Nationality: British
Place and Date of Birth: Oxfordshire (England), November 30, 1874
Date of Death: London (England), January 24, 1965
Profession: Writer, historian, officer, and statesman

MASTER DJWHAL KHUL'S COMMENTARY

Winston Churchill was a remarkable man whose strength and ebullient character disturbed many. He possessed a fairly just vision that sometimes compelled him to trigger a reaction amongst his entourage, who did not always understand him. His straight talk caused him some problems because people feared him and feared his influence. It was preferable to be on his side instead of against him; nothing frightened him except failure.

He liked success and the power that he used fairly well, and being right. Without him, the Second World War would have lingered. A faithful friend, he did not fear to disturb another because friendship for him entailed certain risks when the truth had to be told. He appreciated truth and suffered when lies floated in his "ether." He did not fear words that became, for him, working instruments in his profession where only speech could help to move things forward.

Initiation Level: 2.3

His initiation level allowed him to counter Hitler's influence. If this level would have been inferior, the battle would have been harder. Churchill could guess Hitler's intentions, because his ray 1's and his initiation level gave him a certain vision that often proved to be correct. However, his ray 6's sometimes impeded his work because he would become too fanatic and straightforward. The combination of his rays 1 and 6 made him a man who seemed to be made of tempered steel. However, his ray 2 Soul rendered him sensitive behind an appearance of harshness.

Ray Structure

Monad: 2	Soul: 2	Personality: 1-5
Mental: 1-3	Astral: 6-2	Physical: 3-6

Monad and Soul

His Monad did not really influence his existence, contrary to his Soul that demonstrated an influence on his actions. It guided and inspired him on several occasions. Being part of Koot Hoomi's[1] Ashram, he had to create his destiny through the choice of some key rays.

We have to specify that his life, as England's Prime Minister, was prepared during some of his previous lives, particularly the last during which he made certain choices of rays that allowed him to reinforce his Soul ray. Committed to the service of humanity, he had made this choice while being aware that his life would not be easy. He knew Hitler's Soul for having met him in several lives. They are not Soul mates, but they were regularly in close contact with each other. Churchill's Soul never liked Hitler's, which contributed to increase his warrior's strength.

Personality

His ray 1, sub-ray 5 Personality gave him the ability to make fast, fair and well-thought-out decisions. Ray 1 conferred on him a clarity of spirit favouring decision making. He liked to work alone and did not appreciate the tears of those he considered too "sensitive." He was endowed with a fighting spirit that was not easily impressed. He demonstrated a strong stamina, always ready to serve his country and his people.

---

[1] Koot Hoomi is the *Cohan* of the Ray 2 Ashram.

His ray 1 graced him with the power of speech and commanded everyone's respect. Nothing could stop him; he knew how to lead and listen. He would rapidly sort the information received thanks to the amalgamation of ray 1 (direct and to the point) and ray 5 (more Cartesian, which incited him to go over all the material with the pros and cons). His ray 1 enlightened his intelligence and allowed him to be efficient in his actions. He was feared but this fear commanded respect.

His sub-ray 5 offered him the possibility to demonstrate his strategic ability and to foresee, with the help of ray 1, the strikes that the German army was getting ready to carry out. He could penetrate the enemy's mind and read their thoughts, thus seeing their desire to conquer the world.

Sub-ray 5 also enticed him to demonstrate how "intelligent" he was in his intelligence. He had answers for everything, with logic and vision (thanks to his initiation level). Very arrogant and self-confident (a mix between his Personality rays and his initiation level) and difficult to contain, he could sense what was being plotted. His character made him difficult to live with, even at times unbearable. His mood swings would frighten people but he commanded respect. He suffered a lot from solitude and often felt misunderstood.

Mental Body

His ray 1, sub-ray 3 mental body allowed him to be efficient and fast. The ray 1 influence could easily make him pass for a brute; never at a loss for words, he would often offend without meaning to. He liked power and enjoyed using it, promoting justice and hating treason and indecision. He could see far because of his clear mind. He was not a quitter.

Sub-ray 3 offered him the possibility to dazzle his audience when this proved necessary. He was not afraid to play with words and knew how to master them, becoming then, more magnetic. This sub-ray granted him the faculty to hedge his bets.

Astral Body

His ray 6, sub-ray 2 Astral made him a man dedicated to his country. He defended the "cause" well and, to do so, used all the means at his disposal. Ray 6 gratified him with a lot of eagerness in expressing himself. He liked to impress people, particularly those he respected. While being independent, he remained very attached to his family. As he experienced difficulty in expressing his feelings, he was often considered a cold and stubborn person. He literally swallowed his emotions, enjoyed drinking and smoking, and felt ill at ease with the emotions ray 6 made him live. When he did not get what he wanted, he experienced frustration and anger.

His sub-ray 2 softened his fiery character and instilled in him a love for children. In spite of his roughness, he was full of tenderness that he was unable to express. This caused him a lot of grief. He was sensitive to criticism and felt it difficult to let go.

Physical Body

Due to his ray 3, sub-ray 6 physical, he was a strong and powerful man. Graced with a great endurance, he could work tirelessly day and night. His goal motivated him and his physical body supported him well. His excess weight came from his emotional body that still dominated certain aspects of his life. His sharp intelligence, which sparkled in his eyes, also came from the mix of rays 1 and 3. Ray 1 gave him a strong and powerful expression, and ray 3 added a spark. He could see everything, or almost.

Sub-ray 6 kept alive certain attachments in his life, including his attachment to his family, to whom he was very faithful. His sense of duty also came from his ray 6, which increased in him the desire to work for others. Let's not forget that ray 6, in its enthusiasm, strangely resembles ray 1. He was not a quitter. He did not know how to stop. The world lost a great brightness when he passed away. He is not yet incarnated but will be soon. He is waiting for his wife, to whom he has to repay a small karma. He is still very attached to her. She helped him and supported him a lot in his work and will continue to do so in their next incarnation.

June 20, 2008

 CLINTON, HILLARY

Given Name: Hillary Diane Rodham
Nationality: American
Place and Date of Birth: Chicago, Illinois (United States), October 26, 1947
Profession: Lawyer and politician

Master Djwhal Khul's Commentary

A woman led by her heart but especially by her head, Hillary Clinton brings a lot of solidity to her environment because she is a reliable, honest and solid woman. She usually knows her rightful place and is not afraid of facing the unknown. She takes her work very seriously and gives it her all. People can depend on her. The Masters of the Great White Lodge place a great deal of hope in her because within her rests the expectation of some form of democracy in the United States which will not happen if a certain Republican candidate[1] enters the White House.

She is not without her faults but she has sufficient courage, willpower and rectitude to make a difference in the political balance of the United States. Should Ms. Clinton be elected as the country's president, she will encounter challenges similar to those faced by her predecessor[2] and will lose much of her vitality. It is a sacrifice she seems ready to make for the well-being of the American people. She is more or less conscious of it because this sacrifice stems more from her Soul than her Personality.

Initiation Level: 2.3

Her Soul has started to have some influence; it supports her in difficult circumstances. Ms. Clinton appears to be listening more and more to this small inner voice guiding her in some of her decisions. The challenges

---

[1] We are referring here to Donald Trump.
[2] Barack Obama.

of the past twenty years (as First Lady of the United States, during the Lewinski affair, in her role as Secretary of State of the United States, etc.), from which she emerged stronger, have allowed her to get closer to her Soul and to climb a few decimal points in her initiation level. It is evident that she carries herself with a certain arrogance linked to her status as a young initiate, but she nevertheless remains available to "serve" and she listens to the suffering of others with true sincerity.

Ray Structure

Monad: 2	Soul: 2	Personality: 3-7
Mental: 7-5	Astral: 6-2	Physical: 3-7

Monad and Soul

Her Monad currently exercises no influence, contrary to her Soul which is starting to have one, and will only grow over time.

Personality

With the influence of rays 3 and 7, Hillary Clinton has a stable and strong personality due to the support of sub-ray 7, while also being flexible and adaptable to certain situations (influence of ray 3).

Ray 3 gives her the facility to express herself, to move and to interact with people. It allows her to be diplomatic when necessary but she can also be manipulative to get what she wants. She knows how to use social media to project a faultless image of herself. She wants the public to believe she is close to them while projecting an image of power and solidity. Ray 3 also gives her a quick wit and a sense of humor, which makes her charming when she wants to be.

Sub-ray 7 adds seriousness to the influence of ray 3. At times, when ray 3 tries to get around certain ways of behaving in order to get the desired result, sub-ray 7 puts Ms. Clinton back on the right track. It promotes justice and wants things to be done correctly in compliance with conventions. It allows her to find solutions towards the aspired outcome, without having to resort to questionable activities.

Mental Body

The influence of rays 7 and 5 makes her a very intelligent woman. Ray 7 makes her intuitive and sub-ray 5 gives her a good base to affirm what she says and to take action.

Generally, ray 7 transmits clear and precise ideas to her, which guide her in her daily life. However, if the astral body of Ms. Clinton is unbalanced, ray 6 muddles her vision and the influence of ray 7 then becomes very trenchant and unequivocal. In those circumstances, her words can become "harsh" and hurtful. But she usually pulls together rather quickly and regains her mental polarity free from any emotion. She becomes efficient again and forgets (for as long as it is necessary) what had "emotionally" perturbed her. Ray 7 also makes her attentive to details – this makes her more secure as well as more formidable for her adversaries because she leaves nothing to chance.

Sub-ray 5 gives her solidity because Ms. Clinton is always trying to base her words on verifiable facts. She does not generally make false promises and when she gives her word, she can assume the consequences. Sub-ray 5 sharpens her intuition and allows her to heal herself adequately and rapidly when she takes time to admire nature and let her mind wander, even if only for a few seconds. This helps "recharge her batteries" rapidly.

Astral Body

As for most women, her astral body is her weak point. But with age and the diminution of seduction games and sexuality, she is becoming internally more solid and less fragile. Ray 6 allows her to be loyal to her family, a sentiment which she puts forth to the whole country which then becomes "her" family. If Ms. Clinton is elected, she will fight tooth and nail for the well being of the American people, as much for her poor as for her rich constituents, without regard to the color of their skin.

Sub-ray 2 (which is allied with the influence of her Soul) helps her to remain loving, even in the most difficult moments. She can forgive sincerely though she tries not to get herself into the same situation twice. Ray 6 makes her warm and sub-ray 2 increases that feeling of love she feels more and more towards all. This sub-ray 2 makes her a woman who can listen and express herself clearly.

Physical Body

The rays which influence the energy of her physical body adequately support the rays of her Personality.

Ray 3 provides her with an efficient and intelligent brain which can detect manipulation in others. It helps her control her emotions by allowing her to see and understand what is hidden behind the attitudes and the words of those people she comes in contact with. She can keep her cool when she has to. Supported by sub-ray 7, this ray also gave her a strong nervous system which serves her well. She is not the type of woman who will fly off the handle to satisfy her ego. She prefers observing, listening and analyzing a situation in order to extricate herself from it with as little damage as possible.

Sub-ray 7 refines her thoughts, makes her more apt to speak adequately, and gives her a facility to answer with intelligence and without doubting herself. It sometimes causes her to be harsh or impersonal, but she readjusts fairly quickly, because ray 7 tends to be concerned with appearances, and Ms. Clinton is careful of her image and always wants to show herself as a loving and intelligent woman whom people can trust.

As previously mentioned, Hillary Clinton is not perfect but we believe that she can accomplish work that will allow the American people to once again become an example of peace and harmony. The United States, this super power, must become wiser because other world powers, aligned to dictatorships of all kinds, are starting to create damage which will soon affect the world balance.

January 8, 2016

 COHEN, ANDREW

Given Name: Andrew Cohen
Nationality: American
Place and Date of Birth: New York, New York (United States),
October 23, 1955
Profession: Writer and lecturer

MASTER DJWHAL KHUL'S COMMENTARY

An intelligent man, Andrew Cohen received the first call from his Soul when he was 16. He was put in touch with his light so that his life would be guided towards one of service and assistance to others. However, he is not "Awake" but partly illuminated because his Consciousness is lit with a new spiritual knowledge acquired in this present incarnation. He is young as a Soul, although he is old in terms of incarnations. He has been living on this planet for quite some time and attempts to penetrate its mysteries from all viewpoints. In the past, he was a writer, a scientist, a poet, a business man, a prostitute, a housewife, a North American Indian, a doctor, and so on. He accumulated an extensive knowledge that his atmic memory uses.

Presently, he has to mature and to integrate all he acquired in the past. He likes studying and people; now he must love his spiritual knowledge more and integrate it into his lives, which he has often failed to do.

Initiation Level: 1.8

Andrew Cohen is a mini-*guru* who can bring a lot to mankind. He is still young; until he has not reached his third initiation, which depends only on him, he will remain young in our eyes.

Ray Structure

Monad: 1	Soul: 2	Personality: 6-4
Mental: 3-7	Astral: 4-2	Physical: 3-6

Monad and Soul

His Soul is starting to have a certain influence. In the past, he let it play with his various incarnations. However, once he knows how to integrate the various acquired experiences, particularly in the field of knowledge (which ray 2 loves because, in a way it gives him a feeling of subtle intellectual superiority), he will become more active and evolve more rapidly.

Ray 2 likes to accumulate knowledge, while ray 3 likes to accumulate experiences. Both, in a way, are alike. Contrary to ray 3, which adores experimentation even in more evolved incarnations, ray 2, once it has reached a certain wisdom through accumulated knowledge, ceases to experiment and focuses on a more rapid evolution.

Personality

His Personality, influenced by ray 6, sub-ray 4, makes him a warm man who likes to guide and advise. Ray 6 makes him loyal and devoted. He likes to help because it results in a certain recognition. Sometimes, he seems like a separatist but he always tends towards unification in order to realize the divine plan (influence of ray 3's in the Mental and the Physical).

Sub-ray 4 offers him the possibility to be a good writer, to appreciate the arts as well as the beauty of things without abusing them. His ray 4's make him sensitive and easily influenced. He sometimes experiences ups and downs that are rapidly corrected. He is a good friend who, however, requests a minimum of letting go, since he dislikes the feeling of being entrapped.

Mental Body

His mental body, ruled by ray 3, sub-ray 7, endows him with a brilliant intelligence; he has the faculty to clearly explain the most abstract concepts. He is seeking experience in the accumulation of knowledge. His thinking wants to be flexible because he proves to be a fairly good speaker (thanks to the support of ray 3 in the physical body).

Sub-ray 7 provides an interesting strength and a self-confidence that guides him during his travels and realizations. It allows him not to lose himself and to anchor himself to reality. Ray 3 (assisted by his ray 4's) makes him dream, while sub-ray 7 brings him down to earth. He likes perfection and knows how to surround himself with a good team.

Astral Body

His astral body, tinged with the energy of ray 4, sub-ray 2, renders him a sensitive man easily hurt, who suffers the ups and downs of an emotional body influenced by ray 4. This ray is such that he attracts conflicts, which he hates.

Sub-ray 2 supports him and provides him with a certain intuition that helps him in his work that requires his meeting a lot of people. This sub-ray grants him kindness, sociability, intuition, perseverance and restraint, often fearing to hurt people. It makes him vulnerable, but sensitive to the energy carried by his astral body. Do not forget that he is heading towards the mastery of his astral body at the second initiation. It is important then, that ray 2 be part of his configuration. Frequently, he gives the impression of having a sixth sense, which is, in fact, only the result of ray 2's influence.

Physical Body

His physical body, ruled by the influence of ray 3, sub-ray 6, grants him resistance. Ray 3 gives him a facility to talk, to express himself, and to move. He proves to be almost indefatigable, with a calmness due to his ray 6 Personality (although he moves constantly). This ray ensures him flexibility and adaptability that serve him in various situations that become complicated because of the intervention of the two ray 4's of his configuration.

Sub-ray 6 gives him the impression of being grounded, which is not the case. He perceives a lot of things, thanks to his plexus. He enjoys eating, drinking and enjoying good company.

This man is doing good work. However, he should not, under any circumstance, take on the charge of a Guru, a Light bearer. Admittedly, he enlightens certain aspects of the human personality, but the fact still remains that he cannot "transmit" this Light in man in a way to really transform him. Deep down, these students remain the same, unchanged. On the surface, they evolve in knowledge, in experiences, which is very commendable, but deep within, no authentic contact takes place with their Soul…

September 19, 2008

 # CREME, BENJAMIN

Given Name: Benjamin Creme
Double Nationality: Scottish and British
Place and Date of Birth: Glasgow (Scotland), December 5, 1922
Profession: Painter, writer and speaker

MASTER DJWHAL KHUL'S COMMENTARY

A highly intelligent and proud man, Benjamin Creme serves the Masters very well and thinks he is accomplishing a great deal in his lifetime. He helps humanity by giving man hope for the future. He seems to converse with us regularly, especially with Maitreya. However, you should be aware that this is not the case. Indeed, he converses with a number of Masters, but the impact of his transmissions serves mostly to suppress the fear and hate prevailing within various cultural communities. His contact, which is sufficiently pure, allows him to transmit a rather important truth, as the Truth must be spoken. And he stands ready to do so. However, we must say that he has been accumulating certain errors that sometimes detract from our work. His main handicap is his lack of vision. He leaves too much room for interpretation and accords too little emphasis on transmission.

Did he really receive the intensive training he thinks he did? We will not contradict him; let us simply say that the training was not as intensive as he thought. Nonetheless, it is true that a certain dose of energy was infused in him to allow him to clear his channel, one that was too narrow and polluted. His channel is derived 80% from the Astral (the upper Astral) and 20% from the Mental. Thus, we can say that he channels quite well, as the majority of people on this planet are "astrally" polarized. Therefore, he transmits important information to them. They understand his statements and prove ready to act accordingly. This type of channel, which reaches a considerable number of people, is necessary to us. However, he remains an only partially illuminated channel who is unable to accomplish all of his work.

We might also add that he is less evolved than in his previous life, which was rich on many levels. From infancy, knowing he had a particular destiny, he quickly stopped progressing, only attaining a portion of his preceding initiation level. Struck with the mirage of "serving" at any cost instead of "serving" when the time was right, he will readjust during his next reincarnation. He knows this and will do so. You should also know that his Master is not Koot Hoomi, but actually El Morya Khan. He only serves Koot Hoomi temporarily, and the majority or his teachings are dictated to him by one of Koot Hoomi's closest disciples.

Initiation Level: 1.8

During his last life, his initiation level was 2.8. His current initiation level of 1.8 creates flashes in his vision arising from his prior superior initiation level, which does not find full expression in this present incarnation. He is a Soul that deserves our respect, but he should not be considered a mature Soul that is highly advanced.

We hope he will attain the second level of initiation during his present lifetime. But his destiny may soon dictate otherwise…

Ray Structure

Monad: 1	Soul: 2	Personality: 7-3
Mental: 2-7	Astral: 6-4	Physical: 3-6

Monad and Soul

His Soul exerts a strong enough influence on him to allow him to be receptive to the Masters' requests. Being sensitive, he knows how to receive certain messages, thanks to his ray 2 mental body supported by sub-ray 7, which instills a form of structural clarity into his thinking.

Personality

His ray 7, sub-ray 3 Personality makes him creative and refined. He likes beautiful things and likes to express himself through beauty, although he remains chaotic and almost negligent in his environment (ray 3 physical body). He is a cultivated man whose art finds expression through ray 7. He likes things to be clear, although he often has difficulty expressing himself clearly.

His sub-ray 3 enables him to adapt quickly to events as they unfold, and to respond to questions with apparent ease and in a highly intelligent manner. He has mastered the art of measuring his answers carefully, according to what is asked of him.

Mental Body

His ray 2, sub-ray 7 mental body makes him extremely receptive to superior worlds. He is intuitive and able to receive messages from other planes. His ray 2 enables him to sense the existence of dimensions beyond our own, although it also makes him fragile and prone to certain influences and impressions from "elsewhere". He must be vigilant, even as he remains receptive. Without this ray 2 mental body, he could not accomplish what he does. It gives him an "otherworldly" air. It also confers on him the powers of a medium and, due to his initiation level, he is fairly well attuned to what he receives.

His sub-ray 7 provides him with a sense of structure and allows him to remain coherent. He has an intelligence that proves undeniably reassuring for those who are close to him. He appears structured and very credible. His ray 2 provides him with the "antennae" to receive and his sub-ray 7, with the "hardwiring" to transmit effectively. Without this sub-ray 7, he would appear incoherent and be hard to understand, seemingly coming from another dimension. It thereby allows him to be orderly and structured in the statements he makes.

Astral Body

His astral body, ray 6, sub-ray 4, makes him dedicated to his work and devoted to his life's goal and the Masters, whom he tries to serve well. He can be stubborn and hard to deal with at times, as his sub-ray 4 afflicts him with emotional ups and downs he finds difficult to handle.

His sub-ray 4 also prompts him to be creative and makes him sensitive to beauty. He likes to create, which greatly relaxes him. His painting allows him to strike a kind of balance with his emotional life, which proves very demanding. He endures much solitude.

Physical Body

His physical body, ray 3, sub-ray 6, makes him robust and hard working. He is resilient and knows how to accomplish a great deal without becoming overtired. Intelligent and studious, he has shown himself to be an excellent diplomat with a sense of humour greatly appreciated by his entourage. He knows how to be fair to those who help and support him in his task.

His sub-ray 6 confers him with an unflagging determination. He knows what he wants and what he has to do to get it. He is not a quitter. Obstinate and hardworking, he refuses to rest too much.

We would like to point out that the mention of Maitreya's eventual public appearance is questionable. It is certain that he will not appear in public in the presence of the media. He works in another manner entirely, through the Consciousness of those he tries to awaken.

June 21, 2008

ADDITIONAL COMMENTARY FROM MASTER DJWHAL KHUL

The Return of Maitreya

Benjamin Creme has been briefing us for a number of years on the return of Maitreya, the Buddha of the future. I will not contradict his declarations, because he has effectively returned and is actively working for the global awakening of human consciousness. However, I will add some precisions that will undoubtedly get across the objective of his work and the procedure he is using to reach it.

It is true that human consciousness, in the majority of cases, is not too evolved. One just has to watch what is happening in the world: wars, persecutions, unjustified executions, torture, famine, lack of respect for the Earth and the lack of equitable distribution of the financial capital within the international community. Everything has to be reviewed and corrected before humanity faces its doom, which could happen if such beings as Maitreya were not actively working to awaken this consciousness that is sleeping and too turned in on itself.

Changes must take place slowly and carefully, otherwise chaos will reign on Earth. Man must deprogram his old patterns that he has always known, although harmful for him and his environment. Man very often does not see further than his own life; now, his consciousness must "become aware" that his life is part of a whole in which he returns cyclically in order to become "more conscious" of what he is and what he must become. Man buries his head in the sand and does not see beyond the tip of his nose, which creates in him a fear of change, but mainly a fear of the unknown inside this change. This is the reason changes prove to be long and often painful.

Being afraid of change, particularly of changing, man is unconsciously acting to delay the evolution of his consciousness because this evolution requires self-denial in order to reach the Self, something which he does not demonstrate a readiness to do. He only thinks of himself and sees only through his own eyes, wrongly believing that what he perceives is just and true. He infuses, then, his energy with this belief and imposes his own view, narrow and lacking vision, on the people around him, convinced that he is acting well. This situation stems mainly from ray 6, which will gradually be replaced by Ray 7, more realistic from a worldwide viewpoint because it is less individualistic.

The goal of the influence of ray 6 was to bring man to become more aware of himself, his own consciousness, his own existence, and to assume his own survival. In doing this, he learned to belong to himself and become the perfect expression of some of his rays that spread to nations. Homogeneity was replaced by a differentiation that gradually became a separation. Ideologies come to life and are replaced by the need to survive physically, a necessity that is getting easier to fulfill. Previously, everyone or nearly everyone believed in the existence of several gods manifested through various kingdoms (animal, vegetable and mineral). Some gods were honoured (for rain, abundance, Lakshmi) and vengeful gods who, according to beliefs, brought destruction (Shiva, etc.). Lives were sacrificed in the hope of obtaining the clemency of these gods.

In order to counter this ignorance ray 6 came, favouring the emergence of a more personal and individual aspect. With this ray, monotheism appeared: one God for man's Consciousness to cease being collective. This produced a shock to consciousness but also introduced a separate individualism. Man divided in himself his beliefs, and also his small consciousness, which became narrower and more linear. That is when the fear of not being what he thought he was was born, the fear of not belonging to himself. A more subtle form of slavery surfaced, the slavery to various religious beliefs that, instead of liberating man, made him more of a prisoner to the group spirit. More subtle but also deadlier, these beliefs created the survival of the species, as thinking individuals, and a massive destruction of what did not correspond to these beliefs.

The fear of disappearing did not only touch man's physical envelope but what he believed to be his Soul, which in reality represented his personality. Man is still living this illusion. We, the Masters must accomplish much work, refusing to step back from any sacrifice so that man's consciousness stops being small and narrow.

The advent of ray 7 will bring a new breath to the consciousness that will become not collective but "cooperative" to everyone's awakening, touching his vital space and spiritual life. Each man's personality will be strongly worked, because it is through the personality that change will take place. The physical body will only be used to frighten the personality that will have no other choice but to turn to other personalities if it wishes to survive. The personality represents, in a way, the perfect envelope of the man who does not wish to evolve. It is a hiding place for the ego that manipulates man like a puppet, responding to all its desires.

Maitreya's work will be to awaken man so that he becomes conscious of his illusions that stem from concepts imposed by generations of thinkers who thought they were doing well but only thought individually. Man's ego is hard to destroy because everything brings him back to this fact: the media, leisure, his spiritual life. He thinks of himself only, although he fights in the name of Allah or Jesus. He is only concerned with his own beliefs that do not reflect the reality of what he is. There are many paths leading to liberation. Religions or religious beliefs, that must unite us to our Self, and must not, at any time, enslave us to beliefs built in their entirety by man's personality by way of his primary thinking system. In a sense, religion poorly understood (which is the case in the majority of situations) does not liberate man; it hypnotizes him and renders him powerless in front of his destiny that becomes limited, taken in a context where nothing can evolve. The one who puts man to sleep instead of awakening him commits a grave sin. These sins create the karmic link that compels man to constantly come back while continuously provoking chaos, because the awakening is slow to occur.

The awakening must occur voluntarily and gradually. No one can impose his will and Maitreya knows it. Therefore, he has to work in a way than man understands him, thinking and transmuting his mode of thinking, narrow and individual into a thinking mode more appropriate to what he is: a free being in a world equally free where harmony and the respect amongst differences reign.

Let's not forget that there are several paths leading us to our Destiny and that none, whether or not it is promoting the real liberation of man and the whole of humanity, has more value than the other. We have to understand each other and mutually support each other; the religions to which we adhere have no relation to "the" God as such, but rather touch more the rays of our personality or of our Soul (when we have stepped through the first door of initiation). The rays of the various nations exert a great influence because they act collectively on the human consciousness that lives in them. Rays possess a hold on personalities that, in a particular way, have no distinctive personality and try to differentiate themselves by their beliefs. They then have the illusion of "belonging" to something that defines them as an individual but, in fact, keeps them enslaved and prevents them from becoming who they really are as individuals that then differentiates them by what they really are. Man must cease to define himself according to his beliefs and start to really define himself, with what is beyond what he thinks to be when he prays or ignores God.

Maitreya makes very few public appearances because man's primary consciousness cannot conceive of such a fact. He uses reflections of himself, astral reflections that take shape and impose a harmonious energy that temporarily appeases the spirit of the suffering man. These occurrences do not change man's consciousness and, in certain cases, enslave him more with his own beliefs that include this belief in a "Saviour God that would save them from their sins." Maitreya is not a "saviour" but an "awakener" of consciousness. His rare physical appearances occurred anonymously. They occurred in places where he could influence, in their decisions, the great politicians of the world who, if they are well directed, could change the future of humanity. Occasionally, he appears to some Masters that are actively working to change man's narrow consciousness.

He lives in England but outside London because he cannot bear an energy so materialistic and full of psychic pollution. He lives, most of the time, outside his physical body which is too limiting. He does not appear as himself in public in a crowd. What appears at times represents a pale reflection of what he really is. The creation of these reflections aims at producing an effect, but mainly at entering into a resonance with the people he wishes to imbue with this energy of harmony and hope. Let us not forget that the worldly Consciousness does not want immediate radical changes. It requires preparation, which Maitreya is doing. He temporarily alleviates suffering by his astral apparitions, which do not change the consciousness of those looking at him, as these apparitions are still under the influence of ray 6.

When he uses a physical body, he does it discreetly but efficiently. The energy he radiates is an energy of Strength and Truth with no link to the mystical aspect that these apparitions take. He uses rays 7 and 1 more when he uses his physical body. Ray 6 is used during his astral apparitions.

He works actively and one should not waste time hoping for a public appearance on television. This expectation is dictated by beliefs produced by ray 6 and not the reality. Maitreya is intelligent, mysterious and efficient. He only appears to those who are open to working with him to change the world, and it is not through the media. He never reveals his real name, and strives in such a way as to go unnoticed, because that is where his real transforming power resides.

In doing this, he is neither threatening nor intrusive. He does not create fear that produces judgement, doubt and death, and has nothing to prove. He is what he is. Only those who ignore who they are secretly hope that his work will reveal itself to them through astral apparitions that make them believe they are worthy and apart from the others.

On the contrary, those who know that self-awakening takes place through an internal transformation that requires work, patience and that goes through themselves and not someone else... they give a real importance to the subtle messages transmitted by Maitreya that are not communicated through his astral apparitions. They wish, whenever possible, to receive shocks to the consciousness in order to polarize their beings towards a transformation that, passing through fire, will become real and durable. They know how to "see" behind the mirages and attempt to relentlessly progress, while knowing that He is here and that He is taking care of the whole planet, without consideration for their little selves.

June 20, 2008

 # CROMWELL, OLIVER

Given Name: Oliver Cromwell
Nationality: British
Place and Date of Birth: Huntingdon, Cambridge (England), April 25 1599
Date of Death: London (England), September 3 1658
Profession: Military leader and statesman

MASTER DJWHAL KHUL'S COMMENTARY

Oliver Cromwell was a remarkable man, thanks to his determination and desire to help his country attain a certain autonomy. However, he still remains the subject of controversy today, being a hero to some and a traitor to others.

It is true that he led his country to a degree of liberation and, in order to reach such a result, he sometimes used harsh means. However, his work has redeemed some of the faults committed in his past life as Genghis Khan, also called "The Barbarian." We must add that he remained aggressive and hard to deceive, and was scathing in his comments, particularly towards those he considered to be traitors to his country.

As Cromwell, he used the strength of his mental body instead of the strength of his arms. He fought with less fierceness than during the time of Genghis Khan, because his love for his people was more sincere while being as determined.

He also had a certain refinement that was lacking in his life as Genghis Khan. While being as intelligent, he dominated less while imposing himself more. This may seem paradoxical; let us simply mention that he was less powerful than in his past incarnation. This was the wish of the Masters, who hoped that he would adopt better behaviour.

He feared love less, which was felt in his entourage. This did not prevent him, however, from being a strong man, committed to his duty and who was not often easy to deal with. His life was most interesting, though often contentious. He made mistakes that he regretted later, due to his initiation level, which did not allow him to have a wider vision. However, his vision was sufficient enough to help improve the political conditions within his country.

Initiation Level: 1.8

He worked hard to reach this initiation level because he had many karmic debts. He paid back several, because many souls in incarnation with him from the time of Genghis Khan were in England and Scotland. He helped them while helping himself.

Ray Structure

Monad: 3	Soul: 2	Personality: 1-3
Mental: 5-7	Astral: 6-2	Physical: 3-7

Monad and Soul

His Monad had no influence, contrary to his Soul that exercised a little. He was mainly ruled by his Personality rays, as the strength and the vision of ray 1 were necessary to him. He was reliable and this was mainly due to this ray. Ray 2's influence at the level of his Soul allowed him to be more honest and more sincere. He now knew how to recognize his faults, which was a great progress in his evolution.

Approximately five lives (his life that followed Genghis Khan was very short) have separated these two important incarnations, lives that taught him lessons regarding his arrogance and desire to dominate. A rebel in the first four lives, he suffered a lot during the fifth one, which opened his eyes to this problem he had to correct. The results did not prove to be perfect, but sufficient to allow him to do a better job in his life as Oliver Cromwell. He is presently holding an important position inside the British Government. The only clue I shall give you is that he now occupies a female body.

Personality

His ray 1, sub-ray 3 Personality has supported him well during this incarnation. He could, thanks to this configuration, show flexibility and firmness simultaneously. He had an iron hand in a velvet glove, even if, sometimes, he would take off his glove and become only "iron."

Ray 1 gave him a sufficiently clear vision of what he had to accomplish. He was sometimes plagued by doubts; however, the influence of ray 1 gave him the strength to continue and provided him with the wind in his sails by stimulating his perseverance. He could liberate himself mentally from the work to be brought to fruition. He knew he could accomplish a lot and his goal was simply to reach it.

Sub-ray 3 brought him important support to express himself and see his opponents' games. Endowed, in addition, with a configuration of ray 5, sub-ray 7 in the mental body made him more "strategic," therefore he was not easily fooled. This sub-ray granted him sufficient diplomacy to open important doors for him. He disliked cheating (ray 1) but knew how to discover it in others. This gave him an additional weapon to play his cards well.

Mental Body

He was intelligent and methodical in his approach thanks to the influence of ray 5, sub-ray 7 in his mental body, which allowed him to accomplish his military task. Ray 5 conferred on him a love for "discipline" (his "strategic" aspect) that incited him to gain time. He liked things to be done properly, flawlessly. He would not make a move without having given it enough thought and having well understood the situation in which he found himself. This helped him but also made him lose some possibilities that were beyond this well planned world.

His sub-ray 7 brought him the respect of others because he had a strong sense of refinement. He liked beautiful objects and knew how to surround himself with them, as well as order, which he knew how to implement. An excellent soldier, he knew how to properly lead his men. Often harsh, he aspired to a certain perfection that his men usually failed to understand.

Astral Body

His astral body, influenced by ray 6, sub-ray 2, rendered him dependable and determined with regards to his country's cause. Very faithful to his family that he loved a lot without really showing it, he did not display his feelings, a consequence of his ray 1 Personality. He loved his wife and his children, who without hearing him say as much, knew it and supported him in his endeavours.

Ray 6 gave him the possibility to develop in himself, this love while remaining charming and secretive. He could be aggressive and demanding towards his family, but he deeply loved them while knowing that he could not be the ideal father and husband.

Sub-ray 2 refined ray 6 that would have otherwise become too rigid and difficult to live with. Cromwell had few friends but he was loyal to them. This sub-ray conferred on him a certain dose of intuition with regard to his relations that allowed him to utter the right words in order to nurture and reassure. This sub-ray created an uneasiness concerning the pains felt by his family, such as the pain of his wife's delivery and the illnesses of his children. However, he remained stronger vis-à-vis the pains felt by his troops on the battlefield, thanks to the influence of his Personality rays 1 and 3.

Physical Body

His physical, ruled by ray 3, sub-ray 7, conferred on him a strong body that was, nevertheless, lacking in power. Endowed with strong resilience, his physical strength was somewhat modest. He could accomplish long trips on horseback and fight, but he would tire quickly when it was a matter of working hard with his body (lifting or dragging weights…). Ray 3 gave him speed, as much at the thinking level as at the physical level, which helped save his life on several occasions.

Sub-ray 7 conferred a certain refinement that he needed to win over his opponents and his fellow countrymen. He knew how to appreciate beauty and comfort. He was always a good leader; and thanks to this sub-ray, he knew how to lead well, that is with intelligence.

July 5, 2008

 CRUISE, TOM

Given Name: Thomas Cruise Mapother IV
Nationality: American
Place and Date of Birth: Syracuse, New York (United States), July 3 1962
Profession: Actor and film producer

MASTER DJWHAL KHUL'S COMMENTARY

A man of little faith, except in himself, Tom Cruise is living proof of how big the human ego can grow. Full of himself, a seducer and manipulator, he may seem to have a great heart, but his soul is full of anger. He remains tied to complexes due to his height and infertility, thus confirming his young age.

I mention the word soul with a lower case "s", because he seems to have partially contaminated his human soul (linked to the human condition and not to the divine condition, man having to educate the human soul in order to relate its experiences to the divine Soul that gratefully welcomes them). Too much popularity made him self-centred and not focused on his life's goal which is another matter. A Priest[1] in his Soul, he acts like an immature priest who loves to dominate without really educating. He is ignorant of what real love is as well as his real nature which was enslaved by being in the limelight.

---

[1] "From one incarnation to the next, the soul takes on a set of different traits with the exception of one that always remains the same, the role. This permanent trait allows the essence or heart of the soul to get closer to divinity, when shown in its positive polarity." "The objective of the priest is to preach. His essence is compassion, an inborn compassion for others that expresses itself through service."

Excerpt from: *Les Discours de Michael sur le Tao du Savoir Vivre selon la typologie de Chelsea Quinn Yarbro et développés par D.D.D.*, The Group of 7, Paume de Saint-Germain Publishing, Montreal, 2011, 329 pp.

He could have and should have accomplished more, but his life as an actor and producer blinded him to such an extent that he will be unable to fulfill his destiny. He will have to start all over in more difficult conditions.

His intrusion into the world of Dianetics made him even more selfish, more cynical towards life and the people that make it up. His union with Katie Holmes is like a countdown; she will not be able to live long under the yoke of his impatience and domination. Only her daughter counts; she knows she would lose much if she separates from the almighty God that Cruise believes he is. She will have to choose between her daughter and her freedom of expression. For the time being, her daughter prevails, and as she has the "Soul" of a slave[1]…

Initiation Level: 1.5

He is a very young soul experimenting with fame, success and celebrity. He is secretly thinking of becoming the leader of Dianetics when he would reach retirement from show business as an actor.

Ray Structure

Monad: 2	Soul: 7	Personality: 6-2
Mental: 7-5	Astral: 6-4	Physical: 3-7

A Perfectionist (three ray 7's), he reveals himself devoted to his cause (two ray 6's, and his not so evolved initiation level) while knowing how to adequately manipulate his entourage (ray 3 physical brain). Although he often lacks sensitivity (ray 7 mental body and ray 6 Personality), he knows how to play his role towards his relatives (ray 6 astral body conferring on him an ensured devotion, that in spite of his selfishness, is derived from

---

[1]"The slave's essence is service. He is always seeking a person or an institution to serve. He really likes to help, trying to bring comfort in a material sense to humanity."

Excerpt from: *Les Discours de Michael sur le Tao du Savoir Vivre selon la typologie de Chelsea Quinn Yarbro et développés par D.D.D.*, The Group of 7, Paume de Saint-Germain Publishing, Montreal, 2011, 329 pp.

his initiation level, as well as sub-ray 4 granting him acting capabilities, the whole being supported by a ray 3 brain and a ray 6 Personality).

Monad and Soul

His Monad has no influence, his Soul, a little, although insufficient to make a difference.

Personality

His ray 6, sub-ray 2 Personality endows him with a certain warmth that makes him attractive, because he seems to be sensitive and dedicated to several causes. His ray 6 grants him this dedication but beware of betrayal: he does not forgive easily. Incidentally, a portion of the strange behaviour of Nicole Kidman is a result of his influence. Since the beginning of their relationship, he tried to manipulate her which created a lot of fear, anger and impatience and a great deal of insecurity in her, from which she has not yet healed.

His sub-ray 2 makes him charming and magnetic, conferring on him the wish to save the world — according to his way and vision. His pride is easily hurt, because this sub-ray 2 as well as his sub-ray 4 Astral twinned with ray 6 create a cocktail that makes him hypersensitive and somewhat paranoid.

Mental Body

His ray 7, sub-ray 5 mental body gives him the impression of being intelligent. He reasons and directs easily, believing that he has a just vision and thinks he is helping others by communicating his view of things. Undoubtedly, scientology, which focuses its impact on the mind, does not help him find a balance. Of this "science", he enjoys the fact that it is based on the concrete, on the mind, creating in him this superiority of artificial intelligence.

Ray 7 lends a certain order in his thinking process, and sub-ray 5 gives him the words to explain in a more or less significant way. He believes in thinking and in the fact that everything is managed from there. In a way, he is a non-believer; he does not believe in the divine nature of man but rather in his capacity for reasoning which influences the established order by sending electric and magnetic waves that can change the course of life and intervene in his favour.

Astral Body

His ray 6, sub-ray 4 astral body gives him warmth although he is unpredictable at times. He can change his character as fast as his ideas – which in his case is very fast. His ray 6 allows him to be a good father, though without vision, thus making him possessive and controlling.

Sub-ray 4 confers on him the facility to play different roles, because he is mainly focused, in this life, on his emotions that he is attempting to manage adequately, often without success.

Physical Body

His ray 3, sub-ray 7 physical allows him to accomplish a lot in a day; he proves to be tireless. However, his small size bothers him. To compensate for this, he tries to dominate through his Mental.

Sub-ray 7 gives him the taste of perfection, what Katie Holmes must respect. She has to be perfect in everything, particularly in public. If she does not untangle herself from her complacency, he will succeed in making her give up her career as an actress.

He is a man who possesses a certain power based only on appearances. If he does not wake up soon, he will commit errors for which he would have to pay the price in future incarnations.

January 30, 2009

 CURIE, MARIE

Given Name: Maria Skłodowska
Double Nationality: Polish and French
Place and Date of Birth: Warsaw (Poland), November 7, 1867
Date of Death: Sancellemoz (France), July 4, 1934
Profession: Physician

MASTER DJWHAL KHUL'S COMMENTARY

An extraordinary woman for her time, Marie Curie allowed humanity to take steps forward towards more autonomy. Since then, human beings are in a better position to understand some of the aspects that seemed, until that time, hidden (the atom, X-rays).

The discovery of radium and radiography allowed humanity to become conscious of all the potential that is dormant in the feminine human brain as well as admiring all the marvels of the human body without dissecting it, from the smallest to the biggest of its components.

While Madame Curie was reclusive, she enjoyed studying and working and loved her friends and especially her family. However, endowed with a strong determination, she always acted according to what she believed to be just and equitable. Meeting her husband gave her the possibility to discover family stability, something that always nourished her.

Totally dedicated to her task, she still lives today in a field where the scientific contribution is an important element in her life. She is presently working in chemistry in a female body. This body allows her to be more "human" in the sense of her emotions because ray 7, that influences her tremendously, has a tendency to confine her in a colder, more mental aspect, driving her away from her *feelings*.

Initiation Level: 1.8

With a serious start towards mental polarization, she contributed to advancing science in an exceptional way. Not yet touched by the arrogance of a second level Initiate, she was able to accomplish "more" because she remained open to the ideas and suggestions of others. She felt neither superior nor inferior to other scientists but felt the need to be part of this big family they represented. This humility allowed her to keep a strong bond with her two daughters who admired her a lot.

Ray Structure

Monad: 2   Soul: 7   Personality: 6-3
Mental: 7-5   Astral: 2-6   Physical: 3-7

Monad and Soul

The ray of her Monad had very little influence on her life. In contrast, her ray 7 Soul played a real role in her incarnation, particularly because it was assisted by two other ray 7's. This, then, contributed to Madame Curie's success in the field of research.

Personality

She had a Personality that was both sweet and strong and expressed itself under the influence of ray 6. This ray allowed her to be relentlessly devoted to her task, without forgetting about her children whom she adored. Fortunately, this passion was shared by her spouse who, otherwise, would have suffered tremendously since Madame Currie was an uncompromising person who gave of herself selflessly. We may even say that, sometimes, she could seem obsessed by concepts that constantly bounced around in her head. Warm at times, thanks to the influence of ray 6, she would quickly become a scientist again when she accessed her workplace. This ray granted her the perseverance she experienced throughout her life.

Sub-ray 3 endowed her with a particular fluency of speech, giving her the opportunity to earn the respect of other scientists. In other words, she was never at a loss for words and would use this talent contentedly if it could serve her cause. The influence of this sub-ray also allowed her to be less rigid and love research and experimentation.

Mental Body

Gifted with a ray 7, sub-ray 5 mental body, this woman had no choice but to work for humanity's well-being. The influence of ray 7 conferred to her a certain direction in her research. It gave her a sufficiently strong intuition and a more just vision about the problems that stood in front of her during her research. It also gave her a methodical aspect, facilitating her task.

Her sub-ray 5 made her love science but mainly let her understand the mystery behind it. It compelled her to relentlessly seek answers to her questions. It forced her to succeed and never give up. It also gave her the opportunity to be in contact with the infinitesimal, the atom, as well as the *devic* kingdom, because in the atom shines the mystery of the cosmic fire.

Astral Body

She had an astral body that could have prevented her from accomplishing her work if ray 7 had not influenced her so much. Ray 2 would have created too many fears. However, it conferred on her sensitivity, coupled with an intuition that served her in her marriage as well as in her work. This ray gave her the possibility to quickly understand people's suffering. It led her to go to the rescue of soldiers on the battlefield, and instilled in her the desire to work to help humanity so that a better destiny would take shape for all the people inhabiting this planet.

Sub-ray 6 supported ray 2 well by giving it more strength. It enhanced her devotion to her family, her friends (she did not have many for lack of time) and those closest to her. She would have given anything for them to be happy. However, she knew intuitively that she had work to accomplish and she did it, despite the sacrifices it entailed.

Physical Body

Her ray 3, sub-ray 7 physical body endowed her with a delicate yet strong body. She could accomplish a lot without paying attention to the fatigue that often racked her. Possessing a certain pride, she did not want to appear weak, particularly in front of the men who largely denigrated women. Ray 3 allowed her to survive in a world of men and to "accept" the mockery of these men. If she would have had the time, she would have known how to be a great feminist.

Sub-ray 7 accorded her the ability to be tidy. Although she had little help, she managed to keep her house and her laboratory, without complaint. Often penniless, she succeeded in demonstrating to the whole world that the atom is nothing but a portion of the immeasurable.

April 16, 2010

 # Da Vinci, Leonardo

Given Name: Lionardo di ser Piero Da Vinci
Nationality: Italian
Place and Date of Birth: Vinci (Italy), April 14, 1452
Date of Death: Amboise (France), May 2, 1519
Profession: Painter, sculptor, architect, scientist, musician, philosopher and writer

Master Djwhal Khul's Commentary

Leonardo da Vinci reveals himself to be out of the ordinary by his genius and occult knowledge. He could see the future in his dreams at night and translate it in his writings during the day. Intelligent, an artist and philosopher, he possessed magic at his fingertips. He was not understood by the people of his time, who could not help loving him. He had male and female lovers, but never married. He made fun of conventions and would enter into a relationship only through the links of the soul, without any link to sex. His real love was his art, to which he gave himself entirely.

Initiation Level: 3.2

He had reached a certain wisdom, but still possessed a formidable ego. His painting allowed him to live (and survive); his real passion remained his "art in the vision of the future" to which he practiced without fear of reprisal on the part of the Church that was shocked by some of his remarks.

Ray Structure

Monad: 2	Soul: 4	Personality: 7-3
Mental: 3-5	Astral: 4-6	Physical: 3-6

Monad and Soul

He was very influenced by his Soul, which made him very creative in his writings and paintings. He was often tormented by what he would see in his dreams but was unable to translate into reality. Magnanimous, he was a defender of the weak and the oppressed. Born out of wedlock, he never believed in human hierarchy, but rather in an occult justice. He recognized a hidden meaning in everything and this impression came from the influence of his Soul, now ray 2. He is part of the Ashram of Koot Hoomi.

Personality

His Personality, conditioned by the energy of ray 7, sub-ray 3, infused in him the taste of perfection to the most infinite details. Ray 7 endowed him with the sense of organization and defiance of established laws. It made him more structured and reliable in what he was doing. He demonstrated signs of genius, both in his attention to detail as well as in the way he treated spirit and matter.

Sub-ray 3 allowed him to play with colours and words. He could manipulate others by his speech as well as the Church that frequently disapproved of his work that displayed nudity in his paintings. This sub-ray made him apt to react correctly and circumvent laws without it being a threat to anyone.

Mental Body

The influence of ray 3, sub-ray 5 at the level of his mental body granted him the faculty to direct the energy according to what needed to be said and done, and particularly in front of the Church, who understood nothing of his art. Ray 3 made him intelligent and scientific. Hard to fool because his genius came through in his remarks, he could think of several creations and work on various projects simultaneously. Untiring, he proved to be a great thinker.

His sub-ray 5 made him more "scientific" and active in his speech. This sub-ray enticed him to develop research on various levels and build some solid bases that freemasonry used in its teaching. He liked to believe in the incredible, and his dreams encouraged him to act in that way.

Astral Body

The energy carried by his astral body, via his ray 4, sub-ray 6, made him a misunderstood person who lived the highs and lows of an artist. Ray 4 infused him with passion, creativity and devotion, and made him eternally happy in his art. This art made him live a sexuality that did not appear consistent with the social norms of the time. He liked the expression of bodies with their energy, regardless whether they were male or female. However, he disliked women's emotional overflow and would avoid them like the plague. Consequently, he felt more at ease with men and mixed more with them socially. He had secret lovers, one of which was a woman who was his source of inspiration for the Mona Lisa and who, in a way, was the extension of his Soul's energy.

Sub-ray 6 endowed him with this ardour that sometimes frightened his contemporaries. Qualified as not being lukewarm, he was quick-tempered and gave it free expression. He felt limited in this world and sharply expressed it. This sub-ray motivated him to cultivate the dedication and passion towards his art, which was his only true reason to live.

Physical Body

The energy communicated by ray 3, sub-ray 6 at the level of the physical body conferred on him an intelligent brain, quick on the trigger. Ray 3 gave him a strong resistance and allowed him to have little sleep. He worked relentlessly, only taking a few hours of rest in a day. He did not eat and digest well because of the uncomfortable positions he sometimes had to accept to work. He did not talk to waste energy but always by seeing in advance the effect of his words.

Sub-ray 6 caused him some difficulty with his weight that fluctuated often according to his diet. He was not graced with an extraordinary beauty, which did not really affect him because he had other preoccupations. Of course, he would have liked to have had more delicate features, but as mirrors were not very common at the time, he would easily forget this fact to focus on his art.

This man had never really been happy, but that was not the goal of his life. He lived his life fully sometimes forgetting the constraints of the time that eventually caught up with him at the end of his life, during his exile in France.

August 19, 2007

 # David-Néel, Alexandra

Given Name: Louise Eugénie Alexandrine Marie David
Double Nationality: French and Belgian
Place and Date of Birth: Saint-Mandé, Val-de-Marne (France), October 24, 1868
Date of Death: Digne-les-Bains, Alpes-de-Haute-Provence (France), September 8, 1969
Profession: Orientalist, Tibetologist, opera singer, reporter, writer and explorer

Master Djwhal Khul's Commentary

Alexandra David-Néel was, in actual fact, one of the first white women to cross the Tibetan frontier. She experienced remarkable encounters within lamaseries, although her encounters were less impressive than Helena Blavatsky's, who was a more than remarkable woman, because she was one of my students and my first "secretary".

With a lower initiation level, David-Néel revealed herself to be more "egotistic" in her approach. She only explored the most superficial aspect of Tibet (the culture and a bit of the religion, whose occult aspect she did not understand), her initiation level preventing her from accessing it. However, thanks to her interesting physical strength and determination, she lived adventures that few men and women of her time could have lived.

Not understanding the power of women, she preferred to have a masculine entourage. She felt inferior in a feminine body and experienced some difficulty accepting it, following the example of Helena Blavatsky, who came up against the same difficulty but for totally different reasons. Blavatsky never really wished to be a man, in spite of the difficulties she encountered. This was a sign of the great maturity of her Soul, which was not the case for David-Néel.

Her real knowledge of Tibet being limited, I will, therefore, not treat this subject in depth. I will dwell more on the characteristics of her rays.

Initiation Level: 1.8

Very polarized towards the mental body that she used with intelligence, she, unfortunately, demonstrated much arrogance because of her initiation level. She thought she knew a lot and liked to impress her acquaintances. When she allowed her mind to rest, which unfortunately did not occur often, she displayed great attributes of the heart. She was considered a knowledgeable person, which was the reflection of her ray configuration.

Ray Structure

Monad: 2	Soul: 1	Personality: 6-3
Mental: 1-5	Astral: 4-2	Physical: 3-6

Monad and Soul

David-Néel did not often express sweetness, because she had only one ray 2, (a sub-ray in her astral body). This ray in the Monad had no effect on her life. Her ray 1 Soul exerted a particular influence, which she often managed awkwardly. This influence grew stronger, thanks to a ray 1, sub-ray 5 mental body that made her controlling, heartless at times and judgemental. She judged quickly and rarely changed her mind.

Personality

Her Personality, ruled by the imprint of ray 6 and supported by sub-ray 3, made her a stubborn woman. Ray 6 prevented her from having a truly long-range vision of certain subjects. She liked to be right and would rarely concede a point. This ray also endowed her with perseverance which she exhibited all her life. She could prove to be warm when her emotional body did not clash with her Personality. She would experience emotional ups and downs (influenced by her ray 4, sub-ray 2 astral body) that were difficult on the people around her. It is true she had some hormonal problems which did not improve her behaviour.

Sub-ray 3 granted her an ease of expression. If it was her intention, she could be very manipulative in order to get what she wanted. These two ray 3's made possible the emergence of her intelligence and the assertion of her rights.

Mental Body

Her ray 1, sub-ray 5 mental body made her an intelligent and pragmatic woman. Ray 1 granted her clear ideas and determination. It provided her with a strong will and the possibility to reach the goals she was pursuing. She was not a quitter!

Because of her sub-ray 5, she had a down-to-earth appearance, almost scientific, which gave her the possibility to prepare her expeditions in complete safety. She would plan everything and properly measure the risks to be taken.

Astral Body

Her ray 4, sub-ray 2 astral body gave her a hard time; she often experienced difficulty in controlling her emotions, particularly her fits of anger. Ray 4 made her sink into passing depressions and inspired her to give everything up, which her mind forbade her to do. It also impressed on her the taste for independence; she was unable to properly understand the marriage bond and to conform to it.

Her sub-ray 2 made her sensitive at times, an aspect of herself she did not really appreciate and that she hid fairly well. She ran away from emotional pain, preferring to manage physical pain, with which she was more at ease.

Physical Body

Her ray 3, sub-ray 6 physical body gave her resistance (ray 3) and perseverance (ray 6). Ray 3 conferred on her a certain flexibility and endurance that served her well during her trips. Her curiosity is derived from her two ray 3's (the Personality sub-ray and the Physical ray).

Her sub-ray 6 invested her with a kind of resistance to the cold; it provided her with a strong bone structure and a layer of fat that created a barrier against the extreme cold. This sub-ray increased her stubbornness and her desire to pursue her quest.

Her relationship with her adopted son was not entirely platonic but we will dismiss this delicate subject.

June 15, 2007

DILGO KHYENTSE RINPOCHE

Given Name: Dilgo Khyentse Rinpoche
Other Name: Tashi Peldjor
Nationality: Tibetan
Place and Date of Birth: Kham region (Oriental Tibet), 1910
Date of Death: (Bhutan), September 28, 1991
Profession: Vajrayana Buddhist Master

MASTER DJWHAL KHUL'S COMMENTARY

I know him, or should I say rather, we have known each other. I met him on several occasions without his knowledge. He was a highly educated man and very interesting. I would, with no fear, entrust him with some of my disciples.

Initiation Level: 4.8

He could have undertaken his fifth initiation. However, he chose to help his people by sacrificing a part of himself that prevented him from progressing further. He put himself aside but you should know that self denial results sometimes in a temporary stop on the path. He will recover his path in the next incarnation, which has started some time ago.

Ray Structure

Monad: 2	Soul: 2	Personality: 1-6
Mental: 3-4	Astral: 6-2	Physical: 3-6

Monad and Soul

His Monad had a certain influence on him that guided him all his life. Ray 2 allowed him to be a good listener and also a very good teacher. His Soul ray, also a 2, provided him the opportunity to achieve what he wanted as an instructor within Buddhism. This ray also prompted him to take the *Bodhisattva*[1] vow which temporarily stopped his evolution. He will understand this vow better in his present life. He will know how to grow within his community while evolving to reach the fifth door.

Personality

His Personality, ruled by ray 1, sub-ray 6, endowed him with a strength allowing him to achieve his destiny. These rays also helped him locate certain *termas*. Guided by the rays of his Monad and his Soul, he has, furthermore, drawn his determination from the ray 1 of his Personality that gave him the possibility of subsequently transmitting everything thereafter. Ray 1 granted him vision and determination. He displayed much strength due to the union of ray 1 and sub-ray 6, though expressed gently due to the contribution of his Soul and Monad of ray 2. This allowed him to be heard and respected.

Sub-ray 6 communicated a warmth that he transmitted without limitation. Very devoted to his Masters, he was able to inspire this devotion to those closest to him. He forgave easily but never forgot the lesson learned.

Mental Body

With a mental body influenced by ray 3, sub-ray 4, he was, unquestionably, an intelligent and very creative man. He loved beautiful things but knew how to give them up. Ray 3 gave him the possibility to learn and experiment a lot of things. He taught what he had lived. He liked to reason but in a sensible manner. He could think and act fast; sub-ray 4 could curb his enthusiasm to deepen his knowledge.

Sub-ray 4 encouraged him to tone down several of the impulses in his life. In doing this, through his retreats, he was able to tame the negative aspect of this ray and gain it as an ally. It is thanks to this sub-ray that

---

[1] A *Bodhisattva* is a being who aspires to acquire the Buddha state and who gives up the perfect Nirvâna bliss as long as all beings have not been saved. *Dictionnaire de la sagesse orientale*, Robert Laffont, Paris, 1989, page 762.

158

allowed him to see the two sides of a problem, that he never made a hasty decision. He would think, meditate and then pronounce judgment in a delicate situation.

Astral Body

His astral body, influenced by ray 6, sub-ray 2, increased his sensitivity but also his strength in himself. Ray 6 instilled in him a faith and an unshakeable joy. He would dedicate himself relentlessly, forgetting himself in order to serve those who needed it the most. Always available, he would not hesitate to help and support others. Endowed with a certain stubbornness, he would not let go easily. He would use a gentle approach but when it became necessary, he would become tough and demanding. He could even frighten people who, while respecting him, feared his furious outbursts.

Sub-ray 2 accentuated his softness and tenderness towards every living being on the planet. He suffered a great deal from hypersensitivity that he was able to master thanks to the influence of ray 1 and his two ray 3's.

Physical Body

His physical body of ray 3, sub-ray 6 energies allowed him to live a relatively long life. Ray 3 graced him with flexibility and efficiency. His mind understood quickly and well. He knew how to adapt to different situations and did not fear to live new experiences. He loved life and life returned this love (even if suffering was often there). His constant contact with his Soul infused him with a *joie de vivre* that knew no bounds.

Sub-ray 6 conferred on him a sturdy body during some difficult periods of his life. He was able to resist the cold and the isolation thanks to this ray that allowed him to preserve his faith in his destiny.

This man was an example of perseverance, love and faith. He succeeded in transmitting the art of being a monk while remaining human and close to his disciples. Simple and humble, he knew how to remain a model of wisdom despite all his acquired knowledge and experience gained.

September 26, 2010

 DION, CELINE

Given Name: Céline Marie Claudette Dion
Nationality: Canadian
Place and Date of Birth: Charlemagne, Québec (Canada), March 30, 1968
Profession: Singer / Interpreter

MASTER DJWHAL KHUL'S COMMENTARY

An ambitious young woman, Celine Dion is a bit victimized by her rays because she has not yet learned how to exploit them properly, giving her the impression of being a "victim." This is what triggers in her a separation effect that she has trouble getting rid of: she is torn between the "*glamour*" aspect and the "love of life" aspect. She lives these two polarities simultaneously and does not know how to merge them, which makes her a superficial woman. However, when she concentrates more on her Personality, she knows how to touch peoples' hearts; when she focuses on her emotional aspect, she becomes a victim of her emotions and the resulting *glamour*.

Her ray 4, sub-ray 6 Astral and her ray 3, sub-ray 7 Personality act in such a way that, when she concentrates on her Personality, she becomes dynamic, intelligent, open, and perceives her ambition more; whereas when she focuses on her astral body, she becomes truly manipulative for her cause and thirsty for the desire to be loved and adulated. Emotions and their tempo make her vibrate, thus becoming easily manipulated by ray 4 that uses her like a violin.

Initiation Level: 1.2

Ray Structure

Monad: 2	Soul: 2	Personality: 3-7
Mental: 7-2	Astral: 4-6	Physical: 3-7

Monad and Soul

Her Monad has, of course, no influence, contrary to her Soul that attempts some breakthroughs that she sometimes listen to, allowing her to soften and open up to the suffering of others. Graced with a big heart, she is unaware of how to use it properly, because she remains too perturbed by her desires. It will, undoubtedly, be easily influenced by her Soul in her next incarnation that will once again take place in the musical field.

Personality

Due to her ray 3 sub-ray 7 Personality, she is dynamic, open and understanding, but also occasionally manipulative. She plays with her body and energy in order to serve her emotional body that demands to be loved and adulated. As ray 3 manipulates and ray 7 has affection for just causes and just things, she sometimes corrects herself and transforms herself into a charming woman, warm and captivating. Her Personality then becomes bubbly. She can make people laugh and attract their attention in a healthy fashion without using their emotional bodies. When she strikes this note, which sometimes happens, she reveals herself as being radiant and carrying an energy that temporarily transforms hearts (a metaphor meaning that she can inject hope for a better life).

Ray 7 promotes equity, and ray 3 helps it in this regard, because it broadens a vision that is sometimes too narrow. Ray 3 modulates the environment in order to support the expression of the magical aspect of ray 7. When her attention is focused on her Personality, she demonstrates strength. When it is directed towards her astral body, she appears weak and easy to manipulate, but consequently manipulating others.

Mental Body

Her ray 7, sub-ray 2 mental body makes her an intelligent woman, sometimes experiencing some difficulty to express herself verbally.

Ray 7 confers on her an extraordinary mental discipline; she rarely departs from her duty and acts according to what is demanded of her to remain at the height of her fame. This ray is beneficial with regards to discipline but not innovation; she also reveals herself to be an excellent interpreter, but not a remarkable composer.

Sub-ray 2 offers a sensitivity that sometimes works to her advantage, because she can "feel" the energy of the audience. Although it is often painful for her to adequately translate what she feels, she lets her body move in a way to express what people wish. This sub-ray communicates to her a certain intuition that helps her make the right choices for her career.

Let us not forget that the blending of ray 7, sub-ray 3 of her Personality, coupled with the sub-ray 2 of her mental body, renders her magnetic for people who are astrally polarized. She arouses admiration and envy: the disciplined ray 7 allows her to perform in a show to the best of her ability while dictating to her the way to dress in order to release the maximum amount of magnetism possible. When she is overcome by her emotions and her ray 4, sub-ray 6 astral body dominates, she loses a lot of her beauty and becomes perturbed in her looks as well as in her emotions. Ray 3 grants her the flexibility to properly serve her cause and to slightly reduce the effect of ray 7 that sometimes demonstrates too much rigidity.

Astral Body

Her ray 4, sub-ray 6 astral body creates in her the desire to please, to be cherished, loved and recognized. She wants to be the best while knowing that some others are better than her. However, when her ray 4 is off balance, she fights to prove her supremacy. But when this ray recovers its balance, she accepts to be part of the best. This ray allows her to express herself with emotion and warmth, except when she becomes unbalanced. Then she acts in a cold and distant way. She also vibrates with the sound of her art and would find it difficult to live without it.

163

Sub-ray 6 communicates to her the love of family and children. She nevertheless remains a woman torn between her career and her son who does not really know her because she is always busy. She provides him with love but does not necessarily educate him as a mother would. More evolved than her, he partially understands what is happening to him. Fortunately, Celine Dion's entourage is very warm towards him and provides the family core he is lacking.

Physical Body

Her ray 3, sub-ray 7 physical body allows her to accomplish a lot. Ray 3 confers on her a sound intelligence and a certain flexibility of spirit that offers her the possibility to adapt to her environment. It also endows her with a physical resistance that helps her to accomplish her work.

Sub-ray 7 increases her resistance and her performance. It invests her with magnetism and helps her get the maximum benefit of situations. It also confers on her a certain sense of grace.

Ms. Dion has a lot of potential, but she also has to work very hard to reach a serious balance. She is easily influenced, sensitive and easily hurt in her emotions. Fortunately, ray 7 comes to the rescue and allows her to present herself as a functional woman in a universe that is not always so.

October 17, 2008

 # DISNEY, WALT

Given Name: Walter Elias Disney
Nickname: Walt
Nationality: American
Place and Date of Birth: Chicago, Illinois (United States), December 5, 1901
Date of Death: Los Angeles, California (United States), December 15, 1966
Profession: Producer, director, script-writer, actor and motion picture cartoonist

MASTER DJWHAL KHUL'S COMMENTARY

A talented man, Walt Disney animated the youth with a breath of fresh air. He reminded us that the fairy tale and magical world still exist in everybody's heart and one has to believe it. He has brought back to life in the human spirit, the notion that the impossible becomes possible if one strongly believes in it. He was a magician with words, prints and characters that became familiar in the childrens' eyes. With the help of his characters, he was able to highlight certain messages, such as love, faithfulness, trust in one's star (the Soul), friendship, courage and perseverance.

He remained simple in his being and his joy was to see "magic" in other people's eyes, inspired by a message of hope and optimism. He was not a quitter and he trusted humanity. An eternal optimist, he assured that he would never be forgotten, though this was never really one of his wishes.

He was afraid of death, afraid to have to leave behind everything he loved. However, he believed in the existence of an afterlife. He was never cryogenically frozen as some people thought. He was simply cremated, which reveals in him a certain detachment of the body.

He was not a superficial person, contrary to what some people thought. He accomplished a lot by providing dreams to those who did not have any.

Initiation Level: 1.8

Ray Structure

Monad: 2	Soul: 2	Personality: 6-4
Mental: 7-5	Astral: 2-6	Physical: 3-7

Walt Disney displayed a particular arrogance that he controlled fairly well. His artistic flair brought him closer to nature and to humanity. He had started to polarize mentally, which allowed him to develop the genius we know.

Monad and Soul

His Monad had no influence on him, contrary to his Soul that was starting to exert one. It made him receptive to certain ideas transmitted to him through his emotional body and his Personality. His mental body made practical what he was receiving because his rays allowed him to anchor the images he could perceive through his other bodies into reality. Thus, a bird became a fairy and a grasshopper, a skilled communicator.

Personality

His ray 6, sub-ray 4 Personality made him charming, warm, friendly and very close to children. Ray 6 provided this warmth that he was able to transmit to the majority of his characters, and in doing so bringing them to life. We only have to look at Mickey Mouse to see that this character is inhabited by an aura, making him appear almost more real than he seems.

Sub-ray 4 allowed him to draw, to build a fabulous universe. His immense talent came from the influence of ray 4 added to his ray 7's.

Because of this harmony, he could build a universe in which he himself believed (or almost).

Mental Body

His ray 7, sub-ray 5 mental body provided him with a logic endowed with magic, as the energy of ray 7 represents the magician par excellence, and Walt Disney was one. It also communicated to him this perfection that was translated into everything, particularly his drawings.

Sub-ray 5 introduced form and logic to his mind. It allowed him to be an excellent business man. It helped him manage his business and instilled in him good judgement. One could count on him because he was an honest person and a man of integrity.

Astral Body

His ray 2, sub-ray 6 astral body made him a sensitive and generous man. Ray 2 allowed him to be a good father and a good husband, ready to listen to others and their emotions. He tried to impart happiness through his art and characters.

Due to his sub-ray 6 he remained a just and reliable man. He was faithful to his family, friends and public. He attempted to never deceive anyone, an arduous task he tried to accomplish relentlessly.

Physical Body

His physical of ray 3, sub-ray 7 graced him with a fairly good memory and speed in gesture and action. Ray 3 gave him a brilliant brain that helped him in the making of his drawings. He had an expert eye for detail (sub-ray 7), and the practical aspect of ray 3 was able to transmit the desired message throughout his drawings.

Sub-ray 7 offered him the possibility of reaching a perfection that made him what he became. Disney's international reputation is untouchable.

Ray 7 permitted him to bring out the magic in everything that he touched. He was imbibed with his characters that he projected onto the screen.

Walt Disney made his mark during his era and gave humanity the possibility of living a certain unity of consciousness through his animated cartoons. His characters are well-known worldwide and their messages carry a feeling of hope that opens the door to the magic, so that it may live in each one of us.

May 23, 2009

 # DYER, WAYNE

Given Name: Wayne Walter Dyer
Nationality: American
Place and Date of Birth: Detroit, Michigan (United States), May 10, 1940
Profession: Author and teacher

MASTER DJWHAL KHUL'S COMMENTARY

Mr. Dyer, a very interesting man, brings a new vision regarding the deep motivations that enliven humanity. He is a simple man with a complex vision of what weaves our universe; in other words, he can easily enough explain what may seem complex. His intelligent mind can dissect what appears complex by using just words that demystify what gives the illusion of being mysterious and incomprehensible.

While being sometimes mystical, his approach adapts well to the real need of the human Mind. Through his words, he reassures and prevents chaos from penetrating too deeply into the thoughts of the thinker who listens to him or reads him. In a way, he prevents the emergence of certain fulminating awakenings requiring an unstable climate, to encourage minor awakenings developed in the comfort of a thought cradled by his "reassuring" and "simplifying" aspect.

He encourages people to progress internally and awakens them to an aspect that is closer to their real Personality. In other words, the human soul learns from its mistakes and expands in order that a stable and authentic fusion with the Soul may one day become possible. He is, in short, a first-degree spiritual master. He works on the basis of individuals in order to prepare them for a deeper and more subtle work that will occur in their next incarnations. He is somewhat the "Deepak Chopra" of psychotherapy.

INITIATION LEVEL: 2.3

He possesses the arrogance of the second Initiate, although this arrogance is coming to an end, as life has presented to him some difficulties that have gradually worn out this characteristic. He is, therefore, increasingly cultivating simplicity as well as humility, which is starting an interesting work with him.

RAY STRUCTURE

Monad: 2   Soul: 3   Personality: 6-4
Mental: 5-3   Astral: 2-6   Physical: 3-7

Monad and Soul

His Monad has little influence in his life. On the other hand, his ray 3 Soul has an influence that is becoming more and more important. The Soul coloured by this energy, guides him in making certain choices and in his way of expressing himself in public. It also allows him to probe the most occult aspects of some issues because Mr. Dyer leaves nothing to chance, constantly trying to improve himself and to understand the Universe in its infinitesimally small and infinitely grand aspects.

Personality

Graced with a ray 6, sub-ray 4 Personality, Wayne Dyer can be charming (ray 4) and warm most of the time (ray 6). At times, he could seem tormented (ray 4) and cold (ray 6) when he falls into a more negative aspect of his Personality. The influence of ray 6 provides a great sensitivity that helps him understand others, allowing him to adjust and comfort them. However, when he is hurt, he has a tendency to withdraw and lick his wounds until the wound is healed. He recovers fast, because sub-ray 4 proves to be an outstanding warrior who often comes to his rescue. This sub-ray allowed him to survive a very difficult childhood.

Sub-ray 4 graces him with a "culture" that pleases his public. He is a scholar who loves the arts and music. This sub-ray also confers on him an aura of mystery allowing him to sometimes deal with the most delicate subjects. It allocates to him an inner certitude (when he is displaying his positive aspect) that drives him to fight relentlessly for the human cause. However, if it happens that this sub-ray momentarily falls into one of its negative aspects, Dyer must then demonstrate an uncommon strength (derived from ray 6 dedicated to the cause) in order to escape from a temporary lethargy created by this unbalance.

Mental Body

His ray 5, sub-ray 3 mental body confers a clear and active intelligence. Ray 5 grants him the faculty to study a problem in depth that, thanks to the influence of sub-ray 3, proves to be temporary; this faculty allows him to finally find a solution. Without this sub-ray, his mental body would be more rigid, stricter, and he would suffer from it. He needs the scientific aspect provided by the influence of ray 5, which confers on him a lot of credibility. The influence of sub-ray 3 remains, however, essential to allow him to preserve openness towards other peoples' beliefs.

Sub-ray 3 allows him to play with his "ideas", to reshape and transform them if necessary. Ray 5 provides a solution that his sub-ray adapts to according to the situation and the needs of the time, which proves to be one of his strengths and a quality appreciated by his entourage. Ray 5 grants him important psychic strength on which sub-ray 3 can dance with joy.

Astral Body

His ray 2, sub-ray 6 astral body makes for an interesting combination. The great sensitivity of ray 2 allows him to "have antennas" to capture the ambient energy, making him empathetic, and encouraging him to actively listen to others. However, he must be careful as this ray sometimes makes him too sensitive, causing him to absorb other people's negativity. He had to learn to protect himself adequately because this increased sensitivity caused him a lot of suffering in the past, particularly during his childhood and passage into 'young adulthood."

Sub-ray 6 offers him the possibility to love everybody. He dedicates himself body and soul to the human cause as well as to his family. He does not rest much, spending his time writing and giving conferences and counselling. Besides, he is happier in action than when not active. This sub-ray provides a presence that knows how to arouse and encourage its audience.

Physical Body

His physical body reveals itself to be his weakness. Why? Because he has difficulty feeling good in his body. He would frankly feel more at ease with a more "ethereal" body. Ray 3 provides a certain physical flexibility that compensates for the rigidity of sub-ray 7. It also allows him to work on several projects simultaneously, while sometimes feeling tired; it offers him the possibility of continuing without letting go of the tension necessary to his work. Ray 3 transmits to him a certain speed that he learned to master, becoming more of a perfectionist with age.

Sub-ray 7 allows him to keep in shape without excess weight; it invests in him a sense of order that he uses when needed. It also confers on him solid nerves that give him stamina in spite of the difficulty he encounters. Moreover, the influence of this ray colours his language with a certain magic.

Dyer sees himself as a man full of potential, whose life is passing more and more rapidly. He has not yet finished his task; he has to set aside his physical limitations in order to achieve, before the end of his life, his destiny that will directly influence his future evolution.

June 18, 2010

 # Eastwood, Clint

Given Name: Clinton Eastwood Jr.
Nationality: American
Place and Date of Birth: San Francisco, California (United-States), May 31, 1930
Profession: Actor, movie director, producer and composer

Master Djwhal Khul's Commentary

Clint Eastwood is an intelligent man who is, however, still missing a certain depth. His vision of things, while it is by far beyond the vision of the average American, needs to be broadened further. His initiation level grants him a just vision with respect to some of life's aspects. However, the rays that are presently influencing his incarnation impose on him a narrower vision, preventing him from really opening up more to his inner vision. In fact, he remains too materialistic in spite of his big heart that desires justice for all, particularly from a financial perspective.

He has accomplished a lot; however, he could have accomplished more particularly as a director; He is a good director, but he remains in a way too superficial. Admittedly, he touches emotions but does not transform. He produces good movies, although his movies do not change the consciousness of people as the movies of Spielberg or Lucas do. His movies delve into the emotions, highlight them, make us think but do not change us. I might even add that they are easily forgotten.

Endowed with a big heart, he is still unaware of what love is; he has been working on it for several years. We hope he would have integrated certain lessons into his present life, lessons that would help him make giant leaps in his next incarnation that would occur in France; he will evolve in the political realm. Why France? Because France will need his help and he does not really like the French, which is bound to change…

Initiation Level: 1.8

He is getting closer to his second initiation, which makes him sensitive. Of course, part of his arrogance comes from this fact, but he remains relatively humble in spite of the conflicts that torment him.

Ray Structure

Monad: 2	Soul: 3	Personality: 3-4
Mental: 7-5	Astral: 6-2	Physical: 3-7

Monad and Soul

His Monad has no influence on his life contrary to his Soul that is starting to have a greater one. It provides him with a taste for politics and the desire to become gradually open to various experiences. Gradually, he will become a "dabbler" in his next incarnations, which proves to be good. However, he will need a spiritual guide... something we strongly advise, because he risks losing himself in the various experiences he will live.

Personality

His ray 3, sub-ray 4 Personality makes him a pleasant man, who knows what he wants. Ray 3 gives him the fluidity and ease to live more than one life simultaneously. It also grants him the wish to express himself in various ways as well as the verbal fluency and charm that women find attractive.

His sub-ray 4 inspires him with a taste for the arts. Without it, he would have been unable to have a career as an actor. This sub-ray creates complexity in his life. In fact, it magically complicates his life, something he does not often understand. It also allows him to appreciate beauty and to seek it. Consequently, imagine ray 3 that likes to experiment and sub-ray 4, constantly seeking beauty. As a result, he has trouble resisting women.

Mental Body

His ray 7, sub-ray 5 mental body makes him intelligent, a trait of which he is proud. Ray 7 makes him look for perfection in beauty, which is attributable to his sub-ray 4 Personality. He likes things that are clear and well done. His ray 7 provides him with the possibility of properly manipulating matter, particularly when pertaining to the universe of the film industry. It helps him project into the physical (thanks to the support of sub-ray 5), the image of what he perceives in himself. He possesses, then, a sharpened "sense" of staging.

He is a straightforward man due to his sub-ray 5, which prevents him from taking too many risks, particularly in the financial field. This sub-ray dislikes taking too many risks, which make him insecure. He, therefore, remains cautious in business. However, this proves to be generally different in his love life, influenced in part by his astral body but mainly by his physical body and not his mental body.

Astral Body

His ray 6, sub-ray 2 astral body confers on him kindness, pleasantness and warmth. When he sees himself influenced by his Astral rays, then a warmth arises in him that touches his entire environment. Ray 6 endows him with this warmth, making him passionate and fascinating. However, he knows how to be stubborn, because this ray prompts him to hold his ground and forgive with difficulty.

Nevertheless, when the evidence is revealed, sub-ray 2 allows him to forget and forgive. It softens him and invests him with a real gentleness. Generally, he would not hurt a fly. He loves humanity; however, this love is riddled with certain restrictions since he is inhabited by fears he is trying to reduce. He feels that the end of his life is near and that he should undergo great inner changes. We think he is already preparing himself.

Physical Body

His ray 3, sub-ray 7 physical graced him with a beauty that he knew how to use. Ray 3 provided him with a keen mind and an ease to think about many things simultaneously. It also granted him a certain flexibility that resemble that of a cat; he can move with lightness and rapidity, which is sometimes amazing. Thanks to this ray, he is fearless and adventurous; too preoccupied with the action at hand, he does not always consider the consequences.

Sub-ray 7 gives him the sense of discipline and perfection, also granting him refinement and resistance. This sub-ray also gifted him with the talent of captivating others, one that he used well with the fairer sex. It also instilled in him a certain pride (as well as a nervous system) that allowed him to weather difficult times without falling apart.

He will accomplish much more in terms of spirituality in his next incarnation. He will become a philanthropist/politician who will leave a mark on his era.

August 27, 2009

ECKHART, JOHANNES, COMMONLY KNOWN AS MEISTER ECKHART

Given Name: Eckhart von Hochheim
Nationality: German
Place and Date of Birth: Hochheim (Tambach), circa 1260
Date of Death: 1327 (uncertain information)
Profession: Philosopher and theologian

MASTER DJWHAL KHUL'S COMMENTARY

A great sage and great scholar during his time, Meister Eckhart integrated the occult aspect of Christian teaching at an austere period for humanity, where everything was to be mystical and inappropriate for the joy of the Soul. Intelligent, learned, simple and sincere, he succeeded in seeing the light and fully living in it without damaging the ideal image he projected as a "man of the church".

Initiation Level: 3.5

Ray Structure

Monad: 2	Soul: 1	Personality: 3-2
Mental: 7-3	Astral: 6-4	Physical: 3-6

Monad and Soul

His Monad was starting to have a certain influence on his life, through his teaching that allowed for a glimpse of just and intelligent thought. He was endowed with an inner strength that came from his Soul. He could sometimes appear tough, while he really was not. He could see his "goal" and tried relentlessly to reach it. He would have liked to accomplish more, because he was never satisfied with himself.

Personality

His ray 3, sub-ray 2 Personality conferred on him a flexibility much appreciated by his entourage. Ray 3 made it easier to communicate with others. He had a certain sense of humour. This ray allowed him to act in such a way as to avoid constant harassment by the Church of this time because he brought a new integrated vision that did not always please his fellow members who sometimes considered him a heretic.

Sub-ray 2 softened the influence of ray 3 that occasionally made his speech caustic. It sometimes adorned him with "angelic" overtones and endowed him with a great understanding of others' suffering.

Mental Body

His ray 7, sub-ray 3 mental body allowed him to write with intelligence on the complexity of the human spirit. Ray 7 conferred on him an aesthetic sense in his verbal expression but mainly a precision in his writing and the spoken word. It brought a part of God's speech back to man. This ray allowed him to demystify the occult and make it more accessible. It also bestowed on him a sense of ritual that harmonized perfectly with his Soul's development.

Sub-ray 3 proposed an expanded meaning to his words. It made it possible to demystify better what ray 7 felt, because this ray in its occult aspect can become expressively very powerful and create an even greater mystery… instead of clarifying it. Consequently, ray 7 initiated demystification and sub-ray 3 allowed it to remain efficient and not to go astray in the perfection aspect of what is "hidden."

Astral Body

His ray 6, sub-ray 4 astral body gave him this strength and faith in God that enabled him to pursue his path to priesthood without flinching. Ray 6 provided him with a fervour that never betrayed him. This ray coloured his words with warmth and faithfulness to the Church, even though the Church sometimes ran counter to his deep convictions.

Sub-ray 4 reduced the feeling of oppression he often felt from his peers. It allowed him to be happy within himself and to appreciate God's beauty in all its glory, because this sub-ray may feel what proves to be impossible for other rays.

Physical Body

His ray 3, sub-ray 6 physical body conferred on him a sizable resistance. Ray 3 (supported by ray 1 coming from his Soul) granted him a highly capable mind that thought quickly and efficiently. It gave him a sense of repartee that he used frequently to disarm his detractors.

Sub-ray 6 allocated him important physical support that allowed him to remain realistic, because he could have easily become an ethereal being without substance. This sub-ray increased his human warmth and enticed him to appreciate life's "small pleasures" within the austere measures he often imposed upon himself.

Even today, his writings reveal themselves to be precious sources of inspiration worldwide. He succeeded in giving back to man his dignity and divinity, things that the Church disapproved of during his time.

June 22, 2008

 # EINSTEIN, ALBERT

Given Name: Albert Einstein
Triple Nationality: German, Swiss and American
Place and Date of Birth: Ulm, Wurttemberg (Germany), March 14, 1879
Date of Death: Princeton, New Jersey (United States), April 18, 1955
Profession: Physicist

MASTER DJWHAL KHUL'S COMMENTARY

A very intelligent and discreet man with a rather shy nature, Einstein, did not appreciate praise. His biggest regret is having encouraged, without wanting it, the making of the atomic bomb, although the Masters authorized it. Without this weapon, the Pacific War would have lasted several more years. A lot of blood was shed during World War II, too much.

Einstein, who had fled from Germany, always considered himself more of a citizen of the world than a German citizen. Alone amongst men, we can contend that he maintained contacts with certain dimensions that are forbidden to most humans. He enjoyed drifting into areas where the possibility to enlarge his knowledge of energy prevailed. He did not meditate consciously, but fell into a trance-like state that made him forget everything, including his family that he loved very much. He did not seem to be made for this earth because of his ray configuration. Not yet reincarnated, he will be shortly.

Initiation Level: 3.2

This initiation level allowed him to reach levels of consciousness whose existence is unknown by the common man. He had attained a certain humility conferred on him by this initiation level. Incidentally, he demonstrated a strong attraction to the occult sciences which, he felt, contained a compelling part of the truth.

Ray Structure

Monad: 2	Soul: 1	Personality: 3-2
Mental: 4-5	Astral: 6-2	Physical: 3-7

Monad and Soul

His Monad exerted a certain influence, making him more apt to listen to the "invisible" that contained, according to him, many answers to his questions. However, his Soul's influence pushed him all his life to accomplish his task. Einstein was gifted with determination, particularly in terms of numbers and their occult aspect. In the eyes of some people, they often appeared as an obsession. He would become impatient, quick-tempered and would shove everything around, a bit like Beethoven. Totally absorbed by his passion and driven by ray 1, nothing could stop him. Take heed those who would dare try.

Personality

His Personality of ray 3, sub-ray 2 helped him in his research, because the faculty of analysis of ray 3 and the intuition of ray 2 matched perfectly. He would easily fall into a state of deep thinking without even being aware of it. He liked to reflect about things and would forget everything when he did. Einstein appreciated comparing, explaining and understanding a problem with its many facets, and would not tire from considering all angles. He was an intelligent, brilliant man, also efficient due to his accumulation of experiences. Thoughtful, he would not rush things, enjoying the brilliance of intelligence. Not very tidy on the physical plane, it was the opposite on other planes where everything appeared clear, tidy and "logical" to him. For him, it was simply a matter of opening the right door and everything would be "revealed" to him.

His sub-ray 2 emphasized his intuition and helped him open the appropriate doors. This sub-ray supported him and gave him the patience to continue his work despite the difficulties he was experiencing in his personal life. He was admired but rarely understood. In a way, his family life was a fiasco: too absorbed in his work, he was unable to be a good husband and a good father; he only lived for science which was his life.

Mental Body

His ray 4, sub-ray 5 mental body increased his lack of satisfaction towards life, trying to understand it through numbers. For him, everything was mathematical. His ray 4, though it created unstable states and amplified his moodiness, allowed him to "see" in an unseen way, a problem that seemed impossible to solve. He was not afraid to explore the unknown. He experienced ups and downs and would quickly recover from his downs, since his sub-ray 5 would shake him up and help him find a logical and satisfying answer, even the perfect one.

His sub-ray 5 favored the pure scientific aspect. He loved to rub elbows with some of his scientific colleagues in order to exchange "intelligent" and scientific data with them. He was averse to mundane life and avoided receptions.

Astral Body

His ray 6, sub-ray 2 astral body predisposed him to appreciate women without really getting attached to them. This is quite paradoxical because ray 6 likes attachment, which was not his case. However, he would be devoted to some he believed to be intelligent, but mostly to those who were considerate towards mankind, even if he thought that the majority of these women should be more "educated." He disliked injustice and wars, which he was unable to understand. In matters of love, he could prove to be very hard because his ray 1 Soul combined with his ray 6 Astral did not tolerate any threat that risked interfering with his work and the goal he wished to pursue.

His sub-ray 2 made him a little more human; without it, he would have proven impossible to live with. He loved humanity, and this unquestionable love stimulated his work. He trusted humanity in spite of all the senseless acts it demonstrated.

Physical Body

He had a ray 3, sub-ray 7 physical body because a brain influenced by this type of configuration was necessary. Not really attractive, he had a certain charm or magnetism that came from his intelligence. Completely absorbed by his art, he did not see the time pass. He could be considered quirky, and hated being disturbed from his "creative day dreaming."

His sub-ray 7 refined his intelligence and conferred on him the ability to explain his theories. He liked discipline, even if he seemed undisciplined, as he was not necessarily "logically" disciplined as his entourage would have wished. He could be described as a genius because he allowed a certain light, thanks to his own light, to be carried through him.

He believed in the Masters although he never admitted it openly. For him, there were mysteries that had to remain as such like in the case of the Holy Grail in which he believed.

June 30, 2008

 EPICTETUS

Given Name: Epictetus
Nationality: Greek
Place and Date of Birth: Hierapolis, Phrygia (today Turkey), c. 50-55
Date of Death: Nicopolis, Épire, c. 125-130
Profession: Philosopher of the Stoicism School

MASTER DJWHAL KHUL'S COMMENTARY

Epictetus was a wise man, and he still is. Thanks to his ray 3 Soul, he knew how to develop his wisdom, in order to enlighten others along the difficult path of being human. He felt inwardly immortal. He believed in the existence of the Soul that he felt was something bigger than himself, wiser and with whom he would someday become " one". He believed that this part of him was his immortal aspect, unchanged in its "whole" and that it made man better. He knew that everyone possessed this part in them, and he hoped to guide people by demonstrating the "Path" to follow towards what would qualify each and everyone as a kind and "unique being" in this immense universe.

He dreamed many dreams at night and believed that his Soul was guiding him through them. He loved life and humanity, although man often demonstrated great cruelty, even towards himself. According to Epictetus, man was a free being in himself and nothing could contradict this fact. He preferred the company of men who were often more educated and less emotional than women.

This Soul still lives today. Having now reached his fifth initiation, he continues to work and to watch over humanity as a "Master of thought". Consequently, this Soul is active within the scientific community as a researcher and project director. He presently lives in the United States and manages large-scale projects in agreement with the Will of his Ray Master. We would remain silent about his identity for the moment, but know that this Soul has also been a well-known pope that was murdered soon after his election because his vision frightened Church leaders. This Soul also took the shape of a XVIth century inventor, related to Copernicus. A great friend of the Count of St. Germain, he was, on several occasions, a precious help in the pursuit of his work.

Initiation Level: 1.8

Ray Structure

Monad: 2	Soul: 3	Personality: 3-4
Mental: 7-5	Astral: 6-2	Physical: 3-6

Monad and Soul

While his Monad had no influence, his Soul, however, inspired him a lot. It invited him to always search deeper and deeper within himself in order to exceed the limits of his consciousness. It made him explore man's inner Universe through his behaviour, reactions, relations and way of thinking. Epictetus already knew that everything is a matter of perspective and that man had the possibility of evolving by changing "his perspectives."

Personality

His ray 3, sub-ray 4 Personality allowed him to endure his life that could sometimes be very uncomfortable. Ray 3 granted him the possibility to adapt to difficult conditions, without complaining. He knew (and this knowledge came from his sub-ray 4) that the suffering would not last forever. Despite the difficulties he encountered, he never lost hope in man.

His sub-ray 4 conferred on his Personality a power of lightness or depth according to what he wanted to convey to others. He feared nothing and knew how to transmit his faith in a more evolved aspect of man to those he felt open to new perspectives. Possessing an interesting nature, he knew how to inspire respect from other people.

Mental Body

His ray 7, sub-ray 5 mental body endowed him with brilliant thinking that was "enlightening" for others. He knew how to think and possessed an outstanding intuition that he used wisely. His perception was clear for his times and he suffered tremendously watching human nature behave so "stupidly" most of the time. He lived in a difficult era where equality between men existed even less than today. He witnessed horrifying things. He eagerly wanted man to understand that he had a "divine" and not a "bestial" nature. His task was not easy!

His sub-ray 5 granted him the ability to express himself in a concrete and comprehensible way. He knew how to use simple examples in order to make known more complex aspects of human thought. He truly was a great thinker.

Astral Body

His astral body of ray 6, sub-ray 2 made him loyal and sensitive. Ray 6 invested him with kindness, dedication and sincerity. He was also very warm at times. He appreciated good food whenever possible. Ill at ease with the female gender, he preferred the company of men even if he was not averse to women.

His sub-ray 2 endowed him with a great sensitivity towards other people's suffering, leading him to live like a hermit at times. This sub-ray guided him outside his thought, inciting him to perceive the reality of life, that is to say, human suffering.

Physical Body

His ray 3, sub-ray 6 physical body gave him strong physical resistance. Ray 3 provided him with a highly-efficient physical brain to receive the thoughts sent out by his Higher mind.

Sub-ray 6 allowed him to be more robust at some key moments in his life. In this way, he would appear stronger and more imposing.

We still have a lot to learn from his teachings that always remain true, although his incarnation as Epictetus goes far back in time. His present incarnation will allow humanity to grow in a technological universe more adapted to its real needs that are not necessarily related to the ego.

July 30, 2009

 # FÖLLMI, OLIVIER

Given Name: Olivier Föllmi
Nationality: French
Place and Date of Birth: Saint-Julien-en-Genevois, Haute Savoie (France), 1958
Profession: Photographer

MASTER DJWHAL KHUL'S COMMENTARY

More evolved than he seems, Olivier Föllmi has reached a certain wisdom that shows through his photographs. He loves humanity in its entirety and is fascinated by the occult aspect of things. He is a humble and wise man.

He is accomplishing an important work, allowing humanity to see and understand the beauty inhabiting within, because his photographs emphasize beauty and not suffering. Very artistic in his approach to photography, he knows how to produce through this "medium" a certain inner peace in others, though it is a peace that does not transform. This will take place later in his life.

Initiation Level: 2.2

He should, however, attain 2.3 shortly.

His potential is considerable, and he has much to offer. He is endowed with a particular mental arrogance that will easily correct itself. He has the rays of an artist who bows when facing a more authentic spirituality. Having been a monk several times in the past, he never accomplished so much as in this present life.

Ray Structure

Monad: 2	Soul: 3	Personality: 4-2
Mental: 7-3	Astral: 6-2	Physical: 7-3

Monad and Soul

His Monad has no real influence while his Soul wants to be more and more present. It allows him to experiment with a multitude of things, which makes his photography unique.

Personality

His ray 4 sub-ray 2 Personality favours him with an artistic sensitivity. He likes change and enjoys living experiences that stimulate his creativity that is always present in his life. He appreciates beauty and strives to bring it out through his photography. He detests conflicts, although his ray 4 tends to provoke them in order to promote change in others.

His sub-ray 2 graced him with a great gentleness and provides him with a grand sensitivity that is transmitted in the way he takes photographs. He has an aversion for suffering, although it runs everywhere alongside. He likes to give to others and relieve their pain. He desires, somewhat, to "save" others and often pays the price, because his energy diminishes rapidly when he is not alert and gives too much without discernment.

Mental Body

His ray 7, sub-ray 3 mental body provides him with a logic and a perseverance that are transmitted in his work. He is a perfectionist, demanding towards himself as well as very ritualistic. He leaves nothing to chance when it is a matter of photography that, for him, demands a lot of work and attention. He is, however, surprised at times when the Soul encourages him to take pictures without granting him the time required for his customary preparation. He knows a force is guiding and helping him, a force that he is trusting more and more.

Sub-ray 3 confers on him an agility of thought that nicely completes the work of ray 7, allowing him to be more spontaneous and more creative in his perfection. This agility softens his ray 7 during the thought process.

Astral Body

His ray 6, sub-ray 2 Astral makes him a warm and sensitive man. Ray 6 allows him to appreciate life and humanity and he fights for this cause that is close to his heart. Ray 6 contributes to making him a generous person, a loving father (doting father at times) and a loving husband. He loves to give and be loved. His comments can be scathing at times when he considers a situation to be unfair; it is best not to be against him at those moments as his words can be forceful yet effective.

Sub-ray 2 invests him with an aura of gentleness. He possesses a broad knowledge that he takes pleasure in spreading, but which sometimes prevents him from experimenting. He likes to give advice, is sensitive, too much sometimes, and can be easily hurt.

Physical Body

His ray 7, sub-ray 3 physical body accords him appreciable physical resistance that proves necessary for him to accomplish his work. Ray 7 grants him a sense of order that also helps him in this regard. Very persevering, he does not appreciate having to give up. His joy lies in the accomplishment of the impossible.

Sub-ray 3 endows him with an interesting sense of humour; he likes to provoke a reaction, however, without malice. He can laugh at himself and at others; he does not take himself seriously, except in the field of photography.

He is a kind, loyal and reliable man. He appreciates simplicity, and his work is a tribute to the beauty of this world and of the people that populate this planet.

December 17, 2006

 FRANKLIN, BENJAMIN

Given Name: Benjamin Franklin
Nationality: American
Place and Date of Birth: Boston, Massachusetts (United States), January 17, 1706
Date of Death: Philadelphia, Pennsylvania (United States), April 17, 1790
Profession: Printer, writer, diplomat, scholar and inventor

MASTER DJWHAL KHUL'S COMMENTARY

Benjamin Franklin was a remarkable man, overshadowed by the Masters to accomplish humanitarian work at the heart of the planet. Displaying little conceit, he knew how to transmit knowledge beneficial to the development of the human consciousness. He left an indelible mark on the history of humanity. Without him, humanity would have remained in the dark for another century, not only a physical darkness but an intellectual one as well.

Well ahead of his time, he knew how to face humanitarian problems while trying to counter some himself. While he knew he was not alone as he had friends in many high places of societal and spiritual circles, he suffered much from not being understood.

Benjamin Franklin deserves to be known, as he inspired and still inspires many people. Without him, America would show a different face and undoubtedly be behind in many aspects. America was lucky to have attracted people of great importance in order to be able one day to represent freedom on earth. However, it now has to readjust and increase its vibration in order to liberate itself of the illusion of superiority that presently characterizes it. It is, therefore, not excluded that Benjamin Franklin's Soul would still work for this purpose during the next century. We will see his availability and desire in this respect because he now has the option to choose his destiny.

Initiation Level: 3.2

This initiation level was high for that time. He reached his fourth initiation in his last incarnation as Martin Luther King, a great man who significantly contributed not only to African Americans, but also to all of the American people.

Ray Structure

Monad: 2	Soul: 3	Personality: 2-3
Mental: 7-5	Astral: 6-4	Physical: 3-7

Monad and Soul

His Monad started to have a particular influence; on the other hand, his Soul guided his vehicle fairly well. It spurred him to adapt easily to various situations, motivated him to accomplish several things simultaneously and inspired him with the taste to travel and meet leaders in various fields, whether political, social or scientific. It also endowed him with a great flexibility and allowed him to easily integrate within various communities. We can assert that he was a citizen of the world, which was revolutionary for that time.

Personality

His ray 2, sub-ray 3 Personality conferred to him a great sensitivity, well directed by the rays of his mental body that definitely demonstrated to be at his Soul's service. Ray 2 gifted him with a strong dose of intuition on the level of feelings experienced by men, a taste for research, and the desire to serve in order to diminish human suffering. This ray offered him the possibility to be accessible to the needs of others and to remain humble despite his successes and discoveries. This ray was actually a request from the Soul to remind him not to fall into the arrogance he had experienced during his incarnations as a second level initiate. It also allowed him to transmit and incarnate a wisdom that never left him.

Sub-ray 3 simplified the task of the Soul so that it could become more efficient and diplomatic. It assisted ray 2 so that it remained uncorrupted by the desire to serve and be loved at all costs. Without this sub-ray, it would have been difficult for him to resist some pressures by his entourage. This sub-ray encouraged him to never give in to blackmail and corruption, in the face of his desire to be recognized and loved by all.

Mental Body

His mental body governed by the energies of ray 7, sub-ray 5, shaped him with principles and a remarkable intelligence. Ray 7 moved him to invent, produce, and be perfect in his research while his sub-ray 5 allowed him to make everything a reality. This ray also animated a mental will that never left him. It graced him with this brilliance that helped him perform and make a name for himself in the social and political realms. He was very respected because of this rectitude that emanated from him. When ray 7 feels and acts for the benefit of all, it does not compromise.

His sub-ray 5 gave him a down-to-earth aspect that allowed him to see the consequence of his gestures. It granted him the chance to make manifest what did not seem possible. It conferred on him a mental body always ready to experiment for the good of all. This sub-ray also freed him from a certain fear. Consequently, he could experiment safely because he left no parameter to chance.

Astral Body

His astral body, strongly influenced by the energies of ray 6, sub-ray 4, provided him with this unshakable loyalty towards his country and his relations. However, the contribution of the energy of sub-ray 4 kept watch over him, so that he did not suffer from limitations or from erroneous faithfulness. It invested him with the character of a free man in a world imprisoned by matter and dogmas.

Ray 6 accorded him a communicative warmth. It gave him the taste for service, intelligently sacrificing himself to the causes he was defending (his mental body influenced by rays 7 and 5, properly balanced his emotional body, bringing him back to order if necessary). This ray made him available and reliable because once he gave his word he would never take it back.

Sub-ray 4 slightly coloured the influence of ray 6, preventing him from becoming too rigid. It made him understand the needs of humanity and its difficulty to evolve. If he lived some *downs*, which was rare, because he lacked time, he would rapidly reclaim the torch forgetting his discomfort in order to serve the goals he had given himself. He was also supported by three Masters who helped him in various tasks: Koot Hoomi (social aspect), El Morya Khan (political aspect) as well as Saint Germain (scientific aspect). Paul the Venetian was often present, but his task consisted mostly in supporting his disciple in difficult situations, to inspire him intuitively, while the three other Masters helped him accomplish his task within various communities. He physically met these remarkable men (Koot Hoomi, Saint Germain as well as El Morya Khan) so that they would inspire him during the preparation of the signing of the Declaration of Independence.

Physical Body

His physical body, conditioned by the energy disclosed by ray 3, sub-ray 7, conferred on him a physical brain necessary for the task. Ray 3 allowed him to be self-taught and offered him the possibility to work on several things at the same time. Thanks to sub-ray 7, he could concentrate and not lose himself in the details because his time was counted. This ray 3 endowed him with a flexible and efficient physical body.

Sub-ray 7 granted him strong resistance to tension, both externally as well as internally. It gave him an inner discipline that never left him. Supported by his sub-ray 5 mental body, this physical sub-ray gave him the gift of bringing all kinds of inventions onto the physical plane.

This man was a world pillar and will be once again during his next incarnation that will occur soon. It will take place again in the United States where his help is greatly needed.

November 22, 2009

 GAMPOPA

Given Name: Gampopa
Other Names: Dhagpo Lhaje or Dhagpo Rinpoche (the doctor or the Master of Dhagpo)
Nationality: Tibetan
Place and Date of Birth: Nyal (south of Tibet), 1079
Date of Death: Nyal (south of Tibet), 1153
Profession: Master of Buddhism of the Kagyüpa lineage

MASTER DJWHAL KHUL'S COMMENTARY

A great scholar in his times, Gampopa considerably influenced the generations that succeeded him. He was succinct in his words, but always efficient. This particularity came in part from his ray 7, sub-ray 1 mental body.

He lived in extreme solitude and spent the majority of his life, following the death of his wife, deepening his inner being. He accomplished a lot and disseminated Buddhism in simple terms so that it was within everyone's reach. His teachings, although seemingly difficult to grasp, provide important keys, accessible to all, to living important realizations. It is essential to understand that his teaching is meant as an inheritance that requires several successive lives of work, because it weaves, within the consciousness of the person studying it, a thread maintaining the continuity of the progressive awakening of Consciousness. Correctly interpreted, his work can lead to the gates of illumination, because Gampopa was guided (by Koot Hoomi) when he wrote it.

Initiation Level: 3.2

He could have reached an initiation level of 3.8 but the love he had for his wife constrained him. The vow she made him take to maintain the sacred bond of marriage, prevented the full accomplishment of his destiny.

Ray Structure

Monad: 3	Soul: 2	Personality: 3-4
Mental: 7-1	Astral: 6-2	Physical: 7-3

Monad and Soul

His Monad had a certain influence on him that allowed him to write in an occult fashion. Ray 3 loves to induce thinking and provoke experimentation that arouses a deeper understanding of what is being conveyed through the teaching.

His great sensitivity came mainly from his ray 2 located at the Soul level. He could feel other people's suffering and be inspired by it to write. He would have loved to help humanity more which, according to what he saw and understood, was caught in a web of inner misunderstandings, hindering the progression towards the Light he knew was omnipresent within all those he came close to.

Personality

His ray 3, sub-ray 4 Personality conferred to him the capacity to be fluid and efficient. Ray 3 made him quite social and encouraged interesting exchanges with those who wished to talk with him. He liked to provoke thinking in others and act in such a way that his listener would leave with the impression of having understood a new aspect of his being.

Sub-ray 4 produced in him a certain adaptability initiated by ray 3, but adequately supported by sub-ray 4 that considerably dedramatized the facts that his intense life presented to him. It also offered him the possibility to enormously appreciate Milarepa's unorthodox teaching.

Mental Body

Due to his ray 7, sub-ray 1 mental body, he was a perfect scholar, disciplined, tidy, never giving up when facing difficulties. Ray 7 graced him with a mental refinement that allowed poetic and exact writing. It made him extremely respectful of the intelligence of Miralepa's teaching, because it forced him to think and to integrate what he succeeded in understanding. It also offered him the possibility of expressing in words certain important notions for the future of Buddhism.

Sub-ray 1 awarded him a flawless determination and the desire to accomplish the utmost possible in his life. It also conferred to him great concentration that served him in all the fields of his life.

Astral Body

His ray 6, sub-ray 2 astral body transmitted to him an exceptional sense of devotion, dedication and faithfulness. Once he had given his word, ray 6 acted in such a way that he would never take it back. He was stubborn and quick-tempered. He could be charming and very warm, thanks to the combination of rays 6 and 2. He experienced great pain at the death of his nearest and dearest, pain accentuated by ray 6; in a way, he actually never recovered from such losses.

His sub-ray 2 incited him to become a doctor, mainly thanks to the support of his Soul that motivated him to relieve human suffering. Moreover, it created in him, a temporary mirage that inspired in him the desire to save others at any cost. He finally understood by adequately observing the human psyche and by realizing how much the human being was responsible for his own pain.

Physical Body

His ray 7, sub-ray 3 physical body equipped him with such a resistance that he revealed himself as being almost indefatigable. Ray 7 endowed him with an excellent nervous system, encouraging him to manage certain tensions in his life well. Also, his human brain proved highly efficient and constantly sought perfection in his writings. He was very tidy, both on the physical as well the psychic level.

Sub-ray 3 granted him more resistance by conferring to him an intelligence that provided more flexibility to the perfection of ray 7. He did not have many illnesses, this being the result of the combination of the energy of rays 7 and 3.

This remarkable man actually lives in a Tibetan body in Lhassa. He is fighting for the liberation of the people he loved so much during his numerous incarnations in Tibet.

August 8, 2009

 GANDHI

Given Name: Mohandas Karamchand Gandhi
Nickname: Mahatma
Nationality: Indian
Place and Date of Birth: Porbandar, Gujarat (India), October 2, 1869
Date of Death: Delhi (India), January 30, 1948
Profession: Lawyer, philosopher and statesman

MASTER DJWHAL KHUL'S COMMENTARY

A man endowed with a certain nobility of the Soul, Gandhi accomplished a lot for his country in the political field. He knew how to tame, by force, certain austere aspects of political life in India. He even restored a certain pride and more liberty for the Indian people. He fostered an understanding between Hindus and Muslims, which ultimately cost him his life.

He was tormented all his life by good and evil. He would have wished more justice, love and devotion in the world. He fought with courage, often risking his life, so that more harmony would reign. He always carried feelings of guilt, blame towards himself because he would have liked to be perfect, which, of course, was not the case. He was a sad idealist, who was never able to see the light at the end of the tunnel. He often had the impression he was taking one step forward and ten steps back. He did not like himself and suffered from an excessive ray 6, perceived from outside as the expression of a martyr, which he was not.

He was intelligent, hard-working, dedicated, but he leaned too much towards the austerities he liked to practice, because he thought he was thus purifying his flesh that was too caught by the carnal desires which he qualified as being not high enough, at least in terms of the Soul's expression. Certain illusions guided him but also made him suffer uselessly at certain times. He loved too much, had too many passions he was attempting to master, in vain.

He is undoubtedly the most well-known Indian, the most respected presently. However, he was not the most evolved, although he did a lot for his country. Supported by the Masters, he had a task to carry out that required a faith that he always cultivated, thanks to this invisible support he felt present in his life.

Married too young, he would have without doubt accomplished more if he had not been compelled to live a youth where sexuality, being part of the decor, was accompanied by the obligations of the head of a family. Sexuality was always his weak point, but mainly the aspect of his life he never understood. He would have wished to be a saint while he knew he was only a man on a quest for justice for all!

Initiation Level: 2.3

He was influenced by the illusions that go hand in hand with this level. Heading towards his third initiation, a certain number of illusions qualified him, illusions he had trouble dispelling. He would have needed a master on the physical plane to guide him on the inner planes.

Ray Structure

Monad: 2	Soul: 2	Personality: 3-4
Mental: 7-5	Astral: 6-2	Physical: 3-7

Monad and Soul

His Monad had no influence on him, contrary to his Soul. Truly inwoven with love, he wished to help others, wished the best for all, although he had a vision that would have gained more by expanding because it was dominated by his emotional body that he did not perfectly master. His ray 2, strengthened by his Astral of ray 6, sub-ray 2, was sometimes poorly polarized, revealing then his shyness and giving him little confidence in himself.

Personality

His Personality of ray 3, sub-ray 4 conferred to him the art of being quick-witted and a remarkable intelligence. He did not fancy the strict aspect of culture or studies but gave more value to the intelligence that could result from them. In spite of his deep shyness, he knew how to play with words, whose power and effect on his entourage he appreciated. It is important to keep in mind that his brain was influenced by his ray 3 physical body. It was very difficult to fool him except when it came to emotions that made him very vulnerable and excessively sensitive. He attempted several times to correct this aspect, without success.

His sub-ray 4 gave him the manual dexterity he sometimes needed, mainly to weave his clothes. Furthermore, he was plagued with ups and downs that he tried to hide as well as he could. He sometimes seemed to experience deep depressions that were interpreted by those close to him as existential pains, when facing the injustices he saw that made him suffer.

Mental Body

Thanks to his ray 7, sub-ray 5 mental body, he was a brilliant man, very organized and thoughtful. No gesture was made without thinking first. He liked to think. This is indeed what he did when he was fasting. He could also prove to be very stubborn, abrupt and lacking diplomacy. For him, the only thing that mattered was the task at hand in order to reach the goal to be attained.

His sub-ray 5 allowed him to be an honorable lawyer, because this sub-ray was useful to him in finding loopholes and solutions. However, due to his great shyness, he had difficulty pleading. His sharp intelligence was paralyzed when he had to speak in public, because he was afraid to be judged and misunderstood, which did not eliminate his stubbornness, increased by this sub-ray.

Astral Body

His ray 6, sub-ray 2 astral body made him very emotional and sometimes quick-tempered, pushing him to continuously seek equity in everything. He would give himself body and soul when he knew he had to accomplish an important task for humanity's well-being. His ray 6 made him hard as stone and emphasized his stubbornness more.

His sub-ray 2 increased his shyness, particularly when he entered in a relationship with others. However, he had a loving heart and gave without limit. He had many fears, fears he mastered well enough when they concerned other people. He would forget himself then and, in the same way, forget his own fears that easily paralyzed him.

Physical Body

His physical body of ray, 3, sub-ray 7 endowed him with the aptitudes necessary to accomplish a lot and conferred to him, despite his fragility, a lot of resistance. He enjoyed a certain flexibility in his physical body that did not always transfer to his invariably firm and rectilinear thinking, which gave him the necessary determination to accomplish his task. He preached non-violence and never shied away from it.

Sub-ray 7 increased his resistance and allowed him to keep an efficient spirit in spite of deprivations. He would also attract other people's respect because of his relatively organized mind.

His ray configuration was almost perfect for his task. He has not yet reincarnated, though this should not be delayed too long.

August 1, 2009

 # GATES, BILL

Given Name: William Henry Gates III
Nationality: American
Place and Date of Birth: Seattle, Washington (United States), October 28, 1955
Profession: Computer engineer, inventor, entrepreneur and philanthropist

MASTER DJWHAL KHUL'S COMMENTARY

Bill Gates is a remarkable man because he was able to mold form from the formless, thanks to the life challenge he set himself before his present incarnation. He was able to discover the infinitesimal within the infinitely large. We may consider him a genius because of his extraordinary intellectual ability.

His great strength comes from his humility, even if he often demonstrates a strong obstinance. The humility he knew how to develop in his last incarnations allowed him to increasingly open his energy at the level of the heart. Here is an intelligent man who has a heart.

Thanks to his "mathematical" Soul, he was able to understand, in the course of his incarnations, the universe through mathematics. He was a great mathematician-astronomer (Johannes Kepler), which gave him the possibility to discover the invisible form maintaining the Universe. Then, reincarnated as a great scientist (Robert Fulton), he uncovered, around the 1800's, what we call occult power propulsion that would one day produce nuclear power.

Next, being born as a Buddhist monk in Tibet, at the Ganden Monastery, he began to know man's inner Universe. He was, at the time a creator of *thangkas* and sand mandalas, which provided him with the possibility of continuing to discover what was hidden behind the symbolism of form (and this with patience). He perfected his power of concentration during this incarnation.

Initiation Level: 3.1

Thanks to his initiation level, he is recognized as a powerful man, who demonstrates more detachment towards the world of matter, while still being part of it.

Ray Structure

Monad: 2   Soul: 3-5 (he changed his Soul Ray in this life)
Personality: 3-7   Mental: 7-5   Astral: 6-2   Physical: 3-7

Monad and Soul

His Monad helps him to better manage his life. It is starting to have an influence that will contribute to the accomplishment of his destiny in terms of humanitarian aid. His Soul of ray 3, sub-ray 5 allows him to manage his business efficiently. The Soul can now continue its work with the recent assistance of the Monad that wraps it in the love aspect that was often absent.

Personality

Due to his Personality of ray 3, sub-ray 7, he is active and resourceful. Endowed with a warm Personality, influenced by his ray 6 Astral, he is not easily impressed. Ray 3 makes him a shrewd business man, mainly because of the support of sub-ray 7, which makes him a perfectionist. He can "play" with numbers perfectly. His ray 3 confers flexibility and speed for decision making while sub-ray 7 grants him this magician aspect that attracts success.

Sub-ray 7 qualifies ray 3 by making him more alert and conscious of certain details. This ray 3, sub-ray 7 Personality shapes him into a man who knows where he is heading and how to employ the means to achieve it. This combination is the reason for his wealth.

Mental Body

His mental body of ray 7, sub-ray 5 confers to him intelligence and perfectionism in his projects. Ray 7 endows him with the necessary instinct and allows him to seek the inaccessible on the mental plane in order to realize large-scale projects. Ray 7 attracts and sub-ray 5 manifests!

Sub-ray 5 makes him very realistic and down-to-earth. He understands matter and knows how to manage it adequately. Sub-ray 5 allows ray 7 to perform even better and to quickly check what does not function in the implementation of certain projects. Sub-ray 5 makes him very mental and sometimes drifts him away from his Soul's goal. Fortunately, his initiation level is such that the Soul gets the upper hand and straightens his way.

Astral Body

His ray 6, sub-ray 2 Astral grants him warmth and sensitivity. It is these rays coupled with his Soul's goal that renders him sensitive and charitable. Ray 6 makes him a faithful and loving man. He adores his family, which gives him balance and endows him with the joy that animates him. Ray 6 provides him with the possibility of having sincere friends and to really appreciate them.

Sub-ray 2 allows him to soften, to become "human" and to love humanity. His mental arrogance, because he has it, makes him temporarily forget this "humanity". But he rectifies it quickly and becomes again this Soul aspiring to grow and help others grow.

Physical Body

His physical body of ray 3, sub-ray 7 provides him with the possibility of working hard without tiring. Ray 3 allows him to think and act fast. It makes his intelligence accessible (ray 5 does not always allow it) and grants him a sense of humour appreciated by those close to him.

Sub-ray 7 refines his intelligence and grants him a physical body even more resistant. This sub-ray confers to him a strong nervous system; he can then handle several cases simultaneously.

He is a reliable person, generous but stubborn and arrogant. He is not easily impressed. His weakness is love, or if you prefer his "heart", which only asks to open more in order to become an active instrument for Hierarchy.

July 4, 2009

 GAULLE, CHARLES DE

Given Name: Charles André Joseph Marie de Gaulle
Nationality: French
Place and Date of Birth: Lille (France), November 22, 1890
Date of Death: Colombey-les-Deux-Églises (France), November 9, 1970
Profession: French general and statesman

MASTER DJWHAL KHUL'S COMMENTARY

A man of great talent, Charles de Gaulle allowed France to restore its credentials and to acquire the respect of the whole world, because France prior to de Gaulle is not representative of the France that followed him. This country won recognition among the super powers because of this man who was able to transmit nobility, pride and rectitude to the whole world.

An uncommunicative introvert, Charles de Gaulle was not unanimously accepted by his international counterparts, who often perceived him as dull and uncooperative. De Gaulle pursued only one goal: to serve his country well and to favour a serious and respectful relationship with other nations. His righteousness, his desire to succeed in his life and his life missions, qualified him in the eyes of some people as being an arrogant individual who did not really appreciate life's pleasures. This undemonstrative man was passionate about life; however, he preferred to live this passion wisely instead of wasting it on vain receptions and social events.

In his private life, he demonstrated the same authoritarianism as in public, although his love flowed towards his significant others, which contrasted with his public life. A good father and a loving husband, he always jealously kept his private life private. Not seeking glory, he always gave greater importance to his sense of duty towards his family and his nation, which was an extrapolation of the former. He continuously fought for human freedom in every sense of the word.

Initiation Level: 2.8

He was a great statesman because his profound sensitivity and his "active listening" to others allowed him to work efficiently for his country. A second Initiate at birth (2.3) he demonstrated its related arrogance in his youth; however, when he grew older, on the physical as well as on the initiatory level, he acquired more maturity and his arrogance diminished to a great extent. When he left his body, he did not wish to be either recognized or glorified, but departed with the peaceful Soul of someone who was able to follow his real destiny without flinching.

Ray Structure

Monad: 1	Soul: 2	Personality: 1-3
Mental: 7-5	Astral: 6-2	Physical: 7-3

Monad and Soul

His Monad had a certain influence, but it was mainly his Soul that guided him in this incarnation. His desire to help his nation, to be just and loving, came from this happy influence.

Personality

His Personality of ray 1, sub-ray 3 served him well, conferring to him the possibility of accomplishing his mission. Ray 1 communicated to him this strong iron will and this particular vision that characterized this incarnation. He feared nothing or almost nothing; His weakness was his astral body, thus his family. This is the reason he did not expose it in daylight, thereby protecting this sure value in his life. Recognized for his lack of diplomacy resulting from ray 1, he was impatient to act and always looked ahead.

Sub-ray 3 lightened the influence of ray 1. It endowed him with the sense of humour so typical of ray 3, as well as a certain ease in his personal relations, but not necessarily political. This sub-ray gave him "The Verb" to express himself and allowed ray 1 to loosen up a bit.

Mental Body

His mental body of ray 7, sub-ray 5 equipped him well to govern his country and his soldiers so that he proved to be a good strategist, not flinching when tired, because ray 7 provided him with a great mental resistance. This ray also conferred to him a certain arrogance with regards to his thoughts and the desire to be perfect in everything. He disliked flaws and could not bear disloyalty (due to the combination of rays 7 and 6).

His sub-ray 5 donned him with a strong intelligence and the desire to demonstrate honesty in everything. He appreciated possessing and providing evidence, when necessary. This sub-ray also allowed him to acquire a certain intuition coming from his attachment to properly understanding the hidden aspect of things. He deciphered others by their bodily and facial expressions. Narrow-minded and stubborn, however, because he had strong beliefs, it was difficult to make him change his mind; once his idea or impression was reached, he would not budge.

Astral Body

His astral body of ray 6, sub-ray 2 allowed him to be a good husband and an excellent father, warm and faithful. He appreciated taking care of his family and hosting some close friends. This ray 6 conferred to him a remarkable sense of patriotism towards his country, which he loved more than anything else.

Sub-ray 2 filled him with a great sensitivity that he hid behind his arrogance. He understood human suffering and attempted to reduce it.

This sub-ray conferred to him a certain wisdom in love and friendship, because when he loved it was forever (rays 6 and 2 influence). On the other hand, he could not stand treason and demonstrated obduracy towards those who would betray him or betray the nation.

Physical Body

His physical body of ray 7, sub-ray 3 graced him with the proud appearance that characterized him. His refined traits, particularly his hands, reveal that he did not possess a ray 1 body, contrary to what certain people were tempted to believe. This physical body provided him with resistance, but caused him certain lumbar pains (lower back pain) all his life. Image was important for him because it reflected his desire for perfection in everything. He would therefore always appear well-dressed and took care of himself.

Sub-ray 3 endowed him with a quick wit that compensated for the slowness of ray 7 that prefers perfection to rapidity. He hid this inner turbulence fairly well, which resulted from this sub-ray that sometimes made him impatient. He did not appreciate the undecided and respected those who did not fear him.

This statesman accomplished a lot and his accomplishments will continue to surprise humanity. He will work in the political field in his next incarnation.

May 21, 2009

 GORBATCHEV, MIKHAÏL

Given Name: Mikhaïl Sergueïevitch Gorbatchev
Nationality: Soviet, then Russian
Place and Date of Birth: Kraï of Stavropol (RSFS of Russia), March 2, 1931
Profession: Statesman

MASTER DJWHAL KHUL'S COMMENTARY

A fascinating man because of his determination and desire to help humanity to suffer less and to become freer, Mikhaïl Gorbatchev is a good tool for us, the Masters, in spite of his task, which was often difficult and painful. He is endowed with an immense faith that guides him during painful times.

Never alone, although he lives a profound solitude, his desire and his need to help humanity is persistent in spite of the fact that he is increasingly tired and demonstrates less resistance than before. A man of character, he always displays courage to express himself and to pursue his mission despite the years that weighed down his physical body. Graced with a very acute sensitivity, he can listen to the need of others while keeping himself proud and alert in his thoughts, still striving to be just and equitable for all.

He would love to do more but he knows for a fact that there is a time for everything and that certain negative powers work in the shadows in order to impede humanity's progress. He believes, in a way, in life's process through other lives, although he cannot claim it publicly.

He has lived numerous lives in Russia, a country he still loves in spite of its coarse aspects at times, rendered thus through the suffering of his people. He feels that his next incarnation will not take place in this country but rather in a region that will require the contribution of men such as he to help liberate it. Russia would still be under communist domination; we are thinking of Tibet, but also of Nepal, which will suffer considerable hardships in the coming years.

It is interesting to see that he is working more and more for the Masters and feels ready to become a perfect servant, forgetting his attachments in order to serve better.

Initiation Level: 3.2

Mikhaïl Gorbatchev succeeded, in this lifetime, to get closer to his Self while remaining an active human being in the world of matter.

Previously, he experienced several religious lives that allowed him a certain interiorization. Now he is ready to work relentlessly, while keeping himself far from monastic lives, having succeeded in acquiring a certain trust in the Self that should not diminish.

Ray Structure

Monad: 2	Soul: 3	Personality: 6-4
Mental: 7-1	Astral: 2-6	Physical: 3-7

Monad and Soul

His Monad has little influence; however, a fairly strong bond unites him to his Soul, which, under the governance of ray 3, supported him a lot. He demonstrates a great deal of intelligence and tries to help humanity as much as possible. For him the whole world and education should become accessible to all. He knows that education is an important key; without it people are at the mercy of those that benefit from this deficiency and manipulate them. He suffers sometimes by what he sees and understands.

Personality

His Personality of ray 6, sub-ray 4 makes him obliging and faithful; he appreciates helping and being of service. A dedicated and honest man, most of the time, he has a strong character, efficiently supported by ray 6. He can seem very warm and fervent during discussions, thanks to this ray that warmly colors his remarks. He would give his life to help (if he could perceive its usefulness).

His sub-ray 4 makes him appreciate art, which appears to him as a way of liberation and not as a waste of time. Do not forget that his mental body is endowed in part with a ray 7; he is therefore delighted by good and beautiful things. Due to his ray 6, he lives some attachments to those "things" while his mental brings him back to order if need be. This sub-ray 4 sometimes creates worries (ups and downs) that he controls fairly well. He likes to have a drink, but he properly controls himself.

Mental Body

His mental body of ray 7, sub-ray 1 grants him efficiency and intelligence. He has a fairly wide vision, and he knows how to listen to his intuition (ray 7); obstinate, he sometimes experiences difficulty to listen well, when he is too implied in the "fervor" of a project or a discussion. However, he respects intelligence and knows how to yield in front of a person that seems to be right.

His sub-ray 1 supports him in his task as an efficient leader and enlarges his vision. Fortunately, his ray configuration confers to him an astral body of ray 2, otherwise he would reveal himself to be often hard (the combination of rays 6, 7 and 1). He sees the things that must be accomplished immediately and attempts, thanks to these two ray 3's (the Soul and the physical brain), to act within reasonable, even short deadlines.

Astral Body

His astral body of ray 2, sub-ray 6 makes him charming and pleasant at times; he may reveal himself to be an exceptional host and to be sincerely attentive to the needs of others. He also succeeds in understanding them and realizing the catch twenty-two which these people experience. He often feels powerless and tries to do his best while knowing that nothing can be perfect or be achieved if the timing is not appropriate. In a way, he believes in karma and in the consequences of the acts performed in this lifetime and in other lives.

Sub-ray 6 reinforces his loyalty and his desire to help others. He can prove to be a real driving force capable of destroying the walls that separate people.

Physical Body

His physical of ray 3, sub-ray 7 has strengthened his intelligence and his self-expression. Ray 3 granted him diplomacy, intelligence and an inkling of flexibility. It also granted him a larger view of things, thus balancing his ray 7, sub-ray 1 mental body, sometimes too narrow. This ray endowed him with a good physical resistance although he often lacked sleep.

His sub-ray 7 provided him with a sense of order and contributed to increasing his efficiency and strength. He likes that there is a place for everything and that everything has its place.

Mikhaïl Gorbachev is a distinguished man who works very hard for the benefit of all.

Misjudged and often misunderstood, he deserves our respect and interest.

August 16, 2008

 # GURDJIEFF

Given Name: Gerogej Ivanovitch Gurdjieff
Nationality: Russian
Place and Date of Birth: Gyumri (Armenia), November 1, 1866
Date of Death: Neuilly-sur-Seine (France), October 29, 1949
Profession: Spiritual teacher

MASTER DJWHAL KHUL'S COMMENTARY

A marginal man for his times, Gurdjieff was able to bring a new vision on certain aspects of spirituality, too rigid at the time. Perceived as a libertine by some people, divinely mad by others, he skillfully aroused controversy. According to his vision, only paradoxes could change man and free him from his strait jacket that prevented him from seeing beyond himself. Polarized towards the mental body, he denied emotions that, for him, represented barriers blinding man even more by driving him away from his real path, freedom.

His vagrant years allowed him to see pain and suffering from the point of view of karma, and also allowed him to believe that karma revealed itself to be a game of spirit attempting to maintain a firm hold on human destiny. He denied the power of spirit and declared that man, divine in himself, did not require any outside assistance to his Consciousness. He was young and inexperienced as a master. We hope he will do better next time.

Initiation Level: 3.3

His initiation level was high for his times, however, without a real guide, he roamed in his own consciousness in search of answers related to his inner discomfort. He was very intelligent, perhaps too much and expressed the desire to destroy human slavery in all its forms.

Ray Structure

Monad: 3	Soul: 2	Personality: 1-3
Mental: 7-5	Astral: 4-6	Physical: 3-5

Monad and Soul

His Monad's influence was starting, which provided him with a certain form of divine knowledge and subtle intelligence. His Soul endowed him with a particular sensitivity that he hid behind known vices such as alcohol and sex in which he took pleasure and enjoyed without restrain. However, he respected the people he loved, without letting their fears and desires influence him.

Personality

His Personality of ray 1, sub-ray 3 made him hard and manipulative. He often frightened people, and his working method only suited those who promoted intelligence before anything else. He would easily pass for an atheist, which he was partially. His ray 1 enticed him to make blunt and direct remarks, removing self-doubt and providing a fervour that made him almost magnetic. He was right in the majority of cases and knew which path to take to reach his goals. He would often appear heartless, with a pure intelligence. He did not understand the fervour of Buddhism, Islam's fanaticism, the blindness of Hinduism and the servitude of Christianity. He had a weakness for Tantrism of the left path, which he poorly used and badly understood.

His sub-ray 3 made him intelligent and very ingenious in his approaches. He had an easy speech, was quick at repartee and was not easily boxed in. He hated the idea of a Master, although he was one. He declared to be his own master and helped those who wanted to be masters of their lives, far away from the slavery of emotions. Intellectual people loved his speeches and his writings.

Mental Body

His ray 7, sub-ray 5 mental body conferred on him even more intelligence and hardness in his speech. He liked rituals and accepted disorder with difficulty, particularly at the level of thoughts that needed, according to him, to always be clear and objective, what emotions did not allow. Sub-ray 5 reinforced this nearly scientific approach. He had a sense of humour, bitter and sharp like his thoughts.

Astral Body

His Astral of ray 4, sub-ray 6 made him a man who defied and hated faithfulness. He desired his freedom on all levels. His fits of anger, attributable to the combination of ray 4, and rays 7 and 5 in his mental body, often raged. This ray 4 made him experience ups and downs that his entourage hardly understood. A refined creator, he swarmed with ideas that he had difficulty carrying out, which frustrated him tremendously. His sub-ray 6 granted him a sense of duty towards his relations and a faithfulness beyond question towards his beliefs that he fearlessly defended.

Physical Body

His physical body of ray 3, sub-ray 5 did not grace him with beauty, something he regretted; he used his speech to compensate for this gap. Endowed with a sharp intelligence thanks to this brain influenced by ray 3, he often spoke and acted rapidly. His sub-ray 5 gave him this "strange" air that "came from nowhere". Equipped with a physical resistance and remarkable strength, no one was indifferent to him.

June 8, 2008

 GURUMAYI

Given Name: Malti Shetty
Also called: Swami Chidvilasananda
Nationality: Indian
Place and Date of Birth: Mumbai (India), June 24, 1955
Profession: A Guru of the Siddha tradition

MASTER DJWHAL KHUL'S COMMENTARY

Swami Chidvilasananda demonstrates more wisdom than Mother Meera, although she lacks vision. She is relatively evolved, but would require the help of a guide, otherwise she will not progress in this present incarnation. Too much power was conferred to her and too many responsibilities, which made her a prisoner. Although still lacking perfection, she possesses a capacity to forget herself. A subtle selfishness, of which she is more or less conscious, still gnaws at her; she tries to cure herself of it, without success. She is moving forward like a blind person in a labyrinth composed of her devotees and disciples. To give her back her vision, she would have to be liberated from this responsibility.

Initiation Level: 3.2

Ray Structure

Monad: 2	Soul: 2	Personality: 2-3
Mental: 6-4	Astral: 4-2	Physical: 7-4

Swami Chidvilasananda is very magnetic and very beautiful, which comes partially from her initiation level and her rays. Although she knows that good and evil exist, she does not always understand the "divine" madness that cleverly plays with her two polarities.

She has several ray 2's, which makes her sweet and loving; she forgives easily but never forgets. Her *shakti* is real, but lacks power.

Monad and Soul

Her ray 2 Soul makes her magnetic and easily influenced, because she still does not possess sufficient power to master a ray 2 focused mainly on the "love" aspect and not enough on the "wisdom" aspect, which is lacking in her. Her "love" aspect incited her to commit errors that she is sorry for. The power of her Monad should accomplish more serious work; however, fear coming from her Soul - the fear of losing this "love" aspect she is experiencing - is temporarily slowing down the changes she is seeking.

Personality

Her Personality of ray 2, sub-ray 3 emphasizes this "love" aspect more. She appreciates giving and being loved and wishes to be the "saviour" of this world that suffers from a flagrant lack of love. She could sometimes seem hard, because when ray 2 becomes too crystallized towards the "love" aspect, it hardens and loses the perspective of this aspect.

Sub-ray 3 confers to her a sense of humour that lightens the way she sees life and the people that populate the world. It makes her appreciate her existence while disguising the lack of freedom that distresses her so much. She would like the life of a couple filled with serenity, but her condition prevents it. The sub-ray 3 in the Personality helps her endure this life experience that she sometimes considers difficult.

Mental Body

Her mental body of ray 6, sub-ray 4 makes her a woman who knows what she desires, although she remains tormented within, because, occasionally, sub-ray 4 makes her unstable. As she has three such rays in her ray configuration, she sometimes lives difficult moments. Luckily, her initiation level helps her to keep the "4's" balanced and to get the maximum positive effect. Her ray 4's also give her this fluid and fragile aspect that characterizes her so well. Her ray 6 makes her stubborn, devotional and sometimes incites her to judge.

Her sub-ray 4 in the mental body allows her to be intuitive and a woman equipped with an artistic sense that expresses itself even in thought forms. This sub-ray provides her with antennas that she uses to feel the aura of her devotees and to come to their rescue.

Astral Body

Her Astral of ray 4, sub-ray 2 has made her discreetly tormented, perturbed, and sometimes allotted to her anorexic tendencies that she masters fairly well. Ray 4 invests her with the art of beauty, beauty she seeks in everything and which is difficult to acquire, particularly in the emotional aspect of life. Her ray 7 in the physical body reinforces this trait because she desires perfection without ever achieving it.

Sub-ray 2 provides a sensitivity that allows her to feel people's moods. She suffers from chronic fatigue because she gives too much and excessively absorbs other people's suffering.

Physical Body

Her physical body of ray 7, sub-ray 4 endows her with a remarkable beauty she will keep all her life. Ray 7 awarded her perfection in her traits, emphasized by sub-ray 4. Ray 7 gives her a certain nervous resistance that allows her to manage fairly efficiently the ray 4's she possesses in her ray configuration. Ray 7 feeds her a taste for tidiness to the point that she becomes a nit-picker when this tidiness is not respected.

Sub-ray 4 confers to her a physical aura that leaves no one indifferent. She seduces through this aura that supports her in the accomplishment of her work. However, this sub-ray 4 sometimes creates mental dismay that she nevertheless hides fairly well.

This is a very strong woman who suffers tremendously from solitude in spite of the strong bond that unites her to her Soul. She is achieving good work and offers the Souls who follow her the possibility to hope for a better life in this world, which sometimes seems without hope.

August 8, 2008

HAIG, JUSTIN MOREWARD

Given Name: (unknown)
Nationality: English (according to various sources)
Place and Date of Birth: (unknown)
Profession: Master of Wisdom

MASTER DJWHAL KHUL'S COMMENTARY

A high-standing initiate, Justin Moreward Haig knew, through his different incarnations, how to incarnate the divine in earthly form. He has always been one of my friends as we belong to the same Soul group. We know each other fairly well and the mutual respect we have for one another is infinite.

Presently living in Paris, he works within the western community that he tries, somehow, to educate in the spiritual and occult aspects of life. He succeeds fairly well in spite of the numerous obstacles he finds on his path. It is not an easy task to take charge of the spiritual destiny of students and disciples. He pays dearly for the gift of his vitality; it is for this reason that he has to retire and replenish his energy regularly. Immortal as we all are, he made the commitment to remain in the same body during several centuries, just like myself, in order to pursue his work in the company of particular students that he follows from life to life. This continuity allows him to better understand them and make them progress more justly, because the most crystallized require an occult follow-up demonstrating that their lives are only steps in a succession of lives. In parallel, he pursues worldly work that does not grant him any temporary rest, but demands a continuity that he must honour again for a few years before reincarnating into a female body.

Initiation Level: 7.2

We will say no more.

Ray Structure

Monad: 2	Soul: 3	Personality: 7-3
Mental: 5-6	Astral: 2-4	Physical: 3-6

It should be noted that a Master of this level plays with all rays, which allows him to produce the desired effect at the desired moment. However, in daily life, with his friends and his relations who are unaware of his occult work, he uses these rays to link him to the physical world.

Monad and Soul

His Monad confers on him an unconditional love towards everything and encouraged him to take the *Bodhisattva* vow. It inspires him with a gentleness he often uses to transmit his energy.

His ray 3 Soul allows him to live long in the same physical body that he modifies as needed. He prefers the neat and "well dressed" aspect of ray 7 in the physical appearance because he likes perfection in the form that he uses adequately. He always seems dressed up to the nines, which often amuses his Master who does not pay much attention to his physical appearance, although he is "perfect" in his expression.

Personality

His ray 7, sub-ray 3 Personality confers on him a notion of "fair-play" that he likes without being attached to it. He can easily play the heavy if the script calls for it. He almost always has a refined look and his hair is combed to perfection. He is concerned about details, such as the quality of his clothes, without becoming a slave to this habit. He appreciates warm and silky textures, and occasionally smokes. He calls these details small flaws necessary to his Personality.

Sub-ray 3 gratifies him with a flexibility that grants him the ability to "disguise" himself, making him able to disappear almost instantly in a crowd. This sub-ray affords him a lot of flexibility, particularly in his relations with people. He is an astute manipulator of energies.

Mental Body

His ray 5, sub-ray 6 mental body instills in him an understanding of certain occult topics that he can properly explain to the most skeptic among us. He has an answer for everything and has fun by often adding a touch of humour (arising from his ray 3's). He is an occult scientist and this ray 5 is necessary to him to face the Cartesian mind of Westerners.

His sub-ray 6 feeds his intuition and provides him with sufficient devotion for his hosts and his friends to "feel" his devotion. This sub-ray makes him very intuitive and often grants him the right answer even before the question is asked. This sub-ray grants him a certain compassion for those who suffer a lot from the influence of ray 6 in their lives.

Astral Body

His ray 2, sub-ray 4 astral body confers on him charm and sweetness while allowing him to remain flexible and adaptable to the feelings of those around him. Ray 2 sometimes makes him sad, particularly in terms of the suffering of those he loves the most. He remains sensitive, although confident in himself, never doubting who he is and what he must do.

His sub-ray 4, which demonstrates a remarkable stability, allows him to accomplish a lot in a short time. Versatile while being stable, he is creative and adores art. He appreciates nice things and the objects expressing this beauty that are sometimes more occult than physical.

Physical Body

His ray 3, sub-ray 6 physical equips him with a strong body that adapts easily to all of life's conditions. He is endowed with a sharp intelligence that matches very well with his ray 5 mental body.

His sub-ray 6 provides him with the ability to adapt to the suffering of those that are still under the influence of ray 6. Do not forget that the effects of this ray have accompanied him for several generations, a ray that has experienced its high point at the end of the XIXth century (1800), particularly during the period of the two wars that followed.

May 15, 2008

 # HANKS, TOM

Given Name: Thomas Jeffrey Hanks
Nationality: American
Place and Date of Birth: Concord, California (United-States), July 9, 1956
Profession: Actor, producer and director

MASTER DJWHAL KHUL'S COMMENTARY

Tom Hanks is very intelligent but less evolved than it may seem. He has to work a lot before reaching his second initiation; the first step would be to get out of the acting profession. He is very focused on the mental plane (because of his initiation level), but he is also very intuitive due to his rays.

Initiation Level: 1.7

Ray Structure

Monad: 3	Soul: 2	Personality: 4-3
Mental: 7-5	Astral: 6-2	Physical: 3-6

Monad and Soul

His Monad has very little influence on his life, contrary to his Soul that is starting to have an interesting influence. It infuses a sensitivity that characterizes him, and grants him a particular intuition that helps him in the way he acts and directs his actors. As he ages, his Soul will make him appreciate more the perspective of being "behind the camera" instead of in front, thus reducing his presence on the screen.

Personality

His ray 4, sub-ray 3 Personality makes him a born artist. Ray 4 gives him the modulation necessary to his profession. It confers on him this ability to play parts that allow his performance as an actor to seem credible.

One believes his story even if it seems unlikely. This ray also inspires this spirit that makes him fear almost nothing. He likes to take risks (calculated ones due to his sub-ray 3) and he likes to live life's ups and downs. He enjoys life and wishes that his good luck will last long.

Sub-ray 3 invigorates ray 4, giving it more support. The "intelligence" aspect of this sub-ray allows Tom Hanks to be a formidable businessman, which would have undoubtedly not been the case if sub-ray 3 did not support ray 4, always on a tight rope. This sub-ray allows him to be more efficient and more flexible in his profession and less contradicted by the sometimes difficult aspects of the ray 4 influence.

Mental Body

His mental body, governed by ray 7, sub-ray 5, produces an interesting amalgam. These two rays add to his scientific aspect and reduce the effect of ray 4 on his Personality, thus producing a strong and balanced individual when he is mentally polarized. This combination may also make him appear rigid because ray 7 appreciates things well done and ray 5 adores precision in the scientific aspect. Luckily, ray 7 through its "magical" aspect reduces much of the rigid aspect of sub-ray 5, which often demands proofs before acting.

Ray 7 equips him with a clear mind that knows what it wants and when it wants it. It advocates perfection in everything and suffers when it cannot attain it. This ray's influence complements his ray 4 Personality well because it allows him to be an intelligent actor with excellent discipline. Often ritualistic, ray 7 allows Tom Hanks to remain grounded, even when he is very successful. He knows the wheel may turn against him if he makes bad choices and the combined influence of rays 7 and 5 provides him with priceless support when he must make decisions.

Because of sub-ray 5, he is an intelligent man who cannot easily be swindled. He sometimes reveals himself to be naïve because of the growing influence of his ray 2 Soul that has a tendency to trust too fast. Sub-ray 5 restores order, rapidly.

Astral Body

His ray configuration on the Astral level makes him a sensitive and warm man. Ray 6 creates in him a paternal feeling of a person who loves to see everybody well and happy. It pushes him to work a lot. He feels responsible for all the people who orbit around him and for all who depend on him financially. Totally devoted to his family, he wants to be a faithful man, who doesn't count the time spent in their company. For him, love is more important than money, although sometimes he is awkward in the expression of his feelings.

Sub-ray 2 increases his sensitivity. Consequently, he may feel a potential malaise hovering over his intimate or business relations. He does not appreciate conflicts and disagreements and always tries to solve what does not seem to work, even at the expense of his own feelings. He can "forget himself" if necessary to help the progress of a cause or a project.

Physical Body

Equipped with a physical of ray 3, sub-ray 6, he must be careful about his image. Ray 3 can modulate itself according to the psychic or emotional needs of the person it influences. Therefore, a person with such a ray as a main ray, can be very thin at a certain period of his life and then put on a lot of weight later and vice-versa. Since sub-ray 6 characterizes him in the physical, he will have to be very careful about his weight. This sub-ray has the annoying tendency to cause excess weight that could sometimes be disconcerting. He will therefore have to continuously watch this aspect because this sub-ray will push him to indulge in overeating and putting on weight.

This man has a lot of potential and a promising future ahead of him. However, he has to remain vigilant because he may be at risk of contracting an illness if he does not remain centered and balanced, which could actually shorten his life tremendously.

August 15, 2009

 # HILLS, CHRISTOPHER

Given Name: Christopher Hills
Nationality: British
Place and Date of Birth: Grimsby, Lincolnshire (England), April 9, 1926
Place and Date of Death: Boulder Creek, California (United States), January 31, 1997
Profession: Businessman, professor, philosopher, and scientist

MASTER DJWHAL KHUL'S COMMENTARY

A very interesting man due to his intelligence, Christopher Hills could have accomplished more if an aspect in him related to his mental body had not deluded him. Certain utopian ideas never left him: he would have liked to change humanity, to find equitable solutions, which he did not succeed in doing. However, we may say that his life was a success; only his illusions failed, and it had to happen in order to prepare him for his next life. He will then incarnate as a visionary, more balanced, giving him an increased capacity to act. Let us study him.

Initiation Level: 3.2

He reached his third initiation in this life, but the mirages of this initiation were very active. He wanted to save the world although it was not yet the proper time. This mirage was part of his personal ambition, which he considered altruistic. Everything is very subtle at this level: this type of Initiate thinks he is helping humanity, although he is pursuing the mirage of a saviour and unconsciously seeks recognition. He hopes to leave his mark, a trace of goodness that humanity may choose to follow as an example. His intentions want to be good but he remains self-centered with his unconscious need to "make a difference".

He was a good-hearted man, whose vision was slightly modulated by the mirages that resulted in the fact that he was not listened to or heard the way he wished to be.

Ray Structure

Monad: 2	Soul: 2	Personality: 7-3
Mental: 7-5	Astral: 6-2	Physical: 3-6

Monad and Soul

His Monad was starting to have a light influence, although it was mainly his Soul that really started to influence his life and his behaviour. Ray 2, in its desire to serve, sometimes creates a mirage of wanting to save people in spite of the fact that it is not yet the proper time. If the Soul does not have a stable vehicle, and this was his case, it may tilt in such a way as to influence the individual so that he engages on a path inappropriate for his evolution. The individual then becomes an instrument for the Soul that does not notice the devastating effect of the other rays on his behaviour.

For example, Christopher Hills had a ray 7 in his Personality, which made him just and equitable, although without real vision. Ray 7 in the Personality will experience difficulty in adapting to others and in recognizing their real needs; he would wish them the best without really perceiving their true priorities. Therefore, an individual whose ray 2 Soul wishes to serve beyond what is needed, and who does not possess the balanced vision of a Personality more empathetic to others in their real life experiences, cannot help without falling into the trap of messing up an important aspect of the project related to their real needs. Ray 7 makes him think he knows what is good for another person and more. While his initiation level is important and his Soul is ruled by ray 2, which wishes to soothe other people's misery and strongly motivates him to act, the individual directs himself towards ray 7. It would have been better for Christopher Hills to have had a ray 2 astral body instead of a ray 6, which emphasized this mirage.

Personality

His ray 7, sub-ray 3 Personality granted him fairly accurate vision, although biased. He perceived problems but was unable to find an ideal way to solve them for everyone. In a way, he was ahead of his time. If humanity had been more awake and ready to live through considerable changes within its habits and environment, as will be the case in the ray 7 era, which has not yet reached its total amplitude, processes such as those he proposed would be more effective. However, as humanity is still vibrating within the ray 6 era, these changes proved to be too precocious. His ray 7 gave him a certain rigidity that, in his actions, did not support him in his task.

His sub-ray 3 helped him several times, granting him moments of flexibility that saved him in certain situations which would have made him lose a lot (in terms of his projects). This sub-ray expanded in part his narrow vision, particularly in relation to the environment.

Mental Body

His ray 7, sub-ray 5 mental body kindled an interest in understanding man in a more occult universe. He attempted to scrutinize within him the most intimate aspects of his inner universe, which he partially succeeded in doing. His vision, however, was really disoriented by the hidden desire to understand and to explain the process of human evolution too much, thus leaving no room for divine intuition to imbue itself in him. He acted with an excess of reasoning while the divine man is not "reasonable", hence he cannot be "resolved" like a mathematical enigma.

Sub-ray 5 increased this difficulty by creating a desire to want to explain everything "logically", which gave him a certain notoriety within the scientific community. However, this desire also adversely affected the accomplishment of his inner work, because he was too troubled by rational thoughts.

Astral Body

His ray 6, sub-ray 2 astral body conferred more strength in his research, because he liked to devote himself, body and soul, to his cause. We may also say that he displayed a rather wanton conduct, although he had a sense of faithfulness that was typically his own. He conceived faithfulness in spirit, but not physically. For him, life was love in all its aspects. Ray 7 being very present in his life, his sex life was strongly permeated with it.

His sub-ray 2 sometimes gave him the impression of understanding others but his mental body would rapidly take over and dictate to him not to lose too much time in this regard. He could be charming and warm, for a short while, because for him everything was an experiment, everything!

Physical Body

His ray 3, sub-ray 6 physical body granted him a powerful brain, tough and efficient. He could think and act fast. He did not like to waste his time and worked nonstop. He had the gift of motivating others and giving them self-confidence.

Sub-ray 6 conferred more strength on him, making him practically indefatigable. This sub-ray gave him certain dependencies that he finally got rid of with time.

This man will be a remarkable being in his next incarnation if he accepts guidance that will allow him to see beyond his illusions. He likes to navigate alone, as is the case of these Initiates on the path towards their fourth Initiation. They believe they are the Masters of their lives, in their life, while they are not yet Masters of their ego.

October 16, 2008

 HOWARD, RON

Given Name: Ronald William Howard
Also known as: Ronny Howard
Nationality: American
Place and Date of Birth: Duncan, Oklahoma (United States), March 1, 1954
Profession: Actor, director and producer

MASTER DJWHAL KHUL'S COMMENTARY

A very talented man, Ron Howard is endowed with the necessary qualities that allow him to become an excellent disciple because he likes to serve humanity, thanks to what he knows best: films. He appreciates creating a dream and making it a "possibility". He educates the world population in a certain way and opens new horizons.

He is a very intuitive man, but also very intelligent, demanding and adaptable. He has a great understanding of human phenomena and human feelings. He does not like to make films only for success or money. He reveals himself to be an altruist, but in an intelligent fashion. His weakness, women! Although he is a family man, he is very sensitive to the fair sex. He therefore has to remain constantly on his guard because female beauty fascinates him.

Initiation Level: 2.8

If he works relentlessly, he will reach the third initiation in this life, which will make him a real disciple of the Hierarchy. However, because he has no active and real Masters in this life, we have our doubts that he will succeed in passing through this difficult phase.

Ray Structure

Monad: 2	Soul: 2	Personality: 4-3
Mental: 3-7	Astral: 6-4	Physical: 3-6

Monad and Soul

His Monad is starting to have a slight influence on him, although it is mainly his Soul ray that guides him in the present incarnation. Ray 2 simplifies the contact with others and makes him very intuitive and sensitive, which allows him to efficiently direct actors.

Personality

His ray 4 "artist" Personality prevailing, he enjoys creating and rendering the imaginary real, since this ray makes him productive and imaginary. He can easily adapt himself when the influence of ray 4 is well balanced. He knows how to fight for his beliefs and does not fear to take some risks. He adores beauty, harmony and attempts to transmit them in his films. Moody at times, he quickly takes hold of himself because he loves his work and its diversity.

Sub-ray 3 balances ray 4. It allows him to increase his adaptability in order to respect the moods and demands of the actors with whom he works. Equally intelligent and an astute manipulator, this sub-ray brings incredible support when conflicts and misunderstandings arise on sound stages. He knows what to say and when to say it. This sub-ray also helps him to act fast and make rapid decisions when necessary.

Mental Body

His ray 3, sub-ray 7 mental body makes him intelligent and a perfectionist. His ray 3 allows him to think fast and provides him with a broad vision of the overview of the projects in which he participates. It confers to him the wish to experiment and to try new avenues. He likes to face challenges and this ray helps him to bring them to term.

Sub-ray 7 dictates to him a way of working that is almost ritualistic. It allows him to establish demands and find incredible solutions to problems that may at first appear to be without solution. It helps him to obtain a "quasi" perfection in his art and to appreciate the good and beautiful things. It also offers him the possibility of grasping details that may escape the vision of ray 3 and encourages him to "see" the realization of a project even before it is finished or even conceived.

Astral Body

His ray 6, sub-ray 4 astral body reveals itself to be his strength, but also his weakness. Ray 6 makes him devoted and indefatigable; when he believes in a project, he works at it relentlessly, giving lavishly of his time and energy. This ray makes him appreciate his family, which he cares for and values greatly. Without his family he would not prove to be so efficient; it is an anchor point, the cornerstone that supports him in all fields of his life.

Sub-ray 4 may sometimes create a handicap; very sensitive to beauty, it could haunt him. We are referring here to the beauty of a project as well as the beauty of a woman. He is therefore constantly walking on a tight rope that requires that vigilance always be practiced. The influence of this sub-ray may also cause him periods of high activity or deep depression; vigilance is also mandatory here.

Physical Body

His physical body is strong, thanks to ray 3, which confers energy and a relative absence of fatigue to him. This ray allows him to think fast and well; he can accomplish more than one thing simultaneously and gives the impression that he has eyes everywhere. He moves and acts very rapidly. He does not appreciate inactivity and adores movement.

Sub-ray 6 provides a certain physical stability and, to a certain measure, an anchor that prevents him from committing too many abuses; a well-balanced ray 6 ensures perfect conduct and an ability to listen to his body, which is essential to its proper functioning, However, when his focus is directed more towards the influence of ray 4 in its configuration, he must remain alert because many abuses may appear. Ray 4 likes to experiment with certain substances, thus causing the forgetting of inner struggles sometimes experienced by those governed by this ray.

Mr. Howard is enjoying good years ahead of him. However, he must remain aware and careful, and not let himself be weakened by the unpleasant vagaries of life. Greatly sensitive, he must remain alert, otherwise he may shorten his life by developing a serious illness that will make him leave his physical body prematurely.

August 25, 2008

# Hubbard, L. Ron

Given Name: Lafayette Ronald Hubbard
Nationality: American
Place and Date of Birth: Tilden, Nebraska (United States), March 13, 1911
Place and Date of Death: Creston, California (United States), January 24, 1986
Profession: Author of science fiction books and Dianetics, and founder of Scientology

Master Djwhal Khul's Commentary

A man of a great intelligence, Ron Hubbard is the possible reincarnation of Leonardo da Vinci. Why do I say "possible"? Because with this affirmation, I am going to raise a lot of questions, a lot of queries, which will not necessarily favour my comments.

Similarly to da Vinci, this man of genius accomplished a lot in this lifetime as Ron Hubbard. Do not forget that the Soul likes to understand, to experiment, likes to live on earth, fully in its nature.

As Ron Hubbard, this Soul lived marginally like da Vinci, namely far from all eyes at the end of his life. He suspected all the evil he created through his religious system and he had difficulty bearing such a weight in the last years of his life. He enjoyed power even though he was taken hostage by this power. Haunted by mirages, he had difficulty getting rid of them, like da Vinci.

At the time of da Vinci, he had a ray 4 Soul that then polarized towards ray 2 after his death. After the third initiation, Souls whose rays are spread out between 4 and 7, the Rays of Attribute, must polarize towards one of the three Rays of Aspect (rays 1, 2 and 3). It was not easy for this Soul to change Ashram and to become a ray 2 Soul after having been with the Ashram of Ray 4 for so long, more artistic and warrior-like. This resulted in lives that were interesting but sometimes perturbed because this Soul had trouble finding its path, even under the guidance of Koot Hoomi, who had to ask Serapis Bey[1] to come to his aid.

Therefore, this Soul came back, in this present incarnation, as Ron Hubbard, with all the pride of da Vinci and his taste for art and for the divine. He loved humanity and the fame granted to him by his immense talent in the field of writing. Around the end of his life, he became more of a dictator and was haunted by certain abuses committed in the present life and in past lives. Da Vinci was no saint, but quick-tempered, temperamental and unstable in his thoughts. In other words, he was disturbing to "ordinary people". Hubbard tried to correct this fact by becoming more magnetic, warmer, although he did not become a saint, which he would have truly wished.

Initiation Level: 3.7

Ron Hubbard was unable to reach his fourth initiation. Too attached to life on earth, he was unable to detach himself from this world and make the ultimate sacrifice of his Personality on the sacred altar of initiation. He knew he was wrong in the last years of his life, because the Masters tried several times to put him on the right track, through dreams. He will have to try again in his next incarnation, which will not take place soon because he has first to understand and assimilate certain things.

Ray Structure

Monad: 2   Soul: 2-4   Personality: 4-3
Mental: 5-2   Astral: 6-4   Physical: 3-6

Monad and Soul

His Monad had a certain influence and attempted to guide his Soul through life's multiple journeys. His ray 2, sub-ray 4 Soul – such an

---

1 Serapis Bey is the *Cohan* of the Ray 4 Ashram.

influence cannot be totally erased at the Soul level; do not forget that this is where certain soulmates separate; it's time to give up the Ray of Attribute to choose a Ray of Aspect – made him fragile under the influence of certain energies, because he was caught between two worlds: that of love-wisdom and that of art, as well as harmony through conflict. He did not necessarily feel good but his initiation level allowed him to keep a fairly interesting balance.

Personality

His ray 4, sub-ray 3 Personality made him a creative man with multiple facets and functions. He did not appreciate routine and organized himself to have none in his life.

Ray 4 conferred to him his talent as a writer as well as the taste for adventure. He rested rarely because idleness embarrassed him. We cannot say he was a faithful person, except to some of his ideas. He often did not feel well without understanding the reason, which drove him to write in order to express what he felt.

His sub-ray 3 offered him the possibility to accomplish many things simultaneously. He was tireless in many ways. He could have lived several lives at the same time, and that is actually what he did in part, because he liked to explore and experiment relentlessly. He was a great manipulator, in private as well as in public.

Mental Body

His ray 5, sub-ray 2 mental body allocated to him this mix of the concrete and the abstract. ray 5 gave him an attraction to science and made him very intelligent. It also gave him a taste for learning and understanding. A lively and curious spirit, he liked to impress through his mental body. It is true that he was fascinated by the mind and that ray 5 helped him better understand it, without healing him (he remained perturbed at this level). His mental body practically never gave him a rest, which in the long run made him live periods of intense paranoia. At the end of his life, he confused reality with fiction.

His sub-ray 2 offered him privileged access to the subtle worlds. He could feel the universe around him, feel the energies and coalesce with them. His sub-ray 2, however, did not help him conquer his inner fears and torments. It was mainly the contrary, which produced in him excessive, uncontrolled fears.

Astral Body

His ray 6, sub-ray 4 astral body made him a devoted being, charming and warm although sometimes authoritarian and critical. This provoked in him an excess of enormous kindness followed by excesses of anger and punishments that then made him very unhappy. He was a kind man, having difficulty accepting his rays (which he did not understand); he showed reluctance to really love himself and, thus to love others (although his level of initiation was high).

His sub-ray 4 perturbed him even more, but facilitated his creativity. We wish him less of ray 4 in his next incarnation where he should attempt to balance the abuses provoked by his own teaching, abuse he did not really wish at the beginning.

Physical Body

His ray 3, sub-ray 6 physical body granted him an efficient physical body as well as a brain adapted to his needs. Ray 3 gave him intelligence, an ease with words and a verbal magnetism he used very well.

Sub-ray 6 conferred warmth to him, which made him even more magnetic. However, he did not appreciate the excess weight that this caused him at the end of his life, because, for him, his image was very important.

We hope he will come back equipped with a more balanced aspect in his next life and that he will be more at ease in his ray 2 Soul. He will then be able to accomplish much more while remaining loving and loyal to his Soul.

January 31, 2009

 # HUINENG

Given Name: (Unknown)
Also called: Dajian Huineng or Eno in Japanese
Nationality: Chinese
Place and Date of Birth: Canton (China), 638
Date of Death: China, 713
Profession: Founder of Chan Subitism, known as "Southern Chan" of Mahayana Buddhism

MASTER DJWHAL KHUL'S COMMENTARY

Huineng was a great patriarch, who knew how to demonstrate Buddha's real nature and did not want to be either a bigot or limited to concepts based on man's mental, which is often too limited. He proved to be a perfect mirror without being the mirror. He refused to identify himself with anything, except to the void, to vacuity that, for him, contained everything and reflected everything.

He experienced a lot of suffering to which he was not attached, because for him it was only illusion, illusion that will be resolved in passing years and future incarnations. He knew suffering by having lived it in all its aspects, while being aware that he had also caused a lot of suffering in his past incarnations.

His simplicity demonstrated a great mastery of the environment and a deep knowledge of Buddha's nature, though without having reached it, which he knew. This conferred to him more humility and made him concrete in his approaches. He never believed that he was superior to others, knowing that we are all equal in the eyes of the Creator. He defined himself as the servant of servants and worked to reach this divine potential, which he knew was within him but had not yet emerged. Recognizing that everyone has this same potential, he took the vows of the *Bodhisattva* in order to help all people of this Earth to reach perfection under the loving eyes of the Creator.

Initiation Level: 2.8

Many believed that he had reached his fourth initiation, which was not the case. Do not forget that the average initiation level of the time varied between 0.5 and 0.7. Those who aspired to become disciples came near 0.8; there was therefore a large initiation gap between them and Huineng. He lived in a lot of solitude but never failed to perform his task.

Huineng is presently incarnated in Japan where he is trying to introduce a new philosophy based on an opening of the heart. He is preparing this people for the new world religion to be able to penetrate this earth one day, because without this preparation it will be very difficult.

Ray Structure

Monad: 2	Soul: 2	Personality: 3-7
Mental: 7-5	Astral: 6-2	Physical: 3-7

No ray 4 was part of his configuration, which would have adversely affected his task. His speaking skills came from his ray 3's supported by his ray 7's, which refined his comments.

Monad and Soul

His Monad had no real influence, contrary to his Soul. He knew, thanks to silence and emptiness, how to seek refuge in it and listen to what it whispered in his ear. It guided him during the majority of his life.

Personality

His ray 3, sub-ray 7 Personality allowed him to hide, mainly to hide his real nature, which sometimes frightened others. He appeared strange in this world that largely focused on physical survival, while he thought of many other things. The influence of ray 3 endowed him with certain speaking skills that he used with discernment.

He never talked too much or in an inappropriate way, sub-ray 7 helping him to find the right timing. ray 3 conferred to him a subtle intelligence that lightened his inner being because it dazzled him with a thousand aspects of the same topic and some appeared very funny. He had a good sense of humour that he occasionally showed.

His sub-ray 7 supported his ray 3, giving him a clearer vision of what he had to do. This sub-ray conferred to him a goal, the goal to reach perfection in this life or in another. He had all the time he needed and preferred to act correctly instead of rapidly.

Mental Body

His ray 7, sub-ray 5 mental body gave him fair and balanced thought. He lived a lot in his head and knew how to rapidly distinguish truth from falsity. He reflected much, which he appreciated (this came from his sub-ray 5 that influenced his ray 7 in search of perfection).

His sub-ray 5 endowed him with a strong intellect that allowed him to understand humanity well. The "everything is possible" of ray 7 found itself sometimes in contradiction with the effect of sub-ray 5 that created doubt in him. Luckily he often took refuge in meditation in order to calm down this sub-ray and to favour the vision of ray 7 in him.

Astral Body

His ray 6, sub-ray 2 Astral made him human, which allowed him to understand humanity. With a reserved appearance due to his sub-ray 7 Personality, he was warm and enjoyed life. However, he demonstrated a fairly remarkable mastery of the world of desires except perhaps a craving for sugar that he bravely tried to control. Devoted to his Soul and his superiors, when he had some, he was equally dedicated to his disciples that he loved a great deal.

His sub-ray 2 invested him with great sensitivity. He was able to feel things easily and to use his intuition in order to re-establish energy if this was considered necessary. This sub-ray made him give up public life because his work was, most of the time, very discreet. He did not like fame, which he thought would have pulled him away from his task and his goal.

Physical Body

His ray 3, sub-ray 7 physical body equipped him with a certain resistance that was above all useful for long daily meditations. The influence of ray 3 gifted him with a powerful brain, particularly for solving certain mysteries or koans. It gave him analytical and philosophical thought.

Sub-ray 7 increased his strength and resistance. It inspired in him the need to reach perfection in this world. He liked beauty. As ray 7, that supported ray 3, was not at the forefront, he did not become its slave.

No one knows if his task was totally completed when he left his physical body. He felt his Soul's call and withdrew almost immediately without leaving behind him a worthy successor. This was probably his only real fault, which he later corrected by becoming one of the pioneers of his school of thought during his following incarnation.

February 23, 2010

 JACKSON, MICHAEL

Given Name: Michael Joseph Jackson
Nationality: American
Place and Date of Birth: Gary, Indiana (United States), August 29, 1958
Place and Date of Death: Los Angeles, California (United States), June 25, 2009
Profession: Singer, dancer, composer, producer and actor

MASTER DJWHAL KHUL'S COMMENTARY

Michael Jackson's Soul was a young Soul who will go through its cycle as a mature Soul in the next incarnation. This Soul has experienced fame and fortune in the present incarnation but has also felt a deep solitude and a lack of love that pushed him to various abuses. These abuses incited the Personality related to this Soul to self-destruct. However, certain lessons were learned, essential lessons that will not be forgotten.

During his next incarnation, his life will be less lavish, while undoubtedly happier, because his priorities will change. Returning in a Caucasian body, he will live more peacefully, while keeping his immense talent. He will discover love and will start a real family, so that his heart knows a more authentic love.

This life demonstrated to him that money does not buy anything that can really make him happy. He did not know how to love and accept himself and always wished to live a fairy tale that would transform him into a white prince charming, loved by all. He was unable to really see who he was and the colour of his skin always labeled him. He will be born again as a black man in a future incarnation that will not be the next one; he will then learn to feel better in his skin, a test that he failed in his life as Michael Jackson.

Initiation Level: 1.2

His immense talent resulted from his ray configuration, but also from his ray 4 Soul, which he was unable to master. This ray destined him for fame while making him live an inner hell, from which he is partially liberated. However, he will have to wait for a while because his self-destruction resembled a suicide.

Ray Structure

Monad: 2	Soul: 4	Personality: 4-7
Mental: 3-5	Astral: 6-2	Physical: 3-7

Monad and Soul

His Monad had no influence on him. His Soul, however, provided a certain influence, particularly in the field of music.

Personality

His ray 4, sub-ray 7 Personality subjected him to a dilemma. Ray 4 invited him to live creativity in its perfection and beauty, but also brought *downs* and a lack of acceptance of what he believed to be imperfect. This ray made him magnetic and beautiful in everything he created, while emphasizing his discomfort as a Black American.

Beyond question, sub-ray 7 helped him reach perfection in music, but not in life. This sub-ray created torments emphasized by ray 4 and his Personality lived an inner hell. If a sub-ray other than ray 7 had been part of his configuration, Michael Jackson would have been unable to personify what he was. He would not have experienced fame, which unfortunately made his life painful at times. He wanted to be loved, but he was adulated instead, which prevented him from living a normal life.

Mental Body

His ray 3, sub-ray 5 mental body conferred to him intelligence and efficiency in business. His thoughts wanted to be brilliant, but his too-great sensitivity led him to several deceptions. This ray 3, aided by sub-ray 5, could translate his music onto paper. However, this ray acted in such a way that he was unable to be peaceful in his thoughts: he continuously ruminated. This is the reason he was taking drugs, in order to calm the inner turmoil.

His sub-ray 5 provided him with spectacular intelligence that was ill-omened. It allowed his megalomania to take shape: his logic shaped what he was seeing in his thoughts. Unfortunately, these ideas, although inspired, led him to a destructive state, since they were unable to elicit happiness in him.

Astral Body

His ray 6, sub-ray 2 Astral caused him tremendous suffering: Ray 6 demanded love and affection and sub-ray 2 created insurmountable fears. Michael Jackson could at times prove to be possessive; totally dedicated to music and his family, he suffered tremendously. His family ideal was never realized; he wept a lot and always felt unhappy.

His sub-ray 2 produced in him a sensitivity that allowed him to write magnificent music, but acted in such a way that he was easily hurt. In a way, he felt a malaise in this life where he was simply trying to live; constantly feeling an inner uneasiness, he tried to please everyone. This sub-ray awakened irrational fears in him, including those of illness and old age.

Physical Body

His ray 3, sub-ray 7 physical endowed him with beauty, even if he did not like himself. This configuration provided him with the dancing style so particular to him. Ray 3 inspired the movement and sub-ray 7, the perfection and grace.

Ray 3 conferred to him the capacity to accomplish a lot in a short time. His brain, ruled by the influence of this ray, equipped him with the ability to create several pieces of music simultaneously. It endowed him with speed and ease of movement.

Sub-ray 7 granted him a sense of perfection at the physical level. It made him demanding; he was constantly working until exhausted, which created tension and mood swings he was unable to control.

We hope that his next life will offer more composure and that he will learn to give and really receive love. His life ended on a resounding note of material disillusion that would never have made him happy.

July 3, 2009

 JOHN PAUL II

Given Name: Karol Józef Wojtyła
Nationality: Polish
Place and Date of Birth: Wadowice (Poland), May 18, 1920
Place and Date of Death: Vatican (Italy), April 2, 2005
Profession: Pope

MASTER DJWHAL KHUL'S COMMENTARY

A remarkable man, thanks to his simplicity and his desire to help others, John Paul II was provided with an open enough consciousness that he had to stifle, because of the constraints imposed by the Vatican. He could have done more but he had to remain cautious because the Church, having some slightly unorthodox methods, could have resorted to various schemes not always considered "Catholic"!!! John Paul II was Master of his life, but not in his life.

Modest and devout, he was imbued with great faith in his Soul, in which he believed more than anything else. He would commit his destiny daily into the hands of the divinity he called "God". He respected the other religions without completely endorsing their philosophy. He believed in a just God as well as in the existence of other lives. However, he remained discreet on this last topic, knowing that he never should talk about it in order not to offend the Church, not yet ready to publicly recognize this fact. He would have liked to accomplish great things but he felt his hands were tied. He was strongly criticized, because he was greatly misunderstood. He would have changed certain fundamentalist and outdated ideas of the Catholic Church, had it been possible.

Initiation Level: 3.2

He will certainly reach his fourth initiation in his next incarnation. He suffered a lot from the lack of understanding from his peers but his love for them and for humanity has steeped his pontifical coat with patience. Parkinson's disease developed because he felt a prisoner to imposed constraints.

Ray Structure

Monad: 2	Soul: 2	Personality: 2-3
Mental: 7-5	Astral: 6-4	Physical: 3-7

Monad and Soul

His Monad had an influence on him in the beginning, although it was mainly his Soul that held a strong link with him. He meditated every day in order to contact it in a more conscious way. It inspired him with a love of all and a sense of justice. It also allowed him to keep his cool and to act with more precision in certain situations, particularly when the ray 3's of his Personality and physical were more agitated.

Personality

His Personality, influenced by the energy of ray 2, sub-ray 3, motivated him to cultivate love with intelligence. Ray 2 conferred on him a sweetness and attentive listening that was never disputed. It inspired him with caution that sometimes changed into fear. He knew his task was not easy and he tried to do his best. This ray offered him the possibility to understand others, even when they were silent. He possessed a certain intuition that he used with intelligence (thanks to his ray 3, but also to his ray 7 in his mental body).

Sub-ray 3 ensured a certain fluidity in his speech and a sense of diplomacy that ended up being important for his reign. He could speak with intelligence while demonstrating caution in order not to hurt others unnecessarily, particularly certain heads of states. Gifted with a fairly broad view, thanks to this sub-ray 3, he could accomplish many projects simultaneously.

Mental Body

His ray 7, sub-ray 5 mental body made him intelligent, tidy, far-sighted and efficient. Ray 7 allowed him to carve out a respectable place for himself within the scientific and political community, because he was considered very intelligent. This ray also transmitted to him a sense of honesty, that sometimes disturbed his entourage, but gave rise to the admiration of all those who came into contact with him.

Sub-ray 5 allowed him to acquire a good base in the field of communications, because he liked to be cultured and learn many things. In a way, he never stopped studying in order to understand life's mystery. He would never have someone pull the wool over his eyes with overly mystical events. He would survey someone before granting them his full trust.

Astral Body

His Astral, coloured by ray 6, sub-ray 4, made him a devoted, sincere and indefatigable man. Warm, he could also become firm during certain discussions that required a more balanced adjustment. He loved Christ and believed in this man he knew was still alive as he had secretly met him a few times. He respected Jesus because Jesus in Christ represented for him the perfect man.

Sub-ray 4 offered him the possibility to appreciate the arts but also to understand artists, who are generally little appreciated within the Church. He recognized their contribution to culture and to human evolution. This sub-ray granted him a lot of flexibility; it also taught him to remain constantly open and not to judge others.

Physical Body

His physical body, influenced by ray 3, sub-ray 7, gave him a strong body, resistant and well-adjusted to the task. He ruled for over 26 years, which was not an easy task... Ray 3 refined his intelligence and allowed him to retire into himself when the tension became too strong. It also gave him a sense of humour that saved him from the boredom that reigns within the Vatican, because people take themselves too seriously.

Sub-ray 7 granted him strength and an ethical sense that served him within his task. He had a just and good vision most of the time. He appreciated good and beautiful things without being enslaved by them.

This man will still accomplish a lot of good in his next incarnation. He may choose a more peaceful life in order to rest from this one, particularly if he is canonized one day; the healing requests from his devotees will then take up a lot of his energy. However, we believe he will accept a similar task that will prepare him to cross the gate of the fourth initiation, which necessitates total self-negation!

September 21, 2008

 # JUNG, CARL GUSTAV

Given Name: Carl Gustav Jung
Nationality: Swiss
Place and Date of Birth: Kesswil (Switzerland), July 26, 1875
Place and Date of Death: Küsnacht (Switzerland), June 6, 1961
Profession: Doctor, psychiatrist and writer

MASTER DJWHAL KHUL'S COMMENTARY

A human being of great talent, Carl Gustav Jung enjoyed playing with the psychological aspect of man in order to better understand himself. With a very complex nature, he liked to analyze while trying to be as objective as possible, which is fundamentally impossible for any individual working on the human psyche, because research work is always influenced by the memories haunting the past, of the present life as well as past lives.

A psychologist or a psychiatrist works with a still life, coming from the past, which in reality adversely affects spiritual progression. It is good for man to understand, to realize his potential, referring sometimes to his experience, but this work should not become his life's essential purpose, that on which all else rests. Psychoanalysis helps man to manage his emotions, but it has no direct link with the thought form.

The psychoanalyst utilizes the thought form, believing it is capable of everything, while the thought form constitutes only a temporary reserve of ideas, emerging from everywhere, and does not possess any potential for transformation. It is strictly wrong to believe the contrary, because believing it simply proves our desire of not risking change.

Any psychoanalysis, following a session or two, goes in circles and brings nothing valuable to the person who lives it. We should think about it and grow thus: "Any aspect of a being that is explored in such a superficial way will never reach its peak within its destiny, and what rules this fact is the fundamental fear to really change". Psychoanalysis can sometimes allow one to understand, but it does not possess the energy to transform.

Carl Jung was a man who led a very interesting life and was strongly shaken by the inner nature of man. He suspected man was hiding within himself a part that went beyond appearances, a part that even his colleague Freud tried to explain. He considered Freud to be too limited, which actually put an end to their friendship, because Freud was very narrow-minded and impossible to change, which goes against the occult law of transformation and against what Jung thought. For Jung, everything was, in a sense, movement and progression, although he never really discovered the law of transformation, which made him suffer terribly.

He was seeking a way to reach man's Soul but he continuously came up against man's Personality. He communicated with his own Soul but was unable to identify the Soul of others. The path of psychoanalysis prevented him from finding his real path, which related more to the fields of the spiritual and the occult. He would have liked to prove the existence of the Soul through psychoanalysis, which he unfortunately failed to do. He lived this failure as an inner mourning that he carried with him all his life.

Initiation Level: 3.2

He acted, however, like a level 2.8 Initiate. Extremely brilliant, he did not succeed in taming his ego, which was too powerful. He did a lot of good, although he did not really accomplish his destiny, which was supposed to reach a much higher initiation level by demystifying psychology. He should have worked more on the occult aspect of man, which he did not realize.

Ray Structure

Monad: 2	Soul: 3	Personality: 4-7
Mental: 5-3	Astral: 6-2	Physical: 7-3

Monad and Soul

He possessed an analytical brain, which prevented him from correctly seeing certain aspects of man that fascinated him. He should have trusted his Soul more, it inspired him more than he believed; incidentally, it saved him from many dangers. A faithful friend, it guided him several times without him ever becoming conscious of this help.

His Monad exerted little influence on him, contrary to his Soul, which was under the influence of ray 3, partially explaining his slow progress at the level of his vertical evolution. However, from the viewpoint of the horizontal evolution, which consists of exploring and acquiring experience, we can say that he succeeded in this expression at the expense of the other.

Personality

His ray 4, sub-ray 7 Personality incited him to explore the human unconsciousness. Man's psyche represented a mystery he wanted to understand and resolve. Ray 4 made him live ups and downs that he sometimes had trouble managing. However, we can say that this ray instilled in him the fire of discovery in every sense of the word. It also allowed him to play certain roles efficiently, which served him in his work. This ray also granted him the possibility to go deeper into himself to prove the unfathomable (according to his vision). It also conferred a lot of courage to him, mainly during the hardships he experienced.

Sub-ray 7 granted him refinement, which followed him in all his discoveries. He also had a sense of honour and quite a fair, critical eye. He targeted perfection that he never obtained, which made him suffer terribly. This sub-ray granted him psychic resistance that helped him in his various tasks.

Mental Body

His ray 5, sub-ray 3 mental body supported him from the viewpoint of his Personality, but not of his evolution. Being too focused on the scientific aspect of things, the Soul could not touch him except through his Personality or his emotional body. However, as he tried to mentally scrutinize emotions, the Soul experienced enormous difficulty transmitting to him what it desired to teach him via its expression.

His sub-ray 3 offered him the possibility of playing with thought forms, to manipulate them, to scrutinize them, which he extrapolated from emotions. This played certain tricks on him because often emotions and thoughts have their own "soul" or personality impregnated by the energies of human souls with which they worked and by which they have been influenced.

Astral Body

His ray 6, sub-ray 2 astral body gratified him with faith and a conviction that man is far more than he thought he was. However, he felt a certain fear of committing himself to women, a commitment that implied his submission to the feminine energy he did not understand and in which he had no trust. He liked women a lot but feared the "woman" in each one, which actually partially harmed his research. He was unable to detach his thoughts from the negative emotions linked to his past experiences with women. This prevented him from evolving in this way and mainly prevented women from growing within themselves as a result of the discoveries he "should" have made.

Let us not forget that real commitment has nothing to do with marriage, which remains a superficial commitment for someone who does not experience "real commitment" that requires communion with the other, mutual respect, that Carl Jung seemed to have had but did not really demonstrate towards the women who shared his life. His wife suffered tremendously from it, as did his children.

Sub-ray 2 provided him with a sensitivity he knew how to use occasionally; through this ray he could feel emotional power and understand certain aspects of the human being. This sub-ray gave him the illusion he could help save humanity from certain hidden and negative aspects that characterize us as evolved beings on this planet. He nurtured the illusion that the human being, through understanding, could break the chains that make him suffer, while suffering (still) remains an evolutionary priority on this planet.

Physical Body

His ray 7 sub-ray 3 physical body conferred to him an intelligent brain, powerful, seeking perfection in the world of illusions of this planet. Ray 7 granted him a certain vision he attempted to follow, unsuccessfully, a vision rendered narrow by his desires to deeply understand physical and temporal paths, not to say scientific. Ray 7 endowed him with an attractive body, which he profited from with the female gender, while fleeing serious commitments.

Sub-ray 3 mainly qualified his physical brain and gave him a constant desire to explore various avenues. He liked experimentation and took pleasure in observing his entourage, thus confirming his superiority. He always felt that he was more intelligent, more evolved than the masses, but mainly more than his colleagues, whom he often considered pretentious and too limited in their vision

That a wine, particularly a non-alcoholic one, is now available under his name makes me smile. This proves Jung's very essence, that is without essence or, if you prefer, without real substance toward the real Soul he was unable to really discover.

April 10, 2009

 # KHAN, GENGHIS

Given Name: Temüdjin
Nationality: Mongol
Place and Date of Birth: Province of Hentiy (Mongolia), circa 1155 (uncertain)
Place and Date of Death: District of Qingshui (Mongolia), 1227
Profession: First emperor and ruler of the Mongol Empire

MASTER DJWHAL KHUL'S COMMENTARY

A young Soul thirsting for power, Genghis Khan invaded the East to become "The Great One", the one who would exercise control over this part of the world that he believed to be the entire world. It was better to be on his side than opposed to his vision. All had to submit to his ideas and never object to his words. Stubborn and faithful to certain traditions, he exhibited strong intuition, which he exploited to unify Mongolia under his rule. Did he love his people? No one can say for sure.

He used brute force and sullied many lands with his presence. A violent man, he believed he was invested with a mission; incidentally, he is considered a hero in certain regions of his native land. He could have become a great dictator, since for him human life was of little importance, because all that counted was the goal to be attained.

He maintained certain contacts that guided him in his endeavours; some proved pure in intention, others not. He was highly intelligent and cunning. Did he really know love? We greatly doubt this to be the case, as only his power and his domination mattered for him. Keep in mind that he was a young Soul who did everything within his power to succeed.

He concluded several alliances that helped him pursue his destiny. In some matters, the Masters, by virtue of his Soul ray, supported him to allow a unifying force to emerge in this country, where havoc reigned through wars, fratricides and conflict. They did not however, approve of the methods he employed, as for him it was better to destroy an enemy than convert him.

He partially settled his debt, by reincarnating numerous times in countries where conflicts reigned that needed to be resolved. You will no doubt be surprised to learn that he was Lord Cromwell, who stood against monarchy in England, lost his life doing so and was misjudged, which was all part of his karma.

Initiation Level: 1.5

His initiation level of 1.5 proved quite high for the period. He had engaged in a certain mental focus, which made him even harder and more imperative in his thoughts and deeds.

Ray Structure

Monad: 3   Soul: 2   Personality: 1-6
Mental: 3-3   Astral: 6-2   Physical: 3-6

Monad and Soul

His Monad had no influence on him, and although his Soul had opened the way, he ignored it most of the time. His Personality rays as well as his Astral rays took precedence.

Personality

His ray 1, sub-ray 6 Personality endowed him with a certain harshness, as well as a certain efficiency that ensured he would attain his goals. He wanted to conquer Mongolia, which he accomplished without a single hitch. He never forgave, displaying a pride beyond compare and proved to be bloodthirsty in his need to conquer and exert his power.

All submitted to him. His peremptory ray 1 cut down everything in its path, refusing to admit the existence of distinct possibilities that might contradict his beliefs.

Sub-ray 6 increased his harshness and demanded unconditional loyalty to his beliefs. He is responsible for the killing of many people because of this poorly polarized sub-ray. Let us not forget that this ray was also present in his astral body and as a sub-ray in his physical body, which rendered him cruel and merciless. He only lived for his cause and had no real friends, only people who were loyal to him and feared him. His children, his concubines and his wife also feared him, although his wife did exert a certain influence on him due to the alliance formed by their marriage. He kept his word when he made a promise, except if he realized that he was deceiving himself through this commitment, which infuriated him and gave him a thirst for vengeance.

Mental Body

His ray 3, sub-ray 3 mental body allowed him to act effectively and with mastery in certain key situations. Very intelligent, he was not easily fooled, but he duped others to get his hands on what he wanted. A great manipulator, his ray 3's conferred to him a certain intuition and a capacity to adapt from a mental viewpoint, equipping him to become a fine strategist. His oratory gift both terrified and commanded respect. He could not remain idle and demanded the same of others, with no tolerance for either lethargy or laziness. He slept little, his mind remaining constantly on the lookout; he thought constantly and often efficiently.

Astral Body

His ray 6, sub-ray 2 Astral destined him to become a leader loyal to his cause, but not to his entourage. A possessive man, his intelligence easily overruled his feelings, which often made him ill at ease. He was a hard and demanding father. He never repudiated his wife because he needed her. He loved her in his own way and knew that it was better for her to be with him than without him. She symbolized an important alliance and he wanted to maintain this symbolic bond. Nonetheless, she loved him and supported him while trying to protect her children.

His sub-ray 2 was of little use, except to display certain signs of weakness that, according to him, were undesirable. He was truly confused when faced with feelings he considered useless and disruptive to his destiny.

Physical Body

His ray 3, sub-ray 6 physical equipped him with great stamina, giving him the capacity to face the challenges of the austere Mongolian climate and the numerous battles he waged. His body healed quickly from any wounds he endured. His ray 3 brain also heightened the effects of the ray 3's in his mental body. He was thus endowed with a remarkable intelligence, although quite challenging.

His sub-ray 6 in the physical accentuated his other ray 6's, making him tougher during battles and stirring an appetite for his enemy's blood. Let's keep in mind that one could quickly become an enemy in his eyes.

July 7, 2008

KHAN, HAZRAT INAYAT

Given Name: Pir-o-Murshid Hazrat Inayat Khan
Nationality: Indian
Place and Date of Birth: Baroda (India), July 5, 1882
Place and Date of Death: Delhi (India), February 5, 1927
Profession: Musician and Master of Wisdom

MASTER DJWHAL KHUL'S COMMENTARY

A simple yet remarkable man, Hazrat Inayat Khan was able to transmit to humanity a real, heartfelt wisdom. He believed in Man's potential to become divine, within the sacred confines of the human body purified from its negative aspects. His celestial writing manifested an occult light embodied in the words he wrote.

Thoughtful and highly intelligent, he loved Truth and strove to make it a reality in the hearts of men seeking Awakening. Considered marginal as a Sufi, he was sometimes judged harshly by his peers. Guided by his Soul, he was able to persevere along his unique path, thereby allowing Sufism to open up to new horizons.

Non-sectarian, he believed in Man's universality and respected individual beliefs. He loved art and music, which made him skilled at listening to others. He often used music to transmit a form of energy that is impossible to communicate otherwise. By so doing he affected certain occult systems of the human body, which then resonated at a higher frequency.

Initiation Level: 4.2

Ray Structure

Monad: 2	Soul: 2	Personality: 6-4
Mental: 3-7	Astral: 6-2	Physical: 4-3

Monad and Soul

Both his Monad and Soul had a fairly considerable influence. He preached out of love and desired well-being for all. His vision of his destiny proved quite clear and he pursued it unflaggingly. The power of love always propelled him forward. Only music granted him some respite. He remained optimistic despite the difficulties he faced in his life.

Personality

His ray 6, sub-ray 4 Personality shaped him into a good, kind, helpful and somewhat stubborn man. He was devoted to his Soul and his destiny, which he knew did not belong to him. He manifested strength and devotion to his family. A man alone among men, he knew how to take comfort in his music. Few people really understood his approach. However, he was respected because the energy that flowed from his person had a harmonious effect on his entourage. The bliss that emanated from him constantly touched people.

His sub-ray 4 granted him the capacity to comprehend individuals as well as their personal problems. It also heightened his taste for music and the capacity to be a good musician. He knew how to adapt to situations and people. This sub-ray made him sensitive to the vibrations he received; a very intuitive person, he could see beyond appearances.

Mental Body

His ray 3, sub-ray 7 mental body gave him the ability to converse with anyone who wanted to meet him. He knew how to please while maintaining a respectful distance; he never imposed himself on others and always respected their personal convictions. He knew how to understand them and speak their language; he had the qualities of a talented diplomat. His ray 3 accorded him the possibility of adapting his teachings by making them accessible and, above all, comprehensible.

His sub-ray 7 blessed him with intellectual grace, which made him shine among men. His ray 7, well-channelled on the mental plane, offered him the possibility of building mental configurations that could influence the near future. He was gifted with vision, as previously mentioned, and this sub-ray was partly responsible for this fact. This sub-ray could not be positioned on the first line of his ray configuration, as he would appear too marginal and misunderstood by all.

Astral Body

His ray 6, sub-ray 2 Astral heightened his sensitivity. Loyal to his Soul and the path he wanted to pursue, he was a good father, although he did not live long enough to see his children grow up and see what they would become. He proved to be an affectionate spouse though not sentimental; he was attached with detachment. He knew how to love without impinging on the other's space. However, he became protective when he sensed his family was distressed or in danger.

Gifted with great sensitivity, he displayed understanding towards others thanks to his sub-ray. He loved to love but with the reserve of a 4th level Initiate who loves with intelligence and discernment.

Physical Body

His ray 4, sub-ray 3 physical, which proves to be very rare, motivated him to harness the subtle energies originating from the higher planes. Ray 4 lavished him with "vision" and an extraordinary intuition. He "saw" the invisible as well as the effect generated by his music and his words. He knew how to look without blinking at the moment of his death. He sometimes had *downs*, but who would not, with such a ray on the first line. He was surrounded by discernible grace, giving the impression that he floated rather than walked. His particularly penetrating gaze derived from the influence of this ray.

His sub-ray 3 gave him flexibility and physical strength to allow him to manage major doses of stress and energy. He did not sleep well, as he received a great deal of energy. He did not know how to reduce this impact in order to find some rest. This sub-ray equipped him with a good foundation in physical terms.

He was a remarkable man among men. Presently, he is incarnated in Asia in the body of a Muslim. Although he is still very young, we hope that as he grows, his influence will create the required effect for Muslim religions to exercise moderation.

August 2, 2008

 # KORNFIELD, JACK

Given Name: Jack Kornfield
Nationality: American
Place and Date of Birth: United States, 1945
Profession: Buddhist monk, instructor and author

MASTER DJWHAL KHUL'S COMMENTARY

Mr. Kornfield is a very interesting man. His spiritual interests really go beyond Buddhism. He likes to promote his teachings to the people capable of seeing beyond the traditional aspect of Buddhism that he finds sometimes too rigid. However, he knows that change requires diplomacy and patience; he therefore works slowly and surely.

Expert in meditation, he has access to several interesting energetic platforms. We can say that he can interact with certain Masters located in the higher realms of the astral plane. He has not yet reached the Buddhic plane but this will happen.

His teaching is very beneficial for young initiates on the Path who wish to advance cautiously. He mainly reaches Initiates that waver between 1.5 and 2, because the beginning of mental polarization is necessary to grasp the scope of his words.

He is a simple man, who likes simplicity. Sometimes disappointed with human behaviour, he knows he is not himself perfect, which adds perspective to his life. We can say that he is a dreamer hoping that humanity will grow in wisdom and consciousness in the fastest possible way.

Initiation Level: 2.8

Ray Structure

Monad: 2	Soul: 2	Personality: 3-6
Mental: 7-5	Astral: 6-2	Physical: 7-3

Monad and Soul

His Monad has very little influence; however, it is leaning more and more towards him during his deeper meditations. It detaches him from the present incarnation; he will therefore have to demonstrate vigilance, or he will leave his physical body prematurely. His Soul is near him and increasingly guides him. He knows it overshadows him, which confers to him a very soft and magnetic aura. However, a certain discomfort arises in him because he feels torn between life here on Earth and the life he feels beating within his Soul. He has accomplished a lot and will still accomplish more if he does not feel too attracted by life beyond his physical form.

Personality

He enjoys a very beautiful Personality. His ray 3 acts in such a way that he does not reveal himself easily. He does not appreciate when people try to nose around his private life, preferring solitude for the privacy it provides him. Ray 3 allows him to express himself well, with a certain facility. Although he prefers to write because of the intimacy it provides, he appreciates being in relations with people interested in their spiritual progression.

Sub-ray 6 makes him a warm and fairly humble person. He likes to dedicate himself to a cause and prefers discretion to fame. This sub-ray grants him a certain magnetism, which, combined with ray 3, makes him very charming and engaging, although he is more or less aware of it.

Mental Body

His ray 7, sub-ray 5 mental body makes him intelligent and methodical. Ray 7 inspires him with a certain intuition and an interesting sense of equity. His thought confers to him a way of writing that is very appropriate to western Buddhism: ritualistic and supervised, very simple (which is an illusion because his writing contains a very occult aspect that only one who "can read" may totally decipher). This ray also provides him with a way of thinking that reassures his entourage. He seems to be down to earth, while conversing with the gods.

Sub-ray 5 injects a certain assurance into his words, because he often talks of a subject he has experienced or understood. Ray 7 offers him the capacity to understand and decipher the incomprehensible, and sub-ray 5, the possibility of explaining the incomprehensible, which is a happy union in his case.

Astral Body

Here is a very sensitive man because the combination of his ray 6, sub-ray 2 Astral allows him to feel and understand others. Ray 6 grants him the sense of family, of the group and of dedication toward the task he has to accomplish. It gives him a warm and honest aspect from which he cannot break away.

Sub-ray 2 endows him with a hair-trigger sensitivity. In a way, he wants to be very vulnerable, but his Soul takes care of him and of his destiny. This sub-ray allows him to be accessible to those who suffer and be available for them. However, he must display caution because sometimes he gives too much, therefore draining his energy and his health.

Physical Body

His ray 7, sub-ray 3 physical make him a man with a pleasant appearance; he is not handsome, but an energy emanates from him that seduces whoever comes close to him. Ray 7 allows him to be efficient and tidy in his work. He reflects well and possesses a sense of order (inner) that allows him to carry on a lot of work in a short while. Extremely available, he is equipped with great physical resistance, although he is often tired.

His sub-ray 3 adequately supports his ray 7, which in its desire for perfection, often forgets the essential: communication. This sub-ray maintains this communication, which would often be cast aside by ray 7. It grants him a certain flexibility that helps him in his relations with others.

Mr. Kornfield accomplishes excellent work. He can still live long or cut short his presence on earth, if he so wishes. Why? Because his Monad is displaying impatience and wishes to establish a stronger contact, which will take place during his next incarnation. If he turns towards his Monad and remains under its influence too long, he will quit this world for another and will come back rapidly to continue his work on this planet.

March 6, 2010

 # KŪKAI

Given Name: Saeki Mao
Posthumous Name: Kobo Daishi
Nationality: Japanese
Place and Date of Birth: Byobuga-ura (Japan), July 31, 774
Place and Date of Death: Mount Kōya (Japan), March 21, 835
Profession: Poet, artist, calligrapher and founder of Shingon

MASTER DJWHAL KHUL'S COMMENTARY

A very intelligent and very educated man, Kūkai was able to demonstrate the occult wisdom of what is "real" and "authentic" within the teaching of Japanese Buddhism. He was criticized by some and adulated by others.

He loved his people deeply, but mainly the divinity he saw in everything. He traveled to many places to perfect his education and has always known that the most difficult place to explore would be man's inner being, which he tried to understand and illuminate.

His biggest wish, though, was his own realisation. However, he always gave precedence to other people's needs before his own because he believed his illumination could not take place if he was too self-centered. He wanted to help and understand others above all else.

Initiation Level: 3.4

This initiation level was very advanced for these times, and he revealed himself to be almost like a Buddha. We may say he has since become one. He worked hard and still works hard. He uses his essence as Kūkai, who lives on another plane, which we will qualify as Buddhic (and that has evolved with him) in order to transmit his strength and his transformational energy. However, this emanation, although powerful, cannot lead a disciple to full realisation without physical contact with a Master. This is the reason he is presently incarnated and lives near a monastery, allowing him to easily access the Kūkai essence.

Ray Structure

Monad: 2   Soul: 2   Personality: 4-3
Mental: 7-5   Astral: 6-2   Physical: 3-6

Monad and Soul

His Soul had a certain influence on him. It dictated to him teachings and guidance that he followed almost to the letter. He loved others and was filled with this love that never left him.

Personality

His ray 4, sub-ray 3 Personality was perfectly appropriate for him because it endowed him with a flexibility that helped him all his life. His ray 4 gave him a hard time during his young age. Thirsting to know himself, he worked on himself to master his darkest aspects. This ray encouraged writing and the arts. It made him sensitive to others and to their inner feelings. However, thanks to this ray 4, he could become firm and adjust certain undesirable behaviours in his disciples. This ray produced the discipline and the concentration necessary for his work.

His sub-ray 3 provided him with a subtle intelligence, sometimes too direct (ray 7, sub-ray 5 mental body). He was gifted with a sense of humour derived from this sub-ray 3 that, combined with ray 4, could tremendously relax certain rigid atmospheres.

Mental Body

His ray 7, sub-ray 5 mental body allowed him to adequately define his teachings based on his experience; order and clarity prevailed. He knew how to properly direct the energy so his disciples could understand. Mentally indefatigable, he could meditate for hours, tirelessly.

His sub-ray 5 served his teachings well; he could dissect it to its slightest detail while making it clear and precise. This sub-ray also served him well when he maintained certain important contacts that demanded a concrete, clear-cut and precise intelligence.

Astral Body

His ray 6, sub-ray 2 astral body made him a dedicated and sincere man. He liked to devote himself to his Essence and act in a way that served it well. He appreciated justice and rectitude, which made him a good Master who knew how to adequately guide his disciples.

His sub-ray 2 rendered him sensitive to others and transmitted to him an increased sensitivity in order to better manage his monastery and his teachings. He was gifted with a sixth sense, derived from sub-ray 2 in conjunction with ray 4 in his Personality.

Physical Body

His ray 3, sub-ray 6 physical provided him with a resistant and easy-to-handle body. He could move easily without tiring too much. Ray 3 also gave him speaking skills that served him all his life, even in silence...

His sub-ray 6 offered him additional strength and foolproof determination. He could increase the faith of his disciples and energetically heighten their etheric bodies, thanks to the warmth of the combination of his ray 6's. Warm and loving, he was able, even through discipline, to confer a lightness that favoured a better contact with the Soul.

He was a remarkable man and is even more so today. He deserves our attention and our gratitude. He still accomplishes gargantuan work in the shadows and works more or less consciously with Maitreya's energy.

October 4, 2008

LÉVESQUE, RENÉ

Given Name: René Lévesque
Nationality: Canadian
Place and Date of Birth: Cambellton, New Brunswick (Canada),
August 24, 1922
Place and Date of Death: Verdun, Québec (Canada), November 1, 1987
Profession: Journalist and politician

MASTER DJWHAL KHUL'S COMMENTARY

René Lévesque, was undoubtedly misunderstood, misjudged, and
mainly overvalued by his peers who accorded him with more wisdom
and power than he could possibly take full responsibility for. He was
kind hearted, but his vision was mitigated in the face of the future of
what he called his country. He desired a certain fame and succeeded in
obtaining it by creating his own political party.

He knew how to charm through his speech, because he was gifted with
a lot of magnetism. Not very disciplined, he however took some pleasure
in directing those who worked for him with an iron fist. A diplomat
under certain circumstances, he had a sharp tongue and liked to provoke
his audience. His vision of separatism was the result of his two ray 6's
in the major line, which coloured his vision of Quebec politics. Failing
to obtain what he wished within the Liberal Party, he preferred to
create his own party, thus becoming Quebec premier. He could have
provoked Quebec's separation if he had been gifted with more potential
and power.

However, this project would have adversely affected the Masters' work,
who do not wish the attainment of such a thing for the time being.
Quebec separation would cause a minimum of twenty years of darkness
within the Quebec community; the explosion of fratricide would also be

possible because for the majority of Quebecers the influence of ray 6 is strongly predominant. There would be fights, anger, grudges and chaos, which is distinctly not desirable. Quebec, because of its situation in Canada, holds a mandate of peace within the international community. This country within a country sets a certain example of the appearance and demands of peace. If this link is broken, there will be a split within the country and heavy karma for Quebecers will follow.

Initiation Level: 1.2

He was not yet mentally polarized, which made him very emotional. This handicap caused him a lot of problems in his work. He saw through the mirror of his emotions, which diminished his vision and his sense of equity. He was good-hearted but had an emotional body that was too sensitive and easily manipulated which, because of his ray configuration, did not prevent him from demonstrating his great intelligence.

Ray Structure

Monad: 2	Soul: 6	Personality: 6-2
Mental: 3-7	Astral: 4-2	Physical: 3-7

Monad and Soul

His Monad had no influence. However, his ray 6 Soul started to have a more considerable influence. It inspired him to do group work, for the benefit of all, although his ray 6, sub-ray 2 Personality made him unstable because of the strong influence of his ray 4, sub-ray 2 Astral that interfered with his vision. He had great ideals coming from his two ray 6's and had difficulty accepting failure and rejection. He was also, to a certain extent, resentful because he never forgot either good or bad things.

Personality

His ray 6, sub-ray 2 Personality conferred to him a sense of honour, a pride that was related to the desire to succeed and to be recognized.

Occasionally, he could demonstrate harshness when his ray 6 Personality felt powerless or betrayed. He did not forgive easily, liked things to be done his way and detested those who would not listen to him. He would display anger and impatience when his ray 6 suffered from not obtaining what he wanted. However, he would remain dedicated and loyal to his cause. He liked to fight to defend his ideas and his ideals. This ray 6 gave him a big heart that he used to manifest his affection and his satisfaction towards those he loved and those who served him well. He knew how to forget himself for the cause but rarely for others.

His sub-ray 2 endowed him with a sensitivity that allowed him, when he was willing, to properly listen to others. He could talk in such a way as to put anyone at ease and possessed a certain wisdom that was expressed in his words. Soft-hearted at times, his ray 6 would take over and force him to stand up in spite of the fear that racked him. Born for a modest life, he was never able to escape this programming.

Mental Body

His ray 3, sub-ray 7 mental body conferred to him a certain intelligence, elaborate and structured. He could easily explain the most difficult concepts in a detailed fashion without losing the attention of his audience. A good manipulator (particularly with women), his speech sometimes fascinated, knowing how to flatter, encourage and lie if needed.

His sub-ray 7 provided him with a sense of order in his thoughts, which balanced ray 3, always busy doing several things at the same time. He loved beauty and structure.

Astral Body

His ray 4, sub-ray 2 Astral made him sometimes unstable. He had difficulty remaining constantly balanced. His ups and downs were frequent, conferring to him, in the long run, a "long face". He also had a tendency to complain and act as a martyr (the mix of his rays 6 and 4). All women were attractive in his eyes; therefore, he was unable to be loyal in love. He enjoyed dominating them with his knowledge, would easily tire of them and while, remaining a gentleman, would still be a womanizer.

Because of his sub-ray 2, he loved children, although he never really knew how to demonstrate it. He did not appreciate feelings and his addiction to alcohol helped him forget them. Most of the time he was a good host and liked to have guests. Some irrational fears that he hid well tormented him.

Physical Body

His ray 3, sub-ray 7 physical provided him with an interesting physical resistance that allowed him to manage his daily stress more efficiently. His Ray 3 brain provided him with the necessary intelligence to accomplish his work and his destiny, and sub-ray 7 equipped him with a certain distinction and an acute critical sense.

August 8, 2009

 LINCOLN, ABRAHAM

Given Name: Abraham Lincoln
Nationality: American
Place and Date of Birth: Kentucky (United States), February 12, 1809
Place and Date of Death: Washington, D.C. (United States), April 15, 1865
Profession: Lawyer and statesman

MASTER DJWHAL KHUL'S COMMENTARY

A strange man, Abraham Lincoln comes from the planet Mercury. Endowed with a very active mind, he was ill at ease with his emotions. He wished justice for all, but proved awkward in the expression of human behavior; he did not always know how to express himself adequately. He was a quietly passionate and feared nothing, except himself.

Initiation Level: 2.3

His 2.3 initiation level, very evolved for the time, conferred to him the necessary sensitivity to be a good president.

Ray Structure

Monad: 1	Soul: 3	Personality: 7-3
Mental : 1-5	Astral : 6-4	Physical: 1-7

Monad and Soul

His Monad had no significant influence; however, his Soul started to really guide him. It allowed him a certain flexibility as well as a larger vision. This influence rendered him sometimes confused or discouraged when faced with the work to be performed. He was ill at ease with the slavery system because he had lived it in another evolutionary system. He desired the cessation of this infamous situation, while knowing it was extremely delicate because it could cause the division of his country that he loved beyond anything else.

Personality

His ray 7, sub-ray 3 Personality conferred to him a certain refinement that was essential; otherwise he would have remained a small penniless farmer. Ray 7's influence revived in him the desire for perfection in everything, particularly in his actions. It also inspired him with certain slowness, sometimes not well understood by his entourage. Wishing to do and to act well, he took the necessary time for his actions to be the fairest possible. He appreciated beauty while avoiding to literally fall under its influence.

Sub-ray 3 prepared him to understand a situation fairly quickly and to perceive all its facets. However, he would not let himself be influenced by too rapid a thought, which he knew could suggest to him erroneous choices. This influence allowed him to be alert and cautious in his choices because ray 3, through its brightness, can recognize right from wrong. This sub-ray also offered him the possibility of being a diplomat and of avoiding certain situations that could disturb his work.

Mental Body

His learning difficulties came from his ray 1, sub-ray 5; instead of granting him more mental speed, provided more delays.

Ray 1's influence inspired him with the desire to attain his goal the fastest way possible without necessarily understanding the magnitude of the situation and whatever it implied. This vision of things conflicted with sub-ray 5 that demands understanding before action, something that ray 1 did not always allow. He lived a constant inner duality between the desire to learn "by heart" and the desire to understand. Without the tenacity of ray 1, he would have given up.

Sub-ray 5 allowed him to obtain the respect of his peers when he was able to adequately explain his vision of things. However, his interest was not in the intellectual aspect of things, he would often lose patience and opted for more rapid action without offering any explanation. Aware that sub-ray 5 was slowing him down in his work, he would brilliantly fight to remain on course in his determination without faltering under the weight of the desire to understand or explain everything

Astral Body

His astral body, influenced by ray 6, sub-ray 4, offered him a feeling of love that was essential for the accomplishment of his task. Ray 6 made him loyal to his country and his family. He gave his life and his energy to preserve, as much as possible, a unity within these two sectors of his life that he judged essential to his existence. He was dedicated and knew how to forget himself for others. He was endowed with an enormous compassion, which many abused.

He lived many inner conflicts because of his sub-ray 4. He liked freedom while knowing it was inaccessible in his present life. This sub-ray granted him the strength to defend his ideas to the end. He was afraid of nothing, except of failing in his mandate, which was to allow his people to live in harmony and equality. While being aware that this mission was utopian, he never lost hope, although he was conscious that he risked his life in doing so.

Physical Body

His physical body, influenced by ray 1, sub-ray 7, created a man with a strange body, revealing simultaneously the strength of ray 1 and the daintiness of ray 7. His ray 1's unrefined traits would appear delicate, a paradox that expressed his inner state well. Inflexible because of ray 1, he knew how to manage, thanks to his sub-ray 7. His ray 1 brain reinforced his mental body and provided him with more vision. Goals had to be attained and he took the means to attain them.

His murder, in rather disturbing circumstances, was planned by fellow countrymen who did not wish him to abolish slavery. Unfortunately, slavery is not unique to earthlings. It is also experienced elsewhere, in sometimes better but also in worse conditions.

The murderer did not come from here, although he was born here, but from a brotherhood that wishes to keep slavery in action. As to the murderer of the latter, he was from the white brotherhood who knew what was being plotted. By eliminating Lincoln's assassin, the white brotherhood scored a point: it demonstrated that we do not wish to have slavery on Earth. A lot of work in this regard remains to be done, but as soon as the planet becomes sacred, slavery will disappear.

December 2, 2007

# LUCAS, GEORGE

Given Name: George Walton Lucas Jr.
Nationality: American
Place and Date of Birth: Modesto, California (United States), May 14, 1944
Profession: Film director, producer and scriptwriter

MASTER DJWHAL KHUL'S COMMENTARY

A brilliant man, George Lucas accomplishes a lot for the planet; he comes from a planetary system different from ours and his arrival on Earth is recent. Presently, he has a beneficial influence and brings a new view to the worlds that populate our world.

Initiation Level: 3.2

Ray Structure

Monad: 1	Soul: 3	Personality: 4-5
Mental: 1-3	Astral: 6-2	Physical: 3-7

Intelligent, sensitive and an introvert, he feels embarrassed by social events, as, in a way, he is ill at ease in the company of human beings (earthlings).

Monad and Soul

The influence of his Monad is starting to grow. It pushes him to accomplish the task he has to accomplish in the present incarnation, which is to create an opening towards people living on other planets. His work consists in demystifying "the strange" that can come from elsewhere, because whatever is unknown to us scares us. This fear will have to disappear in order for a union to take place with other planets and other galaxies, some of which are definitely more evolved than ours.

His ray 3 Soul qualifies him as a timeless "traveller": he makes regular inner trips. Memories of his past lives spent "elsewhere" spring up through his dreams, but also thanks to his creative and innovative imagination; he has the capacity to manifest in matter what he sees on other planes.

Personality

His ray 4, sub-ray 5 Personality make him a good receptacle for the information received through his mental and astral bodies. A part of this information comes from what takes place on the astral plane and his Soul is endowed with the capacity to harness it and transmit it to his dreaming or astral body. Ray 4 provides him with great imagination; sub-ray 5 directs him efficiently so that what he can see can be transmitted concretely on the physical plane. Ray 4, that in a way is located in his wild nature, makes him run away from social events. He lives ups and downs that he controls easily most of the time. This ray gives him the imaginary spirit that often staggers his contacts.

Sub-ray 5 provides him with the scientific aspect we can see in his films. It is expressed through his Personality and he acts in such a way that he imposes his vision of things through it. Thanks to this sub-ray, he gives the appearance of a sensible man who knows where he is heading and why. Because of the combination of ray 4 and sub-ray 5, he knows how to put himself in the public's place and seduce their imagination, but also their intelligence.

Mental Body

His ray 1, sub-ray 3 mental body have gifted him with a sophisticated intelligence, although very fluid. Ray 1 allows him to complete his project well and gives him a visionary aspect that is extremely useful. He "sees" what must happen for him to reach his goal. This ray often creates impatience because the obstacles are numerous, and ray 1 detests them. Fortunately, sub-ray 3 relaxes his mind and allows him to outplay these restrictions or transform the situation in order to iron it out.

Sub-ray 3 acts the part of a buffer for his overly bright mental aspect. It grants him flexibility, allowing him to deepen details more, so that ray 1 can reach his goal. Rays 1 and 3 do not like details, but when it is necessary, they become extremely fussy. This requires an effort that brings results. Ray 1 will see the missing detail and sub-ray 3 will act in such a way that this detail will be used efficiently to allow the project to come to fruition.

Astral Body

His ray 6, sub-ray 2 astral body makes him a warm man, even if he sometimes appears awkward in the expression of this warmth. Without this ray 6 astral body, he would not be adapted to human life; it's the only body that makes him "human", in the sense that it confers to him "human warmth". This ray compels him to stay among us, because he loves us; he loves humanity and its largesse of spirit when the Light runs through the consciousness of certain people.

Sub-ray 2 makes him sensitive and able to understand human suffering, which touches him a lot. This sub-ray, because of the pain it provokes in him, compels him to sometimes isolate himself from the world, when it demonstrates to him a less evolved aspect. As in the case of Steven Spielberg, he does not like human suffering and would appreciate "awakening" the human consciousness so that man becomes more "divine" in his expression.

Physical Body

His ray 3, sub-ray 7 physical body grants him resistance and performance, backing him up in his work. Ray 3 gives him a flexible intelligence that allows him to create the characters and objects he captures from other dimensions. It shows him the "possible" aspect of what he perceives and permits him to transmit in the physical the possible side of the impossible.

Sub-ray 7 offers him an interesting nervous system that efficiently supports the enormous energy he receives from his two ray 1's; this sometimes creates in him the effect of an electric discharge that would strike down anyone on this planet. Sub-ray 7 refines the work of ray 3 and lets him perceive "details" of his visions that transform into film productions.

This charming man has enormous potential that can help humanity grow inwardly. Not because he gives rise to wisdom through his work but because he provokes an opening of the mind that will one day allow wisdom to pave the way within man.

June 9, 2009

 # MADONNA

Given Name: Madonna Louise Veronica Ciccone
Nickname: The queen of *Pop*
Nationality: American, Italian origin
Place and Date of Birth: Bay City, Michigan (United States), August 16, 1958
Profession: Singer, writer-composer, actress and music and film producer

MASTER DJWHAL KHUL'S COMMENTARY

Madonna is an interesting person that requires a certain study at the ray level, because she possesses several ray 4's, well placed, that provoke in her cyclic changes in attitude. She could reveal herself to be almost prudish and then explode in an unbridled sexuality. She likes to provoke, but wishes mainly to be recognized and appreciated. Without this public recognition, she would feel of little value. We will make sure that in her next incarnation she evolves in a less public environment, more adapted to her evolution that will operate in a more linear fashion. In other words, with a stability that will not depend on others. Presently, her evolution lags and she is trying to get out of it. But appearing excessively in the limelight, which she adores, she cannot progress in an orthodox fashion. She wants to puzzle others, but this enigma is easily deciphered by those who can see and understand the deep meaning of evolution and rays.

Initiation Level: 1.2

Ray Structure

Monad: 2	Soul: 4	Personality: 4-3
Mental: 7-5	Astral: 6-2	Physical: 3-7

Monad and Soul

Her Monad has no influence, contrary to her Soul, which is starting to be felt: it transmits certain intuitions that Madonna easily captures via ray 4 of her Personality. She is a woman conceived for the arts and music, each of her cells vibrating at that rhythm. When she uses her mental body, ray 7 eases her sense of rhythm but accentuates her sexuality, which becomes very bold because it is influenced by the combination of rays 4 and 7. Her initiation level not being too high, she falls victim to her rays and their drives, which causes a sexual overflow in her.

Personality

Her ray 4, sub-ray 3 Personality transforms her into a stage and scene magician. She can also very easily start a fight that she will rapidly forget. She causes conflicts despite her good will and likes to see things moving. While acting in this way, she remains a bit unconscious of the effects she has provoked, except when she rationalizes and understands the game she is playing. Then she becomes a manipulation virtuoso in order to elicit a reaction.

Her ray 4 Personality makes her creative and demonstrative; she knows how to manipulate matter to obtain an echo that she will use to dazzle others. She also lives ups and downs that she disguises with a bit of alcohol and drugs. This is a woman who loves nature, healthy things, but who allows herself to go to extremes in everything when her ray 4 is in an excessive phase of experimentation of the senses. She takes care of her body because this ray needs it to express itself. As long as her body will allow it, she will evolve on stage. When it is no longer possible, she will dedicate herself to humanitarian work because her ray 6 in the astral body attracts such experiences.

Her sub-ray 3 provides her with endurance and perseverance in order to express and exploit what she desires. It grants her a certain flexibility and a sense of manipulation that she uses beyond measure in order to mystify her public, who adores her.

Mental Body

Her ray 7, sub-ray 5 mental body makes her an intelligent woman. She knows what she wants and where she wants to go; she uses all the aspects of ray 7 to magnetize, control and manifest her desires on the physical plane. She could also hoodwink those she comes across, becoming fascinating and remaining so as long as she wishes to keep the object of her desire.

A serious and efficient businesswoman, thanks to sub-ray 5, she knows how to make a profit; she will become more generous in her old age. She likes to understand and sometimes becomes too demanding, which can tire her environment.

Astral Body

Her ray 6, sub-ray 2 astral body makes her a loving and warm woman. Loyal in her own way, particularly to her family, she sometimes proves to be a mother hen that protects her children and who does not like to see them in the hot seat. She appreciates the private side that she tries to protect. Her family allows her to keep a very necessary balance: it's her shelter. She sometimes acts in a possessive and demanding fashion with her children, who sometimes find her too rough; she is a hardliner through love but does not see it. She also entertains old concepts (due to ray 6) in terms of education.

Her sub-ray 2 confers on her a sweetness necessary for her children. She can become very tender and very funny, but also worries a lot for them. She would die of heartache if she lost one of them, because they are her only solid link with life.

Physical Body

Due to her ray 3, sub-ray 7 physical body, she is also an intelligent and manipulative woman who can make an audience vibrate. An excellent dancer, her success comes in part from this art she knew how to develop; she magnetizes with the movements of her body, a fascination that vanishes when she stops moving. Ray 3 grants her endurance, resistance and flexibility. It confers to her speed, complexity and suppleness.

Sub-ray 7 provides her with a sense of refinement in her gestures, aesthetics and provocation. This sub-ray makes her magical and ray 3 surrounds her with an exceptional aura. It makes her even more vibrant, more real, and more magnificent on stage.

Madonna is not a very "relaxing" woman because it is difficult for her to really stop. She likes movement in every sense of the word, and her ether can make anyone vibrate, positively or negatively; people love her or hate her but no one is indifferent to her.

October 17, 2008

 # MAHLER, GUSTAV

Given Name: Gustav Mahler
Nationality: Austrian
Place and Date of Birth: Kalište (Austrian-Hungarian Empire), July 7, 1860
Place and Date of Death: Vienna (Austria), May 18, 1911
Profession: Musician, composer and conductor

MASTER DJWHAL KHUL'S COMMENTARY

Gustav Mahler was an excellent composer, although some people doubted this. He expressed a deep admiration for the great composers of the world, like Brahms and Bruckner. Endowed with great simplicity, Mahler had always liked to transmit music through his feelings. He was very internalized and his music demonstrates his attachment to what seems impalpable, inexpressible. It carries a message of hope sometimes coloured by sadness and melancholy.

Mahler believed in the existence of the Soul and was often disconcerted by the behaviour of humans. He knew he was imperfect and attempted to transgress this defect by composing music that transported him beyond his human form.

He felt limited by life, by the field of form, the only escape that remained was the music that made him live, hope and grow. Overly sensitive, he was never really happy.

He had contacts with C. W. Leadbetter and, of course, Helena Blavatsky that influenced his music, but above all, his concept of life and death. He could not bring himself to believe that life ceased after the last breath. As in the case of Houdini, he tried to understand what was behind the veil of death intimately linked to life.

Initiation Level: 2.2

Gustav Mahler was endowed with a great sensitivity, amplified by his initiation level. He would let emotion express itself in everything and he was unable to detach himself from it; in a way, all his life was undermined by emotions. He wanted to be perfect and suffered by not being so, which caused severe depression, from which he had trouble extricating himself.

Ray Structure

Monad: 2	Soul: 2	Personality: 2-3
Mental: 7-3	Astral: 6-4	Physical: 3-4

Monad and Soul

His Monad had very little influence on his life, contrary to his Soul that, undoubtedly, began to exercise one. This resulted in enormous fears when confronted with several challenges that he was unable to meet. Let us not forget that he had a ray 2 Personality, which emphasized his malaise.

Personality

His ray 2, sub-ray 3 Personality made him a sensitive man, very sensitive. He felt everything and had trouble to not feel hurt by life's events. The lack of recognition he experienced also undermined his existence, because his excessive sensitivity prevented him from seeing beyond his hardships. He had to learn humility, which this life partially taught him.

His sub-ray 3 gratified him with a Personality that adapted relatively well to certain physical discomforts. Even when he felt unhappy, this sub-ray allowed him to pursue his work by granting him a more global vision of his work. Sub-ray 3 allowed him to flee internally to his music and escape reality.

Mental Body

His ray 7, sub-ray 3 mental body made him intelligent and allowed him to "write" his music. Ray 7 provided him with the mental discipline necessary for his work, because the energy of this ray succeeded in breaking across the fragile (often depressing) energy of ray 2. Ray 7, through its light, allowed him to build his works, no matter what happened to him. It conferred to him good intuition that he used to write his music.

Sub-ray 3 conveyed dynamism to ray 7 so that the Personality, sometimes failing, did not prevent him from writing. This sub-ray conferred to him a certain fluidity that allowed his music to reach certain interesting high-level spheres. However, his music remained in the high astral spheres, due to his mental polarization, too influenced by the astral body.

Astral Body

Due to his ray 6, sub-ray 4 Astral, he was a tormented man. Ray 6 made him even more sensitive, even susceptible. He did not like criticism and despaired of seeing the light one day that would allow him to be recognized as a conductor and valued composer. This ray created a lot of sentimental attachments that adversely affected him.

Sub-ray 4 provided him with the possibility of transmitting a certain harmony in his music. It also gave him the capacity to hear and write music. Placed at the level of his emotional body, with a strong ray 6 in the front line, he composed well with a strong sub-ray 4, which, if placed in the front line, would have destroyed his life because its influence was too powerful. Let us not forget that ray 4 can build if it reveals itself to be strong and well polarized, and that it can destroy if it affects our weaknesses.

Physical Body

His ray 3, sub-ray 4 physical granted him a fragile body (because of sub-ray 4), but also a fair resistance to the inner conflicts he experienced. Ray 3 balanced his fragile mental health, because his brain, influenced by this ray, would recover control when it reached the edges of an inner abyss liable to destroy him. This ray allowed him to survive in this tumultuous life.

Sub-ray 4 was sometimes his ally because it knew how to permit him to listen to the notes of the high spheres. This sub-ray graced his physical body with a great beauty for the time and with a great sensitivity that pleased women. However, too focused on his own suffering and too romantic (because of his ray 6 Astral), Mahler remained faithful to his wife, even though she repeatedly deceived him with other men, because she found it difficult to live with a tormented man.

Mahler recovered his nobility and his authenticity in his next incarnation. He lived in the United States a life worthy of his expectations. He was a famous conductor named Leonard Bernstein.

October 9, 2009

 # MANDELA, NELSON

Given Name: Nelson Rolihlahla Mandela
Tribal Name: Madiba
Nationality: South African
Place and Date of Birth: Mvezo (South Africa), July 18, 1918
Profession: Lawyer and statesman

MASTER DJWHAL KHUL'S COMMENTARY

Nelson Mandela is quite a remarkable man because of his life but also due to his accomplishments. He has experienced poverty, suffering, while remaining serene and friendly towards others. He possessed and still possesses a vision of the world where everything is possible, even if horror lives with wonder.

Africa is a continent populated with young Souls wishing to grow. These Souls need guides to see the vastness of the planet and also the immensity of their being. Still sectarian because of their lack of vision, Africans will still experience a lot of suffering in the years to come. However, from this suffering wisdom will emerge that will pay tribute to those who were able to fight for it.

More "Nelson Mandelas" will be needed for this part of the planet to live happier days, because the older Souls of the black races exploit the younger Souls and repeat what the white man did in the past in certain places. Africa must now know freedom in everything, particularly with regard to "the expression of its thought" and the economic field.

Nelson Mandela did a lot to allow Africa to free itself from certain ill-omened influences. His work had a global effect, even if he worked more ardently for South Africa. Humanity needs men like him who are not concerned with their skin color or the thickness of their wallet, or the education received in order to claim justice for all. His is a noble Soul who will come back in his next incarnation to complete his work.

Initiation Level: 3.3

At this level, arrogance often gives way to humility. He knows he is mandated to help others and he does it brilliantly. While the course of his present life is coming to an end, his footprints will allow others to find and understand themselves and to pursue, in their own way, his work that will become theirs.

Ray Structure

Monad: 2	Soul: 3	Personality: 2-6
Mental: 7-3	Astral: 6-2	Physical: 3-6

Monad and Soul

His Monad exerts a little influence that is helping him during the last years of his life. It inclines him to retire in order to prepare (more or less consciously) his next incarnation that will not be long now, because Africa still needs him. According to his wishes, he will be reborn on this continent.

His Soul exercises a fair impact and helps him adequately accomplish his task. It has supported him during all his political life, even when he was in jail. It made him discover in himself the possibility of changing the world while remaining in the same place (ray 3's spider web)[1], because his imprisonment allowed humanity to turn its eyes towards Africa and to support him in his desire to liberate South Africa from Apartheid.

Personality

His ray 2, sub-ray 6 Personality allowed him to be a loving, charming and warm man, but also very stubborn and very rigid on certain points

---

[1] See page 551

he would not give up. Ray 2 gives him the feelings of love he has for everyone, feelings that strengthened during his incarceration. This ray makes him emphatic and reveals his great simplicity. He loves sincerely and wishes the best for everyone. It also colors his life with great wisdom that he transmits with utter humility.

His sub-ray 6 fed the flame of devotion toward his people. This sub-ray built a will within him that always accompanies him. He desires peace for all and works eagerly towards this goal (and this, in spite of his age, which slows down his occult work because when he was in prison he learned to work through invisible channels).

Mental Body

His ray 7, sub-ray 3 mental body allowed him to accomplish efficient (influence of ray 7) and productive work (influence of sub-ray 3). Ray 7 encouraged him to be organized in his thoughts and not to be too influenced by provoking and threatening words and ideas expressed by his opponents. When balanced, this ray knows how to remain calm in a storm, without making waves, in order not to lose sight of the destination.

Sub-ray 3 granted him dynamism and a certain quickness of reply. It adequately supported ray 7 by granting it additional leeway because this sub-ray can, if positively polarized, find solutions for almost everything. Versatile, it compensates for the rigidity reflected in the perfection of ray 7.

Astral Body

His ray 6, sub-ray 2 astral body makes him a sensitive man, particularly sensitive to suffering and injustice. Ray 6 cannot tolerate injustice and often focuses his work so that all are winners in a project. This ray made him a man passionate for his cause and helped him not to flinch in the face of adversity.

His sub-ray made him very intuitive and empathetic towards others. He sincerely loves his people and this sub-ray allows him to express his wisdom so that his people find and maintain hope.

Physical Body

His ray 3, sub-ray 6 physical equipped him with a resistant body and a performing brain. Ray 3 endowed him with a vivid and efficient intelligence. He likes to reflect on things, although he can make a decision rapidly, if necessary. This ray grants him flexibility of thought that helps him in his projects. He can accomplish a lot of things simultaneously, if necessary.

Sub-ray 6 endowed him with an energy reserve that nurtured him during his incarnation. This sub-ray slowed down his thought process during his incarceration so he could keep balance in his inner world. It allowed him to hope for a better world, in which he believed and still does.

His present incarnation is coming to an end, but it was the measure of the task at hand. He will exit this life in peace, knowing that he will rapidly return in order to accomplish new work for the real liberation of his people whom he loves so much!

March 18, 2010

MARCUS AURELIUS

Given Name: Marcus Catilius Severus
Name after adoption: Marcus Ælius Aurelius Verus
Emperor's Name: Caesar Marcus Aurelius Antoninus Augustus
Nationality: Italian
Place and Date of Birth: Rome (Italy), April 26, 121
Place and Date of Death: Vindobona, today Vienna (Austria), March 17, 180
Profession: Roman emperor and stoic philosopher

MASTER DJWHAL KHUL'S COMMENTARY

Marcus Aurelius was a great emperor and a great philosopher. He had the heart to help others by guiding them with the best of his thoughts and being. He knew that human nature was complex and he attempted to understand it as much as possible. Contrary to what was said, his life was difficult because human behavior was a mystery he had trouble explaining. Sensitive to the jealousy of others, human anger and wickedness, he would have wished to accomplish more: he always felt powerless in the face of human foolishness.

Initiation Level: 1.9

Ray Structure

Monad: 2	Soul: 3	Personality: 2-5
Mental: 3-7	Astral: 6-2	Physical: 3-7

Monad and Soul

His Monad had little influence on him but his Soul definitely had one. It strongly supported him in his work and inspired him in his reflective thinking.

Personality

His ray 2, sub-ray 5 Personality gave him a balanced sensitivity. Ray 2 granted him the ability to understand others and allowed him to display human warmth that nurtured when needed.

Sub-ray 5 provided him with a solid base that rendered it possible for his Personality to be respected and to be fair, without being influenced by the too empathetic aspect of ray 2. This sub-ray sometimes made him appear uncompromising, which was not really the case.

Mental Body

His ray 3, sub-ray 7 mental body made him an intelligent and sincere man. Ray 3 conferred to him the capacity to think about several aspects of a problem in order to see it from all perspectives. It allowed him to "reason" a problem without being trapped by it.

Sub-ray 7 dictated to him a just and loyal way of thinking towards his subjects. It granted him a taste for perfection in everything. He loved beautiful things and knew how to appreciate them.

Astral Body

His ray 6, sub-ray 2 Astral made him loving and warm. The influence of ray 6 gave rise to loyalty and sincerity towards those he thought were sincere like him. He did not accept treason and did not forgive this infidelity, judging that the person who betrayed did it consciously, without ignoring the possible consequences of his actions.

Sub-ray 2 conferred to him a certain sensitivity and empathy. He sincerely loved human beings and wished the best for his family and his people. This sub-ray emphasized his intuition and allowed him to be fair and understanding.

Physical Body

His ray 3, sub-ray 7 Physical gave him style because the fluidity of ray 3 combined with the beauty of ray 7 made him a good looking man. His ray 3 endowed his brain with an energy that supported his work and philosophy well, and granted him good resistance.

Sub-ray 7 made him appreciate beauty and perfection that he mainly sought in its inner aspect. This sub-ray conferred to him a nice elegance and a performing nervous system, which permitted him to seduce while remaining relatively calm in the most difficult moments.

Marcus Aurelius brought a lot to his era and demonstrated wisdom in the following incarnations. However, he lived a few difficult incarnations in which the ego weighed a lot, thus slowing his spiritual progress. He had an interesting incarnation as an explorer in the sixteenth century. He is presently living in America in a female body. He writes literary essays and is well known in the field of psychology.

September 1, 2009

 # McNamara, William

Given Name: William McNamara
Pseudonym: Abba Willie
Nationality: American
Place and Date of Birth: Rhode Island (United States), February 14, 1926
Profession: Monk (Carmelite)

Master Djwhal Khul's Commentary

An honest man, William McNamara has a narrow vision on certain topics. However, he displays great wisdom regarding the laws of the heart, the love of his fellow men, of children, the respect of others and the love of God.

He is passionate, a good man who wishes to deepen his love of God through service to humanity. Although he appreciates living alone, he adores contact with people.

Initiation Level: 3.2

Ray Structure

Monad: 2	Soul: 1	Personality: 3-6
Mental: 7-5	Astral: 6-4	Physical: 3-7

Monad and Soul

A noble-hearted and determined man, he knows what he wants and what is desirable for his community and for himself. He is endowed with a sense of duty and justice that comes from his ray 1 but also from the increasingly growing influence of his Monad. His Soul dictates the path, and ray 2 of his Monad motivates him to follow the paved way with a gentle firmness.

Personality

His ray 3, sub-ray 6 Personality makes him affable and intelligent. Ray 3 grants him a gift for speech and repartee, as well as a sense of humor very much appreciated by his entourage. He likes to laugh, to eat and to have fun as long as it does not affect his spirituality, which for him is the very source of his existence.

Sub-ray 6 was necessary in order to anchor his faith to his Personality. This sub-ray is useful in arousing faith in others, to encourage them and give them hope in their future as Souls existing on this planet. His faith is immense and could easily make him move mountains.

Mental Body

His ray 7, sub-ray 5 mental body makes him intelligent, but also gullible regarding certain non-verifiable data. He likes to believe, but also has "common sense" that served him on many occasions. A born philosopher, ray 7 helps him define himself in this role. This ray renders him occult and reduces the mystical aspect of his religion. He believes in God's mystery and wishes to learn more about this Mystery that tries to reveal itself via his ray 7.

Sub-ray 5 enhances his intelligence and facilitates his writing and his verbal expression. Combined with ray 3, this sub-ray makes him an interesting man who knows how to captivate his audience by presenting convincing facts and examples. His initiation level allowed him to tame his sub-ray 5 and to use it effectively.

Astral Body

Due to his ray 6, sub-ray 4 astral body, he is a divinely loving person. He loves others and wishes them the best. He detests conflicts and wars. He dislikes suffering and to see others' suffering causes him tremendous pain. He would give his life if he knew it would be useful to human evolution. He believes in Christ and in the Christ. He has met him without recognizing him though. This meeting transformed him in such a way that he dedicated his life to the service of his religious community.

His sub-ray 4 makes him receptive and responsive to the occult world of the form. He sees beauty in anything and everything. He likes the sacred arts and respects them. This sub-ray increases his sensitivity and confers to him an "ear" for the feelings and misfortunes of others.

Physical Body

Due to his ray 3, sub-ray 7 physical body, he is a robust man who is not afraid of work and lack of sleep. This allows him to accomplish his task without slowing down his pace. He does not know rest and does not seem to need it. Ray 3 gives him a strong resistance that disregards obstacles. It confers to him an efficient brain that he uses with wisdom. He can think fast and efficiently.

Sub-ray 7 increases his resistance and refines his intelligence. It endows him with a sense of balanced order that allows him to accomplish much more, as this sub-ray channels ray 3 and prevents it from scattering.

This is a good man, but he still needs to heal certain aspects of his vision, because he can sometimes be too aggressive on certain topics. It is true that ray 1 confers to him a hot, spitfire temperament, which does not go unnoticed. This ray saturates his physical body, sometimes revealing its presence in his ray configuration. This man demonstrates respectability and intelligence and we can give him our trust.

October 3, 2008

 # MICHELANGELO

Given Name: Michelangelo di Lodovico Buonarroti Simoni
Nationality: Italian
Place and Date of Birth: Caprese, Tuscany (Italy), March 6, 1475
Place and Date of Death: Rome, Latium (Italy), February 18, 1564
Profession: Painter, sculptor, poet and architect

MASTER DJWHAL KHUL'S COMMENTARY

A renowned artist, Michelangelo still influences our times, thanks to the beauty he transmitted through his paintings and sculptures. Loving life, beauty and love, this man gave everything to his work, which allowed him to express this passion that constantly possessed him.

In those times, it was not unusual for a man to love men, meaning homosexuality, which he experienced in a platonic fashion most of the time. Before incarnating, he had chosen to express his sexuality in this way in order to dedicate himself to his art as much as possible. To have a family would have impeded his work; it would have been impossible for him to live with a woman who would have asked too much of his time. However, this homosexuality temporarily slowed down his evolution, hampering his total self-denial, an essential prerequisite to get to the fourth initiation. He preferred to postpone it in order to fully live an art that was going to influence humanity for centuries.

Initiation Level: 3.8; he was an angel among angels

His level of initiation allowed him to demonstrate a certain humility, which fittingly enough prevented him from feeling superior to others. He knew he was endowed with a talent that was meant to serve others and not him. He would become enraged when human unconsciousness would prevent him from expressing the truth and forced him to betray his art, his path and his destiny.

Ray Structure

Monad: 2	Soul: 2	Personality: 4-7
Mental: 7-3	Astral: 6-4	Physical: 3-7

Monad and Soul

His Monad started to exercise a certain influence that helped him to carry on his task. His ray 2 Soul granted him a gentleness and a love for humanity that sometimes made him suffer.

Personality

His ray 4, sub-ray 7 Personality conferred to him the perfection he transmitted to his art for which he emanated and lived, and that filled every space of his life. Ray 4 afflicted him sometimes with an illness that he would divest himself of with difficulty. Thanks to this ray, he would feel all the beauty of the world but also all its misery. His initiation level allowed him to compose with these lows that, finally, lasted for a very short while. Ray 4 also imbued him with seemingly endless creativity.

Sub-ray 7 provided him with a sense of detail and refinement that shaped the remarkable artist he still is today. Who can brag that he is able to express man's perfection with such beauty? At no time has he been surpassed and he probably will never be. His works of art touch the Soul and temporarily pervade the Personality with his energy. I am not talking about reproductions, but of his authentic works that remain permeated with his essence that he transmitted so well to them.

Mental Body

His ray 7, sub-ray 3 mental body provided him with an intelligence that comes to light in his work. Everything mattered: the choice of the pigment color, the texture on which he painted and sculpted, the lighting effects, the gestures and bodies that had to express what he felt. He could meet all challenges. Ray 7 offered perfection and sub-ray 3, the means to reach it. Ray 7 expressed what he wanted to implement and sub-ray 3 sought what was necessary to express this perfection in the physical realm, be it money, texture or objects (human or not).

Astral Body

His ray 6, sub-ray 4 astral body conferred to him the passion, the buoyancy that animated him. Ray 6 shaped him into a simple, warm and charitable man. He liked to give but detested those who would try to adversely affect his art.

Sub-ray 4 colored his Personality by amplifying his warrior aspect. When he called upon his ray 4 from within, he would fear nothing. This sub-ray made him the rushing type, capable of defending his ideas in order to favour the search for beauty and harmony inherent to his work.

Physical Body

His ray 3, sub-ray 7 physical allowed him to work hard and long hours in sometimes unbearable conditions. Ray 3 provided the flexibility that was necessary to him even at an older age. He worked relentlessly, overtaxing his body, his eyes and his mind. Possessed by his work, he did not succeed in finding rest (very brief) until a project was finished. As one project overlapped another, most of the time, he was deprived of rest.

Sub-ray 7 imbedded in him the desire of the perfection that haunted him. It assured him of an ease in his work and facilitated his calculations, endowing him with a resistant nervous system that allowed him to put up with enormous pressure.

He was a very remarkable man who reached his fourth initiation during his last incarnation. As he is presently incarnated, I will not divulge his identity. I will only mention that he is Canadian, that he does not operate in the world of art but that he manages funds in order to serve humanity. Although misunderstood by his peers, this situation is of no importance in his eyes.

August 11, 2009

 # MILLMAN, DAN

Given Name: Dan Millman
Nationality: American
Place and Date of Birth: Los Angeles, California (United States), February 22, 1946
Profession: Professional athlete, writer and lecturer

MASTER DJWHAL KHUL'S COMMENTARY

I have little to say regarding this author of spiritual fiction. He has a young Soul, fairly pure, but still imprinted with the desire to be recognized. His writings bring a spiritual dimension to everyday life. However, in many respects, Dan Millman still lacks depth, which will come to him in the next years that will not be necessarily easy ones. He will live inner transformations that will shake-up a number of his beliefs, and he will finally start believing in the fantastic related to the spiritual life.

His Master, Socrates, an astral projection of his wishes, is an amalgam of Personalities he has met and used to create his character. Socrates, now, exists on the astral plane. Dan Millman's readers, who believed in his existence, have acted in such a way that Socrates enjoys a certain astral atomic texture, a medium for the emanation of this accumulation of thoughts projected on an image totally fabricated by Dan Millman. We would have wished that the story recounted the life of an authentic Master, but such is not the case. However, Dan Millman's books help direct humanity's gaze towards a spirituality that will become more authentic in the future when it will see the magic that hides behind daily events. We can say that he is performing a basic task that will allow his readers to delve more deeply and become authentic disciples on the path in the future.

Initiation Level: 2.3

Dan Millman's initiation level is quite respectable. Already, his vision of the spiritual path is fairly good. However, he still has to deepen his own progression. At present, his Soul guides him in his writings and meetings, which makes him a good transmitter of the data passed onto him. His meditation, sufficiently intense, allows him to sometimes listen to what takes place in the higher astral planes. He has not yet succeeded in touching the mental plane. This will happen in a future life, if he perseveres.

Ray Structure

Monad: 2   Soul: 2   Personality: 3-7
Mental: 7-5   Astral: 6-4   Physical: 3-6

Monad and Soul

His Monad has no influence on him, contrary to his Soul, whose influence has intensified over approximately two incarnations, one of which took place in Russia. It provides him with the desire to listen to others, which he only partially does in his life.

Too many odd numbers make up his ray configuration, creating a tendency for him to be an extrovert, which actually goes a little against his evolution. It is his ray 3's that make him search and gather a lot of information he uses for his writings.

Personality

His ray 3, sub-ray 7 Personality makes him dynamic, while preventing him from becoming more mature. Ray 3 allows him to act and think fast, and to be a good manipulator at all levels. His ray 3 creates agitation and often causes him many difficulties to meditate adequately. The influence of this ray also allows him to be a good storyteller, because it endows him with a full and active imagination.

Sub-ray 7 instills in him a certain rigor that he sometimes uses to quiet his ray 3; it transmits to him the desire to act well and quickly. He likes perfection and is seduced by beauty in everything. This sub-ray helped him acquire the necessary discipline to perform in gymnastics.

Mental Body

His mental body, ruled by ray 7, sub-ray 5, proves to be brilliant and realistic. Ray 7 once more creates discipline and a sense of order in his writings, wrapping them in mystery and magic. He likes the fantastic and knows how to transmit it through his stories.

Sub-ray 5 adds a note of credibility to his writings, an almost scientific aspect. Thus, his stories prove to be more real.

Astral Body

His astral body, influenced by ray 6, sub-ray 4, shapes him into a gentle and kind man. Ray 6 provides warmth that is transmitted in what he says and writes. He is honest and just. This ray makes him love his entourage and endows him with a sense of honor and dedication that he was able to transcribe through Socrates. In a way, Socrates is the perfect man he wishes to be.

Due to his sub-ray 4, he experiences emotions important for his evolution. This sub-ray also adds a little color and a more sensitive aspect to his life. These effects disturb him often: he could rapidly get depressed and become happy and cheerful shortly afterwards.

Physical Body

Ray 3, sub-ray 6, influencing his physical, make him a man who likes to move (ray 3) and to physically dedicate himself to certain causes (ray 6) that are not necessarily of value from the viewpoint of Hierarchy. Ray 3 gives him a taste for gymnastics, to move, to produce and to write; it allows him to have a brain that thinks and acts rapidly. This ray may sometimes mislead him, but he catches up fairly quickly, thanks to his ray 3, sub-ray 7 Personality (ray 7 always bringing him back on the right track) and to his ray 7, sub-ray 5 mental body.

Sub-ray 6 qualifies his movements, his way of seeing life and of thinking. He has to exercise vigilance because he sometimes becomes too sentimental, too focused on the right behavior, according to the vision of ray 6 that, quite often, perceives in an erroneous fashion the proper actions he has to perform. He is a good man who sometimes lacks vision.

We can assert that at his level he is doing a good job. He still has a lot to learn, which will happen in time…

July 31, 2009

MOZART, WOLFGANG AMADEUS

Given Name: Joannes Chrysostomus Wolfgangus Theophilus Mozart
Nationality: Austrian
Place and Date of Birth: Salzburg (Austria), January 27, 1756
Place and Date of Death: Vienna (Austria), December 5, 1791
Profession: Composer of classical music

MASTER DJWHAL KHUL'S COMMENTARY

A musical genius, Mozart marked many epochs thanks to his music. He knew how to bring down to earth joyous or melancholic notes that deeply touched humanity. He suffered tremendously for being unable to adequately transmit what he heard inwardly. He always said that due to our imperfection, celestial music remained inaccessible to human ears. Music was his life, his love, his accomplishment.

Mozart aroused ardor while Beethoven manifested intensity; the contribution of both composers to music is huge. We may say that like Beethoven, Mozart hit the right notes that touched the Soul, but in a lighter, more crystal-clear way. Beethoven touched the Soul's depth, its more intense aspect, and Mozart touched the Soul's joy, its expression in the world of the form.

Mozart was a colorful character, which was necessary for his music to come to life. The Soul is happy, expressive when allowed to be so; this is what he attempted to do and to become. He was bubbling with an explosive energy that gave him no rest. Money, sex, alcohol were unable to diminish this inner fire that constantly burned and finally consumed him.

Mozart was seeking an answer to life, to "his" life, without success. He knew he was immortal, through his music, while being aware that death would surprise him rapidly. He was an Initiate of a fairly high rank for the times and he suffered from it because he felt misunderstood.

Initiation Level: 2.3

Ray Structure

Monad: 2	Soul: 2	Personality: 4-3
Mental: 5-2	Astral: 6-4	Physical: 7-2

Monad and Soul

His Monad had no influence; on the other hand, his Soul started to have an influence that was increasingly expanding. In its expression, it held out the prospect of notes that sparkled in his mind and invited him to consider their beauty. He was very sensitive to the influence of sub-ray 2 in his physical configuration, which weakened him all his life.

Personality

His Personality, influenced by ray 4, sub-ray 3, made him live excesses of all kinds. He loved life in its form, its expression, and could play with all its aspects. Ray 4 gave him the drive, the courage to act and sub-ray 3, a taste for experimentation. This ray inspired in him the desire to live on this planet and made him appreciate the human aspects of life. Without its contribution, he would have probably left his physical body more rapidly. It also conferred to him the ardor to express the constant joy he felt inwardly.

Sub-ray 3 provided efficiency, rapidity and joviality. He liked social events, which sometimes caused him more harm than good. This sub-ray 3 increased the exuberance of ray 4, and simplified relations. It also allowed him to demonstrate that he was a clever manipulator of his entourage.

Mental Body

His mental body, governed by ray 5, sub-ray 2, motivated him to become the composer we know. Sub-ray 2, similar to a pair of antennae, offered him the possibility to "listen" within himself to the music Ray 5, of course, translated into notes and materialized. Without this ray's solidity that allowed him to remain down to earth, the influence of sub-ray 2 would undoubtedly have made him mad and non-functional.

Sub-ray 2 connected him directly to the Soul. This sub-ray could not be found on the first line of his ray configuration, because the Soul would have directly influenced him and Mozart was not endowed with the energetic capacity to put up with such a contribution. This sub-ray acted like a sensing device and allowed him to feel the beauty of celestial music. Without the support of ray 5, this sub-ray would have left him a prisoner of the musical high spheres without a possibility of escape.

Astral Body

Mozart's astral body, governed by the influence of ray 6, sub-ray 4, provided him with a hair-trigger sensitivity. Ray 6 granted him warmth as well as a dedication to his music and his family, whom he always appreciated in spite of his infidelities, because it was his temporary anchor on earth. This ray also endowed him with a stubbornness that he kept all his life.

Sub-ray 4 communicated to him a taste for frolicking, but also the desire to transmit, thanks to his art, the beauty of the Soul and of music. He liked beauty, to which he was sometimes a slave. Occasionally, his ray 4's created conflicts that revealed themselves to be necessary to his evolution and the writing of his music; to be creative sometimes demands not being "static".

Physical Body

His physical, influenced by ray 7, sub-ray 2, a rare configuration for the times and still rare today, gifted him with an efficient brain. Ray 7 offered perfection and sub-ray 2, intuition. Although ray 7 equipped him with a good nervous system, sub-ray 2 submitted him to fears that created fissures in his aura, causing weakness and sickness. Ray 7 favored the search for beauty, balance and a desire that everything reasoned "perfectly". As everything cannot be perfect on earth, he suffered a lot.

Sub-ray 2 caused him difficulties at the level of his physical and mental bodies. Too sensitive, this sub-ray provoked fears he had trouble managing. He often experienced a lot of insecurities resulting from the delicate and insidious influence of this sub-ray when it is unbalanced.

Mozart presently lives in Austria; he is a well known musician who is unaware who he has been. He has to learn to better manage the energy of his Soul. He is getting closer to the third initiation and has to reduce his vanity in order to humbly pass through this third door, which his life as Mozart did not allow him to do. His last two lives, including the present one, will serve to develop this humility, an essential key to crossing the next stage.

August 11, 2009

 NEEM KAROLI BABA

Given Name: Pundit Lakshmi Narayan Sharma
Other Name: Maharaj-ji
Nationality: Indian
Place of Birth: Akbarpur (India)
Place and Date of Death: Vrindavan (India), September 11, 1973
Profession: Indian guru

MASTER DJWHAL KHUL'S COMMENTARY

Neem Karoli Baba was not from this world. His great strength came from his planet of origin, located not far from Sirius. The planetary impact exerted little influence on him. His origin is as strange as that of Sai Baba; we can say that he was a senior cosmic avatar. He has not yet reintegrated into a human body. He is presently working in the higher realms with the Masters of the White Hierarchy that he has accepted to help.

We have very little information on him. We know that where he comes from, time does not have the same consistency and does not produce the same effects as here. He could play with matter at will because he was not subject to it like we are. A magician of words, used under the cloak of silence, he learned how to love humanity, which he adopted like a big family. He lived a deep solitude, a certain nostalgia, but never a real sadness because he could communicate at will with his planet of origin. We may say that he lived here without being from here.

Initiation Level: Approximately 6

Why "approximately" 6? He had not yet perfectly succeeded in fully assuming human nature in all its complexity, its beauty, but also its limitations. On his planet of origin he was not subject to the system of initiation. Therefore, he could not adequately reflect his real nature, because he had not been able to perfectly adapt the fields of his Monad and of his Soul to the limited roles of the various bodies that compose human nature. Undoubtedly more evolved, the real makeup of his nature will only be revealed once he will have withdrawn from his energy field the veils masking it, thus becoming almost human.

Ray Structure

Monad: 2	Soul: 3	Personality: 4-2
Mental: 3-7	Astral: 6-2	Physical: 3-5

Monad and Soul

He could play with his rays at will. However, he let ray 2 of his Monad constantly guide his life. He was Love, Compassion and Devotion (to the Divinity in each one of us). His Soul helped him brilliantly mock his students. This ray gave him a particular sense of humor that allowed him not to take himself too seriously while remaining an exceptional Being.

Personality

He liked to play with his Personality and his ray 4 offered him this possibility. He could rapidly change the atmosphere in a room simply by changing his attitude at will. This ray also endowed him with a certain clairvoyance towards the predictable behavior of his entourage. It also allowed him to change shape and use the molecules of his physical body like a child playing with plasticine. Ray 4 provides a lot of magic and fantasy to the individual capable of recognizing all possibilities. For him, life was *Lîlâ*[1], Bliss, Love, and this ray gave him the means to express it every moment of his incarnation.

Sub-ray 2 graced him with the energy of a father caring for his children. Some would say that he also had the energy of the mother when he found himself in private with his disciples. He took care of others, of their

---

[1] *Lîlâ* or *leela* in Sanskrit literally means "game".

324

evolution, without carrying everything on his shoulders. He knew how to recognize a disciple's value without imposing his strength, his presence or his influence.

Mental Body

Endowed with a mental body influenced by ray 3, sub-ray 7, he could only be brilliant and intelligent. His enlightened mental body supported his work, which consisted in undoing certain harmful patterns in his students. Ray 3 allowed him to play intelligently with his students' concepts and to study them without their feeling judged. He did not provoke, he entered the game with them in order to "outplay" them and demonstrated the illusions that marked their discipleship. Even in the worst moments, the sincere disciple, whose ego's influence had diminished thanks to the Maharaj-ji's presence, would come to laugh at himself.

Sub-ray 7 endowed him with an unquestionable firmness, respected by all. It created in him perfect vigilance, and an almost "palpable" desire for perfection. His saintly fits of rage that he sometimes displayed were feared by all; the energy transmitted by this anger carried a strength capable of destroying any resistance produced by an ego full of itself. All the disciple's bodies were shaken and a release to the Soul's desires due to the Master's intervention would follow. Rare were those who would refuse to see their imperfections because of their great love for Maharaj-ji and their great trust in him. Of course, Westerners were the most difficult to coax because their ego is often like hardened steel, almost indestructible. However, when such egos wake up and care to forget themselves, they become perfect servants for the Soul and humanity.

Astral Body

With an astral body influenced by ray 6, sub-ray 2, he was, unquestionably, a warm and charming man when he decided to be so. Ray 6 conferred to him this love and devotion towards Hanuman, this white monkey representing the perfect disciple who knows how to forget himself in order to better serve his Soul and his beloved Master. This ray allowed him to wrap his audience in his warmth and to act in such a way that all felt loved, appreciated, accepted and understood by this Being so complex and so simple at the same time. He was not afraid to assert his faith in the Divine that constantly animated him.

Sub-ray 2 instilled in him wisdom and compassion that were never depleted. He did not know discouragement, although at times he seemed weary of the ego game his students played. His inexhaustible love allowed him to maintain hope in each and to guide them with wisdom in their life's journey on Earth. Being very aware that this life is only one life among many others, he would continuously turn his look towards the future, visualizing each person's potential.

Physical Body

His physical, saturated with the energies of ray 3, sub-ray 5, knew how to adapt to various situations of his incarnation. Ray 3 allowed him to shape his body according to the needs of others in such a way that his physical appearance would produce an effect on others. Thus, as of the first encounter, according to the reaction produced, he could qualify the authenticity of the discipleship of the person facing him. Ray 3 also equipped him with a very resistant body.

Sub-ray 5, that strengthened the effect of ray 3, made him a remarkably strong man. This sub-ray gave him powerful muscles resistant to pain. It also allowed him to maintain an intimate link with the world of elementals, with which he communicated easily. They simplified his task when he wished to relocate rapidly.

This exceptional Being is not yet reincarnated. He will do so soon when a task at the measure of his abilities presents itself.

May 6, 2007; January 12, 2011

 # NEWTON, MICHAEL

Given Name: Michael Duff Newton
Nationality: American
Place and Date of Birth: California (United States), December 9, 1931
Profession: Doctor in counseling and hypnotherapist

MASTER DJWHAL KHUL'S COMMENTARY

It is useless to mention that Michael Newton accepted a special mission before incarnating: to prove to a scientific degree the existence of the Soul and its role. It was necessary for him to be agnostic to objectively shed some light on the possibility of this existence. He worked hard and did not hesitate to doubt and to relentlessly start his studies on the subject all over again. He sometimes experienced brief moments of discouragement, of hesitation, but his desire to know and to understand always prevailed. Still misunderstood and ignored, this man deserves our respect.

Initiation Level: 2.3

Because he is mentally polarized, he can adequately carry out his sessions of hypnosis while remaining unattached to the results. Therefore, he seeks less to unconsciously and subtly influence his clients' replies. He can take a step back and act with more accuracy. He guides while remaining out of the way, which allows for answers that are more real. Had he not been mentally polarized, the results would have proven to be very different.

Ray Structure

Monad: 2	Soul: 3	Personality: 6-4
Mental: 5-3	Astral: 6-2	Physical: 7-3

Monad and Soul

His Monad has very little influence on him, contrary to his ray 3 Soul, which helped him a lot in his research and gave him the taste of working in this direction. He does not shy from experimenting and loves to discover new avenues. Ray 3 conferred to him the boldness to continue in spite of his doubts and challenges. Because of its natural curiosity, this ray is very useful during experiences like his. We may add that this ray sometimes brings doubt and creates an aspect of "non believing" that, in a way, joins the influence of ray 5.

Personality

His ray 6, sub-ray 4 Personality makes him warm and adaptable. Ray 6 inspires in him the love of his work and the desire to help others. It impresses on him the desire to dedicate himself to this cause (a cause he does not consider his own) and to his need to transmit what he knows so that the torch and the search do not cease. Well balanced, this ray confers to him a certain humility that he uses wisely. However, he also knows how to demand respect when necessary; he then expresses himself with a certain arrogance that ray 6 allows him to do.

His sub-ray 4 allowed him to keep an open mind, not to take himself too seriously, to be endowed with an intelligent humor; it also provided him with a taste for adventure. However, he sometimes lives ups and downs that he can manage fairly well, being a psychotherapist.

Mental Body

His ray 5, sub-ray 3 mental body offers him an outstanding working tool or, if you prefer, one "made to measure." Ray 5 favors discernment, research, questioning that allow him to do a job that gives rise to respect. He knows what he is saying and does not fear to express himself because he has studied and probed the subject adequately. He knows how to explain intelligently while remaining funny (ray 3 influence) and serious. He likes facts. However, the ray 3 influence brings a certain flexibility, which is beneficial and provides a more rounded and broader vision.

Sub-ray 3 was necessary to add fluidity to his work. It also allowed him to adapt to other people's needs, while keeping his self respect. This sub-ray influenced his desire to know and understand. It removed certain blinders that could have harmed his work, because ray 5, too rigid, sometimes lacks latitude and ceases to progress during research, lingering over details that harm it instead of stimulating it and advancing it.

Astral Body

A ray 6, sub-ray 2 astral body was necessary so that his emotional universe would be comfortable and stable. He likes to love and be loved as well, without becoming the slave of his emotions. His relationship is his base, the pillar that allows him to be solid in the various sectors of his life. Sometimes moody, he knows how to be forgiven and inject some warmth that rekindles feelings. Because of ray 6, he is faithful to his family and to his friends, as well as to his clients, who always remain "human beings" in his eyes.

Sub-ray 2 endowed him with sensitivity so that he could understand and help others. It allowed him to really "hear" the topics his clients wished to discuss. This ability drove him to adjust his sessions "almost to the second" so that his clients would not only be satisfied, but also happy and better in their psyche. This sub-ray granted him an intuition that was necessary and without which he could not have gone so far in his work.

Physical Body

His ray 7, sub-ray 3 physical endowed him with a solidity and an endurance that served him all his life. The influence of ray 7 equipped him with a strong and adaptable nervous system, allowing him to remain concentrated during his hypnosis sessions. His physical brain, influenced by this ray, fostered his work by offering him the possibility to categorize, create images and understand what was going on during sessions. Without this ray, it would have been difficult for him to describe, as a Soul, what happens between two lives. Ray 7 includes a "magical" aspect that favors the expansion of vision towards aspects sometimes unknown to the average person.

Sub-ray 3 endowed him with an endurance that improved the too often rigid aspect of ray 7 in the physical body. The combination of these two energies granted him a healthy body resistant to sickness. The influence of sub-ray 3 also eased the sometimes too linear way of ray 7, allowing him to be less rigid in the logic of things.

This man brought a lot to human beings by making them live and see their immortality through their Soul. This work is starting and some will continue where he left off. However, he will come back in the near future, once he leaves the physical world (which is not planned any time soon) in order to pursue his work that is only beginning.

November 20, 2010

 OBAMA, BARACK HUSSEIN

Given Name: Barack Hussein Obama Jr.
Nationality: American
Place and Date of Birth: Honolulu (United States), August 4, 1961
Profession: Lawyer and Statesman

MASTER DJWHAL KHUL'S COMMENTARY

A man of great intelligence and great simplicity, Mr. Obama is a noble-hearted being who knows how to demonstrate "intelligence" in his approaches. Neither a fanatic nor a dictator, he is dedicated to his people's well being (that is the people living in the United States, regardless of race) as well as to world peace. One may qualify him as an idealist but isn't the contribution of idealists necessary for the planet and the whole of humanity to be well?

Suffering, whatever its nature, disconcerts him and is painful for him. His weak point remains women; he discovers his vulnerable side when he faces their charm and beauty, a frailty caused by his ray 7 Soul. He likes perfection, order and equity in everything. He knows how to behave when faced by the seduction exercised by women who like power and who would do anything to get closer to it.

Disciple of El Morya Khan, although he is presently under the direction of the Count of St. Germain, he is a born politician. Ray 7 remains necessary for his first lives in politics. He will dedicate several incarnations to politics, will learn how to manage it so that it does not destroy his own life. He will have to cultivate caution and at times moderation, which ray 7 will grant him. When he will have accomplished a complete circle of seven lives in politics — he is in his third — he will be able to use the energy of his real Master linked to the Ashram of Ray 1.

Initiation Level: 2.3

He will undoubtedly reach the initiation level of 2.5 in the present incarnation if he lives long enough; his ideas could disturb and endanger his life. He has to learn caution, which is essential in this incarnation.

Ray Structure

Monad: 2	Soul: 7 that will go towards 1	Personality: 2-1
Mental: 7-3	Astral: 6-4	Physical: 7-3-5

He displays a certain arrogance that will be necessary all through his political life. It comes in part from his initiation level, but also from his Soul ray and his mental ray. His ray 2 Personality grants him a simplicity and a humility that are equally necessary.

Monad and Soul

His Monad has little influence on his life and behavior, contrary to his Soul that already manages a part, because he wants to be a good channel for the work of the Masters. He is followed, without his knowledge, in the world of dreams, on the inner planes, by certain Masters that guide and advise him. Some manifest themselves on the physical plane to support him in his work. Presently Mr. Obama proves to be the most able to help humanity through the United States. We hope that one day all heads of states would be at least initiates of level 2.5 and more. Then, Earth's surface will improve and it will finally become a sacred planet.

His Soul, presently influenced by ray 7, favors a descent of energy preparing a future that will be more and more influenced by this ray. Order and harmony, bordering chaos, will be more present because the energy of ray 7, in its first millennium, will act as a catalyst to incredible abuses at all levels. These ray 7 Souls will prove essential to bringing a semblance of order, else the committed abuses would lead us to our doom. However, let us not forget that ray 7 is extremely intelligent and that it knows how to predict the future. It would therefore, we hope, block excesses and favour a better balance at the level of world ecology.

When he reaches his third initiation, if his cycle of seven incarnations in politics is finished, he will be able to choose a Soul under the influence of ray 1. His work would take on a larger scope and he would become an important ally of El Morya Khan's Ashram.

Personality

We suggested to him to adopt a ray 2, sub-ray 1 Personality, his approach having to remain imbued with gentleness and qualified with an unshakable will; he has to rule with a firm gentleness. He has to display warmth, care, responsiveness to others while never losing sight of his mandate and the will to pursue, although at times, discouragement creeps in. Let us not forget that he is dealing with people of all types, of all religions, but mainly of various initiation levels, quite often lower than his. Sometimes, it will be difficult for him to understand the way that some people think and act. As mutual aid is close to his heart, he will adjust and continue to work for the good of all.

One should not forget that he would have the faults of his qualities, such as stubbornness, the mirage of the savior, thinking that he has "the vision" favorable to all. He will know how to adapt, because we will be watchful.

Mental Body

His ray 7, sub-ray 3 mental body makes him intelligent, a visionary, clever and a diplomat. He can talk and mould himself to the public he is addressing. He has the wisdom to rule well while respecting others. He can also work on several projects simultaneously without losing sight of the "whole". Sometimes he will tend to neglect his family but his wife will, most of the time, know how to understand and accept what will occasionally seem "unacceptable". Behind a man of this scope must appear a woman that can support him in his challenges. On the initiation front, she is slightly less evolved than he is, although she is getting close to the second initiation. Consequently, she will be capable of grasping most of her husband's motivations.

Astral Body

His ray 6, sub-ray 4 astral body makes him devoted, faithful and patient. He tries not to judge others too much and attempts to understand their viewpoint. Ray 6 provides him with a certain strength at the emotional level, which helps him maintain a balance in all other aspects of his life. His family remains important because it provides him with priceless support and love that assist him in the pursuit of his mandate.

Sub-ray 4 provides him with a sense of art that will be appreciated and well judged; he is also endowed with a refinement necessary to his work. Sometimes he is afflicted with ups and downs, but they are brief because his ray configuration rapidly brings him back to what is essential, which he knows is no longer his small self.

Physical Body

His ray 7, sub-rays 3-5 physical give him exceptional strength and resistance. Ray 7 qualifies his brain, transmitting to him clear and precise thoughts that allow him to justly perceive the necessary procedures for the accomplishment of his work. Sub-ray 3 characterizes his intelligence by removing some blinders that ray 7 has a tendency to put on to reach its goals. It sharpens his intelligence, preparing him to easily and adequately reply to inner and exterior questioning. We have taken the liberty to emphasize sub-ray 5 that reinforces his physical resistance to counter certain health problems that occasionally drain the energy of his physical body. This sub-ray also confers to him a certain intuition very useful for various decision making.

He is a man of the future who should not be ignored.

June 5, 2008

Master Djwhal Khul's Added Commentary

Barack Obama is presently living a transition period that is necessary. He is not getting the support of all; he often sees himself misunderstood by his peers that remain skeptic towards change through simple fear of losing what they already have. It is to be noted that if Americans do not evolve or, if you prefer, do not change, they will rapidly be deprived of their leadership in the world as well as the respect of other nations. Americans have a lot to understand and to realize, and this, in the shortest time possible.

Barack Obama is a man of the future; he shakes the present to uproot the past; this past keeps captive the consciousness of Americans, who are sometimes still grappling with their cowboy aura that shoots everything that moves without checking facts. The future has to take place and the wind of change must strongly blow on the United States.

The strong influence of ray 6 on the American people is creating disagreement that will have to be ironed out. The too rigid and conformist aspect of the American Southwest is polluting the worldly consciousness. The people must evolve and overcome their fear of change. Supportive when our thoughts are similar to theirs, the Southwest becomes resistant when we express an opposite or different idea. It protects itself by creating situations that are useless and incomprehensible to the most evolved among us. In a way, terror reigns in this region and the contribution of terrorism simply increases the discomfort of their very young consciousness.

The American Midwest is, undoubtedly, one of the American territories the most resistant to change; moreover it poses a barrier to the progression of the United States in its unification from border to border, in the North as much as in the South. The mental rigidity that is there does not allow any opening towards other races, cultures and religions. This part of the United States is a bullet in the American consciousness, a bullet that wanders armed with guns and all kinds of prohibitions. Here is what impoverishes the consciousness unable to evolve in such a context. Beware those who do not share their opinions...

The western coast has wended well and opens itself to uncharted possibilities, more equitable for human consciousness; however, materialism is temporarily handicapping the vision of the people living in this area, which should correct itself in the decades to come. The glamour that reigns there is only the result of young Souls in search of beauty and fame. This aspect, which seduces the whole world, will disappear in a hundred years in order to be replaced by a more authentic community, more developed and fairer in its thoughts and actions.

This coast presents a mix between the past and the future; one can find people torn between their country's past and the future of the nation. A great number of immigrants live there, allowing the creation of new western bases, where the cradle of the next race to come will reign in the future.

The north of the United States is more evolved than the south. People there are more open and ready to work for the benefit of all and for humanity. They set their heart on understanding each other and to adjust, if that is the case.

The State of Hawaii is more centered on the future than the past. People from a spectrum of initiation levels live there, allowing this piece of land to be outlined as a miniature example of the world population.

Certainly, people of all sorts and various initiation levels live in the United States. Adepts and Masters work there, hoping to make the American consciousness evolve. The diagram I have described concerns a global aspect of the population. Advanced Initiates live in California and in the State of New York. Let us emphasize that there are Initiates everywhere who are working hard to raise the consciousness of all.

The United States has to improve. Having become capitalist and self-centered, its people must modify their ways of reacting to life, and include the respect of others more, in all that this represents. Too much racism, financial inequalities and illusions reign there to this day. How is it possible that the death penalty still prevails in such a country? Although it is still the Promised Land, its assets are gradually diminishing.

Barack Obama is a strong man graced with a vision very few Americans have. He advocates freedom of speech and liberty. Although his peers are unconscious, he renders tribute to the American Flag.

His role, from now on, consists of regilding the coat of arms of the United States by using his intelligence to the maximum, but also his conscience and his heart. We, the Masters of the White Lodge, support his mandate and hope that the whole of humanity will do the same.

March 16, 2010

 # ORBISON, ROY

Given Name: Roy Orbison
Nationality: American
Place and Date of Birth: Vernon, Texas (United States), April 23, 1936
Place and Date of Death: Madison, Tennessee (United States), December 6, 1988
Profession: Author, composer and performer

MASTER DJWHAL KHUL'S COMMENTARY

Roy Orbison was a young Soul gifted for music and the arts. He also possessed an interesting link with the angelic worlds in which he believed. His voice, so particular, came from past lives where he had sung as a castrato, at a time when this was still permitted. Moreover, he became famous starting from the year 1870, in Rome, as Alessandro Moreschi. He had two lives as a castrato.

We hope that in his next incarnation, he will have a more manly voice, which would allow him to detach himself from his desire to sing like an angel. He might still have a career in singing, because he seems not to have completed his apprenticeship.

He had a Soul we would qualify as almost mature. He will reach this level of maturity during his next incarnation, if he accepts facing certain truths coming from his Soul. One of them is that he has to learn to trust life and his Soul. He always doubted his capacity to contact the latter, which is what he should learn to do in his next lives because this is his real destiny.

This is a being that seems ill at ease in a human body, which he finds too restrictive. He must trust his Soul and accept evolving as it wishes. As a Soul, he is fine; as a man or a woman, he feels cut off, abandoned.

This malaise will undoubtedly lead him to deepen his real and deep nature because he remains too hypnotized by life's mirages.

Initiation Level: 1.2

Ray Structure

Monad: 2	Soul: 2	Personality: 4-3
Mental: 7-5	Astral: 6-4	Physical: 3-6

Monad and Soul

His Monad had no influence while his Soul attempted to have one through music, the only means it could use. Music was the only important transmitter to which Roy Orbison was receptive. He only lived for music and music (in turn) made him live.

Personality

His ray 4, sub-ray 3 Personality offered him the possibility of expressing himself through music but in a much more balanced way than in his previous lives. Ray 4 allowed him to compose music that would become beautiful and harmonious, thanks to the sound of his voice. It endowed him with a Personality that swayed between solitude and the need for a public. He could be comfortable in either situation, depending on the influence of ray 4. If this ray wanted to be balanced (mainly because of his astral body), he would become at ease alone as well as in public. However, if this ray became unbalanced, he was ill at ease in one as well as in the other.

His sub-ray 3 granted him this flexibility in the voice and in the expression of his songs. This sub-ray contributed to modulating his voice (ray 3 is also in the physical) so that it produced an angelic effect that wanted to be amplified by the influence of ray 4. It was also instrumental in keeping him calm, in spite of the moment's agitation provoked by the influence of ray 4. He was like the spider within its web.

Mental Body

His ray 7, sub-ray 5 mental body allowed him to "intuitively" receive melodies coming from elsewhere. The energy issued from ray 7 offered him the possibility of transmitting the data he was receiving, thanks to his physical brain being influenced by ray 3. He would then become a musician of words and melodies.

Sub-ray 5 served as an anchor to his incarnation. Without its contribution, his life would have been hell, because nothing really tangible could retain him. It offered him the possibility to enjoy "concrete" moments that allowed him to "come" back to earth and to solve things that were very "down to earth".

Astral Body

His ray 6, sub-ray 4 astral body granted him the faculty to dedicate himself to his music and his family. He had a big heart and would have easily given his shirt to anyone who would have asked for it, if his sub-ray 5 mental body had failed. He never recovered from the death of his two sons.

Sub-ray 4 provided him with "wings," allowing him to escape within himself when life seemed too painful. He had a strong imagination with which he often wandered.

Physical Body

His ray 3, sub-ray 6 physical endowed him with a sturdy constitution; however, his internal unhappiness repeatedly undermined his vital energy. Ray 3 granted him a pleasant tone of voice and a good sense of humor.

Sub-ray 6 equipped him with "weight," allowing him to be more rooted in the "here and now" because he often drifted in all sorts of dreams.

This sub-ray allowed him to appreciate the good things in life (food, women, and alcohol).

This Soul is not yet reincarnated, but it undoubtedly will be shortly.

July 5, 2009

 PADRE PIO

Given Name: Francesco Forgione
Nationality: Italian
Place and Date of Birth: Pietrelcina (Italy), May 25, 1887
Place and Date of Death: San Giovanni Rotondo (Italy), September 23, 1968
Profession: Capuchin priest, confessor, mystic and healer

MASTER DJWHAL KHUL'S COMMENTARY

Padre Pio was a man with unshakeable faith, who allowed humans to see and feel the extraordinary manifestations related to the energies of ray 6 in its most mystic aspect. These types of manifestations will diminish with the progressive arrival of ray 7, bringing in its wake not mysticism but occultism, in other words the magic aspect that will reveal itself openly. In as much as ray 6 wanted to mystify and hide information, ray 7 will similarly favour understanding and the apprenticeship of the laws weaving our world. It will materialize what ray 6 rendered mysterious. That will be the real magic of ray 7: revealing truth in all its splendor.

Padre Pio was somewhat a victim of his holiness. He became a world leader from the viewpoint of the accomplishment of "miracles" possible in a human life. He lived a life totally dedicated to the Church that he sincerely believed to be the ideal in this world. This necessary veil provided him with the possibility of conducting his mission well, which consisted of allowing humankind to experience the mystery of human life through an energy other than the one of the physical field. He transmitted hope for a better life, sprinkled with kindness and divine Love.

The ceaseless attacks he had to bear, as well as the *kundalini* manifestation that produced the negative energy necessary for the purification of his faith, of his karma, of his Personality and equally necessary for the holding of his status as a saint within the Church, came from the astral plane. In other words, those fearsome attacks, which had repercussions up to the physical plane, caused him to deepen his being while remaining humble and understanding. These attacks cultivated fear and brought him closer to Christ; thus, those stigmatas were created from the desire to be with God and to be protected from evil forces. This fusion emaciated his etheric and eventually his physical, hence favoring a similitude, an identification with his Savior.

These stigmatas created the illusion of a protection against evil forces, because he believed that by losing all this blood, he would expiate his sins and those of the world. The lost blood created a resonance with his divine aspect that had repercussions in the form of manifestations (bilocation, etc.), increasing in such a way his power in God. These inner shocks created simultaneously by the Astral and by the *kundalini* fostered his evolution, in spite of the obstacles he faced. He was a great man, a great saint and an acceptable disciple for the Hierarchy. He will become an exceptional disciple during his next incarnation, which will be less influenced by the sometimes "judgmental" energy of ray 6.

Initiation Level: 3.7

He did not succeed in passing to the fourth initiation because his devotees claimed all his attention. However, please note that at the beginning of his life, he was a simple third Initiate and that his exceptional life as a saint allowed him to forget himself and to really serve humanity. Thus, this life prepared him for the renunciation that will occur in his next incarnation.

Ray Structure

Monad: 2	Soul: 6 heading towards 2	Personality: 4-3
Mental: 7-5	Astral: 6-2	Physical: 3-7

Monad and Soul

His Monad was starting to have an influence. It succeeded in balancing ray 6 by providing him with certain wisdom. Towards the end of his life, his Soul overshadowed him almost continuously. He was in close relationship with the saints of the Ray 6 Ashram, as well as with Jesus, whom he loved more than anything else. Ray 6 guided him in his monastic and human lives. Devoted and obliging but sometimes quick-tempered, he forgave easily if he saw sincerity in the other party. His "odor of sanctity" came from the constant influence of his Soul in his life.

Personality

His Personality, wanting to be more and more at the service of his Soul, reflected more the influence of ray 6 than that of the rays of his Personality. However, we should not neglect the personal aspect of his rays that influenced him a lot during the first decades of his life.

The influence of ray 4 sub-ray 3 allowed him to have courage, in spite of his trials, and to carry on. Ray 4 inspired him with the will to live despite the fears that tormented him because the attacks he suffered often terrified him. No one could logically explain to him this phenomenon that produced in him a terror necessary to his evolution. It encouraged him to remain on the right track, demanding from him a saintly humility. At the beginning of his life he had a sad expression, which he was able to correct as he aged. Having become stronger and more balanced, he would emit, at an advanced age, a powerful energy of compassion and kindness that would erase any aspect of sadness.

Sub-ray 3 kept him balanced when ray 4 became too shaky. It endowed him with a certain sense of humor, thus ensuring he would not take himself too seriously. As he lived a very serious monastic life, he would rarely let the humorous influence of ray 3 show through.

Mental Body

Endowed with a very rational mental body, thanks to the influence of ray 7, sub-ray 5, he succeeded in remaining balanced in spite of all the phenomena that occurred in his life. Ray 7 fostered his ritualistic aspect and gave him certain mental guidelines necessary to the maintenance of his psychic balance. Without the influence of this ray, he would have probably ended his life in a mental institution.

Sub-ray 5 served as an important base for his daily life. It allowed him to enter into a relationship with elementals and to reduce his food intake. This ray conferred to him a strength that sustained him in the most difficult moments. He knew that he was not mad and always felt a beneficial presence near him protecting and helping him in his life's mission.

Astral Body

His astral body, influenced by ray 6, sub-ray 2, acted in such a way that he revealed himself to be an understanding and, at times, warm monk. However, the influence of ray 6 sometimes made him quick-tempered and very rigid on certain points. This ray linked him tightly to Catholicism and prevented him from having a larger vision of the problems of his devotees. He believed in God, in his religion, and would have wished that everyone would be the same. However, if it proved necessary, he would retire and reflect, in order to correct his vision. He knew he was imperfect and cultivated these imperfections daily in order not to forget who he was: a human among many others.

His sub-ray 2 made him suffer a lot because he displayed great sensitivity towards everything. The influence of this sub-ray allowed him to feel Jesus' suffering and that of his brothers and of humanity. It also gratified him with a certain wisdom in order to balance the influence of ray 6 when it became too "fanatic".

Physical Body

Ray 3, sub-ray 7 equipped his physical with strong resistance, in spite of his physical weaknesses, his deprivations, his attacks from the astral plane and the galvanizing surges of *kundalini*. Ray 3 granted him an inner strength such that he demonstrated a great capacity of adaptation to his stigmatas, to various manifestations and an ease of expressing himself in other languages.

Ray 7 also eased his resistance from the physical viewpoint. It ensured him a stability in this world where everything seemed unbalanced. Ritualistic, thanks to this ray, he could hold onto small details of his monastic life in order to remain anchored here on this Earth. The influence of this ray contributed to the preservation of his physical body after his death.

Padre Pio was a saint full of wisdom, compassion and humility. His next incarnation will take place soon, in a country near China, where he will live a difficult life in order to reach his fourth initiation. He will again be a monk.

April 30, 2010

 # PAUL OF TARSUS

Given Name: Paul of Tarsus
Other Names: Saul or Saint Paul for Christians
Nationality: Roman
Place and Date of Birth: Tarsus, Cilicia (presently Turkey), 10
Place and Date of Death: Rome, Latium (Italy), 65
Profession: Disciple of Jesus Christ

MASTER DJWHAL KHUL'S COMMENTARY

Paul of Tarsus was an intelligent and educated man for the times. The great faith he acquired following his conversion to Christianity never left him. It is true that Jesus appeared to him several times, because Paul had an important mission aimed at solidifying the foundations of this new religion. His writings had an important effect and allowed several Souls to go through the long progression towards their first and their second initiations under the aegis of the Ashram of Ray 6, of which Paul was part for quite a long time. Now Cohan of the third Ray, he serves the Hierarchy with love and devotion.

Initiation Level: 3.2 (As Paul of Tarsus)

Paul of Tarsus was the counterpart of Mary Magdalene, who he met only once. The great beings of these times crossed each other, but rarely shared a similar destiny in a common life, their mission constantly sending them where their work had to be accomplished. In other words, the great Initiates rarely lived together because the time they would have lost traveling would have been immeasurable. The future will increasingly bear witness to great Initiates living together because they will be able to work in sometimes different spheres of activity while still being partners.

Ray Structure

Monad: 2	Soul: 6	Personality: 3-4
Mental: 7-5	Astral: 6-2	Physical: 3-6

Monad and Soul

His Monad had a certain influence, while it was mainly his ray 6 Soul that guided his life. Following this incarnation, he joined the Ray 3 Ashram and worked with the Master of this Ashram until he relieved him.

His ray 6 Soul conferred to him an unshakeable faith. He could easily convert the people who came to him. He trusted God and Jesus, whom he called "the Christ".

Personality

His ray 3, sub-ray 4 Personality endowed him with a lot of magnetism. He was a fluent speaker and knew how to adequately use words to convince his public of the validity of his statements. He played with words and interpreted Christ's words to make his teaching more accessible.

His sub-ray 4 equipped him with an iron will because it allowed him to overcome his fears and to defy those who opposed him. He never ran away from danger but he knew how to be cautious when necessary. This sub-ray granted him a way of expressing himself gallantly, or if you prefer, colorfully with abundant expressions, which pleased the people who came to listen to him. He was not dull and knew how to make his public laugh.

Mental Body

His ray 7, sub-ray 5 mental body made him intelligent, brilliant and learned in many fields. Ray 7 communicated to him a certain perfection in his verbal expression. This ray, as well as his initiation level, granted him the knowledge to see beyond appearances.

Sub-ray 5 instilled in him the taste of always wanting to know and think more. He was seen isolating himself for long hours to meditate on topics close to his heart, such as loving thy neighbors, equality of the sexes and of the races.

Astral Body

His ray 6, sub-ray 2 astral body made him a kind and warm man, welcoming and reserved. His ray 6 gratified him with a strong character, and he knew how to forgive with sincerity. He loved people and was not shy to express it. His voice carried far (the combination of his Astral strength and his physical body, which was quite imposing) and he spoke loudly.

His sub-ray 2 granted him good intuition that he used properly. He could easily understand other people's suffering and say words to console and ease their pain and sorrow.

Physical Body

His ray 3, sub-ray 6 physical body invested him with strength and a great resistance. This body offered him the possibility of traveling without experiencing extreme fatigue. Ray 3 equipped him with an intelligent brain; he also knew how to express himself without hurting others because this ray was at the service of his Soul, which expressed love and devotion.

Sub-ray 6 equipped him with a robust body and a flawless determination. Nothing could stop him, except the suffering of others.

Paul of Tarsus was an exceptional man. His words were equally exceptional because they still inspire and will continue to do so for a long time.

April 24, 2009

 PENOR RINPOCHE

Given Name: Kyabjé Drubwang Pema Norbu Rinpoche
Nationality: Tibetan
Place and Date of Birth: Powo of Kham region (Tibet), 1932
Profession: 11th holder of the throne of the Palyul lineage, of the Nyingmapa school of Tibetan Buddhism

MASTER DJWHAL KHUL'S COMMENTARY

Penor Rinpoche's reputation reached me, and I am conscious of its "theatrical" aspect, as he likes to impress and please. He also believes he is charged with a mission: conquer the world via Buddhism, which he considers the most sacred and the best path on Earth. This is a good man, but he does not yet possess the knowledge required for his awakening. He thinks he can awaken others because he thinks he is awake. He believes himself to be the reincarnation of Vimilamitra, which is false. However, he is the reincarnation of a famous monk named Dzogchen Rinpoche, who lived until the year 1870 of our era.

In this present incarnation, he unfortunately suffers from the mirage of his popularity and the prestige it brings. He knows that his title fascinates and that he can thus receive a lot of recognition. He is a kind man who lacks wisdom and practice within what we call the "Straight line of the Just Middle Way". He can help a lot but he can also delay people's evolution by creating the false illusion of an "evolved" evolution. The majority of those he recognized are not *tulkus*, at least not well-known *tulkus*. We are all *tulkus* to an extent, because we have all lived past lives, as well as interesting and enriching lives. We can find *tulkus* everywhere and they come from different environments and religions. I will discuss this topic in another text.

Initiation Level: 2.8

His initiation level is reasonable. He should have already reached his third initiation, which will take place in his next incarnation.

Ray Structure

Monad: 2	Soul: 1	Personality: 3-7
Mental: 7-5	Astral: 6-2	Physical: 6-3

Monad and Soul

His Monad has little influence on him; on the other hand, his Soul attempts to inspire him, which reveals itself to be difficult because his present Personality is very resistant. However, ray 1 confers to him an iron will and a character sometimes difficult to grasp (and sometimes explosive).

Personality

His ray 3, sub-ray 7 Personality renders him magnetic and funny. He likes to talk, to educate and manage. His ray 3 provides him with versatility and prepares him for almost anything in order to obtain what he believes to be right for himself and his community, which he considers the extension of himself. He is very intelligent and a manipulator.

Sub-ray 7 makes him narrow-minded and a perfectionist at times. He usually gets what he wants. A good storyteller, he can prove to be very persuasive. Having a narrow vision, which he believes to be the best, he likes to guide others and uses all the means he can to do so.

Mental Body

His ray 7, sub-ray 5 mental body increases his intelligence and his magnetism. Brilliant, he knows how to "shine" and dazzle through the art of divine manipulation, which he knows very well. I repeat, he acts this way for everyone's good because he really believes himself to be a savior that can awaken sleeping minds.

His sub-ray 5 makes him more brilliant and allows him to resort to arguments, during discussions that knock out his opponents. He is a charmer and this sub-ray makes him more attractive, because he can explain the most complicated things with humor and wisdom. This sub-ray proves to be a precious help for the understanding of complicated Buddhist texts, because he can understand and dissect almost everything that occurs as a "challenge".

Astral Body

His ray 6, sub-ray 2 astral body grants him charm and warmth. A jovial fellow, he can become blunt and harsh when he is unsatisfied. Proud and faithful to his cause, he also likes people to be faithful to him; he forgives with difficulty but will do it if it serves his cause. Ray 6 loves righteousness when it is convenient but can also deviate from it if it can help the cause.

Sub-ray 2 endows him with sensitivity and empathy towards others. He knows how to listen (with one ear) and provide warmth in return. He does not like to be hurt and would run away from wounds and conflicts, if he could. However, if he has to solve a dispute, rays 1 and 6 will support him and help him in this battle. If he wishes he can be merciless; fortunately, he rarely wishes it.

Physical Body

His ray 6, sub-ray 3 physical body grants him robustness and strength. He can work long hours without tiring. His two ray 6's on the first line make him dedicated, reliable and warm towards his cause (Buddhist). He is not at ease with other religions that he does not consider to be equal to his.

His sub-ray 3 confers to him intelligence, liveliness and adaptability to various situations. He has a sense of humor that honors him and can make an audience laugh or cry at will. A good speaker, he can bring passion back to a tired crowd.

We wish him to reincarnate rapidly after his death that will occur sooner than he thinks. He has a lot of work to accomplish within himself and we hope he will do it with awareness and dedication.

October 3, 2008

 # PRAAGH, JAMES VAN

Given Name: James Van Praagh
Nationality: American
Place and Date of Birth: Bayside, New York (United States), August 23, 1958
Profession: Medium and author

MASTER DJWHAL KHUL'S COMMENTARY

James Van Praagh is an intelligent, sincere and dedicated man. He likes people and likes to help them and give them hope. He is a priest in his Soul, a role[1] he likes to play impeccably. However, this dedication is wearing down his body, which is experiencing certain difficulties: lack of sleep, kidney complications causing high blood pressure. He should be careful, because his feelings of discomfort may get worse in the years to come.

He possesses a precious gift of clairvoyance that he uses intelligently. However, this clairvoyance includes certain gaps we will pass over in silence because his work is more beneficial than harmful. He attempts to open people's consciousness to the existence of other dimensions, which he succeeds in doing fairly well. At the same time, to his dismay, the effect lacks depth. He would like to change people in a more significant way, but people are the authors of their own transformation and there is nothing he can do about it. Although he exercises, through his Soul's role, the mandate of teaching and educating, which he does at his best, he has not yet attained the status of Master.

---

[1] "The priest's objective is to preach. His essence is compassion, an inborn compassion for others that expresses itself through service".

Excerpt from: *Les Discours de Michael sur le Tao du Savoir Vivre selon la typologie de Chelsea Quinn Yarbro et développés par D.D.D.*, The Group of 7, Paume de Saint-Germain Publishing, Montréal, 2011, 329 p.

Initiation Level: 2.2

He will reach the level of 2.3 soon, his self-denial forcing him to grow almost despite himself.

He sustained important losses in his life, losses that helped him grow and understand many things. He is suffering from a certain arrogance, of which he is conscious and that he masters fairly well. However, he gives too much without discernment, which is somewhat harmful to his evolution. Slightly afflicted with the savior complex, he wants to save others before saving himself, which is commendable; however, he must also understand that no one can save others against their will. It is a tough lesson he will learn shortly. We think he will take the vow of *Bodhisattva* in his next incarnation.

Ray Structure

Monad: 2	Soul: 3	Personality: 2-6
Mental: 3-7	Astral: 6-2	Physical: 3-6

His clairvoyance comes from his initiation level, but also from his ray 2's that jointly with his ray 6's create an opening at the level of consciousness and of the third eye. Ray 2 desires to give in an altruistic way and ray 6 to dedicate itself in the same way, which creates, when sincerity is present, clairvoyance, a tool that will serve to the benefit of others.

His heart is open, but still young in the expression of a true love for humanity. He has a lot of illusions about love, illusions presently necessary but which he will get rid of when he reaches his third initiation.

Monad and Soul

His Monad has no real influence yet, which is the opposite for his Soul that guides him increasingly. It should help him get rid of certain illusions — such as, "knowing better than others" (ray 3) — and to become a Master in the art of teaching and balancing people (and their environment).

Personality

His ray 2, sub-ray 6 Personality makes him sensitive and creates the mirage of the savior – a mirage enhanced because of the second initiation. He gives a lot and deeply understands others' suffering. He had to create a certain protection over the passing years, protection that was efficient most of the time but sometimes let some (intruding) feelings that do not belong to him penetrate and temporarily blur his aura and vision.

His ray 2, sub-ray 6 allows him to "see" and to efficiently "feel"; we cannot dissociate them because they rely on each other. Ray 2 feels in a certain way and sub-ray 6, which combines with this "feeling," acts in such a way that he can grasp others in their globality and fairly correctly interpret what he feels and sees. This is what creates in him this visceral need to help and guide in the most efficient way. His Personality and his Astral are very strong; we witness there the same conjugation, though reversed. Why this focus? Because his mandate is to help, mainly at the levels of the Personality and the Astral.

Mental Body

His ray 3, sub-ray 7 mental body allows him to see the person from every angle, or almost, and do a rapid analysis. Ray 3 looks at all the facets, analyzes, and sub-ray 7 organizes. Ray 3 provides speed and sub-ray 7, precision. Ray 3 allows him to see "broadly" and sub-ray 7, to underline priorities. Ray 3 confers to him an interesting intelligence refined by sub-ray 7. Ray 3 makes him act and sub-ray 7 makes him work industriously right to the smallest of details, if necessary.

As we noticed, this man cannot be dissected easily; he proves to be a perfect mix of rays that marvelously complete each other in him. This is a precious gift that he has received and that he uses advantageously, which allows him to be efficient and precise most of the time. We may also add that some invisible helpers, that we may qualify as angels assist him. Why? Because he accomplishes a lot and this support is necessary for him not to flounder. As long as he will remain altruistic, these collaborators will be present because his help is directed towards others and not towards himself.

Astral Body

His ray 6, sub-ray 2 astral body bestows dedication and attention upon him. He can tune in to people and transmit to them the feeling that he understands them and can really help them. He represents for them hope and he knows how to cultivate it. Ray 6 makes him nice, pleasant though stubborn, and sometimes difficult to live with, particularly when the fatigue of having given without restraint takes too much from him. He corrects himself quickly but can have fits of anger fit for a lion.

His sub-ray 2 increases his sensitivity and offers him the possibility of sincerely loving those around him. He gives over and above and this sub-ray makes him a good teacher. He loves people to understand and can easily put himself in their shoes to comprehend their problems.

Physical Body

His ray 3, sub-ray 6 physical body equips him with good resistance. He can achieve a lot without tiring. His rays qualify his thoughts; ray 3 makes him intelligent, quick to reply and sub-ray 6, makes him dedicated to the maximum. He wants to help, save the world, although sometimes he feels ridiculed by people who do not believe him. Ray 3 helps him find an exit, allowing him not to be too influenced by the pronouncements of the people who doubt. He can forget or set aside hurtful words in order to pursue his work.

Sub-ray 6 provides him with his stubbornness, as well as with strong physical resistance. It gives him a sense of humor (paired with ray 3) that helps him not take himself too seriously and control his arrogance fairly well. This sub-ray allows him to put people at ease; he can be a great listener and immensely warm.

This is a man who loves humanity and who tries to demystify the invisible so that it has less control over people. To ignore the invisible world makes us slaves of this world.

November 28, 2008

 PRESLEY, ELVIS

Given Name: Elvis Aaron Presley
Nickname: *The King*
Nationality: American
Place and Date of Birth: Tupelo, Mississippi (United States), January 8, 1935
Place and Date of Death: Memphis, Tennessee (United States), August 6, 1977
Profession: Singer and Actor

MASTER DJWHAL KHUL'S COMMENTARY

A very talented man, Elvis Presley incarnated to allow the "decrystallization" of certain obsolete thought forms. Without his contribution, which was supported by divine forces, the average American would still be under the control of much closed concepts related to the affective and artistic life. He allowed them, so to speak, to get closer to their feelings and their sexuality. He was able to inspire certain dynamism and a certain glamour that proved necessary to the possible emergence of changes.

He represented the perfect medium for the arts. Having had several lives as a musician, he knew how to contact the inner music for it to touch the body of human feelings. He was the reincarnation of Puccini and had kept his tormented character, as well as the "hot blooded" characteristics Italians are recognized for, from that life.

He loved women, all women, and they reciprocated the feeling. We can say that his attachment to "mama" came from his past lives in Italy; he had lived several, although the most famous remains the one as Puccini.

As Elvis Presley, he experienced much solitude and fear, the worst of which was the fear of dying. He would have wished to be immortal, to remain young and handsome all his life. The excesses committed in everything in order to forget his torments, led him to leave this world earlier than planned. He could have lived ten more years but his worn out physical vehicle could not hold out.

Initiation Level: 1.7

The fervor of someone getting closer to the second initiation, as well as a subtle arrogance that sometimes blinds, was necessary to him. Having difficulty mastering his emotional body, he tried to polarize his mental body, without real success. Only his music provided him with a semblance of comfort.

He did not evolve much in the present incarnation because he had to work to broaden the consciousness of the masses by sacrificing part of his evolution. If this had not been the case, he would have diverted too soon from his music and would not have entirely produced the desired effect he had and continues to have. People whose emotional body needs comfort and change still vibrate because of his music.

Ray Structure

Monad: 2	Soul: 4	Personality: 4-3
Mental: 6-2	Astral: 2-6	Physical: 7-4

Monad and Soul

His Monad had no influence on him, contrary to his Soul, which was starting to have a significant influence, which pushed him to question his work and his music. He wished to go deeper, to think, but life wanted him to remain a vehicle of love, energy and beauty, which he thought he lacked. He felt divided in two: the Elvis who brought joy and happiness and who seduced in order to create passing moments of rapture, and the Elvis who, in his personal life, felt powerless and useless. He felt misunderstood and experienced difficulty understanding himself. A guide who could have helped him understand himself better, but mainly help him better grasp his life's objective, would have been beneficial.

Personality

His ray 4, sub-ray 3 Personality did not simplify the task. Indeed, this ray configuration rendered him very creative and magnetic but conveyed a sense of despondency that he tried to forget with alcohol, drugs and women. His feeling of powerlessness, as well as his fear of death, increased as he grew older. He feared punishment, dying alone and poor, suffering, not being recognized, a nobody, which made him impatient, quick-tempered and at odds with himself. He had everything, although he felt alone in this world. Who really loved him? He was adulated for his music, but who really knew the man behind the music? He would have wished to be loved for what he was and not for the image projected.

Very magnetic, engaging and a charmer, he knew how to captivate the public and lead them to a universe where only his music existed. In his presence and by listening to his songs, people forgot their everyday lives and sometimes forgot themselves. This effect was produced in part from the energy injected by the Masters and the skillful blend of his rays. He was endowed with several ray 4's; his sub-ray 3 supported his ray 4 Personality marvelously and the total of his rays equaled 7, which allowed him to maintain beauty in the creation of his shows. The magic was not so obvious in his films, because he was directed by directors who did not at any time respect this configuration. This frustrated him because a part of him felt the lack of respect.

Sub-ray 3 presented him with an ease of speech that ray 4 did not allow. He expressed himself well in songs but often had difficulty to do so in his private life. His mother understood him and supported him; he developed an attachment for her, one that was intensified by his mental and astral ray configuration. In a way, he always believed that she was the only one to truly love him for what he really was.

Mental Body

His ray 6, sub-ray 2 mental body contributed to the fact that he attached himself rapidly but would detach himself just as rapidly when he did not feel loved. Ray 6 emphasized this attachment, which made him harsh sometimes when he knew he was betrayed and hurt; this ray was partially responsible for his attachment to "mama". He needed to be taken care of, to be understood and to be given time. The arrival of a child provoked in him a difficulty in adapting to the role of mother his wife played, now taken up by the newborn who would claim all her attention. He felt abandoned and found it difficult to live with this feeling.

He loved his wife and his daughter tremendously, but following this rejection he erected a wall of protection around himself that he was unable to remove later. He isolated himself more, which resulted in stimulating his writing. Focused on his discomfort and on several subsequent deceptions in love, he translated his feelings into music and touched the masses of people who experienced similar pain.

His warmth came from his ray 6's that expressed themselves in his whole being. His sub-ray 2 mental body increased his intuition and facilitated the writing of his songs. He was "literally connected," thanks to this sub-ray that conferred to him much sweetness and sympathy for people; the latter had the impression that he was singing exclusively for them.

Astral Body

His ray 2, sub-ray 6 astral body gave him the possibility to understand other people's pain, their suffering, but also increased his own sensitivity. Very touchy when faced with the slightest criticism, he had difficulty accepting being told that he was not perfect. He felt like a "King" and enjoyed floating above the people in his kingdom.

As mentioned earlier, he suffered tremendously and felt misunderstood. Ray 2 made him feel what was wrong around him. It would prove difficult to lie to him, because he "perceived" what was wrong. He could give everything, but his sub-ray 6 astral body pushed him to demand a lot in return. Generous with those he believed in need, he would prove to be rough with those who betrayed him or abused him.

Physical Body

His ray 7, sub-ray 4 physical body granted him good looks, but also discipline; he was very disciplined. Ray 7 gave him a sense of rhythm that was avant-garde for the times and this unique way of moving. Sub-ray 4 provided the flexibility and the elegance to which those looking at him reacted. He shook off American puritanism and allowed youth to get rid of a certain self-consciousness of their bodies. He gave back a note of nobility to the physical body and prepared the way for the emergence of ray 7.

Sub-ray 4 also refined the effect of ray 7, granted it an angelic flavor that was only beneficial. This sub-ray finally made him gain weight; the "weight" of his emotion becoming too heavy, the physical body literally absorbed this surplus. Some of his glands, unbalanced, caused a bodily change whose effects he detested. He could have preserved his physical beauty all his life if he had been able to manage his emotional life.

He is presently on stand-by to reincarnate, which should take place very shortly.

July 15, 2008

PROPHET, ELIZABETH CLARE

Given Name: Elizabeth Clare Wulf
Nationality: American
Place and Date of Birth: Red Bank, New Jersey (United States), April 8, 1939
Place and Date of Death: (information not available), October 15, 2009
Profession: Writer, speaker and leader of a religious movement called *The Summit Lighthouse®*

MASTER DJWHAL KHUL'S COMMENTARY

Elizabeth Clare Prophet has accomplished a lot by making certain information concerning the Masters accessible. She worked to make them known without realizing that she was communicating with an astral reflection of these Masters. Because she demonstrated sincerity in her work, the average citizen came to realize that authentic Masters existed and still exist. Regarding her teaching, we can affirm that 20% of her work is truthful, the rest being emanations of the astral potential of the Masters. We do not want to discredit this woman, but simply reestablish the facts. Not being very evolved, she accomplished a lot with a love for humanity that seemed sincere most of the time.

Initiation Level: 1.5

Ray Structure

Monad: 2	Soul: 2	Personality: 4-3
Mental: 1-5	Astral: 6-2	Physical: 3-7

Monad and Soul

Her Monad had no influence, contrary to her Soul, which began a better one. This Soul will still act as a medium in her next incarnation, a medium of a higher quality. The Masters will be closer to her without really providing training, because before reaching the fourth initiation, few mediums are liable to accomplish good work. Her ray 2 Soul endowed her with sensitivity, allowing her to become a good channel for information coming from the astral plane.

Personality

Her ray 4, sub-ray 3 Personality allowed her to be versatile and to write profusely. This was to the detriment of her family life; although she was a loving mother, she did not prove to be an excellent mother because she was too busy writing her books, too preoccupied by her projects and by herself. Ray 4 prevented her from being truly balanced. During her whole life she was afflicted by ups and downs that were harmful to both her family life and her work.

Sub-ray 3 allowed her to perform a lot of work; in her "ups", she was indefatigable. This sub-ray also gave her charisma that added to the magnetism of ray 4.

Mental Body

Her ray 1, sub-ray 5 mental body allowed her to efficiently write the information she received. Ray 1 provided strong concentration and sub-ray 5, the strength to move down to the physical plane the information she received from the astral plane. We repeat, the information she was gathering came from a reflection of the Masters of Wisdom on the astral plane, not going beyond the fifth level, except on rare occasions, where they were emanating from the seventh astral plane.

Astral Body

Her ray 6, sub-ray 2 astral body rendered her a conformist, sometimes narrow-minded. She directed certain aspects of her personal life with an iron fist, and since her Ashram was meant to be an integral part of her intimacy, she would often be quite hard. She loved with little discernment and got carried away at times for projects without real meaning. Ray 6 also created fears that were amplified by her ray 4 Personality.

Her sub-ray 2 made her fragile and easily hurt. She was an arrogant woman and an opportunist who could not bear betrayal and felt personally touched by remarks. However, she also had a love (colored by ray 6) for humanity and a desire to help others, because the mirages of ray 2 (saving the world) were continuously hovering in her life.

Physical Body

Her ray 3, sub-ray 7 physical body, at times helped her control her mental illness, as she had lapses that were far from spiritual. These lapses came from a past life where she had enormously abused drugs, including opium. Ray 3 gave her a mind that offered her the possibility of escaping conventions, which simply means that it allowed her to justify her "lapses" in a more or less rational way. This ray made the use of diplomacy easy in several occasions (except if her ray 6 astral body entered in reaction).

Sub-ray 7 gave her the taste for the beautiful and the luxurious. It also helped her find perfection and discipline in her writing.

This woman loved beauty and was endowed with an interesting ambition. We can affirm that her association with Mark Prophet was not a love association, but one of ambition. Admittedly, she learned how to love him, but she mainly loved his power.

July 31, 2009

 PROPHET, MARK L.

Given Name: Marc L. Prophet
Nationality: American
Place and Date of Birth: Chippewa Falls, Wisconsin (United States), December 24, 1918
Place and Date of Death: Colorado Springs, Colorado (United States), February 26, 1973
Profession: Founder of the religious movement called *The Summit Lighthouse®*

MASTER DJWHAL KHUL'S COMMENTARY

Mark Prophet, like his wife, allowed the whole world to know of the existence of the Masters. However, we must mention that he was less evolved than his wife was and that the majority of his writing was fictitious. His source of inspiration came from the lower astral and did not go beyond the third level. He therefore knew how to enter into communication with almost perfect astral reflections of the Masters.

He is not a Master and will not be one for several incarnations. He is carrying the responsibility of a heavy karma, because the abuses perpetrated within his group stem from his energy. When he created the group, he inspired it with an astral energy that polluted part of the mission of this movement. By encouraging his wife to assist him and by deliberately leaving her his succession, he committed an error he will have to pay for during his next incarnations. The founding principles of this movement was acceptable but the personal abuses that were perpetrated impose individual restitution towards the people affected. The ease with which his wife entered into communication with the Masters made him aware that she was more evolved than he. Unfortunately, he failed to direct her correctly. Sometimes, a being who is less evolved has to place beacons so that the more evolved adequately prepares itself to guide.

Initiation Level: 1.4

Although a single tenth of a decimal separated Mark Prophet's Initiation level from that of his wife, let us not forget that this tenth made all the difference. Numerous lives are often necessary to reach a new decimal.

Ray Structure

Monad: 2	Soul: 2	Personality: 3-6
Mental: 7-2	Astral: 6-4	Physical: 1-7

Monad and Soul

His Monad had no influence on him. Although still minimal, his Soul started to have one.

Personality

His ray 3, sub-ray 6 Personality made him a versatile man, who could adapt to several situations. He spoke well and was endowed with a certain magnetism. His ray 3 granted him credibility, and his intelligence (a mix of ray 7 mental body and ray 1 brain) exuded through this warm Personality, in spite of his ray 1 physical body configuration. His ray 3 transmitted warmth that radiated from sub-ray 6.

His sub-ray 6 made him a charming and affectionate man. However, the combination of his ray 6's (Personality and Astral) made him vulnerable towards his wife, with whom he was utterly in love. He was faithful to her and gave her his total trust. This sub-ray made him sometimes harsh when he felt hurt or betrayed. A ray 6 does not forgive easily and this was the case with him.

Mental Body

His ray 7, sub-ray 2 mental body allowed him to become an instrument capable of astrally channeling certain projections of the Masters. Ray 7 provided fairly good concentration and mental discipline necessary for the accomplishment of his work.

His sub-ray 2 literally endowed him with astral antennae. He could capture information and transmit it via his ray 1 physical brain, which granted him good concentration, thus supporting his ray 7 mental body, active only to a third of its capacity. This sub-ray activated his clairvoyance and granted him credibility.

Astral Body

His ray 6, sub-ray 4 astral body allowed him to be a warm man who inspired trust. Ray 6 created an atmosphere of trust and endowed him with the air of a "benevolent father". He seemed to be listening to all.

His sub-ray 4 created difficulties. He sometimes showed signs of depression provoked by strong vacillations from this sub-ray. He experienced ups and downs that he hid fairly well. This sub-ray also provided him with a sensitivity that was useful during his conferences and his channelings.

Physical Body

His ray 1, sub-ray 7 physical body graced him with significant strength. Ray 1 endowed him with an efficient brain; he could concentrate the time necessary for a channeling. However, this ray resulted in impatience and harshness towards those who were unable to understand him or assist him efficiently. He often lacked finesse because this ray confers a certain clumsiness when it is present in the physical body.

Sub-ray 7 softened ray 1, while giving it a sense of perfection, which sometimes accentuated the effect of ray 1. He liked beauty and to feel invulnerable; however, he feared death and sickness. He appreciated discipline, which his wife strongly encouraged, because through discipline reigned a semblance of harmony.

August 1, 2009

RACHMANINOV, SERGUEÏ

Given Name: Sergueï Vassilievitch Rachmaninov
Nationality: Russia
Place and Date of Birth: Oneg (Russia), April 1 or 2, 1873
Place and Date of Death: Beverly Hills, California (United States),
March 28, 1943
Profession: Composer, pianist and conductor

MASTER DJWHAL KHUL'S COMMENTARY

This man was a great genius, tormented because of music and not by music, although it was indeed the source of his life. He lived for music and experienced a great discomfort when he was unable to compose. His torment came from the fact that he was not always able to express what he desired. His ray configuration also passed onto him mixed feelings: their effect produced an impact he could not master all the time. We would know the cause shortly.

A sensitive and gifted man, he was able to transmit the divine gift of divine harmony through his music; he also expressed man's torment regarding his divinity, which was incomprehensible and unattainable in his eyes. He would experience uncontrollable fears, among which were those of death and the people of the invisible realms.

He loved his family considerably and dedicated all his music to them. Without his family, he would have lived part of his life in the psychiatric institutions of the times. His family balanced him and was his reason for living and composing.

Initiation Level: 2.8

Sufficiently evolved to compose magnificent work, it was not enough to compose adequately with the effect his rays produced on him, his weakness being the lack of mental polarization. Through his incarnations, he had developed a surprising mastery of his physical and emotional bodies, however without succeeding to develop a significant link with his mental body, which often ensures a balance between the higher (the higher subtle bodies, Mental and Soul) and the lower (the lower material bodies, Physical and Astral, because contrary to popular belief, the Astral has a very dense body). As to Personality, it makes the junction between the higher and the lower, of which it sometimes becomes the victim when the latter pulls too strongly.

Ray Structure

Monad: 2	Soul: 2	Personality: 7-3
Mental: 7-5	Astral: 6-4	Physical: 7-4

Monad and Soul

In spite of his initiation level, his astral and physical bodies were predominant while the Soul's effect emphasized his sensitivity. In other words, being very sensitive, his ray 6, sub-ray 4 Astral weakened him if he lost his self-confidence and his capacity to reproduce the music he heard within himself. His ray 6 made him warm with his family and friends, and his sub-ray 4 granted him the capacity to compose his music. However, when he lacked inspiration, this sub-ray produced a depression and took away all motivation for life and for expressing music's truth within the world of matter.

He was also endowed with a sub-ray 4 physical body that qualified his physical brain. When he was unable to reach the perfection demanded by ray 7, and sub-ray 4 took more place, he would become depressed again and would become passive.

Had he had a higher mental polarization, his ray 7, sub-ray 5 mental body would have balanced the effect of his sub-ray 4's. He would then not have been subjected to these intense moments of depression.

Personality

His ray 7, sub-ray 3 Personality incited him to seek perfection. His great sensitivity came from his Soul ray, which made him sensitive to criticism. He was targeting perfection and displayed an apparently cold nature, which was far from the case. Ray 7 produced in him the push that was necessary for him to work relentlessly on his music. It gratified him with a grace that translated (with the help of his ray 7 physical body) very well into his gestures, particularly as a conductor.

His sub-ray 3 granted him a certain flexibility that people sometimes mixed up with too great a sensitivity. He disliked suffering, which he feared. This sub-ray endowed him with prudence concerning certain topics he did not want to address.

Mental Body

His ray 7, sub-ray 5 mental body made him a perfectionist and helped him in the writing of his music. However, it did not produce the desired effect on his Personality, a fact he will correct in his next incarnation. Ray 7 offered him the possibility of working long hours, often until exhaustion.

Sub-ray 5 provided him with the capacity to write music and to transmit the notes he was hearing in his head to the material world; he received the music via his mental, which produced an effect on his emotional and physical bodies that had to transmit this music. Because of his lack of mastery of the mental body, he would somehow become a victim of the music because the strong thrust of energy coming from the mental body relentlessly affected his two other bodies.

Astral Body

His ray 6, sub-ray 4 astral body qualified his life. Kind and charitable towards his entourage, he would display jealously and possessiveness in his private life. He resented being disturbed and detested public outings. However, because he had to earn a living, he would reason with himself and accept giving concerts. This ray 6 created in him a lot of attachment for his close relations, his country, his friends and his music.

Sub-ray 4 granted him the possibility of writing music (because it transmitted in melody what originated from the mental body) and of being a good composer. It provoked downs he had to fight all his life.

Physical Body

His ray 7, sub-ray 4 physical body equipped him with a certain resistance and also gave him the strength of his weakness. Ray 7 gratified him with perfection that sub-ray 4 attempted to translate into music. It provided him with distinction and granted him the respect of others. Meticulous, he disliked being ridiculed. He loved beauty in all its forms.

Sub-ray 4 provided him with this ease to write music and to transmit the beauty that fascinated him so much. He could experience difficult periods where everything had no importance. However, the love of music and of his close relations always brought him back to life.

This Soul is not yet reincarnated, but will soon be. He will have to face certain unresolved fears from his previous incarnations. He will probably still be a musician and will most certainly come from Russia, a country he still cares about very much.

April 24, 2009

RAJNEESH, BHAGWAN SHREE

Given Name: Rajneesh Chandra Mohan Jain
Other Name: Osho
Nationality: Indian
Place and Date of Birth: Jabalpur (India), December 11, 1931
Place and Date of Death: Poona (India), January 19, 1990
Profession: Zen, Sufi and Tantric Master

MASTER DJWHAL KHUL'S COMMENTARY

Rajneesh is a very interesting man who attempted to enlighten humanity through the mental aspect of his being. Very educated, he strived to "educate" the most educated people of the planet by trying to bring them "out" of their concrete mind so that they could discover their real Self that has no link with the concrete mind.

He liked to shock in order to break too rigid mental concepts. Believing in the fluidity of beings and the human Spirit, he knew that man was capable of big things, particularly on the inner planes. He attempted several times to awaken humanity to its greatness, but he was greatly disappointed by the slow evolution of his disciples. For him, a disciple was meant to be saved from his dark aspects and to be accompanied by his Master towards his own mastery.

His great disappointment was in not finding the expected disciples, those who would have had a real desire to change. He gathered devotees who were dedicated but little inclined to truly transform. Losing hope, he lost the taste for life and gave up his exterior power to disciples who took over without really taking into consideration his desires.

Did he abandon his group to its fate? In a way yes, because his suffering from seeing them evolve so little in spite of the efforts he made to help them created in him a wound he will have to heal in his next incarnation. In a way, he failed as an authentic Master, being unable to bring out the best in the majority of his disciples.

Nevertheless, one cannot deny that he inspired them all and that several among them now inspire through their writings and their music. However, few have succeeded in climbing a decimal point in initiation; at the same time, several have recognized their divine Soul and have begun to serve it from their level of initiation, which has changed little.

He would have liked to transmit his succession to someone of confidence, who would have pursued his work, but no one in his entourage had the capacity or required initiation level to take on such a charge. He therefore left this responsibility to all his disciples, who continue to make him known through his numerous books. However, none can claim to be the leader or the Master of the group.

We will mention that he has entrusted the succession of his group, on the other planes, to two living Masters who are monitoring the group via the inner planes. One of them is my beloved disciple, who is taking care of the western aspect of his teaching and the western disciples and the other is a woman, an Indian Master who supervises the Indian aspect of his practice. Both of them are doing remarkable work and the decline of the Osho ashram in India will occur when they cast off their mortal shroud.

Initiation Level: 3.2

Osho is now an accepted disciple within the occult Ashram of ray 3. He was preparing himself in this incarnation to work as an authentic Master, a work he found extremely painful. His enlarged vision allowed him to see everyone's deficiencies and he was desperate to see them change. In fact, he demonstrated impatience.

Ray Structure

Monad: 2   Soul: 3   Personality: 2-6
Mental: 7-5   Astral: 6-4   Physical: 3-7

Monad and Soul

His Monad had little influence, contrary to his Soul, which had a lot. It was part of his mirage to want to save the world through the divine manipulation of the world of thought, a mirage he experienced difficulty getting rid of. For him, well-directed and coordinated thought towards the divine Plan, became a powerful weapon of progression. He manifested a certain spiritual pride that came at the same time from his ray 3 Soul (making him feel superior to others as a "thinker"), but also because of the fact that he was really more evolved than the masses. He will have to correct this situation in his next incarnation. On the other hand, we believe that this contributed to creating in him the illusion of having failed.

Personality

His ray 2, sub-ray 6 Personality made him a loving man who communicated a lot of warmth, however, always in a detached fashion due to his ray 3 Soul, but also due to his ray 7, sub-ray 5 mental body that rendered him at times a bit dry in the way he loved.

His ray 2 endowed him with great sensitivity that disturbed him at times. He could feel others, their embarrassment, their discomfort and tried too often to come to their help. This ray marked him with chronic fatigue that he was never able to get rid of. It created irrational fears in him that he had to fight on several occasions.

He could have found strength from his sub-ray 6, which, too polarized by ray 2, had a tendency to increase the effect of fatigue. The influence of this sub-ray created a solitude that he was never able to come to terms with. It caused, towards the end of his life, a separation between his students and himself when he was overcome by discouragement.

Mental Body

His ray 7, sub-ray 5 mental body allowed him to say and write words that still generate reflection today. Very organized in his mind (ray 7), he sought an answer to everything (sub-ray 5) and attempted to give an answer to everything. He was an idealist (let us not forget that he had two ray 6's, one of which is on the first line). This increased his disappointment when the ideal did not occur.

His ray 7 allowed him to be a remarkable speaker and writer at times, as this ray in the mental body can create a real magician of words. When ray 5 supports such a ray, the mental body sometimes creates a genius of words in ones chosen field. His style is very interesting and can arouse a consciousness that is willing to be awakened. It does not, however, awaken the Consciousness that requires another source of energy than the one coming from the higher mental.

Astral Body

His ray 6, sub-ray 4 astral body made him a man tormented between the search for authentic Love, the one coming from the Soul, and the human weaknesses in which he was wrapped up. He would have loved to be a God rather than a human. He appreciated beauty (his ray 7) and would temporarily become enslaved by it, which shamed him when he became aware of it. He would then cut off all the sources that could increase this attraction. He loved beautiful things; how could he resist all these gifts (Rolls-Royce, jewelry and clothes) that were offered with so much love? He knew his weaknesses, which he often detested and tried to forget, because life presented too many beautiful objects for which desire would crop up (the mix between ray 6 and 4 it created in him a battle and an uncomfortable gnawing).

Physical Body

His ray 3, sub-ray 7 physical, equipped him with brilliant intelligence. His ray 3 conferred to him a subtlety that seduced all who heard him. He could play with words and incite a vibration that would provoke sparks in the consciousness of those listening to him. This ray endowed him with a fairly resistant physical body, although the Personality rays had succeeded in gradually undermining this resistance, to the point of affecting his way of thinking and provoking the discouragement that followed.

His sub-ray 7 lent him a grace that served him all his life. His nervous resistance, which could be great, allowed him to accept a lot of stress on his shoulders unless he decided otherwise.

He died of poisoning because he had had enough of this life, which did not suit him anymore. He knew he was going to die and that was his wish. I will not dwell on this subject because I may risk shocking some of his devotees, who are partially responsible for his premature death.

February 28, 2009

 ROBERTS, JANE

Given Name: Jane Roberts
Nationality: American
Place and Date of Birth: Saratoga Springs, New York (United States), May 8, 1929
Place and Date of Death: Pennsylvania (United States), September 5, 1984
Profession: Author

MASTER DJWHAL KHUL'S COMMENTARY

Jane Roberts revolutionized the esoteric and occult writing of the times. She led the way to writing in cooperation with the parallel worlds around us. Thanks to her, a new dimension opened, allowing us to realize that our Universe is vast and complex.

The Entity Seth exists, and its implication within the world of matter attracted our attention. More highly evolved than our planetary species, the world from which Seth emerges is our probable future and destiny. According to the choices we will make as people of this Nation, that is Earth, we will evolve towards a sphere that will become our temporary landing place between our earthly and celestial evolution.

I had the possibility of visiting his Universe on a few occasions; however, I have to admit that I am not yet ready to access it permanently, because the atomic adjustments require a constant and vigilant effort. When my destiny guides me towards this precise atomic form, so different from ours, I will be ready and happy to accede to it. For the moment, my evolution remains here and I am meticulously accomplishing my task.

Jane Roberts was a reliable channel for Seth, although she remained basically stubborn and difficult to maneuver at times. She invested a certain strength to Seth's transmissions. Her mental body was endowed with the energy of ray 1, energy necessary to the reception of the high vibrations communicated by Seth. One has also to take into consideration that it was painful for Seth to work with her. He had to reduce his vibration frequency in such a way that the cerebral cells of Jane Roberts could, through their etheric extension, capture the waves and the messages he transferred to her. He did not overshadow her but used her body as a communication vehicle. For Jane Roberts, these energy descents demanded a constant effort because they could have rapidly destroyed her. Certain destructive defects such as smoking reduced her longevity; she did not know how to remain grounded and feared sinking into madness.

Initiation Level: 2.2

She was gifted with a mental polarization that proved necessary for her transmission work.

Ray Structure

Monad: 2	Soul: 2	Personality: 3-7
Mental: 1-5	Astral: 6-4	Physical: 3-2

Monad and Soul

Her Monad had no real influence on her, contrary to her Soul, which encouraged Jane's Personality to somewhat move aside in order to allow Seth to really establish a contact with her. When a person's initiation level is lower than 3, it is practically impossible for this person to be overshadowed, to remain perfectly conscious during the transmission of messages or information from more evolved entities. When the initiation level fluctuates between 3 and 4, it is then possible to transmit the received information while remaining more and more conscious, by not being in a "trance" mode but rather in an "overshadowing" mode. In contrast, the person beyond the 4th initiation, will only be able to receive through the overshadowing vibrational mode, and no longer through trance, because he would have acquired the capacity to do so, and will make it a duty to receive the information in an awakened state, which he must keep at all times. Of course, there are exceptions to any rule; let us say that what I have mentioned is in accordance with the norm.

Personality

Her ray 3, sub-ray 7 Personality allowed her to be flexible and available for the work she has accomplished. Ray 3 equipped her with autonomy while offering her the possibility of living an exceptional experience, one that would mark the century to come. This ray inspired in her the taste for experimentation and adventure and wiped out her fear of failure. Supported by her husband, she knew how to go beyond the known world.

Sub-ray 7 anchored her in the physical world. Through its ritualistic aspect, it also allowed her to establish a certain procedure that would activate in her the "trance" aspect. It made her travel from point A to point B in all "safety" and in all "probability", because in this type of work nothing is certain! Therefore, Ray 3 favored and attracted the experience, sub-ray 7 prepared the ground for the experience to take place and ray 1 in the mental body allowed the conjunction of all elements for the merge between Seth and her.

Mental Body

Jane Roberts' mental body configuration allowed her Soul to become allied with Seth's work. Ray 1 facilitated the contact and permitted her cerebral neurons to become potential and efficient receptacles, to gather Seth's intentions to communicate to her certain information. This ray prevented her from scattering and favored a good mental focus.

Sub-ray 5 established precise and efficient bases for the mind not to fall into temporary madness following her contacts with Seth. This sub-ray made Jane Roberts rational and down to earth, too much according to Seth. If she would have let go more and fought certain effects of the trance and of the concepts carried by Seth less, she would have lived happier and much longer. She often felt ill at ease in her body and tried to escape the "boring" aspect of life. However, she appreciated these foundations that kept her prisoner of concepts that prevented her from going beyond the known world. This is the trap of this sub-ray that, while trying to understand, fights the inevitable instead of efficiently becoming allied with it. This sub-ray does not appreciate the unexpected, but greatly prefers what is known, understandable and sound, which Seth rejected light-heartedly.

Astral Body

The influence of ray 6 combined with sub-ray 4 instilled in her the desire to serve while leaving a certain margin to maneuver; she disliked feeling imprisoned. Ray 6 cultivated her dedication to Seth and sub-ray 4 incited independence. She loved her husband but sometimes had difficulty with the notion of faithfulness. In spite of a semblance of shyness, she was a fighter who was not easily impressed.

Sub-ray 4 gave her a taste for the arts and music and enticed her to write and compose. It allowed her to adapt well to Seth and to feel in harmony in his presence. However, this sub-ray also transmitted to her certain faults or weaknesses she was unable to get rid of. Very sensitive, she was not always able to remain balanced during difficult times. Her difficult childhood had partly tarnished her sentimental life, causing her to live in insecurity and making her fragile at times.

Physical Body

Her ray 3, sub-ray 2 physical transmitted to her a shaky vitality. Ray 3 equipped her with a small body and sub-ray 2, made her fragile. She had trouble being in good shape and accessing an abundance of energy. However, this ray provided her with perseverance and a certain endurance; it made her move continuously, because she had difficulty remaining seated and tranquil.

Sub-ray 2 endowed her with a strong fragility that never left her; she did not have any serious illness, but was never in perfect health. This sub-ray also equipped her with a sensitivity that was necessary to capture Seth's energies. Thanks to this sub-ray, which favored contact with Seth, in conjunction with her ray 1 mental body, she could feel him, express him, and give herself up to him. In other words her brain cells could adapt to Seth's energy, allowing her mental body to more efficiently capture the transmitted messages.

Jane Roberts has not reincarnated yet, but it should not take long. A period of rest was necessary. Seth has not yet recontacted us; he is patiently waiting for her return because a precious link was created between them, one that should reunite them again in her next incarnation.

July 3, 2010

 # ROERICH, HELENA

Given Name: Elena Shaposhnikova
Complete Name: Helena Ivanovna Roerich
Double Nationality: Russian and American
Place and Date of Birth: St. Petersburg (Russia), February 13, 1879
Place and Date of Death: Kalimpong (India), October 5, 1955
Profession: Author, philosopher and public figure

MASTER DJWHAL KHUL'S COMMENTARY

A woman of letters, Helena Roerich lived a most interesting life. A disciple of El Morya Khan, she succeeded in transmitting a small part of his teaching. She was a woman of strong character who tried to promote the value of women, who were at the time considered inferior beings. She displayed much eagerness in doing so, an ardor that will have to be better measured in her next incarnation.

Initiation Level: 3.8

She should reach her fifth initiation during her next incarnation, if she is guided. She will manifest a high degree of stubbornness that should correct itself at her fourth initiation.

Ray Structure

Monad: 1	Soul: 2	Personality: 7-4
Mental: 5-3	Astral: 6-2	Physical: 7-3

Monad and Soul

The influence of the Monad will be felt more during her next incarnation. However, one has to note that this influence was already present and had furthermore almost eclipsed her Soul ray influence to allow her to be a good channel for El Morya Khan. It gave her the strength to accomplish her mission without flinching in the face of adversity. She will be endowed with the same drive at the time of her next incarnation, which should occur soon.

Her ray 2 Soul granted her a gentleness that she transmitted without embarrassment to her students. She would reveal herself to be like a caring mother when her students asked it of her. Her ray 2 Soul softened the influence of her ray 1 Monad, which became more apparent towards the end of her life. As a result, she became less feminine, but more of a feminist. She always liked male bodies. However, she will have to select a feminine body again in order to finish what she started in her last incarnation. Her rays will most likely be:

Personality: 3-4   Mental: 7-5   Astral: 2-6   Physical: 3-7

Let us now continue to study the rays of her last life.

Personality

Her ray 7, sub-ray 4 Personality shaped her into someone efficient, tidy and a perfectionist appreciating beauty in everything. Ray 7 granted her the possibility of developing an occult side that enjoyed seeing beyond form. She liked perfection in form and tried to transmit it through her writings. This ray 7 granted her a discipline that never failed her.

Sub-ray 4 instilled in her a taste for adventure. It also allowed her to be an excellent companion for her husband, a renowned artist. She appreciated his paintings and shared with him this "passion" for life.

Mental Body

Her ray 5, sub-ray 3 mental body made her a very intelligent woman who knew what she wanted. Ray 5 conferred this great intelligence that wanted to be down to earth in spite of the occult experiences she was living. Let us even say that the fact that she was heading towards her fourth initiation allowed her to be more spiritual than scientific.

This ray gave her the taste to live far away, in nature, sheltered from the noise of cities. It granted her the great concentration that was necessary for the work she was accomplishing with El Morya Khan.

Her sub-ray 3 made her intelligence more fluid and stronger. The mixture between rays 5 and 3 acted in such a way that it was difficult to fool her. We will also admit her tendency to always wish to have the last word in a conversation. However if she discovered that she was wrong, she would immediately excuse herself and change her idea without embarrassment or holding a grudge.

Astral Body

Her ray 6, sub-ray 2 astral body allowed her to be a woman devoted to her family, her friends, her students and the Masters. She deeply admired her husband whom she believed to be more evolved than she, which was not the case (she eluded him by a few decimals). Her ray 6 made her warm when she would let her emotions surface. She enjoyed being a host and sharing her knowledge while having a good meal. She jealously protected the intimacy that allowed her to write and to be by herself.

Sub-ray 2 provided her with great sensitivity that she controlled fairly well. However she did not truly like to be polarized to her emotional body, which she considered her weak point. The influence of this sub-ray offered her the possibility of understanding others in their daily lives. She could feel their distress, their suffering or their joy. It made her very intuitive, an intuition that served her all her life.

Physical Body

Her ray 7, sub-ray 3 physical granted her the necessary brain to support her in her writing and endowed her with an interesting physical resistance. She was tidy and proud to be so. Talking was easy, thanks to these two sub-ray 3's (mental and physical) that provided her with the art to maneuver between the most difficult to understand concepts.

Helena Roerich will soon reincarnate and will continue her task for women. She will be more feminine while remaining a feminist. Helping the cause of feminism is dear to her and her work will take an international dimension.

August 18, 2007

 ## ROOSEVELT, FRANKLIN D.

Given Name: Franklin Delano Roosevelt
Nationality: American
Place and Date of Birth: Hyde Park, New York (United States),
January 30, 1882
Place and Date of Death: Warm Springs, Georgia (United States),
April 12, 1945
Profession: Statesman

MASTER DJWHAL KHUL'S COMMENTARY

Franklin D. Roosevelt was a good president, calm and pleasant. His presidency was "clean", which means without too many flaws. He led his country to the best of his abilities, discreetly, firmly, without accomplishing big things. Of course, he worked well but he never demonstrated the qualities of a real leader. His strength resided in his calmness and his tenacity, because he would not let himself be easily discouraged.

He was kind-hearted and knew how to listen, although he sometimes lacked the courage and the necessary strength to knock down certain walls. Proud, he respected conventions, and appearances were very important to him. He was quite ambitious, and we can assert that his was a marriage of convenience to ensure a place on the American political stage. He saw far, but not always well...

Initiation Level: 2.8

Ray Structure

Monad: 1	Soul: 2	Personality: 3-7
Mental: 7-3	Astral: 6-4	Physical: 7-2

Monad and Soul

His Monad had very little influence on him except in the last years of his life when he had to engage his country in the Second World War, which he did with great reservations. He was then compelled to use the strength of ray 1 to face the music and to put aside his ray 2 Soul, which was too sensitive at times. In a way, at the end of his life, ray 1 allowed him to acquire more stamina.

His ray 2 Soul made him a charming man, pleasant and sympathetic to human suffering. He loved humanity and wished to serve it well, as well as his country that he fervently defended. He disliked conflicts, which put him ill at ease. He had charisma that often served him. People liked him and appreciated him as President of the United States, because he gave them the impression that he liked them all.

Personality

His ray 3, sub-ray 7 Personality granted him the power of speech to express himself and the intelligence to act. He was an astute manipulator and a good diplomat. Ray 3 allowed him, at times, to lie or to conceal certain truths that could have shocked or hurt. He had several affairs and his ray 3 brushed off all feelings of guilt. His rays 3 and 7 led him to have a marriage of convenience. He loved his wife in his way, although he never felt any passion for her. A good companion and a good mother, she lacked the spark to arouse him. Do not forget that he loved beauty and perfection, which she did not have, at least physically. Too shy, she was overshadowed by his career. A martyr[1], she did not know how to really tame the man that she nevertheless loved a lot.

---

[1] The "martyr" is one of the seven major faults or Personality traits that slow down a person's evolution. The main characteristic of this fault is self pity. For the martyr, everything is suffering, misfortune, drama: he feels like a real victim and acts as such.

Excerpt from: *Les Discours de Michael sur le Tao du Savoir Vivre selon la typologie de Chelsea Quinn Yarbro et développés par D.D.D.*, The Group of 7, Paume de Saint-Germain Publishing, Montreal, 2011, 329 p.

Sub-ray 7 made him proud and arrogant. His illness was quite an ordeal that he was able to overcome with his characteristic stubbornness, produced by his ray 7's and his ray 6 astral body. He always displayed a proud bearing and always took care of himself. He liked to be noticed and have things done well. Sometimes he would adopt a rigid attitude when he became aware of a lack of order, order that he appreciated.

Mental Body

His ray 7, sub-ray 3 mental body increased his arrogance and his stubbornness, sub-ray 3 supporting ray 7 to obtain what he desired. Ray 7 allowed him to think adequately before making a decision. He would not make a gesture lightly. A perfectionist, mainly in his work, he would at times become impatient when he detected faults in certain projects or documents. He would then use cutting and offending remarks — sub-ray 3 allowing him to aim accurately and well.

His sub-ray 3 mental body was very useful to him because it strengthened his ray 3 Personality. Endowed with a keen intelligence, he was never in a hurry to make a decision, preferring to think… and reflect further.

Astral Body

His ray 6, sub-ray 4 astral body instilled in him fervor and devotion to his family and his country. In spite of his infidelities, he remained, in a way, faithful to his wife. Clearly, he did not want to divorce because of social conventions — if he had made such a gesture, he would have never have accessed the presidency — but part of him was married for life and he intended to respect this fact. He was a good spouse but a lousy husband!

His sub-ray 4 made him appreciate the arts and increased his desire for beauty. A socialite, he appreciated outings and good meals. However, this sub-ray 4 invested him with an air of melancholy. Although he loved life, he knew full well that he could have had better and been happier, which did not really happen. He did his duty at all levels — to obtain what he wished, at the expense of his feelings.

Physical Body

His ray 7, sub-ray 2 physical made him weak at times. Sub-ray 7 endowed him with a strong constitution that was undermined by sub-ray 2. If in his ray configuration, sub-ray 2 had not been placed in this strategic place, he would have suffered no illness. He had to contract this illness "karmically," which explains this ray 2 placed as a sub-ray.

Sub-ray 2 softened the too perfectionist and too ambitious ray 7, thus allowing the link with the Soul to be maintained in a more concrete fashion. This sub-ray made him "human" in the eyes of his fellow countrymen and planted in them the seed of admiration, which he did not detest.

During World War II, he was Winston Churchill's shadow — he sometimes found the latter crude. He did not want to take part in this conflict and Churchill, who had more stamina than he, acted in such a fashion that he had to rally to the cause. These two men respected each other without really liking each other.

June 9, 2008

 ROOSEVELT, THEODORE

Given Name: Theodore Roosevelt
Nicknames: Rough Rider, Teddy, Trust-Buster
Nationality: American
Place and Date of Birth: New York, New York (United States), October 27, 1858
Place and Date of Death: Oyster Bay, New York (United States), January 6, 1919
Profession: Statesman

MASTER DJWHAL KHUL'S COMMENTARY

Theodore Roosevelt was undoubtedly one of the most evolved American presidents. He was committed to opening America to new, less conservative ideas. He wished to cooperate with other countries while keeping America's identity. He disapproved of war and favored balance in everything.

He was a man one could trust because when he gave his word, he kept it. Proud of his country and of his countrymen, he believed in his strength and often felt invincible. Proud, he would never yield ground and hated defeat.

His Achilles' heel was his pride, as well as his family. He did not tolerate anything to be said against the members of his family; he would then become furious and could verbally destroy any attack. We can confidently say that he had a fiery character and that he would not be imposed upon. He seemed fearless and we can assert that this was partially true.

Initiation Level: 2.3

Ray Structure

Monad: 1	Soul: 6	Personality: 6-3
Mental: 7-5	Astral: 2-4	Physical: 3-6

Monad and Soul

His Monad had no influence while his Soul exerted an ever increasing hold. It instilled in him the desire to succeed and to guide his homeland for better or for worse. He would have given it everything or almost… He had a certain intelligence (ray 7, sub-ray 5 mental body) that prevented him from making major mistakes with serious consequences. His Soul guided him to become a good president; he would have liked to be the best. He gave a lot but he also received a lot.

Personality

His ray 6, sub-ray 3 Personality allowed him to be dedicated towards his immediate and extended family (the Nation). Ray 6 made him stubborn, a manipulator (particularly with the support of sub-ray 3) and a dashing orator. He liked to give the impression of power, but mainly of control over the power he thought he managed well. Thanks to this ray, he projected the image of a man sure of himself and of his actions; we can add that his initiation level helped this projection. This ray incited remarkable fits of anger at times, as any source of frustration for him was best to be avoided. He was a loving, although demanding, father.

His sub-ray 3 made him a very cunning man, who was neither afraid of words nor of their effects. He had a certain sense of humor that he always knew how to use with intelligence. Let us mention that he was a tongue-in-cheek type, particularly in privacy. He appreciated good food and was considered a jovial person.

Mental Body

Respected for the clarity of his thoughts, thanks to the contribution of his ray 7, sub-ray 5 mental body, clarity he enjoyed in his explanations, he would become impatient when his remarks were not grasped. He also liked this quality in people, who according to him, favored good communication. A stickler for details, he grumbled when he detected too many errors. He liked to participate in projects and would prove to be fairly strict with regard to their execution.

His sub-ray 5 made him particular and difficult for his opponents to fool, which augmented his pride. A skilled hunter, he would relax his mind in the pursuit of an animal that he considered to be sly and intelligent; he then would forget his problems in order to hunt down the challenge before him.

Astral Body

His ray 2, sub-ray 4 astral body shaped him into a very sensitive person, a sensitivity he hid, thanks to his rays. He hated to see people suffer, particularly those close to him. The loss of his first wife was a tragedy for him. Fortunately, his strong ray 6, sub-ray 3 Personality allowed him to have a fresh start and to have a large family. He was very intuitive, which once more boosted his pride.

His sub-ray 4 inflicted on him a wave of melancholy that would dissipate rapidly. He appreciated nature, which re-energized him, the arts and beautiful things. However, he would not revel in emotions that, according to him, could annihilate a man who was balanced and in good health. He liked to remain in control and his emotional body would at times see itself set aside for the benefit of his fiery Personality.

Physical Body

His ray 3, sub-ray 6 physical made him a beast of burden, always ready to work and indefatigable; he committed himself relentlessly for a cause that, among others, was his country. He experienced satisfaction defending those that seemed the most impoverished. He knew one should not rely on appearances and would become suspicious if someone complimented him too much.

His ray 3 made his intelligence shine and would sometimes entice him to discuss certain hot "topics" with fervor, particularly when sub-ray 6 would get involved. He would then become more fervent in his debates and buoyant in his remarks. One can say that with a calm demeanor, he did not mince his words.

His sub-ray 6 gave him the healthy and lively appearance that characterized him so well. He thoroughly enjoyed good food and would not refuse a drink. However, he knew his limits and did not transgress them, being too proud to do so. He would have hated to be the subject of mockery. A faithful friend, one would not get bored in his company.

He was a good president, less full of himself than most of those who succeeded him. Had he extended his mandate, his life would have been longer and the United States would have been in better shape.

November 3, 2008

 # SAKYONG MIPHAM RINPOCHE

Given Name: Ösel Rangdrol Mukpo
Actual Name: Sakyong Mipham Jampal Trinley Dradül Rinpoche
Nationality: American
Place and Date of Birth: Bodh Gaya (India), December 11, 1962
Profession: Spiritual Master of Tibetan Buddhism

MASTER DJWHAL KHUL'S COMMENTARY

Sakyong Mipham Rinpoche is a young man who is extremely interested in the fate of suffering humanity and has not yet succeeded in accomplishing his destiny. The desire of his Personality to be recognized and to be worthy of being his father's son delays him in his progression. Dependent on high hopes, he has very little real power, because he first has to become himself, that is to say, the dignitary of his own Soul that wishes to merge with him. He possesses great wisdom but he still lacks much depth. His destiny is to teach, to educate, but he has difficulty in being a good transmitter, a great transformer. He should go on a retreat and meditate for his destiny to be accomplished, which we would hope for, although we doubt that it will take place during the present incarnation.

Initiation Level: 1.8

His initiation level explains his life dilemma. He would want more but cannot accomplish more because the spiritual guidance and energy to reach it are lacking. He meditates well but not efficiently because he lacks depth.

Ray Structure

Monad: 2	Soul: 3	Personality: 2-4
Mental: 5-3	Astral: 6-2	Physical: 3-7

Monad and Soul

His Monad has no influence, contrary to his Soul, which is starting to have one and is attempting to guide him in "Buddhic" affairs requiring protocol. He got married by convention, to protect the lineage, which partially indicates his initiation level. His father, Chögyam Trungpa Rinpoche, would have never acted in this way because he could not care less about convention, his desire being to "awaken" the consciousness of those who granted him their trust.

Personality

His ray 2, sub-ray 4 Personality makes him a loving and loved man. He wants to be likeable and knows how to please. His ray 2 makes him gentle, friendly, empathic and loving. One can feel his warmth and his desire to help others. He can at times become "cold" if he feels threatened or too tired.

His sub-ray 4 makes him capable of appreciating beautiful things, including the arts. However, he may at times feel invaded by certain demons that torment him and make him regret certain choices he made in his life. He can appear funny, but could also become uncontrollable regarding certain dependencies, such as sugar, which he is fond of. Sugar is detrimental to his health: it weakens his immune system, investing him with a certain weakness harmful to his emotions.

Mental Body

His ray 5, sub-ray 3 mental body grants him intelligence and stubbornness. He sometimes appears narrow-minded because ray 5 does not appreciate being wrong, rather preferring to prove that he is right. He likes to study and educate himself on all subjects. Attentive and endowed with a sharp eye, he has the capacity to rapidly grasp certain complicated data that he can then teach adequately, thanks to his ray 2 Personality. Consequently, he is considered a scholar and a wise man.

His sub-ray 3 imbues his intelligence with subtlety and finesse. Thus, he can play with words and concepts, which consequently bestows on him a more flexible mind. Sometimes he shines, this radiance resulting from the union of rays 5 and 3, making him temporarily more luminous; he then appears "illuminated" because in this particular moment his intelligence radiates with strength and power.

Astral Body

His ray 6, sub-ray 2 astral body emphasizes his sensitivity and makes him capable of becoming a good spouse and father. However, everything is derived from his Personality and his mental body. If one of these two aspects become too powerful, his marriage will suffer because he will fall victim to his sub-ray 4 Personality, or to his mental configuration, which will make him harsh and insensitive to the moods and desires of his wife. Ray 6 offers him the possibility of remaining faithful to his wife (according to their Soul link) and to be a father who knows how to appreciate his children and would love to watch them grow up.

Sub-ray 2 grants him kindness and warmth. He can appeal to women, who reciprocate the feeling. However, he is intelligent and knows how to perceive feminine manipulation most of the time; he exercises caution and, I repeat, demonstrates intelligence.

Physical Body

His ray 3, sub-ray 7 physical endows him with a certain magnetism that he uses frequently. Although he is quite robust, his body has certain deficiencies that are sometimes detrimental. He is flexible and appreciates the company of people. His ray 3 brain serves him well and supports him when he gives speeches. He thinks and acts fast, thanks to this ray.

His sub-ray 7 allows him, once more, to appreciate beauty and perfection in form, a perfection he is constantly seeking while remaining skeptic because he knows it is not of this world, although he wishes to find it and merge with it. Who knows when he will reach it?

This is a good man with no ill-intent. Naive at times, he is basically proud with a humble attitude that knows how to subjugate his peers.

October 29, 2008

 # SARANDON, SUSAN

Given Name: Susan Abigail Tomalin
Nationality: American
Place and Date of Birth: New York, New York (United States), October 4, 1946
Profession: Actress and producer

MASTER DJWHAL KHUL'S COMMENTARY

Susan Sarandon is a young Soul awakening to spirituality. Still controlled by a lot of glamour, she is leaning more and more towards humanity's needs. She revolves around the spiritual universe, without yet being part of. Aware that she is getting older and discovering that life possibly has a hidden meaning, she is attempting to discover it without really engaging on the path of discipleship.

She wishes to help, without, however, giving her shirt. One should not be surprised, because it is very fashionable in the world of stars "to help suffering humanity"; it is now part of discussions in intimate circles and… it sells newspapers!

Ms. Sarandon has a good heart; she is starting to see beyond her small world, although she does not yet understand the real meaning of karma and of self-sacrifice. Certain mirages are lying in wait for her and, without a real guide, she is lost. She is more interesting, however, than those who claim they are concerned about humanity's suffering. In addition, she has a knack for business that would embarrass many businessmen. Her husband helps her a lot in her progression. Moreover, he is a few decimals more evolved than she.

Initiation Level: 1.2

Ray Structure

Monad: 2	Soul: 3	Personality: 4-6
Mental: 5-3	Astral: 6-2	Physical: 7-3

She will grow a few decimals between now and the rest of her present life if she continues to work for the greater good. Her progression resembles that of Audrey Hepburn, who became concerned with humanity's pain toward the end of her life. This opening to others allowed her to be reborn rapidly in a body more adapted to her new work of a worldly scope. She (Audrey Hepburn) would give her life to defend a cause dear to her heart and that concerns South Africa.

Monad and Soul

Susan Sarandon's Monad has no influence on her but her Soul is starting to have one. Because her Soul is ruled by ray 3, an aspect of it takes its time and accumulates experiences. I did not say "assimilate", because she assimilates little through these experiences. Moreover, this is not the wish of ray 3, which likes to experience for the pleasure of doing so. She will have to wait a few lives, perhaps two or three, it will all depend on her motivation, before reaching her second initiation.

Personality

Her ray 4, sub-ray 6 Personality makes her an artist to the core, because it takes precedence over the Soul. Her ray 4 being fairly balanced, more so in recent years, she is less subject to fear and depression.

Sub-ray 6 supports her efficiently in her work and makes her capable of adapting very easily. One can rely on her, because she will give her maximum. This sub-ray favors inner work, thus allowing ray 4 to remain more balanced. If this were not the case, she would be very unpleasant to live with. Her heart is opening more and more in harmony with her destiny and the work, which will bring her to several countries to support various humanitarian causes.

Mental Body

Her ray 5, sub-ray 3 mental body makes her an extremely intelligent woman, difficult to deceive. She likes to understand things in a clear and precise fashion, does not appreciate duplicitous games and hates to be made fun of. She advocates honesty and likes to "dot the i's" and "cross the t's".

She is gifted with intuition coming from her sub-ray 3 that combines well with her Soul, thus allowing her to be an excellent diplomat when her emotional body is not affected. She knows how to talk to people in an intelligible way and to make them understand that she understands them!

Astral Body

Her ray 6, sub-ray 2 astral body reveals a woman sometimes possessive, which is attributable to ray 6, but devoted to her cause (her family, her friends etc.). She invests herself well in her profession while knowing increasingly how to detach herself from it. Ray 6 makes her a good leader for certain causes. A fanatic leader at times, she controls herself fairly well thanks to her ray 5, sub-ray 3 mental body, that keep a tight hold, bringing her to more down-to-earth matters.

Her sub-ray 2 gives her a good heart that sometimes makes her very emotional in conjunction with her ray 6's. Fortunately, her mental brings her back to more acceptable emotional limits once more.

Physical Body

Her ray 7, sub-ray 3 physical gives rise to a beautiful woman with a good head on her shoulders. She has a sense of order and aesthetics that allow her to grow older with beauty while suffering from this aging that is tarnishing "her perfection". She is searching for perfection in everything and this desire causes her a lot of headaches. Fortunately, her husband has more than one ray 7, which offers him the possibility of understanding her and not judging her too much (and vice-versa).

Her sub-ray 3 provides her with certain flexibility, mainly on the level of her thoughts, which sometimes become too rigid. Her two sub-ray 3's confer more flexibility; otherwise she would be a true little dictator (for the good of others). Fortunately, this is not the case; ray 3's, accomplishing their work well, act in such a way that they demonstrate enough flexibility to understand humanity and to see a little of the *leela*[1] of successive incarnations that we must live and relive. She believes in past lives and hopes to create a good karma in her present life.

June 20, 2009

---

[1] *Leela, lîlâ* in Sanskrit literally means "game"

 # Scott, Cyril

Given Name: Cyril Scott
Nationality: British
Place and Date of Birth: Oxton (England), September 27, 1879
Place and Date of Death: Eastbourne (England), December 31, 1970
Profession: Musician, poet, writer and philosopher

Master Djwhal Khul's Commentary

Cyril Scott was the disciple of one of my dear friends. He could have accomplished more but he stopped progressing shortly after his marriage. Why? No one really knows; however we believe that he had reached the apogee of what he thought he could become. He continued to progress horizontally, but all vertical progression ceased. In other words, he acquired experience, but it stopped ripening into wisdom. Moreover, ten years after his marriage, physical contact with his Master ceased, only occurring sporadically on the inner planes.

The break was very hard for him to endure, and little by little he left the group, using his work and his age as excuses. Very proud, he had difficulty accepting imperfection, especially his own. However, he accomplished excellent work by transcribing his encounters with Moreward Haig, who was his guide and his Master in the present incarnation.

Initiation Level: 2.3

His initiation level explains his arrogance and false humility. Gifted with a certain vision suited for the work he had to accomplish, he also demonstrated a blatant lack of wisdom. However, he loved his Master and was very loyal to him, in his own way, until the end of his incarnation.

Ray Structure

Monad: 1	Soul: 2	Personality: 7-4
Mental: 3-2	Astral: 4-6	Physical: 7-2-3

Monad and Soul

His Monad exerted no influence on him, which was the opposite for his Soul. He often felt torn between the choices of his Soul and those of his Personality, which were diametrically opposed. Without this hold of the Soul, he would never have written the books that allowed him to grow so much. We will not touch upon his poetry here, which we consider rather "average". He showed more talent for musical composition, although its effect did not produce anything extraordinary.

Personality

His ray 7, sub-ray 4 Personality instilled in him a love of poetry, music and literature. However, he was ill at ease in meditation, preferring to write and listen to speeches rather than "sitting down" to meditate. He liked for things to move in a certain order. A distinguished ritualist, he was naturally fond of beautiful things and beautiful women.

Sub-ray 4 ensured his attraction for the arts and their expression. This ray sometimes made him nostalgic; he liked to withdraw alone in his office. He had a hard time surrendering to certain concepts, such as marriage, as he wanted to be free of any constraint.

Mental Body

His ray 3, sub-ray 2 mental body allowed him to write intelligently. Sub-ray 2 granted him intuition that was then channeled by ray 3. Without this ray, which permitted him to express himself quite clearly, he would have gone mad. Sub-ray 2, in alliance with his ray 4's, enabled him to write profusely and be "inspired", as he said so well. He was made for art. Although he was not always easy to understand and follow, one had simply to love him.

Astral Body

His ray 4, sub-ray 6 astral body made him a man who sought perfection in his relationships, something he never found except with his Master. There again, he was disappointed on several occasions because his Master did not always proceed as he would have wished. He was not a man faithful in love, as he was too dazzled by beauty. He loved female beauty without necessarily loving women.

Sub-ray 6 allowed him to become an acceptable spouse and a good father. It also inspired in him a devotion towards his Master. He occasionally became short-tempered when this sub-ray rebelled against various emotional injustices.

Physical Body

His ray 7, sub-ray 2 Physical shaped him into an attractive man, delicate and sensitive. As a young man he seemed charismatic and almost angelic. Sometimes he would cry for nothing and he would marvel at everything. Then he hardened, and adopted more of the characteristics of a ray 7, little inclined to sentimentality.

July 18, 2008

SEAGAL, STEVEN

Given Name: Steven Seagal
Tibetan Names: Chungdrag Dorje, Takeshigemichi
Nationality: American
Place and Date of Birth: Lansing, Michigan (United States), April 10, 1951
Profession: Actor, producer, director and musician

MASTER DJWHAL KHUL'S COMMENTARY

A man of action, Mr. Seagal's roots reveal themselves to be more Japanese than Tibetan. He was a remarkable killer in the army of the 6th emperor of China and a similarly virulent samurai. His lives, and he had several, started as a samurai during the epoch of Kamakura. He lived several lives as a Tibetan monk, but, in fact, is more Zen than Buddhist.

Initiation Level: 1.6

He did not evolve during his lives as a samurai, but he developed pride, bravery and a sense of honor, qualities that were missing in him. However, this inheritance prevents him from acquiring humility, which he will have to integrate sooner or later before becoming a realized being.

This pride is also linked to his initiation level and it will be difficult for him to get rid of it before several lives.

Ray Structure

Monad: 2	Soul: 2	Personality: 7-4
Mental: 3-7	Astral: 6-2	Physical: 3-6

Monad and Soul

His Soul is starting to exert a certain influence that will direct him towards more judicious choices. It also allows him to develop a certain sensitivity that was unknown to him in the past.

Personality

His ray 7, sub-ray 4 Personality makes him a man who can be charming while being controlling. He appreciates things done his way. He can prove to be rigid and uncompromising when it comes to certain aspects of his life. Music allows him to flourish much more than his films.

His sub-ray 4 instills in him a taste for the arts and for becoming an actor. If his sub-ray had been placed on the first line, he would have proved to be a better actor, but would have moved further away from his center. This sub-ray sometimes makes him unstable, a condition he manages, thanks to his meditations and his physical discipline of the martial arts.

Mental Body

His ray 3, sub-ray 7 mental body makes him intelligent, manipulative and controlling. He does not like to meet resistance and lack of respect. He believes he is superior on many levels, especially with thought, which he thinks he manages well. His mental body strengthens his arrogance. We wish him a better ray configuration in his next incarnation, which because of the links created in this life, will take place in Tibet.

His sub-ray 7 grants him mental discipline that proves necessary to the implementation of his art; thus he can concentrate and brush against perception. We may qualify him as a master of martial arts but not of self-mastery.

Astral Body

His ray 6, sub-ray 2 astral body allows him to live a fairly normal life. Ray 6 grants him a sense of dedication and loyalty. He can give everything for his cause (while ensuring that he doesn't lose his shirt). He likes to dedicate himself to the less fortunate, which increases his sense of honor and responsibility. He appreciates feeling useful for causes that he considers valid.

His sub-ray 2 endows him with an excellent sensitivity that dazzles women. At certain moments, he seems "vulnerable", a particularity that women adore. However, this "weakness" does not last long and Mr. Seagal recaptures his arrogance and sense of perfection rapidly.

Physical Body

His ray 3, sub-ray 6 physical body endows him with flexibility, agility and great endurance in the mental and physical bodies. His ray 3 allows him to excel in the martial arts, and sub-ray 6 in the field of music, where he lets his "heart" talk. Ray 3 provides him with speed in movement and in thought; it sometimes makes him blunder, which he seeks to correct afterwards.

As he ages, sub-ray 6 slows down his movements, which he does not appreciate and the importance of which, he attempts to diminish as much as possible. However, it confers to him more humanity, gentleness and serenity.

This is a man who requires a certain study, but who still has a lot of work to accomplish before reaching the desired perfection. He will undoubtedly be a woman in his next incarnation because he has certain lessons to learn.

October 30, 2008

 SHAPIRO, ROBERT

Given Name: Robert Shapiro
Nationality: American
Place and Date of Birth: (information not available)
Profession: Author, medium and shaman

MASTER DJWHAL KHUL'S COMMENTARY

I do not know this man well, but I can state that he is considered an eccentric of the intemporal and spiritual world. He does not belong to this system and even less to the one he is channeling. He is indeed human and has lived on this planet for centuries. He lived in Egypt and has known Atlantis. However, a part of him never landed on Earth and remains in relation with a planet located in the Orion Constellation, near Betelgeuse. In a way he is *Zoosh*[1].

He has always kept this link with this part of himself and believed he was mad during several incarnations. At times, he had the possibility of forgetting this condition, one that reappeared in the following incarnation. He never stopped grieving for this dear planet, which resulted in delaying the evolution of his Soul on our planet. He remains a very sensitive being, very close to nature and the *devas*, but far from his "beingness". He was notably Nostradamus (1503-1566).

His Soul, through the influence of the rays, attempts to link him to this planet, without success. He likes this Earth quite well, but feels constantly attracted by something else.

Initiation Level: 2.2

---

[1] *Zoosh* is a character described in the forthcoming book *Conclave of the Cryptic 7*, Volume 2, Klaire D. Roy, Paume de Saint-Germain Publishing.

Ray Structure

Monad: 2	Soul: 3	Personality: 4-6
Mental: 7-5	Astral: 2-4	Physical: 3-6

Monad and Soul

His Monad exerts no influence on him, contrary to his Soul, which tries to exert one. He has not really progressed since his arrival on this planet. In a certain epoch, he was adulated because he was clearly more evolved, which is less the case now. Perhaps, these repercussions will help him focus more on what he really has to learn, in other words, humanity and the love principle that follows when one opens up to this energy.

His ray 3 Soul reveals itself to be patient, although the time that has passed is significant. It wishes a more real and deeper awakening. This man is interesting and much appreciated in certain circles, which has no bearing on his evolution. He has to learn to turn to his Soul, towards a more occult and more present aspect of himself.

Personality

His ray 4, sub-ray 6 Personality contributes to reducing the influence of the energy from the part of himself generated in this other place, to better manage it and to live in harmony in its company. He uses it like a tool and becomes more eccentric as he grows older. This ray 4 acts a bit like an antenna that helps him to better capture the information that is transmitted via other dimensions both inside and outside himself.

His sub-ray 6 invests him with the capacity to ground himself a little, to face the earthly reality and to prove functional in this world. He must inevitably possess a ray 6 in his configuration if he wishes to have his feet firmly on the ground and to pay his dues (at all levels, even karmic) like everybody else. His sub-ray slightly reduces the effect and grants him the possibility of directing his thoughts towards things useful for survival in a practical way in this world. In a way, he wants to be self-sufficient because he could very well function without establishing human relationships; that is not his destiny and he knows it.

Mental Body

His ray 7, sub-ray 5 mental body provides him with remarkable intelligence and the possibility of expressing himself with fervor and persuasion. He could not care less about conventions but knows how to talk well and describe facts that, in general, reveal themselves to be incomprehensible for the average citizen. His ray 7 helps him to create a semblance of order in his life and grants him the necessary refinement for his work.

Sub-ray 5 creates order "in an orderly" fashion and allows him to be very persuasive. He can become very mental, talking of perfectly abstract subjects and conceptualizing them for those listening. Sub-ray 5 also creates a link with the *devic* kingdom that assists him in the accomplishment of certain tasks. The *devas* feed his intuition to a large extent, and he uses them wisely.

Astral Body

His ray 2, sub-ray 4 astral body wraps him in sensitivity and increases his intuition. He may sometimes experience emotional confusion, rendering it difficult for him to express his feelings. He hides this fact well, thanks to his mental body, and gives the illusion that he is a strong and balanced man. He dislikes emotions and rarely gives in to them. He manipulates others well and maintains an interesting control, thanks to his Mental.

His sub-ray 4 makes him equally sensitive and subject to ups and downs on the emotional plane. Not always easy to live with, he is a passionate man who likes to intensely live the present moment.

Physical Body

His ray 3, sub-ray 6 physical body grants him speech and intelligence to express himself. A bit of a loner, he occasionally appreciates good company. Ray 3 makes him versatile; he does not really like the unexpected, but he knows how to adapt to all situations. He is known to be "tongue-in-cheek".

Sub-ray 6 helps him once more to "ground" himself, which allows him to be functional. He is a man devoted to the extraterrestrial cause in which he firmly believes. He does not fear these worlds that gravitate around us and we know why.

Here is a man that wants to be kind, endowed with a nature difficult to grasp. Enigmatic, he sometimes believes himself to be beyond everything. He, however, has a good heart that he is trying to open more and more.

September 5, 2008

 SINATRA, FRANK

Given Name: Francis Albert Sinatra
Nickname: Frank or *The Voice*
Nationality: American
Place and Date of Birth: Hoboken, New Jersey (United States), December 12, 1915
Place and Date of Death: Los Angeles, California (United States), May 14, 1998
Profession: Singer, actor and producer

MASTER DJWHAL KHUL'S COMMENTARY

Frank Sinatra was a great singer who produced an important effect within America through his political commitments. Without him, America would not quite be what it is presently. Why? Because he pushed, sometimes with charm and sometimes brusquely, American ideals in order to change them. He made Americans more sensitive to the racial condition and the condition of minorities. He exerted a strong influence and brought logical, down to earth viewpoints to the political men who sometimes lose sight of the good of all. He would have been a great president but this was not his mandate. He loved music too much and the effect it produced on others.

He juggled with good and evil because he knew that one had an impact on the other. He would have liked the two to unite in order to overcome evil, which proved to be a more arduous task than he believed. Ill judged by those who pretended to be America's defenders, he accomplished a difficult task, which was to allow communication between society's two extremes.

An excellent mediator, he allowed certain problems to be solved behind the scenes. He knew the name of John F. Kennedy's murderer, but to preserve his life and the life of his family, he kept this information secret until his death. Simply note that the problem resided within the government that considered John F. Kennedy a danger for the survival of the United States as a feudalistic nation (subtle but real meaning), because favoritism was very high. Kennedy advocated freedom in its largest sense, like president Barack Obama wishes to do now. However, Kennedy realized that this task was almost impossible to fulfill since the financial stakes were too great. A lot of work still remains to be done in order for the United States to become a nation in which authentic freedom prevails that includes all races, religions and social and economical statuses. Everything revolves around financial abundance and not spiritual abundance that is composed of the highest aspect of our lives as human beings.

Let us return to Frank Sinatra. Italian to his core, he has always been passionate and devoted to his entourage. He suffered much from not being as loved and understood as he wished to be.

Initiation Level: 1.5

He was more advanced than the average person was, and his new mental polarization gave him a more global vision of his environment. More evolved that his artistic counterparts, he was able to increase the commercial value of the musical world because he had the ability to bring down a magnificent energy of resonance in himself.

Ray Structure

Monad: 2	Soul: 2	Personality: 3-7
Mental: 1-5	Astral: 6-4	Physical: 3-7

Monad and Soul

His Monad exerted no influence on him, contrary to his Soul that began to have one that guided him all his life. It made him intuitive, sensitive and open to the needs of others.

Personality

His ray 3, sub-ray 7 Personality made him an intelligent and well groomed man. Ray 3 provided him with an intensity of spirit that served him all his life. He would manage adequately in the most difficult situations. He was well spoken and possessed an interesting, quick wit. He was afraid of nothing, a state that he exhibited and expressed without fear.

His sub-ray 7 gave him a proud appearance. He had a natural distinction that women liked a lot. He loved refined things and things well done. Nothing was left to chance. He appreciated perfection in everything and proved to be very demanding towards himself and, of course, towards others.

Mental Body

He was endowed with a strong mental body. Ray 1 provided him with clarity of mind, guiding him in his choices, except in his emotional choices that were more influenced by his immature astral body. This ray endowed him with concentration, which helped him all his life. It allowed him to appreciate and rapidly recognize the songs that suited him. He naturally knew the type of interpretation he had to adopt and the way to execute it.

Sub-ray 5 served him mainly in his business, which did not always progress the way he wanted. It also allowed him to be practical, especially in the field of politics. He knew what he wanted and what he did not want. This sub-ray provided him with the necessary arguments during his "serious" discussions.

Astral Body

This was unquestionably his weak point. Unable to manage his emotions, he rather became their victim. He would take refuge in his mind and in his Personality, which allowed him to recover his balance and become functional.

His ray 6 equipped him with a warm aspect he would have liked to exploit. Too fragile, this ray made him jealous and possessive (a condition he detested); he did not succeed in managing his emotional field until the end of his life. This ray made him search for the ideal woman. Married first to a woman he considered a good "mama", he was disappointed. He then married a "femme fatale" who almost destroyed him; then he married a "woman child" who disillusioned him, and he finished by marrying a woman whose feminine values were more balanced. We can say that he was happy with her, but that he would have preferred to experience happiness earlier in his life, his sentimental deceptions having caused a lot of damage to his emotions.

His sub-ray 4 increased his discomfort towards love (the ideal that he sought) and towards life in general. This sub-ray could sometimes provoke almost uncontrollable mood swings, occasional depressions and the desire to destroy everything and to start all over. However, when this sub-ray found its balance, it would awaken in him the volition to fight and not to let himself be defeated by what he considered unjust.

Physical Body

He had a pleasant physical body that served him in his profession. Ray 3 ensured flexibility, which allowed him to perform in dance, although this was not his strong point. This ray endowed him with a sharp and active mind. He did not mince his words, but sub-ray 7 sometimes controlled his ardor, thus preventing him from shocking those listening to him.

Sub-ray 7 provided him with a seductive aura and almost irresistible charm. It allowed him to keep a resistant and powerful body. He experienced more difficulty towards the end of his life; we will say that his alcohol abuse was the reason, but mainly his sentimental deceptions, of which there were many, if we include his amorous adventures outside marriage.

Did he serve the mafia? We would say that he did; however he considered the government the mafia as well, which he also served well!

March 20, 2010

 # SPANGLER, DAVID

Given Name: David Spangler
Nationality: American
Place and Date of Birth: Columbus, Ohio (United States), January 7, 1945
Profession: Philosopher and writer

MASTER DJWHAL KHUL'S COMMENTARY

It is interesting to see how a man of this caliber was able to build his life concretely. He possesses enormous potential that has only been partially explored. He is the reincarnation of Master Suzuki Shôshan (1579-1655) who lived in Japan and brought a new vision to Buddhism, which he practiced with fervor.

From this incarnation, David Spangler retained a firm faith in what he believes and practices. He also retained a lively intelligence that is not easily fooled. Having developed clairvoyance no longer astral but rather etheric, he is able, in this incarnation, to see and hear things that he previously believed without actually having to experience them.

Initiation Level: 3.4

Ray Structure

Monad: 3	Soul: 2	Personality: 6-4
Mental: 7-5	Astral: 2-6	Physical: 3-7

Monad and Soul

His Monad only exerts a slight influence; however, his Soul acts more and more efficiently in his life. It dictates the right choices to make and supports him in times of hardship. He rarely judges anyone severely, preferring to defer to the Divine in him so as not to interfere with energy circulation, which he actually sees very clearly. He knows how to assume responsibility for decisions taken that may sometimes adversely affect others, recognizing that perfection is not of this world, although he tries desperately to live and understand it.

Personality

His ray 6, sub-ray 4 Personality shaped him into a good, sincere, devoted and loyal man. He is reliable and when he gives his word, he never takes it back. He is gifted with good intuition that he uses to serve others. In a sense, he dedicates his life to the service of humanity by trusting the most sacred part of himself, related to the Divine.

His sub-ray 4 grants him flexibility and a sense of creativity that proves useful to his writing. Although not an artist, he has all the qualities of one. He sometimes experiences inner conflicts that he tries to resolve in the most harmonious way possible.

Mental Body

His ray 7, sub-ray 5 mental body confers to him intuition and intelligence. He knows how to keep his feet on the ground and does not let himself be fooled by unrealistic facts. Hard to manipulate, he knows how to keep his cool. His ray 7 gifts him with an aesthetic sense that has followed him throughout his life. It also brings him closer to the kingdoms of nature because this ray holds a magical aspect, mainly on the mental plane, making him receptive to receiving energies from various realms of the invisible world. He can detect the invisible and describe it easily, thanks to this ray that is well settled in his mental body.

His sub-ray 5 gives him a scientific air much appreciated by those he comes in contact with and those who enjoy people who demonstrate an acute intelligence not based on unfounded intuitions. He has a powerful mastery of language that he uses intelligently, to the delight of his listeners.

Astral Body

His ray 2, sub-ray astral body makes him sensitive and ready to listen not only to others but also to other worlds. He is not afraid of his emotions, which he controls quite well. He "feels" others and can intervene effectively. Nonetheless, he has certain irrational fears that he tries to master as best he can. He fears suffering and death, especially a violent death without warning. He is a charming and warm being.

His sub-ray 6 makes him a gentle, likeable and comforting man, unafraid to get involved. He works hard and tirelessly, and likes to give without expecting to receive in return. He is a passionate person, a man of action who only judges when necessary.

Physical Body

His ray 3, sub-ray 7 physical reveals an intelligent, refined, strong and hard–working man. Ray 3 grants him flexibility, a sense of organization in the disorder of life, and an interesting sense of humor.

Sub-ray 7 confers to him a sense of rhythm that he exploits through his writings and speeches. He is a ritualist and does not hide it. Not a conformist, and someone who likes to stray off the beaten path at times, he knows how to discipline himself and accomplish his work within the allotted deadline. This sub-ray offers him a sense of rigor he sometimes takes pride in.

He has proven to be a good man, at times complicated in his explanations, but always sensible. He loves the planet and humanity, which he tries to understand and free from its conceptual shackles.

August 16, 2008

 STEINER, RUDOLF

Given Name: Rudolf Steiner
Nationality: Austrian
Place and Date of Birth: Donji Kraljevec (Croatia), February 25, 1861
Place and Date of Death: Dornach (Switzerland), March 30, 1925
Profession: Philosopher, teacher, occultist and social thinker

MASTER DJWHAL KHUL'S COMMENTARY

A man of science and ecology for his epoch, Rudolf Steiner was fearless and very knowledgeable in esotericism. He has effectively fought Hitler in the invisible, without beating him. He helped us because he possessed a certain vision coming from his initiation level and his ray configuration. He benefited from the "eye and the intuition".

Initiation Level: 2.4

Ray Structure

Monad: 2	Soul: 2	Personality: 7-3
Mental: 5-3	Astral: 6-2	Physical: 7-5

Monad and Soul

His Monad did not exert a very strong influence on his life, which was not the case for his Soul, which granted him this love for humanity that he has transposed in his schools. He wanted the best for man in an equitable system.

He had succeeded in developing a certain humility (thanks to his ray 2's), which allowed him to counteract the arrogance of the second initiation while desiring humble recognition from mankind.

Personality

His ray 7, sub-ray 3 Personality made him a magician of the form, which allowed him to fight Hitler in the occult. He was ritualistic and believed in the existence of the invisible world. The influence of ray 7 enticed him to seek perfection in everything, particularly on the physical plane.

Sub-ray 3 allowed him to work on several planes simultaneously, to appreciate experimentation and facilitated his research. This sub-ray also offered him the possibility to accelerate his research at the expense of ray 7, which prefers perfection even if it slows him down.

Mental Body

His Mental, guided by the ray 5, sub-ray 3 energies, incited him to develop a very occult scientific aspect. He knew how to handle certain magical formulas that he would recite in order to accomplish his destiny among the suffering humanity that he loved to love (ray 6, sub-ray 2 Astral), an illusion of a certain romantic love for the planet. Ray 5 rapidly brought his feet back on the ground so that he remained alert in the invisible.

Sub-ray 3 granted him the faculty to think fast. It helped him to make certain rapid decisions and encouraged him to experience different avenues. It accentuated his intelligence and simplified the sometimes too rigid work of ray 5.

Astral Body

His astral body, polarized by ray 6, sub-ray 2, made him a loving man, dedicated to his cause and fundamentally engaged. Ray 6 blessed him with great moral strength, rendering him almost fearless; when he undertook a crusade, he became an impeccable warrior.

Sub-ray 2 conferred to him great sensitivity. He could feel the needs of others and act in such a way that they would feel better. This sub-ray also instilled a strong intuition in him, which he used to start relationships with others.

Physical Body

His physical, endowed with the ray 7, sub-ray 5 energies, gave him the ease of conversing with chemical as well as etheric elements. He was able to build a whole esoteric life through purely Christian or down–to-earth beliefs.

A visionary who appreciated what was noble and occult; he was a maverick for his time. Mr. Steiner is not yet reincarnated.

July 7, 2008

 STONE, SHARON

Given Name: Sharon Vonne Stone
Nationality: American
Place and Date of Birth: Meadville, Pennsylvania (United States), March 10, 1958
Profession: Actress, producer, director and writer

MASTER DJWHAL KHUL'S COMMENTARY

An intelligent woman, Sharon Stone also has a heart that caused her a lot of trouble, because she is a woman who loves much, but poorly. Her wounds allowed her to keep an open heart in a universe centered on glamour and corruption. She has a head on her shoulders, a head that is well balanced and matches her open heart.

In spite of the fact that she has participated in films that have sometimes shocked, she is generally a discreet woman who does not like to reveal, even if she did it more than once physically. This comes in part from the influence of her ray 7, sub-ray 4 physical. You will therefore understand that this is a fearless woman who acts according to a conscience that is really hers and that we would qualify as being fairly balanced.

Initiation Level: 2.1

This initiation level is recognized as being a dangerous phase that she handles fairly well.

Ray Structure

Monad: 1	Soul: 3	Personality: 4-3
Mental: 7-5	Astral: 6-2	Physical: 7-4

Her initiation level gives her a certain arrogance and the desire to seduce, yet not to a point of perilousness. She likes to appeal to everyone and to be loved, although she also knows how to withdraw and become a warm and authentic woman in private. Her ray 4's allow her to be comfortable in her roles as a public and private woman.

Monad and Soul

Her Monad exerts very little influence; however her Soul is beginning to hold her vehicle in place, i.e. it effectively influences her Personality, which is more and more balanced. Ray 3 gives her flexibility and the capacity to bounce back efficiently after experiencing failures and bereavements. It allows her to capably master the influence of her ray 4's, which give her a bit of a headache.

Personality

Her ray 4, sub-ray 3 Personality allows her to be versatile and not remain hooked on her roles and partners. A faithful woman in private, she likes to flirt out of pleasure. She appreciates art, beauty and beautiful things; however, she knows how to content herself with little, if necessary. Although she is an idealist, she is aware that reality is often different from what things appear. She believes in karma and in the need to act correctly in life.

Ray 4 endows her with harmony and magnetism that are accentuated by sub-ray 3, which allows her to express herself well, in an intelligent fashion depending on the circumstances. She remains elegant even when she is provocative. Seductive and a bit shocking to provoke a reaction, she knows it is a game with which she has a lot of fun — sub-ray 3 allowing her to get away from the influence of ray 4, to see the game and to create it. She is often the master of the game in so far as she does not abuse it.

Mental Body

Her ray 7, sub-ray 5 mental body makes her an intelligent woman, which her IQ of 154 has demonstrated. She likes order and modernity.

She appreciates beautiful things and knows how to surround herself with them. She possesses a certain intuition that serves her well; she is a challenging businesswoman. Her mental body allows her to easily assimilate her roles and to interpret them well. It also makes her respect hierarchy when she sees that the goal sought is noble and the leaders are honest and work towards this goal. If this is not the case, she becomes tough and troublesome. Her ray 7 grants her the ability to rebound and face the music.

Sub-ray 5 emphasizes her intelligence and increases her intuition, making it difficult to fool her. Quite often she sees things as they really are. She is an excellent friend, as long as one is reliable and honest with her. Otherwise, she breaks off relations and directs her energy elsewhere. Conscious of how precious time is, she does not like to waste it. Fearing getting old, she hopes to keep her intelligence more than her beauty.

Astral Body

Her ray 6, sub-ray 2 astral body makes her a devoted and loyal woman. She likes to give of herself, and does it generously. However, her ray 6 confers on her a fault that she detests: jealousy. Very sensitive and sometimes susceptible, her weak point remains her astral body, which she has not yet mastered. Sometimes, she can display fanaticism with regard to certain questions, such as those related to human rights and religion. In that sense she possesses certain fixed ideas that she accepts to give up with wisdom when she is given evidence to the contrary.

Her sub-ray 2 increases her sensitivity and some of her fears, including the fear of growing old. However, this sub-ray makes her loving and a good mother. Endowed with a sense of empathy rare among people in show business, she likes to listen and knows how to do it properly. She detests violence and fights against it. Her adherence to Buddhism corresponds well to her life choice, which wants peace.

Physical Body

Her ray 7, sub-ray 4 physical makes her very beautiful, displaying well-defined proportions. Her ray 7 brain qualifies her intelligence in a "structured and well organized" fashion, to counter balance sub-ray 4 which often isn't. Ray 7 awards her elegance in the physical body, accentuated by sub-ray 4 that renders her very magnetic. Few men can resist her; she is graceful and her beauty is natural. She will probably keep this beauty all her life.

Sub-ray 4 efficiently accentuates ray 7. It often instills in her a melancholy that she masters fairly well. It gives her gait the illusion that she is floating. She does not pass unnoticed, which pleases her!

June 20, 2009

 # Suzuki, David

Given Name: David Takayoshi Suzuki
Nationality: Canadian
Place and Date of Birth: Vancouver, British Colombia (Canada), March 24, 1936
Profession: Zoologist, geneticist and environmental activist

Master Djwhal Khul's Commentary

David Suzuki is a young Soul who is a militant for the good of all in order for our planet to recover its credential as a hospitable planet for life: animal, human, vegetal and mineral.

Few planets in the Universe have such a mandate because several remain at a latent state with regards to life "with a physical beating heart". The majority of these planets welcome life in different forms (gaseous, mineral, etheric). They work in concert with these forms in order to be able to one day develop within their space a materially more conscious form of life. The etheric forms of life are not necessarily more evolved than we; to attain that goal, they have to have the capacity to materialize matter at will, from ether, a potential and necessary source of physical life. Without ether, there could not be life or any possibility of life. Destroy the ether and you remove all possibilities for energy to live, to grow and to reproduce. This is black magic.

David Suzuki, who has the unconscious capacity to converse with the worlds populating the ether, receives appropriate guidance for his work from the *devas* that are constantly accompanying him, without really being conscious of it. This contact helps to keep him young in appearance and in consciousness, favoring a non-crystallized mental. Of course, he is narrow-minded and difficult to live with because he is too absorbed by his task. However, be aware that he knows it and that he is working at it with some humor that lightens his daily life.

Initiation Level: 2.2

He has a certain arrogance that comes from the fact that he reached his second initiation during his last incarnation. At that time, he lived in Japan as the son of a great land owner. He fought in the Boxer war in China, which cost him his life. However, all the suffering he witnessed, including the absurdity of massacres and the cruelty of war, allowed him to open his eyes to human suffering and sharpened in him the desire to evolve in order to change and serve a cause bigger than his.

Ray Structure

Monad: 3	Soul: 2	Personality: 3-6
Mental: 7-5	Astral: 4-6	Physical: 3-5

Monad and Soul

His Monad exerts little influence on his present life. However, in a future incarnation that reveals itself to be sufficiently close that it deserves to be mentioned, he will radically increase his communication with it. He will become an important instrument of the influence of ray 3 in our human culture. He will work within the international community as a scientific businessman in the most advanced fields of molecular and nuclear technology. The fourth dimension will become accessible, thanks to his research. He will still be Canadian.

His Soul is starting an interesting guidance that will be even stronger in his next incarnation. Enhancing his sensitivity, he will be more open to everything that touches upon human life. At present, his consciousness is sheltering certain inaccessible compartments. He is hiding secrets linked to wounds of the past within himself. He will transcend these wounded memories with a special gift that will support decision making that will prove accurate and consistent with the wish of his Soul.

Personality

His Personality, governed by the ray 3, sub-ray 6 energies, grants him a great opening on planet Earth and on all that lives on it. He is, so to speak, more at ease with nature than with humans, whom he sometimes considers as exploiters without brains in regards to the kingdoms of nature. The influence of ray 3 allows him to express himself with a certain confidence. He can easily navigate from one topic to the next without losing the thread. It confers to him a certain magnetism that he uses with dexterity. This ray also allows him to appear relaxed when he is under enormous stress.

Sub-ray 6 helps him stay on course when faced with the fights he has to take on to safeguard nature. It gives him this dedication, a desire to persevere in spite of difficulties. It incites him, when he is not influenced by his mental body, to demonstrate human warmth. The influence of this sub-ray makes him very persuasive and grants him credibility; this warm fire that only ray 6 can display in the tensest moments, is dear to his heart.

Mental Body

His mental body, governed by the ray 7, sub-ray 5 energies, grants him an intelligence he has used well. Ray 7 allows him to be reserved while being efficient in his work. It fosters in him, a mystery always ready to be revealed. It provides him with the mental energy, almost inexhaustible, that he needs to accomplish his work. This ray also gives him logic, a process that makes him orderly while keeping a certain intuition, the influence of this ray but also of his initiation level.

Sub-ray 5 offers him the scientific ability that he needs. While being in a certain way near nature's mystery, he can, in an almost Cartesian way, explain and promote his viewpoints.

This sub-ray makes him love the scientific aspect of his research that is necessary to explain and understand his discoveries.

Astral

With an astral body influenced by ray 4, sub-ray 6, David Suzuki reveals himself to be passionate in everything that touches his life, personal as well as professional. Emotional, although he controls it fairly well, he loves what he does and he includes it in his daily life. The influence of ray 4 makes him appreciate beauty in nature, which presents itself like a constant revelation to his eyes. He appreciates and understands the fact that every second, everything transforms itself and changes. He has an aversion to stagnation and likes that everything moves in his life. Experiencing ups and downs at times, he is quite able to control himself.

Sub-ray 6 provides him with the emotional stability that he needs. He likes that everything moves around him, while maintaining a central and solid point. This point is his family, which he tries to keep together in spite of difficulties. This sub-ray makes him warm in private when there is no tension in the air; otherwise the energy of ray 4 takes the upper hand and turns him into a "warrior". He is then ready to fight in order to awaken what is asleep in each of those around him.

Physical Body

His Physical, governed by the ray 3, sub-ray 5 energies, provides him with excellent health. Ray 3 confers to him a great resistance and offers him the possibility of spending, in spite of his age, well-filled days. In a way, his passion for everything he touches makes him indefatigable. He is always ready to help, to fight for the causes he believes to be just.

This ray grants him a powerful brain that helps him think fast and effectively. It allows him to see problems from different angles in order to find equitable solutions.

Sub-ray 5 increases his link with nature and the deva kingdom. He perceives what few among us are able to perceive. He "feels" things; he "hears" in himself the inexpressible in nature. He converses on various planes with Mother Nature, whom he tries to save from the barbarian invasions that man subjects her to.

David Suzuki is a loyal and honest man, rugged in his work. It is preferable to be at his side because his work is like water that clears its way through obstacles without stopping. Water always gets its way in the end, in spite of those opposing it. Giving sometimes the impression that it is dormant, it remains alive and agitated in its depths, similarly to David Suzuki, who will achieve his ends, thanks to his flawless determination.

May 14, 2010

 TAGORE, RABÎNDRANÂTH

Given Name: Rabîndranâth Thâkur
Nationality: Indian
Place and Date of Birth: Calcutta (India), May 6, 1861
Place and Date of Death: Calcutta (India), August 7, 1941
Profession: Poet, writer, philosopher, composer and painter

MASTER DJWHAL KHUL'S COMMENTARY

Rabîndranâth Tagore was a great contemporary philosopher. He was able to transmit a certain light that enlightened some of our greatest minds, directing and inspiring them towards a little frequented path at the time: the inner path of perfect balance in everything. He advocated a wisdom that went beyond the borders of his country but also the mental borders of the majority of people.

Judging no one or almost no one, he considered all humans equal within a Soul that wanted only to express itself. He feared nothing except himself because his great inner strength had to be continuously held back.

Cautious in his approaches, he would confide with difficulty. His very rich inner life did not transpire much through his writings. He felt limited by the verbal expression that was never able to express entirely what he lived or felt.

He would have liked to see human beings more unified and less divided by selfish desires. Presently incarnated in the political field, he still lives in Calcutta and helps his fellow men as best he can. He is still young but will undoubtedly leave his mark.

Initiation Level: 3.2

Ray Structure

Monad: 2	Soul: 3	Personality: 3-4
Mental: 7-3	Astral: 6-2	Physical: 7-5

Monad and Soul

His Monad was starting to exert a certain influence that grew with years. However, his ray 3 Soul influenced his life and his relations tremendously. This ray made him curious and a diplomat. He liked to explore this planet but also everything that concerned the human spirit that remained, to a large part, a mystery for him until his death. He was unable to understand the chaos that was raging within various people, countries and religions.

Personality

His ray 3, sub-ray 4 Personality granted him a fluidity that allowed him to mold to people. He liked to meet with them, talk to them and desperately attempted to understand them. However, similar to every self-respecting ray 3, he kept secret a great part of what he really thought until they matured, considered and realized certain facts. Then he would make decisions without fearing retaliation, because his sub-ray 4 turned him into a real inner warrior.

His sub-ray 4 also conferred to him a prose and wisdom in his writing, because thanks to his initiation level, he was able to adequately balance certain facts, certain remarks or thoughts. In addition, this sub-ray granted him a lot of courage and also guided him in some decision making. Well managed, it becomes a faultless sign of what is good or bad, according to the consciousness of the Spirit, or the Monad, located beyond the Soul that governs the first true stage of human evolution.

Tagore was starting to go beyond that stage. He would see and understand things he was not always able to understand. He realized that the platform of human evolution was multiple and complicated.

Mental Body

His ray 7, sub-ray 3 mental body made him an intelligent, proud and adventurous man. Ray 7 endowed him with discipline that never left him. It provided him with almost infallible reasoning because ray 7 sees far and in detail, which served him well in the task he had to accomplish. This ray also instilled in him the desire for perfection that accompanied him throughout his entire incarnation.

Sub-ray 3 illuminated the work of ray 7 which sometimes experiences difficulty expressing what it feels, because it sees the complexity of the "whole". Sub-ray 3 communicated more flexibility to the energy of ray 7 and allowed a certain light to circulate between the thoughts, at times too organized of the latter. This allowed Tagore to have a more opened spirit, less censured by the sometimes more rigid forms of ray 7.

Astral Body

His ray 6, sub-ray 2 astral body conferred to him a great sensitivity doubled by a limitless devotion to his close and extended family (humanity). A defender of the weak and the oppressed, he would roam the planet to see with his own eyes (ray 3 influence) what was happening elsewhere and what was reflected in his country. He would have liked to change the face of the world; on several occasions, he realized his powerlessness, which rendered him temporarily morose. However, he would quickly pull himself together and go back to the task at hand.

Sub-ray 2 made him a kind and sincere man, ready to do anything to help others understand, but also to expand their horizons beyond the unknown that is so frightening. He was persuaded that the fear of this "unknown" was the only reason responsible for the miseries of the world. To educate humanity at all levels was, for him, an essential key to human evolution.

Physical Body

His ray 7, sub-ray 5 physical body endowed him with a very pleasant physical appearance (the influence of ray 7) but also with a penetrating gaze giving the impression that he was coming from another world (ray 5 influence). Ray 7 equipped him with finesse, perfection and integrity in his thoughts (his brain) and his physical. It inspired him with the wish to reach perfection on the spiritual level, which in his opinion, did not sufficiently occur.

Sub-ray 5 gratified him with a certain strength that allowed him to accomplish a lot in his life. It mainly provided him with intuition that served him all his life. Occasionally, he would see in the invisible an influence coming from this sub-ray in a direct link with the *devic* world that also conferred to him a moral strength that never left him.

September 10, 2009

 # Tesla, Nikola

Given Name: Nikola Tesla
Double Nationality: Serbo-Croatian and American
Place and Date of Birth: Smiljan, (today Croatia), July 10, 1856
Place and Date of Death: New York, New York (United States), January 7, 1943
Profession: Inventor, electrical engineer

Master Djwhal Khul's Commentary

A man of great intelligence, he was misunderstood by his peers and misjudged by those who did not understand his vision of things. Nikola Tesla was a visionary, an incomparable scientist whose intelligence would have made the greatest scientists of our time tremble. From the technology viewpoint, he allowed humanity, which he would have liked to free from darkness (at all levels including the spiritual), to make a giant leap forward.

Some people considered him mad, others, a genius. He perceived the invisible but was unable to express it adequately on the earthly plane. He only lived for science while being very alert to life on earth, which he was discovering with passion. He loved life, but he mainly loved what was impossible in it. Too much in his head, he had never really been in love, although he enjoyed visiting friends who shared his visions and respected him. He believed in the afterlife and in other lives.

We may mention that he never knew rest because his brain was always ready to act, continuously receiving information coming from other planes. He was a perfect receiver of data coming not from the extraterrestrials but from certain Masters such as El Morya Khan and Saint Germain.

Initiation Level: 3.2

This initiation level was necessary for the work he had to accomplish. The stability this initiation level provides allowed him to live his solitude completely. Certainly, he was working towards his next incarnation, which will undoubtedly allow him to reach his fourth Initiation. He has not yet reincarnated, but this should no longer be delayed.

The quantity of damage to his neurological system, following his experiments, had enormously exhausted his body and the link that united him to his Soul; it has weakened him in certain areas and strengthened him in others. He has to repair and adjust this link before coming back; he will be a man of science again and will come from an eastern country. He will remain as reckless and stubborn, but will no doubt succeed in becoming better understood.

Ray Structure

Monad: 3	Soul: 2	Personality: 7-5
Mental: 5-3	Astral: 3-6	Physical: 1-7

Monad and Soul

His Monad exerted almost no direct influence on him; it worked directly in concert with the energy of his Soul to allow him to receive more information supporting the implementation of his experiments. On the other hand, his Soul demonstrated that it was close to him and guided him in his research. It provided him with this love for humanity that never left him.

Personality

His Personality, ruled by the ray 7, sub-ray 5 energies, made him an intelligent man, who knew what he wanted and what he had to do. Not very emotional, which was, in a way, a gift for him, he worked relentlessly trying to discover the mystery of the invisible world. For him, everything was energy and he tried to prove it on several occasions, while being ridiculed by his peers. Ray 7 gave him a sense of detail, refinement and a desire for perfection.

Sub-ray 5 allowed him to acquire vision and the desire to see beyond this vision. The union of ray 7 and sub-ray 5 offered him the possibility to see his projects in detail before they descended into matter.

Mental Body

His mental body, clearly influenced by the ray 5, sub-ray 3 energies, motivated him to refine his work even more. He was relentlessly busy trying to comprehend the incomprehensible, dissecting and examining all in minute detail. Ray 5 imbued him with desire to understand and analyze everything. It made him very "scientific" and "experimental". He liked to seek proofs supporting his theories.

Sub-ray 3 conferred to him a certain flexibility that allowed ray 5 to be less linear, less mundane. It granted him an extraordinary mental mobility motivating him to make tremendous leaps of consciousness. He was never bored because his mind kept him in a constant state of effervescence.

Astral Body

The energy of his astral body, influenced by ray 3, sub-ray 6, often made him ill at ease in society. It created a certain mistrust when confronted with affective links that, for him, represented danger. These links could not be "studied and understood" scientifically, which baffled him. He did not want to become the victim of his emotions and chose his connections well, which created the isolation he learned to like.

Sub-ray 6 generated in him the feeling of being faithful to his ideas and his friends, although he lacked confidence in them; he always feared that his discoveries might fall into the wrong hands. Therefore, he remained faithful to himself and to the inner voices he heard. These voices always guided him and served him well. Some would say they came from the effect of ray 3 in his astral body; we would rather say that the conjunction of ray 3 and sub-ray 6 allowed him to properly receive certain information that helped him all his life. This information came from the Masters who wished for the advancement of the planet.

Physical Body

His physical body, ruled by the ray 1, sub-ray 7 energies, provided him with resistance, strength and intelligence. He disliked wasting his time. Ray 1 equipped him with a strong, intelligent and remarkable brain. He would go straight to the point and would see the final result (in his mind) from the start. Therefore, he would work relentlessly to reach the goal fixed in his mind.

Sub-ray 7 offered refinement, a sense for detail, order, and conferred to him an air of mystery. He resembled a magician more than a scientist.

Too direct and too much in contact with the other dimensions, he seemed quite strange and sometimes dangerous.

His planet of origin is not in our system, even though he spent a few centuries on Venus. He comes from a planet located in the constellation of Aries. People who live there are more advanced than we, particularly at the mental level.

His direct link with the Masters made him what he became. He wanted to be a perfect instrument to receive the information that was communicated to him, via his brain, in a topographic fashion. The Masters would transmit, in detail, the projects that could help humanity over several decades. He felt limited by the world of matter and often surprised by human behaviour.

He had close ties with the *devic* worlds that contacted him via the animal nature (pigeons), their externalization. The communication would take place thanks to these pigeons that talked to him and dictated to him certain notions that helped him in his research.

He did not meditate; this was not necessary because he was in constant contact with the Masters who, on several occasions, provided their help even in the physical. Contrary to what was mentioned, he did not die alone, but surrounded by his real friends, the Masters and their guardians. Towards the end of his life, he knew how to listen to them and to hear them. He recognized having received an exceptional brain that was not at his service, but at the service of the Masters. Every day, he would get in contact with one of his friends, though unaware of their real identity. Some of their writings were among the papers that burned in his laboratory, and those that were found near him, at his death. Unsigned, no one found out who wrote them. We can also state that Koot Hoomi helped him several times. The most important remains Saint Germain, who had known him in a previous life while he lived in Cairo, Egypt, as Ibn Al Haytham. At that time, he was known for his work on physics and light, which always fascinated him.

He then reincarnated three times. Among others, he was a powerful woman in the Arabic world, which was rare at the time. He would have known Rûmî. He granted himself a life of rest and then came back as the founder of the Budapest School of Sciences.

We have to admit that he does not like to incarnate, finding that life on Earth is too limited. He knows, however, that he has to earn his "stripes" and act in such a way as to evolve on the planetary scale in order to reach his sixth initiation, which would free him from this planet. Subsequently, he will work elsewhere, because we consider him a cosmic *Bodhisattva* who helps Souls everywhere in the Universe, integrating into their world and living their suffering and limitations.

December 31, 2008

TRUDEAU, PIERRE ELLIOTT

Given Name: Joseph Philippe Pierre Yves Elliott Trudeau
Nationality: Canadian
Place and Date of Birth: Montreal, Quebec (Canada), October 18, 1919
Place and Date of Death: Montreal, Quebec (Canada), September 28, 2000
Profession: Lawyer, professor of law, and statesman

MASTER DJWHAL KHUL'S COMMENTARY

Pierre Elliott Trudeau would have better succeeded in life in the field of spirituality than that of politics. He was a very good Prime Minster, but suffered tremendously from the lack of understanding of those with whom he worked. His initiation level was respectable, which did not simplify his task in this controversial and corrupt world.

Initiation Level: 3.2

Ray Structure

Monad: 1	Soul: 2	Personality: 7-3
Mental: 1-5	Astral: 6-2	Physical: 3-7

Monad and Soul

His Soul exerted a huge influence on him, and he suffered much from human cruelty appropriating faces he hated. He was quick-tempered because ray 1 energy from the Monad, was beginning to influence his way of thinking and of acting. He could be very direct and blunt.

He was a fearless man, thanks to the united strength represented by his 7's and his 1's. Better supported, as much by his wife, (whose initiation level was 1.2 at the time) as by his friends and fellow countrymen, he could have accomplished much more. He lived a great loneliness, often prompting him to withdraw within himself.

Personality

His ray 7 Personality incited an interest in perfection and beauty in everything. He loved beautiful things and appreciated using them, without getting attached to them. For him, life should not be so complicated; it is people and their way of thinking that complicate everything. He was fascinated by human behaviour and the relative differences related to these various actions.

Sub-ray 3 conferred to him a certain flexibility that allowed him to intervene adequately in delicate situations that often required a lot of intelligence. He was very intelligent but above all very intuitive.

Mental Body

His ray 1, sub-ray 5 mental body was a very useful gift in his life; it gave him a clarity of mind that allowed him to penetrate mysteries. We already mentioned that he was very intuitive, which was quite useful to see behind mysteries.

Ray 1 made him a frank man, too much sometimes; he said what he thought without fear. This ray made him determined and deliberate; he would express himself very directly, without using kid gloves. He saw the goal and tried, as far as it was possible, to reach it. He believed in human justice while knowing it was difficult to apply. His material wealth never tarnished his humanity. Although he projected a certain arrogance in public, he was quite different in private; he knew how to be kind, attentive and loving (the influence of his astral body). A very good lover, which pleased his conquests, he possessed the art of seduction, with intelligence, while respecting the other as much as possible.

Sub-ray 5 gave him a "down to earth" aspect and he would not easily be thwarted by his emotions. This sub-ray conferred to him logic that sometimes troubled his hosts, and great intuition. This man wanted to be close to nature, thanks to this sub-ray 5, one of whose characteristics is this proximity with the kingdoms living in nature.

Astral Body

His ray 6, sub-ray 2 astral body made him a man loyal to his cause, sincere and an appreciated father. A good husband, his political responsibilities nevertheless damaged his life as a couple because his wife, due to her immaturity, did not tolerate being considered second fiddle. Ray 6 gave him the taste for family, and he adored his children. It made him warm although at times his mind, whose nature was colder, would sometimes take over. He would have given his life for his sons, as he was totally devoted to them.

Sub-ray 2 transmitted to him great sensitivity that served him all his life. He could easily be hurt, although his initiation level would allow him to rapidly regain his self-countenance. This sub-ray instilled in him the desire to teach and help others; he could have become a remarkable teacher.

Physical Body

His rays 3, sub-ray 7 physical equipped him with great physical resistance. Ray 3 granted him charisma and remarkable intelligence; due to his great ability to play with words, he knew how to address people and convince them. This ray allowed him to manage several things simultaneously and, in a way, to demonstrate he was indefatigable. It granted him some ease in conflict resolution.

Sub-ray 7 transmitted to him a constant thirst for perfection. He liked details because he knew that, without them, his work would be incomplete. This sub-ray gave him the taste for beautiful things and luxury.

This man was underestimated. However, we can mention that he appreciated life, that he died at peace with himself and that he will return as such.

November 15, 2007

 TRUMP, DONALD

Given Name: Donald John Trump
Nationality: American
Place and Date of Birth: New York, New York (United States),
June 14, 1946
Profession: Businessman

MASTER DJWHAL KHUL'S COMMENTARY

Donald Trump is a very young Soul who evolves in the world of finance in order to taste "power". He experiments with a flagrant lack of discernment, well demonstrated through his attitude towards humans. For him, everything revolves around his fortune; he is even obsessed with it. This denotes a fairly low level of evolution, for which he could not care less because he only likes the power that money provides him with.

Not having any real friends, he lives a solitude that he arrogantly ignores. If his arrogant attitude does not diminish before his mental polarization begins (starting from approximately 1.5 initiation), it will become difficult for him to progress on the spiritual path. He will remain trapped in a universe where his progression will no longer take place vertically, but simply horizontally. Anyway, this holds no importance for him because he believes it is preferable to be materially rich than spiritually. On the other hand, he believes neither in spirituality nor in God. He is a man to be pitied from our viewpoint, but not from his.

Initiation Level: 1.2

He has reached, in this incarnation, the height of "the experience of power" through what wealth can provide. He will start to live with more difficulty, materially in the next incarnation. As he is dependent on money, he will live a very painful transition.

Let us not forget that at this initiation level, the Initiate creates much karma through carelessness and recklessness. He will consequently have to repair the errors committed since the beginning of his incarnations on this planet. Note that if we take the time to talk about it, it is because he makes too many people react in the world. His worldly influence reveals itself to be coloured by arrogance, contempt, lack of heart and compassion. He is not for us an example to follow but an example to understand.

Ray Structure

Monad: 3	Soul: 4	Personality: 3-7
Mental: 7-5	Astral: 2-6	Physical: 1-6

Monad and Soul

His Monad does not exert any influence on him and his Soul very little. He is mainly influenced by the warrior and gambler traits of the ray 4. As he does not have sufficient strength to master this ray, he is a bit of a victim of it, the energy of the Soul being too far from him.

Personality

His Personality, governed by the ray 3, sub-ray 7 influence, makes him into an intelligent man and a manipulator. Ray 3 provides him with an ease of expressing himself in public. However, it does not confer to him a great distinction. Even if he appears distinguished, he is not. He likes to impress with his speech, loves to have the last word and becomes furious if this is not the case. This ray provides him with the ability to work on several projects simultaneously. He very much resembles a spider in the center of its web, ready to devour anyone who comes too close to him.

Sub-ray 7 allows him to be organized, efficient and punctual most of the time. He loves things well done and perfect. The influence of this sub-ray instills in him the taste for beautiful things, not necessarily those that have great class. He likes to impress and be impressed in his inferior chakras (the power of the hara; beautiful women, from the sexual chakra; strong emotions, from the solar plexus).

Mental Body

His mental body, influenced by the ray 7, sub-ray 5 energies, has little influence on him because he is uniquely focused on his physical body and his Personality, his astral body being embryonic. He does not know how to really love, except money, which seems to bewitch him. We would say, however, that the influence of ray 7 increases his desire for order and perfection. He shows no nuances in his desires; he wants more, to go higher and further than everyone else.

Sub-ray 5 increases his harshness towards others and sucks up every shred of compassion in him. It makes him very mundane, practical and manipulative.

Astral Body

His astral body reveals little evolution. Very selfish, he rarely understands others. He detests the influence of ray 2 that sometimes makes him sensitive. He tries to remain on top of his emotions, creating the illusion that he controls them, although in fact it is the contrary. He escapes his emotions or lets them dominate him by exploding. For him, sensitivity is a threatening weakness; it can ruin him. If this were the case, he would die.

His sub-ray 6 provides a devoted aspect towards his causes, especially financial ones. He thinks he loves his children. He is proud of them most of the time but has no idea how to treat them properly.

Physical Body

His physical body, impregnated with the ray 1, sub-ray 6 energies, influences all his life and that of others. Ray 1 confers to him a resistant and tireless body. Because this ray rules the brain, hence his way of thinking, it allows him to be clear, direct and straightforward. He is rarely diplomatic, which he considers a waste of time. This ray allows him to delegate while remaining attentive to what takes place. He can detect an important detail and correct it if necessary. He shows no pity when he is entirely under the influence of ray 1, becoming impatient, uncompromising and demanding. He does not know how to stop, because the push of this ray, over which he has no control, forces him to advance constantly without stopping. He loves power, which he uses over others, and becomes violent when he faces resistance. One has to be strong to share his life. Very selfish, he does not know how to see what happens around him and he could not care less about it.

This sub-ray 6 increases the effect of ray 1, what makes him even more demanding. If you are not on his side, he thinks you are against him. He does not like to face resistance. He thinks he is the strongest and he believes it. Immortality: it is for him and not for others. He is convinced he will survive this life through his companies. He will die as unconscious as he was when he was born, even more.

This man is not a model for humanity, even if he seems at times to have a heart. Let us wish he never goes into politics, which is not his destiny in this present life.

April 1, 2010

 TWAIN, MARK

Given Name: Samuel Langhorne Clemens
Nationality: American
Place and Date of Birth: Florida, Missouri (United States),
November 30, 1835
Place and Date of Death: Redding, Connecticut (United States),
April 20, 1910
Profession: Writer, humorist and essayist

MASTER DJWHAL KHUL'S COMMENTARY

Mark Twain was a very interesting and very intelligent man. He brought to his community a contemporary vision of writing. An outsider, he has always been attracted by the inexplicable and the unknown. He disliked the beaten track and suffered all his life from the misunderstanding of his peers. The little extended vision that the masses possessed often dismayed him.

We can contend that he maintained a close link with certain Masters without knowing it. These contacts were established during his sleep and sometimes through physical encounters that seemed unimportant. This man had a beneficial effect through literature and the guidance of certain Masters proved necessary. I will only mention Hilarion and Saint Germain.

Initiation Level: 2.6

His initiation level gratified him with a certain vision that dissociated itself from the masses. It conferred to him a certain arrogance that verged on impertinence. He did not fear shocking others because for him humans who favorably reacted to this type of "shock" had a chance to change for the better.

Ray Structure

Monad: 2	Soul: 3	Personality: 4-6
Mental: 7-3	Astral: 6-2	Physical: 7-3

Monad and Soul

His Monad exerted just a slight influence on him, while his Soul established a link more and more closely with his Personality. It guided him on several occasions and served him humorously to provide a newer vision of the literary meaning of the time.

Personality

His Personality, governed by the combined ray 4, sub-ray 6 energies, made him a proud man, who would not go unnoticed. Ray 4 transmitted to him the volition of writing and of fighting for his ideas. He liked to meet challenges and never complained about the sense of adventure that animated his life. He loved to see everything moving and detested stagnation. This ray inspired him to discover what was hiding behind what appeared visible. Always active, he was gifted with a flamboyant, even eccentric, Personality.

Sub-ray 6 conferred to him warmth and a boldness that never left him. He appreciated what was intense and devoted himself body and soul to what he loved. A man faithful to his convictions, he would often reveal himself to be narrow-minded. The union of ray 4 and ray 6 provided him with unfailing willpower. We have to mention that sub-ray 6 helped him maintain his course and not to fall into the *downs* that are sometimes caused by ray 4's influence.

Mental Body

The energy carried by ray 7, sub-ray 3 of his mental body allowed him to acquire a keen intelligence. Ray 7 granted him the sense of perfection and detail. He also wanted to be very ritualistic in his writing. This ray assigned to him this mysterious aspect that characterized him very well. No one could really predict what he would say or do. Quite a gentleman, the pride of ray 7 dictated to him irreproachable conduct in all the fields he particularly cared for.

Sub-ray 3 granted him the art of repartee. It was difficult to fool him. As we said, he was brilliant and intelligent. This sub-ray offered him the possibility to play with words, in order for them to become his allies and to defend his ideas well, ideas he had to sell.

Astral Body

The energy of his astral body, ruled by ray 6 and sub-ray 2 allowed him to be sensitive, very sensitive and devoted to his family and his causes. Warm and cordial, he could also become cold and lose his temper. Ray 6 made him highly critical with his comments when he had to say things. On the other hand, his ray 3's allowed him to encapsulate the passion created by ray 6's and to resort to humour.

Sub-ray 2 endowed him with great sensitivity, but also gifted him with a lot of intuition. He felt "things" and liked to understand them (the influence of ray 7). This sub-ray communicated to him the sense of detail, which helped him in his writings and his research.

Physical Body

His physical body, influenced by ray 7, sub-ray 3, equipped him with a productive body that met his expectations. Ray 7 provided him with discipline and a sense of drama that he transmitted well in his writings. It granted him this ease of creating images through words in his writings. It also conferred to him a sense of the sacred in everything, because for him everything represented a mystery.

Sub-ray 3 allowed him to be phlegmatic and productive. Ray 7 offered him the possibility of hiding his emotions when necessary and sub-ray 3 added verbal spice. This sub-ray gifted him with a fast thinking process that often exasperated his detractors. He could play with words and their meaning. It was preferable to count him as a friend than an enemy.

This man is not yet reincarnated but it should happen soon. He was waiting for technology to be more advanced in order to progress more efficiently, because ray 3 pushes him now to rapidly move forward. He will become a prominent person not in art but in science. He will be a forerunner of time travel.

October 23, 2009

 **VERNE, JULES**

Given Name: Jules Gabriel Verne
Nationality: French
Place and Date of Birth: Nantes (France), February 8, 1828
Place and Date of Death: Amiens (France), March 24, 1905
Profession: Writer

MASTER DJWHAL KHUL'S COMMENTARY

Jules Verne was and remains a prominent figure in the literary world. He was endowed with a great imagination that allowed him to dramatize what he perceived on the other planes (astral and mental). He had the ability to see the future, through his dreams, and to almost live a double life, because he would cheerfully wander throughout the high astral spheres and the lower stratas of the mental plane during his nocturnal trips. What he described in his books narrates the adventures he derived from this nocturnal world that populated his nights.

He never took himself seriously, even if he knew that what he described contained a part of the truth. He would distinctly see the details of every object, of every character, and he could describe them at will simply by drawing upon his inner world where everything was printed and retained.

He was a visionary of his time, almost similar to Leonardo da Vinci. He knew how to dramatize, within the pages of his books, the future and the possible in what seemed, at the time, impossible. However, Jules Verne did not always have an easy life, because his extreme sensitivity was such that he was sometimes hurt and bruised by what happened to him. Yet, his optimism, the travels in his dream states, and his books often compensated for this too harsh world that he found inappropriate to the development of human life.

Initiation Level: 2.3

Ray Structure

Monad: 2	Soul: 3	Personality: 3-7
Mental: 7-5	Astral: 6-4	Physical: 3-6

Monad and Soul

Monad and Soul

His Monad exercised virtually no influence on his life, unlike his Soul, which held some and influenced his visions. His ray 3 Soul created a dynamic that favoured inner travels. This ray enjoys exploring, which is what he did via his dreams. The influence of ray 3 allowed the opening of certain astral doors, but also mental; he had a sense of detail that was very noticeable in his writings ("The Poseidon", in *Voyage to the Bottom of the Sea*, *Around the World in Eighty Days*, *A Journey to the Center of the Earth*...).

Personality

His ray 3, sub-ray 7 Personality allowed the pursuit of perfection in the details of his writings (the ray 7, sub-ray 5 mental body strongly supporting his Personality rays). Ray 3 granted him a fluid Personality, adaptable to various situations, whether real or not, because his astral body remained impregnated with the energy of his ray 3's during his inner voyages. This ray allowed him to be alert to anything that could nurture his imagination. It also gave him a certain humour, perceptible in his writings.

Sub-ray 7 polished his writings and revealed in the description of his adventures an acute sense of perfection. This sub-ray gave him the taste for beauty in everything. It refined his intelligence by allowing him to be clearer and more radiant in his writing.

Mental Body

His ray 7, sub-ray 5 mental body was very useful to him because, like an antenna, it allowed him to bring back into the physical world what he had experienced on other planes. Ray 7 reflected an almost perfect image of the details he perceived and allowed him to remember them, because this ray has an extraordinary photographic memory.

Sub-ray 5 rendered plausible what he described and enhanced the accuracy of the situations described in his adventures. This ray has the ability to convince, through explanations almost always scientifically proven, the most skeptical people. It could prove to be a very good salesman, like ray 3, because it encourages the art of persuasion. Ray 3 likes to impress, while ray 5 dazzles by its brilliance that seems intelligent.

Astral

His ray 6, sub-ray 4 astral body conferred to him the sense of responsibility and duty. Ray 6 imbued him with faithfulness and sub-ray 4, with a sense of wonder that transpired from his writings. Ray 6 gave him a sympathetic and warm air; he was generous and liked to help others.

Sub-ray 4 coloured his writings and gave life to his characters. It made them endearing and diverse. This sub-ray engendered some emotional discomfort that he mastered quite quickly thanks to his mental strength (rays 7 and 5) that put him back on the right track and to work.

Physical Body

His ray 3, sub-ray 6 physical instilled a certain fluidity into his words and allowed him to conceal sufficiently well what he was living on the inner planes. — The brain, qualified by ray 3, authorizes a fair value of proportions between what seems real and what really is. This ray keeps a certain inner balance and provides a sense of humour that can defuse everything. — He did not take himself too seriously, knowing instinctively that what he lived elsewhere really existed. His wish was to encourage as many people as possible to experience these worlds parallel to ours.

Sub-ray 6 allowed him to remain anchored in the world of matter and to be functional. This sub-ray made him like family life, solitude and good food.

Jules Verne is a pioneer that children should rediscover. He allows imagination, even today, to flourish to the rhythm of the reading of his works. It awakens imagination and gives back wonder to the world, thus creating an inner movement instead of paralyzing it like video games do.

June 4, 2009

 # VIVALDI, ANTONIO

Given Name: Antonio Lucio Vivaldi
Surname: *Il Prete Rosso* (The Red Priest)
Nationality: Italian
Place and Date of Birth: Venice (Italy), March 4, 1678
Place and Date of Death: Vienna (Austria), July 28, 1741
Profession: Violinist and composer of baroque music

MASTER DJWHAL KHUL'S COMMENTARY

Antonio Vivaldi was a great devotee of God and a great composer. He conveyed sincerity of the heart to humanity thanks to music. He had certain contacts with the world of angels in which he firmly believed. He suffered a lot from solitude and sickness. However, thanks to music, he was able to transmute his discomforts into something constructive.

I will not discuss his personal life; I will only mention that from certain viewpoints he was avant-garde, while from others he was really linked to his era. He experienced certain fears, including the fear of God's punishment. However, he believed in his divine mercy and knew that the entity called "God" did not foster sexual discrimination. He believed in women's equality although he never dared touch one intimately. He knew that if he did that it would be the beginning of many problems in his life (of all sorts) and he felt he already had enough of them. On the other hand, he liked to imagine music as his mistress, the one that would make him forget everything.

His music transmitted a more majestic aspect to the "religious" aspect, increasing the depth and the variety of what he saw as a tribute to God and his creations. He could play with bass and deep tones and all of a sudden switch to more joyous and sparkling notes, like his life and Life in general (according to his vision).

Initiation Level: 1.9

Vivaldi was getting near his second initiation, which caused him intense inner discomfort. He was ill at ease with himself and often sought refuge in his music to "heal" or reduce this discomfort he felt.

Ray Structure

Monad: 1	Soul: 2	Personality: 2-4
Mental: 7-1	Astral: 6-4	Physical: 3-6

Monad and Soul

His Monad exerted no influence; it was just dormant. His Soul started an influence that guided him in his music. Because his configuration included two ray 2's in the front line, it is exactly these two rays that efficiently increased his sensitivity and created in him a breach that allowed him to listen to others' needs. They also favoured listening to higher spheres, including the angelic realm, that thanks to the energy of his ray 7, sub-ray 1 mental body, captured his attention (the magical aspect of ray 7) and favoured extreme concentration (the effect of ray 1) in order to bring down into the world of matter what he heard in his inner world. Because he was working towards his second initiation, his music will mainly reach those who are also striving ardently to reach their second initiation.

Personality

His Personality, ruled by rays 2 and 4, gave him a bit of the artist's soul. He was sometimes obsessed by the art of creating and would become bewitched by the music he wanted to put on paper. He often went astray in daydreams that allowed him to listen to angels. In part, this is the reason he introduced women's voices in his music, voices he judged to be close to the angelic realm. Ray 2 gave him a certain shyness he was trying to counter. He suffered from pulmonary problems attributed to the stress resulting from the fears caused by the influence of this ill-channeled ray.

Sub-ray 4 increased his creativity but also made him live more difficult periods internally. Certain events tormented him and at times caused an almost unhealthy insecurity, particularly on the financial front. However, he was able to live through this discomfort, thanks to the strength and courage to go on that he managed to draw from this sub-ray. This also served as a support for his stubbornness, derived from the influence of his ray 7, sub-ray 1 Mental and ray 6, sub-ray 4 astral body.

Mental Body

His mental body, under the influence of rays 7 and 1, allowed him to transmit to the world the celestial music he heard "in his head". Ray 7 favoured the desire for perfection in his music and instilled in him the right intuition to transcribe the appropriate notes. It also created in him the desire for order that he expressed in his scores.

Sub-ray 1 provided him with the will and the concentration he needed to write. It also granted him the necessary moral strength. This sub-ray almost always succeeded in getting rid of the doubt created by the influence of his ray 2 Personality.

Astral Body

His astral body influenced by ray 6, sub-ray 4, transmitted to him this devotion to God but also the dilemma to live in a world that did not necessarily correspond to the image he had of God. Ray 6 endowed him with warmth and love of neighbor, but mainly of God. Although he loved man, he loved his God and his music more. This ray made him stubborn, sometimes vindictive and quick-tempered (do not forget that he was red haired, thus revealing a strong character).

Sub-ray 4 created an existential malaise. Even though he felt attracted by women, because ray 4 likes beauty, ray 6 prevented him from getting too close. The influence of this sub-ray instilled in him the desire to know beauty and harmony, which his life did not often allow. He was often in conflict with the Church and certain people did not understand his passion for music.

Physical Body

His physical body, imbued with the ray 3, sub-ray 6 energies, equipped him with a rather powerful brain. Ray 3 allowed him to think fast and to rapidly get out of certain situations that could have caused him problems. This ray endowed him with great flexibility of expression in gesture and speech.

Sub-ray 6 gave him stability, which allowed him to mature his music even into his physical. He would live the warm and devotional aspects in his body through the influence of this sub-ray vibrating to the notes that he succeeded in conveying on paper.

This man lived an interesting life, although often painful. During the following incarnation, he reached his second initiation but not without difficulty. At that time, the physician of Bonaparte (Jean Nicolas Corvisart), he had a passionate life, but there also, not very comfortable in many regards. He became as gifted for medicine as he had been for music.

This man is presently incarnated in the body of a woman in the south of Japan, where he is learning the art of meditation and service in preparation for his third initiation. He lives within modest means but still adores music. The desire of his Soul was not to be "known" in order to deepen acquired experiences and learn humility and simplicity. This Soul is presently teaching music and painting.

August 15, 2009

 VOLTAIRE

Given Name: François Marie Arouet
Other Name: Voltaire
Nationality: French
Place and Date of Birth: Paris (France), November 21, 1692
Place and Date of Death: Paris (France), May 30, 1778
Profession: Writer and philosopher

MASTER DJWHAL KHUL'S COMMENTARY

A man of immense talent, Voltaire had an impact on his era due to his originality and his literary ardour. A great scholar, he was able to accomplish his mission of demystifying the Church, which was too powerful at the time and stood in the way of just liberty for all. He denounced injustice through his prose and became a devil's advocate for many causes, which earned him a somewhat mixed reputation among the French people. Adulated by some and hated by others, Voltaire was always true to his ideas, despite the storm constantly raging around him. A believer in the goodness of human nature, despite the cruelty he witnessed and endured, he never wanted to resort to half measures or to appear weak.

His taste for luxury and beauty resulted from his ray configuration, for ray 4 needs such traits to survive and flourish in this world that it often finds absurd and incomprehensible. Voltaire had three ray 4's, including one on the first line, which produced incredible ups and downs in him. Fortunately, his fairly elevated initiation level allowed him to meet the challenges fearlessly. He could be provocative due to his arrogance (linked to his initiation level) and his ray 4's.

Initiation Level: 3.2

Ray Structure

Monad: 2	Soul: 3	Personality: 4-2
Mental: 5-7	Astral: 2-4	Physical: 3-4

Monad and Soul

His Monad exerted influence at an early stage, although his Soul ruled his life for the most part. It gave him a way with words that sometimes cut to the quick of the matter and guided him in several of his choices. He loved to experiment, no matter what it cost him. The Soul, his ally, gave him the tools to be what he became, which is to say, a prosperous writer who knew how to transmit a form of wisdom that offered the intellect the possibility of reacting to the energy coming from the Soul. A key note can be heard if the individual sets aside his rational aspect, thereby leaving room for a more elevated aspect.

Personality

His Personality of ray 4, sub-ray 2 made him love beauty in all that life offered. Ray 4 sprouted this artistic aspect along with the desire to seduce that characterized him. It also conveyed to him a sense of adventure and graced him with his fearless quality; he liked to provoke and meet a challenge.

Sub-ray 2 conferred to him a noticeable sensitivity that allowed him to feel and understand human nature. He could probe the emotional nature and transmit it through his writing. He loved to love but disliked being attached (the influence of ray 4); he loved his freedom while deeply loving those close to his heart.

Mental Body

His ray 5, sub-ray 7 mental body equipped him with a rational mind that was in tune with his Soul and efficiently transmitted words to express his creativity. His ray 5 made him intelligent and logical. It offered him the possibility of understanding the various aspects of life's events.

Sub-ray 7 refined his thoughts and his writing, granting him the ability to be prolific and to enjoy strong mental resistance. It endowed him with the tenacity necessary to perform his work and his mission in this world. It made him love perfection even more in the art of expression.

Astral Body

His ray 2, sub-ray 4 Astral gave him charm, sensitivity and magnetism, particularly with women who adored him. He made husbands jealous and suffered from temporary jealousy. This jealousy stemmed from his great sensitivity, which created fears of losing a loved one, of losing his fame and of losing the comfort in which he lived… However, as he aged, he acquired more maturity, which helped dissipate his fear and greatly diminished this transitory jealousy.

His sub-ray 4 sometimes perturbed his emotions, but it also allowed him to write with greater depth. This sub-ray made him unstable, inconsistent in his expressions or quick-tempered at times; however, thanks to his initiation level, he always succeeded in rapidly regaining his equilibrium.

Physical Body

His physical body of ray 3, sub-ray 4 graced him with a certain beauty, supported by the union of rays 3 and 4, which total 7. This beauty was more evident in his youth. As he aged, ray 3 gained in amplitude, which slightly dulled his traits and made his appearance less delicate.

Sub-ray 4 offered him an appreciable assistance in his work. Ray 3 gave him quickness of thought and facility in verbal expression; he was never at a loss for words. He could also produce written work in record time when he had to.

This man had certain contacts with the Count of Saint Germain who guided him in his work and helped his consciousness evolve. Saint Germain respected him and never imposed a way of thinking on him. He never presented himself as a Master, as Voltaire would not have accepted it.

June 7, 2009

WALSCH, NEALE DONALD

Given Name: Neale Marshall Walsch
Nationality: American
Place and Date of Birth: Milwaukee, Wisconsin (United States), September 10, 1943
Profession: Speaker and author

MASTER DJWHAL KHUL'S COMMENTARY

Mr. Walsch is a channel, a medium of a similar caliber as Edgar Cayce. He does not really converse with God, but with an astral reflection of what we call "God". He really accomplishes good work because he gives hope and guidelines to humanity, or at least to those who accept putting their trust in him by reading his books.

God is inaccessible, but Mr. Walsch allows a certain understanding, thanks to his writings, of the divine nature of man when he embarks on the evolutionary path (until the third initiation). The entity that dictates the messages originates from one of the higher astral planes and fluctuates between the fifth and the sixth level. He slightly colours the messages received; however, we may mention that he is doing a good job, and will continue to do so as long as his ego remains sufficiently humble not to interfere.

Channels, such as Mr. Walsch, prove necessary in order to reach the mass consciousness. The great ordeal he suffered at the end of his 49 years allowed his Soul to get closer in order to transmit to him the inspiration of his real work. The astral entity, whom we can call an Angel carrying messages from the higher realms, maintains a link with him that allows the transmission of information adapted to the human condition, but mainly to the evolution of the human mass. Some data are obsolete, even false, but their positive effect remains the most important link with God, with faith, and with the human soul evolving within matter.

Mr. Walsch's initiation level will surprise many, because his channel allows him to receive messages beyond the capacity to capture them from this initiation level, as was the situation for Edgar Cayce.

Initiation Level: 1.3

His mental polarization is starting; but what makes him such a good channel remains his Personality that does not obstruct the divine intervention within the communication. He is straddling between the divine intervention of the mental plane, that is not quite ready, and his Soul communicating with the mental plane in order to convey to him messages coming from a high level astral entity that, for some, appears like God. In other words, he possesses the necessary humility in order not to interfere with the divine mental nature, overriding his Personality which, except on rare occasions, offers no obstruction. However, if it happens, he acknowledges it and corrects himself quite rapidly, thanks to the influence of his Soul and his ray 2 Personality. This is also a way to correct several errors made in past lives, among which was having abused the power of money to acquire other people's possessions during the First World War, when he lived in Spain. We will not dwell too much on that topic, the important thing being that he is doing considerable good in this present incarnation. In spite of his weariness and his great fatigue, he knows he cannot stop his work, which he will carry until his death.

Ray Structure

Monad: 1	Soul: 2	Personality: 2-3
Mental: 3-5	Astral: 6-2	Physical: 3-7

Monad and Soul

His Monad exerts no influence, contrary to his Soul, which overriding the Personality, allows the astral entity to reach the mental plane and to transmit fairly correct information. The ray 3 mental body, through its speed, captures the information and communicates it to the physical brain, also ray 3, which then adapts and transmits this information to the vocal cords and to the hands. The speed of ray 3 allows this miracle.

Personality

His ray 2, sub-ray 3 Personality shapes him into a gentle, loving, and rather sensitive man. He knows how to listen to other people's problems, thanks to this ray 2, that now helps him to accomplish his mission.

Previously, sub-ray 3 took too much space and lined up excessively with his other ray 3's (mental body and brain), which made him a good facilitator and manipulator, with an interesting sense of repartee. Thanks to this influence, he remains very magnetic, a fluent speaker, and at times jovial.

Mental Body

His ray 3, sub-ray 5 mental body makes him a brilliant, intelligent man who likes to think. He thinks fast but protects his back by taking the time to think (the influence of ray 5) before talking or writing information that may shock his public. A great thinker, he likes to help others but sometimes forgets basic, simple love. In spite of his great capacity to love, he sometimes remains too much on the mental plane, therefore becoming inaccessible during his conferences. He has the ability to transmit information but not to transform his audience. He nourishes their Mental, eases their Astral, but cannot reach their central point that we will name Consciousness, located beyond the small consciousness. He works hard and we are grateful. His work remains basic but essential because it will allow one day the real awakening of Consciousness.

Astral Body

His ray 6, sub-ray 2 Astral brings him warmth and sensitivity. He likes to give of his time and his money but ignores how to give real love. He loves, of course but in a still subjective and subtly conditional way. However, we will not discuss the magnitude of his love for humanity, which necessarily remains purely astral. He is endowed with the glamour of the savior, the one who would give his shirt, although he should abstain from it. Discernment is still lacking but it will come with time. Ray 6 makes him loving and attentive to others. He is a good host, endowed with a big heart. Sub-ray 2 provides him with refinement, intuition and a good sense of humour.

Physical Body

His ray 3, sub-ray 7 physical body equips him with a fairly resistant body and a healthy appearance, in spite of difficulties. Ray 3 allows him to act and think fast whenever necessary. However, if this proves impractical, he will remain in his ray 2 Personality to teach, which gives him a laid-back, gentle, and attentive approach.

Sub-ray 7 makes him appreciate good things and creates in him the desire to reach perfection. It allowed him to go through the tough trials and tribulations of his life without developing too many psychological and physical consequences.

This is a good man who likes to help and comfort human beings. He will accomplish great things in this life, but mainly in the next one, where he will hold an important place within the Buddhist community.

May 4, 2009

 # WESSELMAN, HANK

Given Name: Henry Barnard Wesselman
Nationality: American
Place and Date of Birth: New York, New York (United States), 1941
Profession: Doctor of Anthropology

MASTER DJWHAL KHUL'S COMMENTARY

Hank Wesselman is an interesting man who speaks about topics as interesting. However, it is to be noted that he still has a lot to learn and to build; he is only at the beginning of his quest and we believe that he knows it. He is a perfect medium that the Masters use to transmit a certain wisdom.

His contact, whom he calls "Nainoa", is an astral projection from his future, meaning that he projects his consciousness via this energy body; in fact, it is one of his possible futures, a parallel of himself that he constructs from life to life. Presently, he does not see himself strong enough to use another vehicle. We strongly doubt that this reality is probable. However, this may occur. This man has a strong imagination, and that pleases us; we still have to recognize that a part of the truth resides in his writings.

His Shamanistic aspect acts in such a way that it is in a close relationship with *devas* linked to the world of time and space through the mineral world. These *devas*, linked to ray 7, a world of ritual and magic, are guided by the Count of Saint Germain as well as their own *devic* Master working on that ray. These two Masters cooperate closely so that the future of the Earth still conforms to its purpose.

This planet is not called upon to involute but to evolve, in all viewpoints, even technologically. We do not believe that a humanity focused on

Shamanism will exist in 5,000 years. Life will be exhilarating and the physical body will have taken on another aspect, more ethereal, less dense. Man will prove to be more intelligent; he will not only use his brain but also increasingly his intuition, linked to the Soul that will gradually turn to the influence of the Monad.

Man is not destined to disappear. He will transform like the planet that will remain similar while being very different. Highlands will become temporary havens during upheavals that will not destroy man but will allow him to deepen, to settle down, although some period of disorder will sometimes make him bitter. While learning from chaos, man dislikes chaos and tries to escape from it instead of getting closer to and learning from it. A lot remains to be said, but let us get back to the topic at hand, Mr. Wesselman.

Initiation Level: 2.2

His initiation level allows him to be a good transmitter for the *devas* that try to teach him, in accordance with his Soul, certain lessons that induce consciousness to perceive something different from what is apparent. His mandate, among other things, consists of opening the scientific consciousness, in order to recognize the existence of other facts that cannot presently be logically proven, but will be in the future. His scientific approach lost a bit of credit when confronted by other scientists who do not believe in a parallel world. Time will be needed, a lot of time, before concrete science will unite with the subtle science of our being, which will prove to be as rewarding.

Ray Structure

Monad: 2   Soul: 3 (under the temporary influence of Ray 7)
Personality: 3-6   Mental: 7-5   Astral: 6-4   Physical: 7-3

Monad and Soul

His Monad exerts very little influence on him, contrary to his Soul, whose influence is more than interesting. This alliance of rays 3 and 7 proves to be particular; without it, he would experience difficulty in accomplishing his work as a medium. Ray 3 serves as a sensor and ray 7 as a transmitter. Therefore, he receives messages from the Ashram of the seventh ray, messages that have to pass through the third ray of the Ashram to which he is linked. Why ray 7? The *devic* world that inspires him is affiliated to this Ashram as well as to the Count of Saint Germain, who in this life is momentarily in charge of its evolution, in agreement with the Master of the Ray 3 Ashram. This seems complicated for the lower mental but not for the higher mental.

Personality

His ray 3, sub-ray 6 Personality makes him an intelligent and practical man. Ray 3 motivates him to act with simplicity and diplomacy; it allows him to express himself with ease and to be understood. He can explain certain facts while giving the illusion that these notions are neither complicated nor strange. This ray can render tangible, by word manipulation, what is not; ray 3 is a great manipulator for good, but sometimes also for evil (which is not Mr. Wesselman's case).

His sub-ray 6 gives him the warm and cheerful aspect that characterizes him. A good motivator, he can easily fire up crowds, because he is brilliant and interesting. He can materialize almost anything while instilling the totality of his faith in what he is saying. He could easily sell a refrigerator to an Eskimo if he wanted. Fortunately, his motivation is not to profit from others but to educate them.

Mental Body

His ray 7, sub-ray 5 mental body gives him his scientific aspect. Ray 7 grants him a certain ease with the non-tangible world, this world that belongs to the unknown and almost to magic. It makes him ritualistic and close to nature. He "feels" things and possesses great intuition.

Sub-ray 5 brings him his "reasoning" and sometimes naive aspect. It is an indispensable tool for the accomplishment of his task; he asks himself the right questions and thus reveals himself to be credible. This sub-ray pushes him to analyze, to search and finally to find intelligent answers to his questions. The union of rays 7 and 5 gives him a good memory; let us not forget that ray 5 also possesses affinities with the world of the *devas*. This sub-ray 5 reveals itself to be an essential support to the work of ray 7.

Astral Body

His ray 6, sub-ray 4 Astral makes him sensitive and lovable. The influence of ray 6 conveys to him this warmth and love he feels for humanity. It instills in him a faith that guides him in his inner explorations and endows him with a determination that pushes him, because of his love for all that lives on this planet, to always go further within. In addition, this ray reassures him with the certainty that he is doing a good job.

Sub-ray 4 invests him with strength and courage. It supports him in his work and allows him to face his fears (particularly those related to ridicule). He possesses a certain pride of the soul and does not like to be laughed at. This sub-ray gives him, on the other hand, a great sensitivity that could destroy him if he is not alert. Without the attachment created by the influence of this sub-ray, he would experience difficulty coming back to his body and would remain lost in the parallel world he is exploring.

Physical Body

His ray 7, sub-ray 3 physical body gives him priceless support. Ray 7 allows him to be disciplined and sufficiently down to earth. It brings him back to reality and the magic found in our daily lives. It equips him with an efficient nervous system, which is essential to his work.

Sub-ray 3 grants him flexibility in every sense of the term. He has better muscular resistance, a brain that offers him the possibility to live his experiences elsewhere while remaining here. This sub-ray gives him the possibility of accomplishing several things simultaneously. It grants him flexibility in his thinking, which helps him accomplish all his tasks.

This is a sincere and reliable man. Progressing steadily, he will accomplish a lot for his own destiny in his present life and in the following one, because the link he has created with his future will remain.

August 29, 2009

 WILBER, KEN

Given Name: Kenneth Earl Wilber Jr.
Surname: Einstein of Consciousness
Nationality: American
Place and Date of Birth: Oklahoma City, Oklahoma (United States), January 31, 1949
Profession: Thinker, writer and spiritualist

MASTER DJWHAL KHUL'S COMMENTARY

Ken Wilber is an extremely interesting and intriguing man because his intelligence demonstrates a recent extraterrestrial origin. This situation indicates that he comes from a system different from ours, whose goal is to help humanity progress from a cerebral technological viewpoint; the brain for man is only a tangible tool, used to browse the world of matter that contains in itself mysteries yet unresolved to this day. You will gradually witness the birth, on this planet, of beings such as him, coming from elsewhere, wishing to learn our behaviour and, in exchange, contributing answers to these interventions sometimes considered incomprehensible in other universes.

Man possesses a unique brain, endowed with concepts unique from one another that are shaped by beliefs passed from generation to generation. Man's brain evolves according to the concepts learned and passed on genetically from father to son, from mother to daughter. Rarely do genes transmit through the opposite sex; polarities admittedly attract each other, but in the case of genetics, fertile ground remains indispensable, which indicates that, from the subtle viewpoint, the *anima* will sow in the *anima*; and the *animus* in the *animus*. One could allow the other to broaden its field of activity, but the fact would still remain that the transmission would be less productive and efficient.

As to Mr. Wilber, his work will allow men in general, to broaden their vision and their belief in themselves (from a potential viewpoint). He will not really help man evolve in his infinite divine wisdom; however, he will help him evolve from the human consciousness viewpoint. These characteristics acquired and not transmitted will allow humanity to see far in its planetary future, not necessarily divine. Another inherent phenomenon, a phenomenon that Mr. Wilber cannot transmit, although a part in him understands it perfectly. He can, however, recognize that it is truly impossible for him to transform others, deeply, which frustrates him a lot. He sees all human limitations, but does not know how to solve this dilemma for others. Certain parts of him remain a mystery he cannot solve, which immensely motivates him.

He is experiencing his first incarnations on Earth. He comes from the Andromeda galaxy, from a planet similar to ours. The Souls living there are endowed with exceptional intelligence. However, as they do not have a physical body as dense as ours, their adaptation here is not always evident. They often suffer from claustrophobia, which is not the case for Mr. Wilber, and they hate large cities.

Initiation Level: 2.3

His extraordinary IQ is close to 200.

Ray Structure

Monad: 3	Soul: 2	Personality: 3-4
Mental: 7-5	Astral: 6-2	Physical: 7-1

Monad and Soul

His Monad exerts little influence on him. However, his Soul attempts somehow (more or less satisfactorily) to guide him in his research orientation and often inspires him with instructions that help him in this direction. However, it cannot favorably and continuously influence such a brain that possesses the potential to understand and destroy everything. Such a type of brain proves to be merciless in its research and experiences. The Soul succeeds, but with difficulty, to dive into the aura network of such a brain; however, it cannot merge with it easily because too many by-pass tracks run in this brain. It analyzes everything and believes that everything is up to science.

Personality

He is graced with a very magnetic Personality, provided by the joint energy of rays 3 and 4. Ray 3 favours research, particularly experimentation. It allows him to be versatile and to work on several projects without experiencing great fatigue. It makes him rapid in action and expression.

Sub-ray 4 confers to him a strange aspect, artistic, that suits him well. It imbues him with the taste for being in the spotlight and appreciating a certain fame. Although he has solitary tendencies, he likes people, thanks to the influence of this sub-ray (combined with ray 3) that creates in him the need to exchange with others. If he were not equipped with such a brain, he would be easily influenced and would become easily depressed. His brain is his anchor in this life and his Personality motivates him to use it well.

Mental Body

His ray 7, sub-ray 5 mental body reveals an honest man. Ray 7 endows him with a magical sense in his thinking and motivates him to believe that the future is at our door. He already lives in the "Star Trek" era. This ray allows him to "see" man's future, to scrutinize it and to understand what "logically" prevents him from becoming superhuman. He believes in Divinity, tries to analyze it and explain it without really succeeding. Human complexity fascinates him. He would feel at ease living in a temporal universe different from ours. Here he feels limited and a prisoner.

Sub-ray 5 activates the "concrete intelligence" without really adding to it. This sub-ray proves to be preferable to his ray 3, because it provides him with a stability that ray 3 is unable to offer. Ray 5 likes to navigate in safe waters, which ray 3 does not really wish to do. As he already possessed a sub-ray 4 Personality and a ray 3 in the front line, he needed solid support in the mental body to conduct his research on reliable and tangible paths, which ray 3 often ignores. Ray 5 brings him a fame that ray 3 could not have provided.

Astral Body

His ray 6, sub-ray 2 Astral grants him the possibility to be "human" and to feel what the term "affection" really means. He really experienced love with his first wife, Terry. She opened his heart and, in a way, left with it. He never was able to love with the same abandonment afterwards. A part of him feels betrayed by life. He knows how to love but can no longer let go and completely trust love and life, which gives and takes. He tries to scrutinize, to understand, to analyze the inexplicable with great difficulties. This is how he progresses and makes things progress.

Ray 6 invests him with endless loyalty towards his friends. He is dedicated to his cause and tries to help people to the best of his "knowledge", that is, of course, limited. He cannot really "embrace" the individual but he can understand and try to help. He is a kind man who, in spite of a marked arrogance, will try to act humbly in order to remain accessible to others, which is only an illusion! He is inaccessible and will remain so until his death. He will have to change his ray configuration and possess fewer odd rays, which he will dislike…

Sub-ray 2 grants him intuition that he uses astutely. It provides him with a bit of compassion in his words but does not diminish in any way his arrogance, when he thinks he is teaching "others". Because it is very versed in details, this sub-ray is accompanied by a subtle mental arrogance by impressing others and often believing oneself to be superior to others (or beyond the average citizen). Mr. Wilber fell in this trap a bit but we concede that his position brings a lot of difficult situations that are hard to manage well.

Physical Body

His ray 7, sub-ray 1 physical body provides him with a robust and resistant physical body. Ray 7 endows him with beauty that served him well and a powerful physical brain for his research (meticulous, perfectionist, indefatigable and sometimes tyrannical). It simplified his task in the writing of his books, allowing him not to omit any details necessary for the proper progress of the understanding of the work. This ray makes him appreciate the good things, and gives him authority in his field, if not the only authority. Ray 7 supports inventors, innovators, those that make "a difference".

Sub-ray 1 offers a potential and complementary constant thrust produced by the other rays, it gives him the possibility to never flinch and to keep ideas clear even in the worst moments. Similar to ray 7, this sub-ray makes him love challenges, puts him at ease in confrontations and allows him to appreciate solitude.

Ken Wilber deserves to be known, studied, but he should never be "known" and "treated" as a Master, a *Guru* or a Guide, because he is none of those. He wants to be a brilliant researcher, a man who makes humans progress without making them too divine.

February 15, 2011

WILLIAMS, ROBIN

Given Name: Robin McLaurin Williams
Nationality: American
Place and Date of Birth: Chicago, Illinois, (United States), July 21, 1951
Profession: Actor and producer

MASTER DJWHAL KHUL'S COMMENTARY

An actor in all areas of his life, Robin Williams experiences difficulty in being himself because he does not know, in fact, who he really is. Of course, he likes art and likes to act in comedy or drama, and this, in a way represents all his life. A young Soul of ray 4, he does not know how to entirely manage the particular energy he is subjected to.

We cannot say that he is really happy, because he often feels like a stranger on this planet, with reason, because he does not come from here and a portion of him cannot forget it. I do not wish for the moment to mention his planet of origin, which must remain a mystery for a certain time. Why? Because this will trigger in him an even stronger desire to leave this evolutionary platform that is Earth and his destiny is presently to evolve here. However, as he ages, he will experience a certain well-being (relative), because he is starting to better integrate into the world of matter he considers dry, "incomprehensible," too cast in a mould from which he has difficulty to depart. He is an outsider who does not know how to get out of the shackles that life imposes on him, here on Earth, which he likes a lot but into which he has difficulty integrating.

Initiation Level: 1.2

A young Soul, he experiences a lot of difficulties adapting to this new energy that circulates in him as well as in integrating to the artificial system that initiations represent on this planet. He will have to choose a ray configuration in his next incarnations that will help him react less and soften more.

Ray Structure

Monad: 2	Soul: 4	Personality: 6-4
Mental: 3-7	Astral: 6-2	Physical: 5-3

Monad and Soul

His Monad does not exert any influence on him. His Soul's energy slightly colours his life (mainly with the presence of a sub-ray 4 Personality) and makes him uncomfortable. This will provoke in him either a difficulty to evolve or a speedy evolution. Everything will depend on his focus and on his ease in managing the energies well.

Personality

His ray 6, sub-ray 4 Personality makes him stubborn, funny and uncontrollable. Why? Because ray 4 is too present and colours everything. A ray 6 combined with a ray 4 creates a clown easily frustrated and offended. Ray 6 likes to be loved, recognized, appreciated and to be amusing. He can reveal himself to be a champion of laughter, through his warm, touching nature. However, a ray 6 who does not feel at ease, or who feels he is judged by others, will become sarcastic and cutting, even uncontrollable, if ray 4 (which cannot reason with it, because it increases its folly) has too much influence.

His sub-ray 4 Personality, his ray 4 Soul, and his young Soul makes him a continuously perturbed being because of the madness of ray 4. He loves beauty, is enslaved by it, but does not know how to really appreciate it. He remains uncontrollable although he is gradually improving with time.

Mental Body

His ray 3, sub-ray 7 mental body makes him a being that thinks fast, acts fast and disappears fast. Ray 3 accelerates his speed and takes away the possibility of quieting his thoughts. Intelligent and tongue-in-cheek, he rapidly captures the energy of a room, of a meeting, and uses it to evoke laughter. He has difficulty being serious because if he falls into a depression, his ray 4 becomes a real hell. He therefore continuously lives between heaven and hell. He tries to forget this polarity, which seems almost impossible.

His sub-ray 7 saves him, giving him some structure, which he follows in order not to reveal himself as excessively strange. He knows that to get up and get dressed in the morning is important and to eat is equally important. He is becoming more conventional and easily accepts life's limitations (while rebellion is never too far).

Astral Body

His ray 6, sub-ray 2 Astral helps him maintain balance within his relations because he likes to love and be loved. He enjoys some stability in his emotional life, although he experiences some difficulty expressing it. He is proud of his children, even if he sometimes only demonstrates it with reluctance. He can be charming and warm but fickle in his demonstrations. Those close to him occasionally go through an emotional roller coaster that ends up harming their relationship.

His sub-ray 2 makes him sensitive, and he can easily cry because ray 4 emphasizes the sensitivity of this sub-ray 2. Unfortunately, this confers to him an increasing discomfort towards emotions he cannot understand and control. Sub-ray 2 makes him very sensitive to criticism.

Physical Body

His ray 5, sub-ray 3 physical body provides him with solidity as well as the capacity to self-destruct for lengthy periods. He has a strong capacity for resistance and rapidly gets back on his feet when necessary. Ray 5 makes him awkward in his approaches to others and does not facilitate his verbal expression. He often seems to be coming from another world. Ray 5 confers to him intuition and the desire to escape the world and isolate himself.

His sub-ray 3 reinforces his physical body and diminishes the logical and Cartesian aspect of ray 5. This is a man who likes proofs, who likes to discuss scientific subjects, and ray 5 inspires him with very interesting mental humour. Sub-ray 3 refines ray 5 and endows him with intelligence less "in accordance with the rule".

This is a being who is interesting to know but who requires a dose of patience when we are in his presence. He is not ready for spirituality or spirituality may not be ready for him?

November 12, 2008

 # WINFREY, OPRAH

Given Name: Oprah Gail Winfrey
Nationality: American
Place and Date of Birth: Kosciusko, Mississippi (United States),
January 29, 1954
Profession: Actress, producer, literary critic, television show host

MASTER DJWHAL KHUL'S COMMENTARY

A self-willed woman, Oprah Winfrey is a young Soul, thirsting to be loved, recognized and understood by the whole world. She has an ardent desire to be "the" woman who could change the world, particularly, the female condition. She considers herself more as a woman, not necessarily of colour, although she is often confronted with the subject of the colour of her skin.

Please note that if she would have been white, her success would have been less. Of course, she has enhanced the image of black people, but she always experienced difficulty in accepting the judgment of others regarding her skin colour.

Be aware that Ms. Winfrey was an activist named Tom Watson for the Ku Klux Klan. At this time, she passionately wanted power and to become president of the United States. Fortunately, she failed because the nation would have greatly regressed in its achievements.

The present incarnation allows her, so to speak, to clear some karma. She questions herself and tries to help black people to free themselves from the limitations that have stayed with them for centuries. Due to the abuses perpetrated during her incarnation as Tom Watson, Oprah Winfrey devotes a lot of time to helping those that suffer from oppressions of all sorts (racial, financial and political).

Ms. Winfrey, suffers from a certain arrogance, and we hope she will one day see herself touched more by the energy of her Soul, and less by that of her Personality.

Initiation Level: 1.2

She has every trait of a very successful young Soul. She possesses financial power and attempts to find her place through it. She will have reached greater depths during her next incarnations and be more at the level of the heart, although she seems to be there already.

Ray Structure

Monad: 2	Soul: 2	Personality: 6-3
Mental: 7-5	Astral: 6-4	Physical: 3-6

Monad and Soul

Her Monad does not exert any influence on her. However, her Soul is starting to have one. Ms. Winfrey is more "guided" or influenced by the ray 6 of her Personality, which dictates her behaviour and her way of thinking. This very strong Personality, who was also quite intense in her past life, will have to quiet down towards the end of her life, or she will become even more authoritarian in her next incarnation, thus difficult to influence by her Soul.

Personality

With a Personality influenced by ray 6, sub-ray 3, Ms. Winfrey can be nothing but stubborn and manipulative. She knows what she wants and what she doesn't.

Ray 6 provides her with interesting willpower. It also endows her with a sense of loyalty that, once betrayed, does not forgive easily. She is obstinate in terms of certain ideas and does not let go easily with regard to her prejudices. Ray 6 confers to her the desire to help others (according to her vision) and she can offer a lot of her time, energy and money to please herself. She seems to give generously but note that everything she does is calculated and planned. She has a ray 3 brain (ray 3 in the physical body), which is not easily manipulated but knows how to manipulate others.

Her sub-ray 3 confers to her fluidity of movement; it also allows her to act and think fast. She can work on several projects simultaneously without getting tired, while maintaining control. This sub-ray is such that she does not really appreciate working in a team; however, she likes to manage a team. She feels at ease in public, because sub-ray 3 helps her to express herself and ray 6 gives warmth to her voice. She defends causes, sub-ray 3 manifesting in her the feeling that she is intelligent and useful, while ray 6 inspiring in her the need to "save the world", in spite of itself.

Mental Body

Her ray 7, sub-ray 5 mental body makes her an intelligent woman, organized in her thoughts and down to earth. Ray 7 provides her with an aesthetic sense that she exploits well. It helps her create organized thoughts and precise goals. She likes to direct, because she believes her way is the best. She does not hesitate to use cutting words because she is not conscious of doing so. She believes she is working for everyone's progress and likes to provoke, if it will serve her cause.

Her sub-ray 5 makes her practical and efficient. She likes to explain the why of the why and sometimes gets lost in the twists and turns of her efforts to understand. Hard to manipulate, she needs to see to believe. However, her ray 6's influence her way of seeing and believing, because this ray believes what it wishes to believe. It can easily convince crowds, because it possesses the words to reassure and ensure that it has the evidence that confirms what is presented.

Astral Body

Her ray 6, sub-ray 4 Astral makes her a passionate woman. She likes to love and be loved. The influence of ray 6 makes her dream of the ideal love that, according to her, must exist. She has often been deceived by love because she loved badly and too much. She still has illusions regarding love, illusions regarding the ideal man, desertion and the faithfulness of her partner. She would have liked to have children and would have proven to be a good mother, very protective, although demonstrating a disciplinary attitude at times. She would have been demanding, similar to the way she is with her lovers and her working team.

Her sub-ray 4 equips her with a sixth sense she has for artists and for what might work in her career. She feels good in this environment, even if at times she is fed up. This sub-ray makes her versatile and, in association with ray 6, gives her the capacity to easily change ideas and turn around a situation if it does not suit her. She is not always easy to be around, because sub-ray 4 communicates moods that are not always pleasant for her entourage.

Physical Body

Her ray 3, sub-ray 6 physical body provides her with fairly good resistance. Ray 3 offers sharp and fast thought. It helps her to work on several fronts at the same time. She is a gifted speaker, who does not get easily flustered. She is remarkable at repartee. Ray 3 gives her an ease of expression during her interviews and produces in her the quality to win her audience's trust.

Sub-ray 6 provides her with communicative warmth when she so wishes. Otherwise, it can make her cold and distant. The influence of this sub-ray endows her with unrefined features and causes a weight problem. It confers to her a strong bone structure. However, it inspires her with a certain softness when she lets go. She can reveal herself to be a very passionate lover if she drops her defenses, which are, unfortunately, numerous.

Ms. Winfrey will live to be quite old. We hope she will open to a deeper and more authentic spirituality, because presently she remains on the surface of things.

March 25, 2010

 YESHE, LAMA

Given Name: Thubten Yeshe
Nationality: Tibetan
Place and Date of Birth: Tolung Dechen (Tibet), 1935
Place and Date of Death: Nepal, March 3, 1984
Profession: Lama of the Gelugpa tradition

MASTER DJWHAL KHUL'S COMMENTARY

Lama Yeshe was a wise Master but not a Master of Wisdom. He enjoyed discoursing but did not appreciate honors, which made him ill at ease. He would have liked his life to be more modest, more withdrawn. He did his duty while trying to guide the people who came to him to the best of his knowledge. He knew himself to be limited as a Master, because he knew he had not accomplished the long path leading to full Realization or to Awakening. This is the reason we can say that he was wise, but had not attained full Wisdom.

He knew the "path", because he was living it. He guided people less evolved than he while knowing that he still had a lot to learn. He always had the impression that people believed him to be more evolved than he was, which, in a way put enormous pressure on him. It is partially for this reason that he left his body rapidly. He wished to accomplish his mission on Earth, known for what he really was and not for what people hoped he would be.

This explains why, in his present incarnation as Osel, he rebelled and suffered a lot. The path of Buddhism sometimes deprives the Soul of freedom, when other Souls seek it out as a *tulku*. Osel will have a lot to do and we hope that he will succeed in finding peace and the liberty he is seeking in order to achieve his future in a more balanced fashion.

Initiation Level: 2.8

While he was approaching a certain realization, he knew he was still far from his goal. This fact indicates the emergence of an authentic humility, ready to serve the Soul's real intention.

Ray Structure

Monad: 2	Soul: 2	Personality: 3-7
Mental: 3-5	Astral: 6-2	Physical: 3-7

Monad and Soul

His Monad exerted little influence on his life. His Soul, on the contrary possessed an influence that was growing more and more. It made him sensitive, and increasingly activated his humility that sometimes verged on self-depreciation. It made him a good Master who knew how to listen and to get in tune with his disciples. It also provided him with a certain clairvoyance that helped him accomplish his task.

Personality

His Personality, ruled by ray 3, sub-ray 7, conferred to him a disciplined sense of humour. Ray 3 made him agile in his speech and a very likeable person. He liked to laugh and make people laugh. For him, humour was an essential key to his survival and his spirituality, motivating him to defuse the sometimes too dry aspect of spirituality. Ray 3 allowed him to accept his situation more easily.

Sub-ray 7 brought inner discipline that helped him progress on the Path. He liked rituals that surrounded him with a sense of security in his practice. He believed that without them, he would have been lost in the twists and turns of daily life. This sub-ray also conferred to him certain rigidity intended to balance the carelessness sometimes induced by ray 3.

Mental Body

His mental body, impregnated by the energy of ray 3, sub-ray 5, graced him with remarkable intelligence that was once more hidden behind humour. Ray 3 sometimes motivated him to be rapid in his thoughts and replies. It gave him the capacity to be good in debates.

Sub-ray 5 provided him with a solid base to explain the founding principles of Buddhism. He came to understand and assimilate them, in order to better convey the Knowledge. He could then demonstrate that he was down to earth. He was venturesome and feared very few things.

Astral Body

His Astral, influenced by ray 6, sub-ray 2, gave him an unstinting love for his native land that he never ceased to love. Ray 6 conferred to him a sincere love for his people and for humanity. He felt very small and insignificant in this immense Universe of which he was a part. This ray enticed him to be devoted, sincere but also stubborn and a rebel at certain times. When he had an idea, it was difficult for him to change it.

Sub-ray 2 gave him great sensitivity. He loved others sincerely and sometimes would forget himself too much for them. He experienced irrational fears he could control fairly well because he considered himself to be without fear, yet imperfect.

Physical Body

His physical body, shaped by ray 3, sub-ray 7, strengthened his Personality and provided him with a very stable backbone. He was therefore twice as "happy" to be alive and to see life through humour, which was a real gift for him. However like most people strongly influenced by ray 3, he would feel a great inner and inexplicable sadness that he would hide behind his laughter. This discomfort inspired in him a hope of something bigger than himself, more sincere and more real.

Sub-ray 7 supported his physical body well by equipping him with fairly good resistance. He appreciated order and discipline, liked beauty and sought it in everything. This sub-ray also gratified him with fairly good intuition that guided him in certain life choices. It allowed him also to have a much larger vision of his discipleship that he often found a bit limited.

This mortal man, remarkable through his simplicity, gave a lot to his friends and disciples. We hope that his present incarnation will measure up to this humility that qualified him well during his incarnation as Lama Yeshe.

October 22, 2009

TABLE OF INITIATIONS AND RAYS

Name	Initiation Level	Rays					
		Monad	Soul	Personality	Mental	Astral	Physical
1. Addams, Jane	2.5	2	2	1-6	7-5	6-4	3-7
2. Ashoka	3.2	2	2	3-1	7-5	6-2	3-7
3. Bach, Jean-Sébastien	2.4	2	2	2-3	7-5	6-4	3-6
4. Bailey, Alice Ann	3.5	2	2	2-3	1-7	6-4	3-6
5. Beethoven, Ludwig van	3.2	2	2	1-3	4-7	6-4	3-4
6. Blavatsky, Helena Petrovna	4.5	2	1	3-6	1-5	6-2	3-6
7. Brother Andre	1.3	2	6	6-2	3-7	6-4	3-2
8. Bruckner, Anton	1.8	2	2	2-3	7-5	6-4	3-2
9. Bush, George W.	1.0	3	2	6-3	5-3	6-2	3-5
10. Carrey, Jim	1.8	2	7	4-3	7-2	6-4	7-4
11. Castaneda, Carlos	3.2	3	4[1]	3-6	7-5	4-2	3-7
12. Castro, Fidel	1.8	2	3	1-7	7-3	6-4	3-7
13. Ceausescu, Nicolae	0.9	2	3	3-7	5-4	6-2	3-6
14. Chia, Mantak	2.5	2	2	3-4	7-5	6-4	3-6
15. Chödrön, Ani Pema	2.2	3	2	2-3	7-5	6-2	3-5
16. Chögyam Trungpa Rinpoché	4.2	3	2	4-2	3-2	6-3	6-1
17. Chopra, Deepak	2.3	3	2	2-4	7-5	6-2	3-5
18. Christie, Agatha	2.2	2	4	3-7	7-5	6-2	3-5
19. Churchill, Winston	2.3	2	2	1-5	1-3	6-2	3-6
20. Clinton, Hillary	2.3	2	2	3-7	7-5	6-2	3-7
21. Cohen, Andrew	1.8	1	2	6-4	3-7	4-2	3-6
22. Creme, Benjamin	1.8	1	2	7-3	2-7	6-4	3-6
23. Cromwell, Oliver	1.8	3	2	1-3	5-7	6-2	3-7
24. Cruise, Tom	1.5	2	7	6-2	7-5	6-4	3-7
25. Curie, Marie	1.8	2	7	6-3	7-5	2-6	3-7
26. Da Vinci, Leonardo	3.2	2	4	7-3	3-5	4-6	3-6
27. David-Néel, Alexandra	1.8	2	1	6-3	1-5	4-2	3-6
28. Dilgo Khyentse Rinpoche	4.8	2	2	1-6	3-4	6-2	3-6

[1] Castaneda, Carlos – Soul moving towards Ray 1.

Name	Initiation Level	Rays					
		Monad	Soul	Personality	Mental	Astral	Physical
29. Dion, Celine	1.2	2	2	3-7	7-2	4-6	3-7
30. Disney, Walt	1.8	2	2	6-4	7-5	2-6	3-7
31. Dyer, Wayne	2.3	2	3	6-4	5-3	2-6	3-7
32. Eastwood, Clint	1.8	2	3	3-4	7-5	6-2	3-7
33. Eckhart, Johannes, Meister Eckhart	3.5	2	1	3-2	7-3	6-4	3-6
34. Einstein, Albert	3.2	2	1	3-2	4-5	6-2	3-7
35. Epictetus	1.8	2	3	3-4	7-5	6-2	3-6
36. Föllmi, Olivier	2.2	2	3	4-2	7-3	6-2	7-3
37. Franklin, Benjamin	3.2	2	3	2-3	7-5	6-4	3-7
38. Gampopa	3.2	3	2	3-4	7-1	6-2	7-3
39. Gandhi	2.3	2	2	3-4	7-5	6-2	3-7
40. Gates, Bill	3.1	2	3-5[1]	3-7	7-5	6-2	3-7
41. Gaulle, Charles de	2.8	1	2	1-3	7-5	6-2	7-3
42. Gorbatchev, Mikhaïl	3.2	2	3	6-4	7-1	2-6	3-7
43. Gurdjieff	3.3	3	2	1-3	7-5	4-6	3-5
44. Gurumayi	3.2	2	2	2-3	6-4	4-2	7-4
45. Haig, Justin Moreward	7.2	2	3	7-3	5-6	2-4	3-6
46. Hanks, Tom	1.7	3	2	4-3	7-5	6-2	3-6
47. Hills, Christopher	3.2	2	2	7-3	7-5	6-2	3-6
48. Howard, Ron	2.8	2	2	4-3	3-7	6-4	3-6
49. Hubbard, L. Ron	3.7	2	2-4	4-3	5-2	6-4	3-6
50. Huineng	2.8	2	2	3-7	7-5	6-2	3-7
51. Jackson, Michael	1.2	2	4	4-7	3-5	6-2	3-7
52. John Paul II	3.2	2	2	2-3	7-5	6-4	3-7
53. Jung, Carl Gustav	3.2	2	3	4-7	5-3	6-2	7-3
54. Khan, Genghis	1.5	3	2	1-6	3-3	6-2	3-6
55. Khan, Hazrat Inayat	4.2	2	2	6-4	3-7	6-2	4-3
56. Kornfield, Jack	2.8	2	2	3-6	7-5	6-2	7-3
57. Kūkai	3.4	2	2	4-3	7-5	6-2	3-6
58. Lévesque, René	1.2	2	6	6-2	3-7	4-2	3-7

[1] Gates, Bill – A change of the Soul Ray in this life.

Name	Initiation Level	Rays					
		Monad	Soul	Personality	Mental	Astral	Physical
59. Lincoln, Abraham	2.3	1	3	7-3	1-5	6-4	1-7
60. Lucas, George	3.2	1	3	4-5	1-3	6-2	3-7
61. Madonna	1.2	2	4	4-3	7-5	6-2	3-7
62. Mahler, Gustav	2.2	2	2	2-3	7-3	6-4	3-4
63. Mandela, Nelson	3.3	2	3	2-6	7-3	6-2	3-6
64. Marcus Aurelius	1.9	2	3	2-5	3-7	6-2	3-7
65. McNamara, William	3.2	2	1	3-6	7-5	6-4	3-7
66. Michelangelo	3.8	2	2	4-7	7-3	6-4	3-7
67. Millman, Dan	2.3	2	2	3-7	7-5	6-4	3-6
68. Mozart, Wolfgang Amadeus	2.3	2	2	4-3	5-2	6-4	7-2
69. Neem Karoli Baba	approx. 6	2	3	4-2	3-7	6-2	3-5
70. Newton, Michael	2.3	2	3	6-4	5-3	6-2	7-3
71. Obama, Barack Hussein	2.3	2	7[1]	2-1	7-3	6-4	7-3-5
72. Orbison, Roy	1.2	2	2	4-3	7-5	6-4	3-6
73. Padre Pio	3.7	2	6[2]	4-3	7-5	6-2	3-7
74. Paul of Tarsus	3.2	2	6	3-4	7-5	6-2	3-6
75. Penor Rinpoche	2.8	2	1	3-7	7-5	6-2	6-3
76. Praagh, James Van	2.2	2	3	2-6	3-7	6-2	3-6
77. Presley, Elvis	1.7	2	4	4-3	6-2	2-6	7-4
78. Prophet, Elizabeth Clare	1.5	2	2	4-3	1-5	6-2	3-7
79. Prophet, Mark L.	1.4	2	2	3-6	7-2	6-4	1-7
80. Rachmaninov, Sergueï	2.8	2	2	7-3	7-5	6-4	7-4
81. Rajneesh, Bhagwan Shree	3.2	2	3	2-6	7-5	6-4	3-7
82. Roberts, Jane	2.2	2	2	3-7	1-5	6-4	3-2
83. Roerich, Helena	3.8	1	2	7-4	5-3	6-2	7-3

[1] Obama, Barack Hussein – Soul moving towards Ray 1.
[2] Padre Pio – Soul moving towards Ray 2.

512

Name	Initiation Level	Rays					
		Monad	Soul	Personality	Mental	Astral	Physical
84. Roosevelt, Franklin D.	2.8	1	2	3-7	7-3	6-4	7-2
85. Roosevelt, Theodore	2.3	1	6	6-3	7-5	2-4	3-6
86. Sakyong Mipham Rinpoche	1.8	2	3	2-4	5-3	6-2	3-7
87. Sarandon, Susan	1.2	2	3	4-6	5-3	6-2	7-3
88. Scott, Cyril	2.3	1	2	7-4	3-2	4-6	7-2-3
89. Seagal, Steven	1.6	2	2	7-4	3-7	6-2	3-6
90. Shapiro, Robert	2.2	2	3	4-6	7-5	2-4	3-6
91. Sinatra, Frank	1.5	2	2	3-7	1-5	6-4	3-7
92. Spangler, David	3.4	3	2	6-4	7-5	2-6	3-7
93. Steiner, Rudolf	2.4	2	2	7-3	5-3	6-2	7-5
94. Stone, Sharon	2.1	1	3	4-3	7-5	6-2	7-4
95. Suzuki, David	2.2	3	2	3-6	7-5	4-6	3-5
96. Tagore, Rabîndranâth	3.2	2	3	3-4	7-3	6-2	7-5
97. Tesla, Nikola	3.2	3	2	7-5	5-3	3-6	1-7
98. Trudeau, Pierre Elliott	3.2	1	2	7-3	1-5	6-2	3-7
99. Trump, Donald	1.2	3	4	3-7	7-5	2-6	1-6
100. Twain, Mark	2.6	2	3	4-6	7-3	6-2	7-3
101. Verne, Jules	2.3	2	3	3-7	7-5	6-4	3-6
102. Vivaldi, Antonio	1.9	1	2	2-4	7-1	6-4	3-6
103. Voltaire	3.2	2	3	4-2	5-7	2-4	3-4
104. Walsch, Neale Donald	1.3	1	2	2-3	3-5	6-2	3-7
105. Wesselman, Hank	2.2	2	3[1]	3-6	7-5	6-4	7-3
106. Wilber, Ken	2.3	3	2	3-4	7-5	6-2	7-1
107. Williams, Robin	1.2	2	4	6-4	3-7	6-2	5-3
108. Winfrey, Oprah	1.2	2	2	6-3	7-5	6-4	3-6
109. Yeshe, Lama	2.8	2	2	3-7	3-5	6-2	3-7

[1] Wesselman, Hank – Soul under temporary influence of Ray 7.

Part II

THE RAY STRUCTURES

Introduction

This second part of *The Circle of Initiates* presents a resume of the attributes of the Seven Rays that influence our evolution on Earth, and is also intended as a valuable guide for the understanding of this book. The expertise of Master Djwhal Khul is its Source of Inspiration.

WHO IS MASTER DJWHAL KHUL?

The Science of the Seven Rays was introduced at the beginning of the 20th Century by the Tibetan Master Djwhal Khul. Working jointly with Alice A. Bailey, he wrote, through her, several volumes on this topic. *A Treatise on the Seven Rays,* composed of five Volumes is one of the main pieces.

Very discreet, this Master who presently lives in Tibet in a physical body, in spite of his very old age (he would be over 300 years), is the abbot of a monastery situated in the North-East of Tibet. Djwhal Khul, whose real name remains a secret in order to protect his identity and his life, works in harmony with the Great White Brotherhood, who watch over our evolution on Earth.

My husband and I had the chance to briefly meet him twice in Tibet. At his request, we kept silent about our interactions with him. However, please note that we work in close cooperation with him, that we are his disciples and that I have resumed, at his request, the work started by Alice A. Bailey and Helena P. Blavatsky. I serve him to the best of my ability and knowledge. The book *The Circle of Initiates* is therefore his work and not mine.

The origin of rays

According to Djwhal Khul, the source of the rays is located within the seven major stars of the Big Dipper. From this source spring seven cosmic energies characterizing the different ray qualities.

These rays influence all the kingdoms that compose our planet, kingdoms of which we are part. For each of us, six major rays influence our lives during our incarnations. These rays condition our Monad, our Soul, our personality, our mental body, our astral body and our physical body.

Added to this picture are four sub-rays that support the major four rays governing the personality, the mental body, the astral body and the physical body. As an example, here are the rays that qualify Elvis Presley:

Monad: 2   Soul: 4   Personality: 4-3
Mental: 6-2   Astral: 2-6   Physical: 7-4

The interplay of the rays, according to our polarization in a given time, characterizes what we are. Therefore, a person dedicating his attention mainly to his physical body will be dominated, most of the time, by rays qualifying his physical body. They will colour his actions. However, if his emotions form the center of his life, he will be subjected mainly to the influence of the rays characterizing his astral body, rays that in turn will affect his daily actions. Although this seems complicated, the study of the rays of different Personalities appearing in this book will help you to better understand the scale of their influence in our life.

The different parts that compose us

We are composed of different parts that cooperate in our evolution. Each one of these parts plays an important role in our life; their sum contributes to define us as humans on this planet and allows us to accomplish our destiny.

The Monad

The Monad, being the most evolved part, reveals itself to be particularly difficult to define. Also called "Spirit", it observes the evolution of the Soul that must return to it when its destiny is accomplished.

Too evolved, it exerts no real influence on our existence for the majority of us. For the Monad to bless us with its magnetism, we have to have reached the third initiation at a minimum.

The Soul

The role of the Soul is to serve the Monad. Our merging with it personifies our first step towards our divinity. When this union is accomplished, our gaze turns to the Monad, so that our human nature, becoming increasingly perfect, merges with it, thus achieving our real Destiny in God. The Soul, in fact, is a necessary bridge, allowing access to the Monad.

The Soul's influence generally begins after the first initiation, which corresponds to the first real opening of the heart, and reaches its pinnacle with the fourth initiation, representing the great sacrifice. Then, it gradually yields its place to the influence of the Monad, although it remains constantly available in order to serve us, as well as the Monad.

The Personality

The personality expresses our being, our daily behaviour. It incarnates our life in movement, when we establish contact with people. It incorporates all the other bodies and allows them to express themselves. Generally, it provides the first impression other people have of us.

Therefore, during an evening out, your personality will mainly express itself through the ray that influences it. However, if your beloved is flirting with someone else, then the ray ruling your astral body will infiltrate via your personality to express itself. People around you will then perceive not the radiance of your personality but that of your emotional body.

The same will apply to the other bodies. For example, if during this same evening, you discuss business, your mental body will rapidly take over within your personality. You will place yourself not at the level of your emotions, but rather at that of the creation of your ideas and of their expression, thanks to the use of your physical brain. You will appear as a totally different person to those who observe you. At the end of the evening, you will, without doubt, find your personality, which will have allowed you to express all the facets of your being.

The Mental Body

The mental body is often confused with the intellect (brain), governed by the physical body. Here are the elements that differ:

Mental Body	Brain
• Thinks	• Does not think, registers data
• Creates via thought	• Carries out what it believes his thoughts are
• Learns lessons	• Gathers information
• Ensures a favorable control on emotions	• Is subject to the influence of emotions, mainly negative
• Is not subject to the physical quality	• Directly receives the influence of the physical
• Receives information from the higher planes	• Transmits the information received from the mind

The Physical Body

The ray linked to the physical body will directly influence the individual's morphology, vitality and movement.

The ray influence depends on the Soul's maturity

Each ray possesses an influence one needs to learn to properly master. A lack of maturity will often prevent the individual from acting correctly in agreement with the energy transmitted by the ray. Let us not forget that a ray is a force we have to channel, but mainly master. If we remain unconscious, we become the victims of rays, as each ray, like yin and yang, possesses a positive and a negative aspect.

Therefore, a more evolved individual will often work with the positive aspects of the ray while a less evolved individual will be subjected to the influence of the ray's negative aspects. Consequently, our task is to acquire sufficient light and maturity in us, in order to easily sail on the energies transmitted by the rays to allow their influence to be beneficial for our evolution as well as that of the people surrounding us.

In other words, to understand the real influence of rays within an individual in particular, one has first and foremost, to look closely at his initiation level, which allows us to discern his maturity, or the contrary, his lack of.

Ray 1

The "Leader" incarnating Will and Power

The individual influenced by the energy of ray 1, who wants to be very powerful, may reveal himself to be an outstanding leader, or a true dictator if he has not acquired a certain maturity.

Well polarized, he appears as a real catalyst, motivating his "troops" in order to rapidly achieve the projects he wishes to realize. To reach the intended goal efficiently and rapidly seems to be all that he cares about.

However, without being conscious of it, he generally reveals himself to lack diplomacy. Thus, to avoid causing harm to others, he has to be particularly cautious with what he says.

Influence of Ray 1 according to the initiation level

The individual whose initiation level fluctuates between 0.8 and 1.4 **can be qualified as a beginner in his apprenticeship of good leadership**. Quite often deprived of wisdom and discernment because of his young soul, he may repeatedly behave like a small dictator with the people around him. Often possessing a very narrow vision and showing himself to be centered on what he believes to be just, he works without perceiving other people's needs.

This individual generally prefers to work alone, feeling ill at ease functioning in a group. However, if he has to surround himself with a team to achieve a project, he will often be feared and misunderstood by his peers. Usually impatient and demanding, he can be daunting and makes people pay dearly for any act of disobedience.

The individual who is more advanced on the path, whose initiation level fluctuates between 1.5 and 2.2 **reveals himself to be a fairly good leader**. At this stage, to learn to lead is not yet so easy. His vision is generally restricted because he has not totally succeeded in grasping the perspective of an overall view. Thus, he appears incapable of perceiving the real priorities.

Frequently, this type of individual works alone, isolating himself, because he does not accept anyone's help. He manages his projects causing malaise around him and can, without being conscious of it, transform himself into a real tyrant. Consequently, he leads with an iron hand, sparing no one, including those who surround him.

The individual whose initiation level fluctuates between 2.3 and 3.3 **reveals himself to be a good leader**. More conscious of being at the head of a group of people when he manages a project, he learns how to listen to them and takes their suggestions into account. Although still awkward in his interventions, he demonstrates a desire to learn to lead for the good of all while offering proof of a vision that constantly expands. He is gradually aware that he is invested with the power of management and attempts to bring to fruition all the projects he is nursing, overcoming any obstacles encountered. Finally, respecting others, he is in turn respected. Thus his entourage starts to love him.

The individual whose initiation level is higher than 3.3 **is considered a visionary, an excellent leader**. He has finally acquired a sense of diplomacy that he uses with mastery. From then on, he possesses a clear vision of the future, develops projects, directs them, checks their progress and manages them with a firm hand, with intelligence and love. He sees potential obstacles and can therefore try to avoid them. He works in a team without constraints, because he knows that the team is an integral part of his projects and remains indispensible to their success. He shows respect towards everyone and receives respect and admiration from all.

The influence of Ray 1 on the different bodies

Here is a brief overview of the influence of ray 1 on the five bodies that compose the human being in his entirety.

The physical body under the Ray 1 influence

It should be noted that very few people on our planet have a ray 1 physical body. However, if this were the case, it would be preferable if the individual had reached an initiation level higher than 1.

Characteristics:

+ Generally sturdy, imposing and possesses a robust frame. May however be slim, tall and endowed with great strength.
+ Does not usually go unnoticed.
+ Easily eliminates the obstacles that arise on the physical plane.
+ often expresses himself with abrupt gestures, because he is not inclined to be delicate.
+ Possesses a strong capacity to organize his environment, to reach the targeted goal the same way the physical body influenced by ray 7 would act. Will therefore logically do everything necessary to put everything in place to be the most effective.
+ Is endowed with a great organizational capacity since the physical brain is under its influence. This will be reflected in his environment, but also in his way of expressing himself verbally and in writing.
+ Abounds with clear and precise ideas.
+ Emits heat.
+ Does not like to be confined, needs space and can display aggressivity, impatience when this need is not satisfied.
+ Generally does not like to be touched without his permission.
+ Occasionally transmits the following subliminal message: "get closer if you dare!"
+ Sometimes makes abrupt gestures due to the tension always present in him.

+ Tends to be mental and not sentimental, because his logic does not leave room for sentimentality.

Here are some examples of people whose physical body was under the influence of ray 1: Abraham Lincoln, Mark L. Prophet.

THE ASTRAL BODY UNDER THE INFLUENCE OF RAY 1

It should be noted that it is excessively rare to meet individuals with a ray 1 influence at the level of the astral body. If it happens, the individual will be equipped with a very uncomfortable astral body.

Characteristics:
+ Controls his emotions or suppresses them.
+ Feels anxiety and is under constant tension, although it is hidden.
+ Tends to cut himself away from others (division).
+ Is inclined towards very destructive emotions, especially if the individual is at a low initiation level.
+ Experiences an almost morbid fear of attachment.

THE MENTAL BODY UNDER THE RAY 1 INFLUENCE

Fairly widespread, this influence offers the individual the possibility of being a good leader in the field in which he evolves.

Characteristics:
+ Is endowed with a great capacity for concentration, never loses the thread.
+ Is graced with a great capacity for decision and synthesis.
+ Is not easily influenceable.
+ Entertains critical and impersonal thought.
+ Possesses a great organizational sense.
+ Acts with much realism.
+ Has great mental endurance.
+ Appears very active.
+ Expresses himself with clear ideas that are right on target.

- May reveal himself to be either inflexible or very flexible, a quality often linked to his initiation level.
- Is equipped with a strong will to live and a great capacity to bear difficulties.

Here are some examples of people whose mental body was or is under the influence of ray 1: Helena Petrovna Blavatsky, Winston Churchill, Abraham Lincoln, Georges Lucas, Pierre Elliott Trudeau.

The Personality under the Ray 1 influence

One can frequently meet people whose personality is influenced by ray 1. When it is well mastered, this ray allows the individual to occupy a management position very efficiently.

Characteristics:

- Is disciplined, in control and not too demonstrative.
- Does not feel any fear and proves to have tremendous drive.
- Displays an independent character.
- Demonstrates confidence and firmness.
- Speaks with a firm voice and walks with good step.
- Detests being disturbed without a valid reason.
- Can easily get angry.
- Has an impatient nature.
- Summarizes his thoughts and translates them into few words.
- Expresses himself without flattery, even with a bit of coldness.
- Does not appreciate teamwork.
- Demonstrates endurance.
- Keeps his word.
- Is a reliable individual.

Here are some examples of people whose personality acted or acts under the influence of ray 1: Ludwig van Beethoven, Fidel Castro, Winston Churchill, Charles de Gaulle, Gurdjieff, Genghis Khan.

THE SOUL UNDER THE RAY 1 INFLUENCE

Characteristics:

* Encourages the liberation of self and has the courage to "be" and to "become".
* Conveys a strong dose of spiritual will.
* Wishes to liberate humanity from all forms of slavery.
* Possesses a great sense of the sacred.
* Affirms that "there is only the Whole, the One".

Here are some examples of people whose Soul was or is under the influence of ray 1: Helena Petrovna Blavatsky, Alexandra David-Neel, Master Eckhart, Albert Einstein, William McNamara, Penor Rinpoche.

In short, the general characteristics of individuals under the influence of ray 1 express:

In their positive aspects:

* will;
* dynamic power;
* power to synthesize;
* power to destroy for good;
* great concentration;
* power to govern and to lead;
* fearlessness;
* great detachment;
* strong independance;
* a lot of strength and courage;
* power to liberate;
* wisdom in the implementation of laws.

In their negative aspects:

- selfishness;
- pride and arrogance;
- isolation and separatism;
- thirst to destroy, to dominate;
- strong fits of anger;
- harshness, coldness that could become cruelty;
- a desire to control and oppress;
- impatience;
- stubborness;
- strong ambition;
- a thirst for power;
- a tendency to feel lonely and abandoned.

What distinguishes the individual under the influence of Ray 1

Master of Ray 1: El Morya Khan.

Associated colour: red.

Symbol: sword.

Strong points: sees the goal to be reached and expresses a strong will.

Weak point: often lacks diplomacy.

What he likes: efficiency and speed.

What he dislikes: details, because, according to him, they make him waste too much time.

Gait: determined.

Clothes: often classic, demonstrating assurance. Does not necessarily like jewelry and prefers simplicity, because he does not like to waste time getting dressed.

Profession: often attracted by positions of responsibility or power, will generally be a good politician, a company executive, a leader, an entrepreneur. He will preferably choose a profession allowing him to work alone and to manage his time, because he cannot stand a boss constantly supervising him.

Teamwork: has a tendency towards individualism; often experiences difficulty integrating into a group and being directed by a third party; prefers to work alone; generally does not like to delegate; often wishes to keep control on everything; does not often give his trust; detests wasting time. On the other hand, the mature individual under the ray 1 influence, proves to be a good leader, capable of entrusting certain powers to the members of his team because he knows he will need help to solve certain details. He easily allies with individuals under the ray 3 influence that act with speed and to those of ray 7 who bring the desired perfection. He likes working less with those under the ray 2 influence because they often have a tendency to get lost in details and seldom make fast decisions. It is also with some difficulty that he will work with people influenced by ray 6, because according to him they seem too emotional and too mystical. In short, he is definitely more at ease with individuals influenced by odd rays; he considers them more logical, more down to earth.

Verbal expression: people influenced in their action by ray 1 are, in general, less talkative because talking or troubling yourself with details is synonymous with a waste of time. They express themselves most of the time in a concise fashion, thus exposing themselves to a lack of understanding, because the notion or the thought they wish to share lacks enough explanation to be well understood. These individuals at times suffer from impatience when listening to the speeches of those influenced by rays 2 and 3. Belittling the long speeches wrapped in non essential details, they then switch their attention elsewhere.

Qualities: strength, perseverance, honesty and loyalty. Likes to work and is endowed with the power to govern and to handle people. No fear assails him.

Faults: often arrogant and displaying fits of anger, not much of a diplomat, easily impatient and sometimes stubborn and hard. On several occasions, he likes to dominate and control situations and people. When he feels trapped by time or by too many constraints, he becomes stressed and impatient.

Qualities to acquire: tenderness, humility, sympathy, tolerance and patience.

Mirages: physical strength, personal power. He often suffers from a Messiah complex in politics (the wish to save the world).

Ray 2

The "Leader" incarnating Love and Wisdom

The energy of ray 2 possesses the capacity to express love with wisdom and to understand people. The primary cause that prevents people influenced by this ray from expressing themselves with compassion and empathy is fear, mainly the fear of not being loved or of being misunderstood.

People influenced by ray 2 do not display the confidence of individuals shaped by ray 1. They usually have a nice and attractive aspect. Generally touched by great sensitivity, they are naturally disposed to offer an attentive ear; in return, they could be afflicted with great suffering because everything can affect them.

Ray 2 likes Truth, the truth that touches the essence of things and not the truth based on reasoning. The higher the initiation level of an individual, the more he will intuitively feel this Truth that will guide him in his decision making.

Influence of Ray 2 according to the initiation level

An individual whose initiation level fluctuates between 0.8 and 1.4 **is learning about love in all its diverse facets** without knowing the face of authentic love. He searches for love at any cost, forgetting its real meaning. In his desire to be loved and to feel constantly esteemed, he reveals himself to be, most of the time, nice, well intentioned, devoted and discreet. He generally demonstrates hypersensitivity and his great shyness prevents him from affirming himself. Fearing rejection and displeasure, he may even compromise his integrity. Not appreciative of solitude, he may engage in doubtful relations that will often make him suffer.

The individual whose initiation level fluctuates between 1.5 and 2.1 is a bit more mature and **starts to catch a glimpse of true love and wisdom.** At this stage, he will undertake work that increasingly requires a genuine selflessness. He will acquire more self-confidence and will usually feel less fear; he helps his fellow men with an ease and a joy unknown until that time. He still likes to please and to feel indispensible, which increases his self-esteem and his subtle arrogance. Generally, he seeks comfort and what is agreeable because his hypersensitivity remains; ordinarily, he escapes suffering, at any price. He still dislikes solitude, which he tries to tame. He still loves too much, although a new vision begins, allowing him to better love himself and therefore sincerely appreciate others more.

When he reaches an initiation level between 2.2 and 2.8, the individual, under the influence of ray 2, **starts to live a more authentic love and wisdom** for humanity. His life changes, because his priorities change. Generally, less assailed by all sorts of fears, he feels better in his skin. Depending less on other people's opinions, he works to become progressively more authentic. He reveals himself to be more sincere and happier because he loves more with authenticity; he thinks less and less of his personal needs and his comfort. He discovers a trust that was previously lacking, a trust that will gradually replace his less-and-less-useful arrogance.

After reaching an initiation level that fluctuates between 2.9 and 3.5, the individual **develops a love-wisdom** that constantly evolves. His altruism gains in sincerity, and one can notice that the wisdom acquired during his evolution guides him increasingly. He forgets himself more and turns his focus towards the real needs of humanity; he becomes a good teacher, helping others to progress on the path. Suffering less from insecurity, he progressively becomes a warrior of wisdom and love who fights for his evolution as well as that of others.

Finally, when he reaches an initiation level superior to 3.5, he **transforms into this Sage full of love** that he is meant to become. He works tirelessly to alleviate the suffering that still has free reign across our world and still suffers as a witness to so much suffering; he will dedicate his life to fighting injustice and unhappiness that are still rampant on earth. He works without respite in order to serve humanity efficiently and to become, one day, when he will reach his fifth initiation, a Master of Wisdom.

The Ray 2 influence on the different bodies

Here is a brief overview of the ray 2 influence on the five bodies that compose the human being in his entirety.

The physical body under the Ray 2 influence

It should be noted that the physical brain that allows us to think, thus to govern the lower mental, will be influenced by ray 2. It should also be considered that very few people, presently in incarnation, have a ray 2 physical vehicle.

Characteristics:

- Is generally fragile and delicate.
- Is quite vulnerable and often sick.
- Generally possesses little resistance and frequently complains of fatigue.
- Is often slightly stooped.
- Feels the environment ("The Princess and the Pea").
- Displays a strong attachment to his environment.
- Reveals himself to be very sensitive to touch and strongly feels pain.
- Is slow and does not like speed, being too fragile.
- Loves preliminaries in love, because it is sensual.
- Fears to disturb and prefers calmness, wants to be patient and can remain motionless for a long time.
- Asks to be touched.
- Requires a healthy physical body that evolves in comfort and security.

Ray 2 physical bodies are permeable and defenceless against external energies, contrary to ray 1's that erect fences to protect themselves.

Here are some examples of people whose physical bodies were under the influence of ray 2: Wolfgang Amadeus Mozart, Franklin D. Roosevelt, Cyril Scott.

THE ASTRAL BODY UNDER RAY 2 INFLUENCE

It should be noted that it is not rare to meet individuals whose emotions are under the influence of ray 2.

Characteristics:
- Reveals himself to be understanding, loving and affectionate.
- Discloses calmness, sweetness, serenity and patience.
- Manifests great sensitivity that can provoke deep joy or, on the contrary, deep suffering.
- Sometimes experiences a lot of fears based on an inner sense of weakness, powerlessness, vulnerability or extreme sensitivity.
- Is a warm reliable friend.
- Is often protective and very endearing.
- Easily feels what others feel, which makes him empathetic and compassionate.

Here are some examples of people whose astral body was or is under the influence of ray 2: Marie Curie, Walt Disney, Wayne Dyer, Mikhaïl Gorbatchev, Justin Moreward Haig, Elvis Presley, Theodore Roosevelt, Robert Shapiro, David Spangler.

THE MENTAL BODY UNDER A RAY 2 INFLUENCE

It is a little uncommon to find the influence of ray 2 in the mental body; however, when this happens, it allows the individual to generally respond more easily to the Soul's impulses.

Characteristics:
- Appears abstract, sensitive to ideas and impressions coming from the astral plane. When the initiation level of an individual with such

a mental vehicle is not very high (initiation level of less than 1.8), he often experiences difficulty in translating what is transmitted to him and shows confusion in his explanations.

- Possesses intuitive capacity on the Buddhic plane.
- Absorbs everything and accumulates knowledge, which can often result in him not understanding.
- Tries to understand, therefore he includes everything and rejects nothing, becoming a living encyclopedia, a real bookworm.
- Is the most analytic of all rays, the synthetic processes appear naturally and without efforts.
- Experiences a lot of difficulties in making up his mind on a particular point or in expressing a solution, because for him everything is good.
- Does not criticize.
- Expresses himself with a lot of details.
- Is slow and soft in the way he expresses himself.
- Is illuminated by the light of abstract and shapeless intuition. A light carrier, he experiences difficulty translating it into words.

Here are some examples of people whose mental body was or is under the influence of ray 2: Benjamin Creme; and as a sub-ray, Jim Carrey, Céline Dion, Ron L. Hubbard, Wolfgang Amadeus Mozart, Elvis Presley, Cyril Scott.

The Personality under the Ray 2 influence

This influence is very common. Part of this category includes well intentioned people at the service of humanity, who cause few afflictions to others.

Characteristics:

- Expresses love wisely and deeply understands others.
- Appears magnetic.
- Coordinates his activities with patience and tact.
- Is compassionate and respectful of people's real nature.

- Manifests himself most of the time as benevolent, kind, sympathetic, sweet, loving and comprehensive.
- Maintains honest interpersonal relationships.
- Is an excellent teacher.
- Likes to work in the health field, where he excels.
- Adopts a shy, weak and fearful nature.
- Has a tendency to be overly tolerant or permissive.
- Is too attached to people and to the comfort of his environment.
- Demonstrates reactions that are generally slow and tends to lack dynamism.
- Possesses a fragile and sensitive temperament.
- Sometimes engages in self pity.

Here are some examples of people whose personality acted or acts under the ray 2 influence: Alice Ann Bailey, Deepak Chopra, Gurumayi, Gustav Mahler, Nelson Mandala, Marcus-Aurelius, Barak Hussein Obama, Bagwan Shree Rajneesh, Sakyong Mipham Rinpoche, Neale Donald Walsch.

THE SOUL UNDER RAY 2 INFLUENCE

Many people are influenced by ray 2 on the Soul plane. This energy provokes the increasing activity of the Christic principle in the heart of humanity. It is particularly active in these times where humanity prepares itself for a "love crisis" and for a major planetary initiation.

Characteristics:
- Serves towards an altruistic goal of love.
- Teaches and heals for the good of others with love and wisdom.
- Uses love and empathy to help others "grow".
- Forgets himself and places others before his own needs.
- Qualifies as a constant source of joy the fact "of being in love".
- Wishes to "Merge One with the All, the One".

Here are some examples of people whose Soul was or is under a ray 2 influence: Ashoka, George W. Bush, Winston Churchill, Céline Dion, Walt Disney, Gampopa, Gandhi, Charles de Gaulle, Gurdjieff, Ron Howard, Genghis Khan, Gustav Mahler, Michelangelo, Serguëi Rachmaninov, Franklin D. Roosevelt, Cyril Scott, Steven Seagal, Neale Donald Walsch.

In short, the general characteristics of individuals under the ray 2 influence express:

In their positive aspects:

* love wisdom;
* magnetism;
* empathy, sympathy and compassion;
* great sensitivity;
* receptivity;
* impressionability;
* love of truth;
* the power to teach and "enlighten";
* patience, tact, serenity;
* tolerance, faith;
* power to heal through love;
* power to forgive and save;
* sociability.

In their negative aspects:

* full of fears;
* self-pity;
* hypersensitivity;
* vulnerability;
* inferiority complex;
* immoderate attachment;
* appreciation for being loved;

- outrageously protective;
- slowness to react;
- coldness and indifference;
- contempt for others' limitations.

WHAT DISTINGUISHES THE INDIVIDUAL UNDER THE INFLUENCE OF RAY 2

Master of Ray 2: Koot Hoomi.

Associated colour: blue.

Symbol: 2nd violin.

Strong point: endowed with great sensitivity that allows him to listen to people.

Weak point: numerous fears that prevent the Soul's free expression.

What he likes: to be surrounded by people.

What he dislikes: to be alone.

Gait: subdued, very soft, slightly stooped.

Clothes: sober and discreet, because he often dabbles in self-depreciation.

Profession: will direct himself towards a career where he can serve. He will excel in medicine, in research and teaching.

Teamwork: at ease working in a team. He likes to be surrounded by people and will feel happy sharing his knowledge. In fact, an individual under the ray 2 influence will very well adapt to other rays. It is the individuals influenced by the other rays that, on the contrary, sometimes find it difficult to adapt to this ray. The individual under ray 1's influence will tend to find that he is too lost in details; the individual under ray 3's influence, will find him too slow; the individual under ray 4's influence will see him as too fearful; the individual under the ray 5's influence may be irritated by the fact that he cannot make a decision; the individual under the ray 6's influence will sometimes find that he lacks motivation and audacity; and the individual under the ray 7 influence will find that he lacks structure.

Verbal expression: a tendancy to express himself in a soft, lengthy and detailed way, as he often fears being misunderstood.

Qualities: calmness, strength and patience. He puts all his energy towards helping others. He has a serene character. When he reaches a high initiation level, he reflects divine love, radiance, attraction, the power to save, and wisdom.

Faults: too many fears that make him complain. He sometimes feels vulnerable and incapable of going forward. He lets himself be excessively absorbed by his studies. As warm as he can be, he similary can, when he feels misunderstood or unjustly treated, become cold, distant and indifferent. He often despises the mental limitations of other people, due to the fact that he accumulates a lot of knowledge.

Qualities to acquire: love, compassion, selflessness, energy.

Mirages: the necessity to be loved and personal wisdom. He suffers from the messianic complex in the field of religion and the needs of others (the world savior).

Ray 3

The "Leader" incarnating Activity, Adaptability and Active Intelligence

The key word representing the main ray 3 influence is undoubtedly "action". This ray transmits the urge to move, to be in constant movement and to experiment. It provides a certain facility of adaptation and allows one to act adequately according to situations.

Ray 3 adores exploring all the possible avenues of a situation or of a given life, and hence, it adores taking its time to undergo its apprenticeships. The reverse of this inclination in the individual influenced by ray 3 sometimes is an obstacle to his Awakening, because he can choose a longer path leading to realization. However, when this same individual's Soul decides to evolve the most rapidly possible, then ray 3, no matter what the price, will become a real catalyst for the consciousness. Its speed of movement will start being implemented, and offers the individual the possibility to evolve at the speed of lightening.

In addition, this ray's energy wants to be a force that stimulates progress and discoveries. A person ruled by ray 3 posesses the power to manipulate shape, time and energy. Thus, when used properly, it could be useful for the Plan and also contribute to the progress of humanity. On the other hand, if this person demonstrates a lack of maturity, then there are risks of manipulations, exaggerated criticism, and a refusal to cooperate, which could cause delays in the projects instead of insuring a participation in their realizations.

THE RAY 3 INFLUENCE ACCORDING TO THE INITIATION LEVEL

An individual whose initiation level fluctuates between 0.8 and 1.5 **is an explorer without a precise destination**. He drifts from one experience to another, enjoys feeling, and looks down new avenues without necessarily committing to one path. Like any young soul he is centered on the pleasure of experimenting at the detriment of others' needs. A refined manipulator and excellent calculator, he tries to get the maximum from situations, while investing himself at a minimum. With an overflow of energy, ray 3 creates in the individual a permanent agitation that incites him to live his life at 200 kilometers/hour, ignoring the speed limits and the warnings. At this stage, wisdom is not his lot because he prefers to handle several projects simultaneously without really investing himself. Ill at ease when he deeply internalizes, he refuses to reflect on his actions and prefers to drift on the surface of things.

When he finds himself more advanced on the path and his initiation level fluctuates between 1.6 and 2.2 then **a more conscious experimentation starts for him**. He begins to perceive exploration differently. Becoming conscious that speed and experience do not bring any real depth, he tries to seriously engage on the path to change. Still embarrassed by what again surfaces and necessitates an inner change, he uses humour to get out of it. A refined diplomat, if he wishes, he can then progress on the path to realization while helping others progress at his side. Slightly less centered on his personal needs, he begins to experience the pleasure of giving. However, pride remains his weak point and even risks increasing, because his intelligence is also increasingly activated, becoming more alert and effective. He possesses the art of speech and how to say what is necessary to have the last word.

When an individual has reached an initiation level fluctuating between 2.3 and 2.8, **experimentation and intelligence become necessary tools for evolution,** resulting in a more enlarged vision of what surrounds him. He opens up more to the needs of others and starts to find solutions in order to reduce their suffering. He increasingly becomes a more valuable ally in solving conflicts or in completing projects. Quick-witted, he easily adapts to all situations, turning them to his advantage. Less sparing of his time, he devotes himself more and more to work for human evolution in all fields. Always involved in several projects, he sometimes loses sight of his own needs, which slows down his spiritual progression. Pride always remains his Achilles' heel, although he masters it better. His verbal manipulation becomes more a tool than a handicap in his relationship with others.

The approach of the third initiation heralds an important inner crisis that will shake things up for this entire period of his life; the external focus changes into a focus more centered on the internal, which indicates the increasing influence of his Soul. The individual whose initiation level fluctuates between 2.9 and 3.5 **sees that his progression is not achieved only through experimentation, but also through internalization,** which often creates the illusion of a temporary halt. The cruising speed seems reduced, when it is more concentrated, allowing an energy focus that pierces through the marked depth of ignorance. Becoming more of a philosopher, he begins to develop a taste for reflection particularly focused on inner evolution. His external search diminishes while he discovers a whole inner universe that fascinates him.

When his initiation level goes beyond 3.5, he **uses his intelligence in a more altruistic fashion and directs it more towards the good of all.** He seeks to perfect himself, to circumvent obstacles, without harming others or his own evolution. He travels for knowledge, to acquire depth and to help those in need. He also accesses inner travels that demonstrate to him another aspect of what he believed Life to be. He increasingly puts his charm at the service of his Soul thus suppressing the demands of his ego. He is preparing himself to live the full renunciation that will be realized when he steps across the door of the fourth initiation. He is starting to have an inkling and to understand the Master Plan of the Divine Purpose. He becomes conscious of the vast display of energies that travel through the universe to which he is affiliated and the forces that characterize it. He now takes pleasure in creating and intelligently carrying out the plan of Divine manifestation.

THE RAY 3 INFLUENCE ON THE DIFFERENT BODIES

Here is a brief overview of ray 3's influence on the different bodies that compose the human being in his entirety.

THE PHYSICAL BODY UNDER THE RAY 3 INFLUENCE

It is to be noted that the physical brain that allows us to think and manage the lower mental will also be influenced by ray 3. Note that more than one third of the world population presently has that type of body. Because this ray does not present any definite physical form such as rays 1 and 6, it can adopt all shapes, which sometimes causes confusion. However, what really distinguishes this body is its speed as well as its generally well balanced proportions.

Characteristics:

- Reveals himself to be very active, needs to move and act fast.
- Demonstrates great endurance.
- Acts and thinks fast, thanks to his brain.
- Is voluble and talks with rapid delivery.
- May resemble any shape.
- Cannot sit down for a long time. frequently changes position; seems to have pins and needles in his legs.
- Appreciates change.
- Possesses the capacity to do many things at the same time.
- Skillfully produces refined things.
- Sometimes becomes awkward because of his speed of action.
- Manifests fluidity in his thoughts and movements and reveals himself to be a good dancer.
- Does not feel fatigue and is insensitive to pain.
- Often demonstrates a lack of concern for detail and a lack of attention.
- Does not care about appearances.
- Is not disturbed by noise or a chaotic ambiance.
- Is more resistant to pollutants than other rays.

- Manifests a mesomorphic tendency (strong, muscled, active).
- Enjoys life, likes to eat, to drink and have sex.
- Expresses himself with gestures.
- Generally is down to earth.

Here are some examples of people whose physical body was or is under the ray 3 influence: Ashoka, Alice Ann Bailey, Ludwig van Beethoven, Helena Petrovna Blavatsky, Georges W. Bush, Carlos Castaneda, Fidel Castro, Deepak Chopra, Winston Churchill, Celine Dion, Gandhi, Tom Hanks, Rene Levesque, George Lucas, Madonna.

The astral body under the Ray 3 influence

It is excessively rare to meet individuals whose emotions are under the ray 3 influence, because the effects of this ray would then be extremely perturbing.

Characteristics:

- Presents a particular type of psychic make-up, may hear voices due to a strong connection between the throat and the solar plexus.
- Risks manifesting through multiple personalities.
- Feels very complex and emotionally confused.
- Experiences very materialistic desires, but is also very malleable.

Here are some examples of people whose astral body was under the ray 3 influence: Nikola Tesla, Chögyam Trungpa.

The mental body under the Ray 3 influence

Finding the influence of ray 3 in a mental body is fairly frequent. This is due to a period of intense activity that actually manifests itself by an accelerated development of intellectual faculties and by a marked intensification of creative work.

Characteristics:

- Is always active, thinks constantly.
- Demonstrates a great ability to reason and solve problems.
- Posesses a great analytical capacity.
- Seems like a great manipulator.
- Acts in a complex fashion.
- Is an intellectual.
- Is interested in everyhing.
- Possesses a very critical sense.
- Wants to communicate, possesses a verbal and linguistic facility.
- Has a creative and inventive mind.
- Could be abstract.
- Is a shrewd strategist, because he plans and evaluates everything.
- Could be fluid, flexible and versatile.

Here are some examples of people whose mental body was or is under the ray 3 influence: Ron Howard, Michael Jackson, Genghis Khan, Hazrat Inayat Khan, Marcus-Aurelius, Neem Karoli Baba, James Van Praagh, Cyril Scott, Steven Seagal, Neale Donald Walsh, Robin Williams.

THE PERSONALITY UNDER THE RAY 3 INFLUENCE

It is frequent to meet personalities ruled by the ray 3 influence.

Characteristics:

- Demonstrates an intellectual vanity and believes he is more intelligent than others.
- Possesses a great capacity for adaptation, intelligent creativity and resourcefulness.
- Knows how to coordinate things well.
- Manipulates using an intelligent strategy.
- Can carry a heavy load on his shoulders.
- Loves challenges.

- Sometimes tends to be too critical.
- Does too much, sometimes appears vague, occupied and preoccupied.
- Sometimes lacks continuity and assiduity.
- May rapidly change his mind.
- Often demonstrates arrogance and has a tendency to believe in his own superiority.
- Often feels discomfited working in a group, because this demands more effort to "manipulate" or "lead" everyone.

Here are some examples of people whose personality acted or is acting under the ray 3 influence: Ashoka, Helena Petrovna Blavatsky, Agatha Christie, Celine Dion, Clint Eastwood, Master Eckhart, Albert Einstein, Gampopa, Gandhi, Bill Gates, Jack Kornfield, William McNamara, Paul of Tarsus, Penor Rinpoche, Jane Roberts, Franklin D. Roosevelt, Frank Sinatra, Rabîndranath Tagore, Jules Verne.

The Soul under the Ray 3 influence

Characteristics:

- Experiments with the influx, versatile, intelligent energy of the Divine Plan.
- Stimulates the intellect and mental creativity of others.
- Expresses immense joy in understanding the Master Plan of the Divine Purpose.
- Demonstrates altruism by helping others becoming more intelligent and expert in the planning of their achievements.
- Inspires more activity.
- Wishes to work for God's Plan and contribute to it.

Here are some examples of people whose Soul was or is under the ray 3 influence: Wayne Dyer, Clint Eastwood, Bill Gates, Mikhaïl Gorbatchev, Justin Moreward Haig, Abraham Lincoln, George Lucas, Nelson Mandela, Michael Newton, Rajneesh, Sakyong Mipham Rinpoche, Susan Sarandon, Robert Shapiro, Sharon Stone, Hank Wesselman.

In short, the general characteristics of individuals under ray 3 influence express:

In their positive aspects:

- abstract thought;
- understanding of relativity;
- a broad view on abstract questions;
- powerful intellect;
- capacity to understand and explain complex facts;
- great mental activity;
- facility to speak;
- ability to communicate well;
- capacity to manipulate;
- adaptability;
- understanding of the economy of numbers;
- philanthropy, ability to manipulate money;
- excellence in business.

In their negative aspects:

- intellectual pride;
- very critical spirit;
- confusion;
- vague expression;
- lack of finesse, particularly in details;
- calculation, manipulation;
- opportunism;
- chameleon-like nature, tendency to lie;
- amoral materialism;
- over preoccupation with business;
- hyperactivity, no rest.

What distinguishes the individual under the influence of Ray 3

Master of Ray 3: Paul the Venetian.
Associated Colour: yellow.
Symbolism: spider web.
Strong point: adaptability.
Weak point: intellectual vanity that places him above others.
What he likes: to experiment and live fully.
What he dislikes: teamwork.
Gait: at ease and fluid.

Clothes: functional, helping him to accomplish his task. He is therefore at ease in a costly garment if he has to impress others but equally at ease in a garment of less quality if he has to perform a task requiring more ordinary attire.

Profession: a great manipulator of matter, he is attracted by construction positions, i.e. architect, engineer or construction worker. He is also interested in performing work focused on the improvement of living conditions and the good utilization of natural resources, which directs him towards fields related to the economy, ecology, industry, commerce or communications. Less affected by all types of pollution, he is at ease working in factories, doing work that requires a speedy implementation, while accomodating the repetition produced by chain production.

Teamwork: inclined to place himself above others, he experiences difficulty accepting other people's ideas, to work with a team. If he can carry out his work alone without relying on a colleague, then he feels good in a group.

Verbal expression: speaks with volubility, makes lengthy explanations, "listens to himself a lot", in short expresses himself very well according to the needs of the moment, an asset for any good manipulator.

Qualities: capacity to adapt to any situation, to act promptly, to understand rapidly, good analytical spirit, power to manipulate matter for the good of humanity.

Faults: negative critical mind; intellectual pride that allows him to shine at the others' expense; manipulator (calculating, opportunist and sometimes dishonest) in order to satisfy his personal needs instead of helping others.

Qualities to acquire: tolerance, sympathy towards others, precision, common sense, devotion to the Plan.

Mirages: needs to be active and busy, to cooperate with the Plan in an individual way rather than in a group formation; believes in his good intentions that are fundamentally selfish and in the importance of the self from the viewpoint of knowledge and efficiency.

Ray 4

The "Leader" incarnating Harmony, Beauty and Art

The key words expressing the main ray 4 influence are undoubtedly "harmony through conflict". An individual under this ray influence experiments with life through opposites, seeking beauty and balance in everything. He possesses the more or less conscious desire to understand life's complexity through what seems to be in opposition: white and black, action and inaction, joy and pain… This predisposition makes him imaginative and sensitive while developing in him great creative potential. The attraction of art and its expression in all its forms will often dominate his life.

Ray 4 energy is often uncomfortable because it leaves in its wake the constant of opposites. Sometimes a warrior, the individual under this influence fears nothings, charges through life and knocks down obstacles without giving up. Sometimes sensitive and vulnerable, he feels incapable of acting, becoming paralyzed by the pairs of opposites that harass him.

Under the influence of ray 4, the individual may be described as greatly sensitive, drifting on an ocean where the two universal polarities that influence life on Earth are travelling. He learns to understand the ocean, to admire all its beauty through the waves that influence his navigation. His maturity will colour his way of reacting to the surprises that life reserves for him. He will see it either as a challenge to meet or as a calamity to be subjected to. When he reaches a point of stable balance, he will become an excellent diplomat, always ready to rescue others in spite of the obstacles liable to harm his work

The Ray 4 influence acccording to the initiation level

An individual whose initiation level fluctuates between 0.8 and 1.4 **begins the apprenticeship of the development of constant harmony in** spite of the conflicts he frequently encounters in his life. Previously influenced by the ray 4 roller coaster journey, he often finds himself the unconscious victim of life's game. With this starting maturity, he becomes more and more attentive to life's ups and downs, which he learns to manage. Because he is obsessed and fascinated by beauty in everything, he is forced to acknowledge the fact that it is not everything but part of a whole of which it is an integral part.

Having acquired more skills to play with this ray's energy, the individual whose initiation level is between 1.5 and 2.1 **begins the discovery of this flamboyant game of life through the search for harmony.** Life for him becomes a play in which he takes part as an actor and a stage director. This individual becomes conscious and is preoccupied by the degree of harmony or lack thereof he experiences in his relationship with others and with his environment. He constantly cultivates vigilance towards his "emotional states" that still dominate him and often generate a personal instability that could create a subtle resistance to his evolution. Too often trapped by beauty in everything, which veils his vision of the world, he is now undertaking the tough apprenticeship to see beyond this beauty in order to discover the real nature hidden within.

When he reaches an initiation level between 2.2 and 2.8, **he becomes more and more conscious of the perpetual conflict in his life, and develops a more critical eye with regard to life's game and its implication.** He starts assuming responsibility for his actions and his feelings, and becomes more solid with regard to this ray's influence. He prepares himself to be an extraordinary tightrope walker, on the continuous razor's edge of his life. He starts to cultivate a sense of equanimity and to develop in him the warrior aspect that has to fight for unity and the union of opposites. However, the fight to reach real harmony is only in its preliminary stages and discouragement may surface at any time. Vigilance and constancy remain a priority, otherwise everything may tip over and ruin his efforts. As to beauty, this individual perceives its influence and deficiencies more and more when he falls in its trap. He learns to tame the influence of beauty on his life by becoming less and less its victim.

After reaching an initiation level fluctuating between 2.9 and 3.5, the individual **starts to sail through conflicts with grace.** He becomes conscious that the sense of balance and of just measure exists and that he can acquire this sense in the middle of forces that seem to oppose each other. His life invests itself in harmony, despite the conflicts that emerge, because he feels more at ease on board his ship, whose operation he better understands. He even succeeds in helping others to introduce a certain harmony in their lives. He incarnates art and beauty in everything he touches and experiments. Very creative, he now plays with opposite pairs; while appreciating beauty in everything, he remains vigilant towards its eternal influence.

Finally, when he reaches an initiation level superior to 3.5, the individual **understands the duality game more clearly and starts to transcend opposites.** He feels more at ease in life's game, which he appreciates more and more. Becoming strong himself, he presents himself as a pillar, a base on which to rely. He does not judge according to appearances, knowing how they could be misleading. Accepting life's diversity, he allows those that run by his side to develop a sense of balance in everything. He teaches them that harmony can emerge from conflict and that beauty is hidden in everything and that the art of living is a priceless gift. Thus, harmony emerges from chaos, and the full potential of ray 4 is reached.

Ray 4 influence on the different bodies

Here is a brief overview of ray 4's influence on the five bodies that compose the human being in his entirety.

THE PHYSICAL BODY UNDER THE RAY 4 INFLUENCE

It is very rare to find the ray 4 influence in the physical body. If this happens this body will be gracious, fluid and endowed with great beauty.

Characteristics:

- Appears very gracious and well proportioned.
- Radiates with an almost perfect beauty, surrealistic.
- Seems ethereal and very fluid.
- May cyclicly become active and inactive.
- Is afraid of getting old or dying prematurely because of life's unrest, or may possess a young appearance and lives long if he learns to remain calm with regards to the torments that life sends to him.
- Possesses a brain that favours intuitive and not linear thought.

Here are some examples of people whose physical body was or is under the ray 4 influence: Hazrat Inayat Khan; and, as a sub-ray, Ludwig van Beethoven, Jim Carrey, Gurumayi, Gustav Mahler, Elvis Presley, Sergueï Rachmaninov, Sharon Stone.

THE ASTRAL BODY UNDER THE RAY 4 INFLUENCE

Few individuals are subjected to the influence of this ray in their emotional body before having reached an initiation level greater than 2. This is due to the difficulty of managing this body with regards to the emotional upheavals provided by the constant search for harmony through conflict.

Characteristics:

- Generates emotional battles and conflicts almost continuously.
- Is subjected to frequent emotional ups and downs.
- Displays an emotional ambivalence, because he is always attracted by opposites.
- May display an excessively changing mood.

THE ASTRAL BODY UNDER THE RAY 4 INFLUENCE WHEN THE INDIVIDUAL HAS REACHED A HIGH INITIATION LEVEL

Characteristics:

- Acts rapidly in order to solve conflicts harmoniously.
- Seeks beauty that favours a better balance.
- Is endowed with a strong intuition.
- Rapidly adapts to diverse situations.
- Likes life's challenges and its opposites.
- Demonstrates a strong solidity in his emotions, because he has learned to sail over or with them.

Here are some examples of people whose astral body was or is under the ray 4 influence: Carlos Castaneda, Andrew Cohen, Alexandra David-Neel, Celine Dion, Gurdjieff, Gurumayi, Rene Levesque, Cyril Scott.

THE MENTAL BODY UNDER THE RAY 4 INFLUENCE

Few people are subjected to this ray's influence at the level of their mental body, unless they desire to experience ups and downs that will enormously perturb their way of seeing and reacting. However, high-level Initiates will choose this possibility in order to evolve more rapidly in their search for balance in everything.

Characteristics:

- Often tormented, which is characterized by stress and constant tension.
- Is frequently undecided, ambivalent and shaky in decision making.
- Is intuitive and irrational, is rarely attracted by the linear side of thought.
- Is provocative, likes to obtain a reaction.
- Has a tendency towards fiction, because it embellishes life's experience.
- Possesses an impressive imaginary world.
- Appears refined, is receptive to beauty, music and poetry.
- Appreciates the subtle and the intangible.

THE MENTAL BODY UNDER THE RAY 4 INFLUENCE WHEN AN INDIVIDUAL HAS REACHED A HIGH INITIATION LEVEL

Characteristics:

- Proves to be a good mediator, sees the value of both sides and positions.
- Favours harmony and peace.
- Is rapid and changing, constantly finds possible links.
- Demonstrates an openness to impressions and is receptive.

Here are some examples of people whose mental body was or is under the ray 4 influence: Ludwig van Beethoven, Albert Einstein; and, as a sub-ray, Gurumayi.

THE PERSONALITY UNDER THE RAY 4 INFLUENCE

Many individuals like to experiment with the ray 4 influence at the level of their personality. It seems that the more or less subtle game of this ray at this level favours the apprenticeship of the game of life as well as the creative aspect that will reflect on the individual's entire life.

Characteristics:

- Can be unstable, unconscious, diffcult to live with and displays fits of anger when this ray is not balanced.
- Is funny, likes to please and entertain.
- May become a fighter or, on the contrary, make many compromises.
- Tends to live inner torments and conflicts.
- Is often absorbed by his personal dramas.
- May rapidly change mood.
- Is gifted for the arts and the expression of beauty in everything.
- May easily create conflicts and feel misunderstood.
- Tends to create melodramas and play the victim.

THE PERSONALITY UNDER THE RAY 4 INFLUENCE WHEN THE INDIVIDUAL HAS REACHED A HIGH INITIATION LEVEL

Characteristics:

* Tends to create beauty and harmony in relations.
* Favours unity in diversity.
* Detests conflicts and seeks to dissolve them.
* Has acquired the ability to find equitable solutions.
* Proves to be pleasant to live with because it expresses joy and adaptation in everything.

Here are some examples of people whose personality acted or acts under the ray 4 influence: Jim Carrey, Olivier Föllmi, Tom Hanks, Ron Howard, Ron L. Hubbard, Michael Jackson, Carl Gustav Jung, Kūkai, George Lucas, Madonna, Michel-Ange, Roy Orbison, Elvis Presley, Susan Sarandon, Robert Shapiro, Sharon Stone, Voltaire.

THE SOUL UNDER THE RAY 4 INFLUENCE

Very few Souls under the ray 4 influence are presently in incarnation.

Characteristics:

* Contributes to the harmonization of other people's lives.
* Transforms conflict into harmony, dissension into agreement, war into peace.
* Helps include all the diversities so that real unity reigns in all.
* Creates beauty and becomes it.

Here are some examples of people whose Soul was or is under the ray 4 influence: Agatha Christie, Michael Jackson, Madonna, Elvis Presley, Robin Williams.

In short, the general characteristics of individuals under the ray 4 influence express:

In their positive aspects:

- facility to re-establish harmony;
- evolution through conflicts and crises;
- capability for compromise and mediation;
- the power to create;
- love of harmony and beauty and the capacity to express it;
- fighting spirit;
- refinement;
- strong sense of drama;
- musical aptitudes;
- capacity to amuse and entertain;
- spontaneity, improvisation;
- ability to create peace.

In their negative aspects:

- constant torment;
- fusion with suffering;
- agitation and desolation;
- worries;
- lack of confidence;
- changing moods;
- constant exaggeration;
- instability in activities;
- unpredictability;
- indecision;
- irregular passions;
- inertia, inaction;
- apathy, laziness.

What distinguishes the individual under the influence of Ray 4?

Master of Ray 4: Serapis Bey.

Associated colour: orange.

Symbolism: chameleon.

Strong point: his warrior spirit fights constantly in spite of his misfortunes.

Weak points: his ups and downs make him fickle in his actions; sometimes passive, sometimes active, he has difficulty finding a happy medium.

What he likes: beauty.

What he dislikes: inaction.

Gait: light and distinguished; he seems to be floating.

Clothes: very colourful and extravagant.

Profession: artist, actor, singer, painter, fashion designer, writer, sculptor, soldier, diplomat, negotiator.

Teamwork: generally likes to work with people, is stimulated by it. However, often under the grip of his "moods", he has to work hard to keep a certain constancy in his work and meet deadlines. According to his attitude, he can lighten teamwork or make it heavy, become a pleasant or unpleasant companion, depending on his mood.

Verbal expression: often theatrical and dramatic. He likes to entertain and to be the center of attention. He rarely goes unnoticed and has a sharp tongue. He likes to provoke, to make people react for the best or for the worst. He catalyzes action by his language.

Qualities: capacity for compromise, mediation, reconciliation and easy creation of links. Very creative and expressive, he knows how to entertain and to lighten the atmosphere. Very generous, he gives a lot of himself in order to help others. Being afraid of nothing, he is always prepared to fight for a good cause.

Faults: egocentrism, tendancy to torment himself, lack of precision, lack of morals, strong passions that could lead him to self destruction, apathy, unconcern, extravagance.

Qualities to acquire: serenity, self-confidence and confidence in others, self-control, unselfishness, precision, balance in everything, wisdom.

Mirages: harmony at any price, focusing on comfort and personal satisfaction, the necessity of war to defend his ideas, conflict with the goal of imposing justice and peace, musical and artistic sensitivity, possessing a 6th sense allowing him to "feel" what others cannot feel.

Ray 5

The "Leader" incarnating Concrete Knowledge and Science

The individual under ray 5's influence is, above all, interested in understanding with precision the way things are made and what makes them work. He will not hesitate to submit his hypotheses to practical experimentation in order to prove or demonstrate what he understood.

For him, only truth counts. When he tries to understand or study one of his points of interest, he can become extremely demanding and rigorous and demonstrate a sharp intolerance towards error or lack of precision. Little inclined to emotions, he easily becomes cold and insensitive to human suffering.

When he is not very evolved, he can prove to be very rigid, critical and full of prejudices, possessing a narrowness of mind that yields with difficulty to the unexpected and to novelty. In contrast, if he wants to be more evolved, his concentration and discriminating qualities may stimulate his intuition, thus leading him to break through the secret of creation and to contribute, through his discoveries to the evolution of humanity.

Ray 5 influence on the initiation level

An individual whose initiation level fluctuates between 1 and 1.4 **has a tendency to submit everything to detailed analysis.** Trusting the information received by his five senses, he mistrusts any reality he cannot scientifically demonstrate. Thus, everything that is part of the invisible and the intangible, such as feelings, intuitions or subtle perceptions, will be rejected because they cannot be proven or captured by concrete intelligence.

Trusting his rational mental that gives him the impression of knowing everything, the ray 5 individual defends his convictions with arrogance and sharp criticism. He easily negates everything which, in his eyes, has no "common sense". As the bridge between the personality and the Soul is not yet fully built, the love of the Soul cannot easily manifest itself through such an individual, who expresses very little compassion with regard to others' limitations. He will easily isolate himself, judging, rationalizing and condemning all that seem strange, thus destroying communication, spontaneity and the appreciation of what is simply good in life.

When his initiation level fluctuates between 1.5 and 2.2, the individual **begins to admit that another reality than the one he can prove exists.** Waking up his interest for the spiritual process, he will inevitably attempt to understand and master all the technicalities underlying such a process, trying, however, not to submit to it. He may then, through an accumulation of often quite correct mental knowledge, become an excellent guru or teacher, while remaining hooked to the limitations imposed by his knowledge; however, he will not succeed in allowing himself to be guided by intuition, but only by what he believes to be true.

The individual, whose initiation level fluctuates between 2.3 and 3.3, is a more evolved being **who lost his intellectual mistrust related to the enigma of existence.** Now, by using his discrimination and reasoning faculties, his desire is to know the truth that expresses itself through form. Guided by his intuition, he perceives life like a big puzzle, and every little step to solve it provides him with considerable joy, that in itself becomes his only reward. No longer needing to glorify himself with knowledge, he is not attached to his discoveries, but seeks to improve the quality of life for all through them. At this level, the love of the Soul uses such a vehicle in order to work in very precise spheres of specific expertise, which could be useful for the evolution of humanity. Research in the spiritual field often becomes his field of research par excellence. It is said that, thanks to ray 5, the Soul's existence will one day be scientifically proven. This is why one of the names of the fifth ray is "The Revealer of Truth".

The Ray 5 influence on the different bodies

Here is a brief overview of the ray 5 influence on the five bodies composing the human being in his entirety.

The physical body under the Ray 5 influence

It is rather rare to actually find ray 5 physical bodies on our planet.

Characteristics:

- Appears quite firm, compact, somewhat stiff, rigid and awkward.
- Sometimes has the appearance of a gnome.
- Likes to work alone and often in nature.
- Is inclined to isolate himself to avoid establishing links.
- Tends to be more mental than sentimental.
- Prefers to work on something concrete.
- Is induced to cooperate with the mineral kingdom and the world of the *devas*.
- Can project thoughts and use telepathy.
- Can receive and transmit light through his *ajna* center (third eye) at a higher initiation.

Here are some examples of people whose physical body was or is under the ray 5 influence: Robin Williams; and, as a sub-ray, George W. Bush, Deepak Chopra, Agatha Christie, Gurdjieff, Neem Karoli Baba, Rabîndranâth Tagore.

The astral body under the Ray 5 influence

It is equally extremely rare to find an astral body under the ray 5 influence.

Characteristics:

- Colourless expression, coupled with an often failing feeling sense.
- Reveals an apparent absence of emotions.
- Experiences difficulty being emotionally stimulated by another.

- Displays emotional detachment and a lack of emotional interest that allows the mental body to pursue its activity without distortion.
- Experiences emotions easily controlled by the rational aspect.
- Feels an emotional interest for the concrete and tangible.
- Connects to the *ajna* center and the solar plexus, the combination creating an ease for visualisation, mainly for objective things.

THE MENTAL BODY UNDER RAY 5 INFLUENCE

Ray 5 influence at the level of the mental body is fairly wide spread, which has permitted technological progress in today's world.

Characteristics:

- Aims at being scientific, precise, just, correct and right.
- Is focused and concentrated, like a laser beam.
- Is sharp cutting, defined.
- Is analytical, discriminating, "divisive"; rejects whatever reveals itself to be illogical.
- Uses a detailed and meticulous thought process.
- Verifies through experimentation.
- Displays mechanical ability.
- Targets a goal (sometimes overly) rational and technical.
- Demonstrates objective detachment and selflessness.
- Is an inquisitor, an investigator and curious.
- Possesses a mathematical mind.
- Lacks imagination, is not much of an intuitive.
- Criticizes harshly.

Here are some examples of people whose mental body was or is under the ray 5 influence: George W. Bush, Wayne Dyer, Justin Moreward Haig, Ron L. Hubbard, Carl Gustav Jung, Michael Newton, Helena Roerich, Sakyong Mipham Rinpoche, Voltaire.

The Personality under the Ray 5 influence:

Few incarnated people on Earth have such an influence in their personality.

Characteristics:

- Reaches exact knowledge through research and experimentation.
- Possesses a sense of realism and common sense.
- Needs to know how things are made and why.
- Demonstrates a sharp sense of observation and discrimination.
- Focuses too exclusively on reasoning.
- Is too down to earth.
- Connects with the concrete and material world.
- Has a tendency towards separatism and criticism.
- Manifests a constant need for proofs and mental certainty.
- Demonstrates clinical objectivity void of emotions.

Here are some examples of people whose personality acted or acts under the ray 5 influence: in sub-ray, Winston Churchill, George Lucas, Marcus-Aurelius.

The Soul under Ray 5 influence

It is very rare to meet Souls influenced by the ray 5 energy.

Characteristics:

- Wishes to penetrate and understand matter and its secrets.
- Makes scientific discoveries for the good of humanity.
- Tries to know the keys and solutions to nature's mystery.
- Wants to discover, beyond all doubt, the truth expressing itself in form.
- Tends to improve the quality of human life.

Here is the example of a Soul under the ray 5 influence: in sub-ray, Bill Gates.

In short, the general characteristics of individuals under the ray 5 influence express:

In their positive aspects:

- capacity to think and act scientifically;
- utilization of the intellect to understand;
- ability to explain and to define;
- ease with mathematics;
- great capacity for analysis and discrimination;
- precision in thought;
- mechanical abilities and practical inventiveness;
- rejection of what is not logical;
- verification through experimentation.

In their negative aspects:

- an extremely mental attitude;
- analysis too present;
- a thought too rational;
- too objective viewpoint;
- excessive scepticism;
- lack of intuition;
- harsh criticism;
- emotions scarcely present;
- attachment to the senses;
- narrowness of spirit and prejudices.

WHAT DISTINGUISHES THE INDIVIDUAL UNDER THE INFLUENCE OF RAY 5

Master of Ray 5: Hilarion.
Associated Colour: green.
Symbolism: rod of power.
Strong point: sharp and precise intellect that allows him to acquire knowledge and verify it through experimentation.
Weak point: excessive rationalism with a pattern of rigid and fixed ideas.

What he likes: expertise in a restrictive field of interest.
What he dislikes: lack of precision.
Gait: is often controlled and rigid.

Clothes: dull colours, shapeless clothes.

Profession: often attracted by positions requiring a certain intellectual expertise — lab rat, doctor, psychologist, scientist — or positions requiring a certain mechanical ability — mining work, iron works — and any field related to nature.

Teamwork: tends to focus on small details and acts only after having verified all possible avenues. With a rather reserved nature, he is a great help for whatever requires technical or scientific abilities. In contrast, his often narrow-minded thinking and critical approach, as well as his tendancy to work alone may tremendously affect a group's unity. More evolved, such an individual will support the group by seeking to always promote the truth, rectitude and justice in all circumstances.

Verbal expression: is generally extremely practical and methodical. He appreciates precise explanations and puts a strong emphasis on details. He detests drama and exaggeration in comments. Less enclined to emoting, his conversation is often informative and impersonal; when he gets in contact with a person, he prefers to keep his distance.

Qualities: intelligence, precision and straight common sense. When he is interested in a subject, he perseveres, sometimes until exhaustion. He ends up finding the hidden truth in the researched field. Independent, justice, for him, leaves no room for compromise.

Faults: often arrogant, rigid and full of prejudices. When vexed, he has a tendency to cut all contact, to isolate himself. He has a lot of difficulty forgiving; his lack of sympathy for others' limitations sometimes pushes him to express a caustic criticism that he justifies very easily. Individualistic by nature, group work is far from being his favorite activity.

Qualities to acquire: respect, love and sympathy for others, broad-mindedness and devotion.

Mirages: confidence based on knowledge and a narrow viewpoint. He believes that the intellect can solve everything, and that it is absolutely necessary to see in order to believe.

Ray 6

The "Leader" incarnating abstract Idealism and Devotion

The key words incarnating ray 6's influence are undoubtedly "devotion" and "idealism" because they are constantly present in the lives of individuals guided by this energy. These people possess an unshakeable faith and a persistant optimism that helps them nourish the ideal of their choice.

In their positive aspect, these people demonstrate a great capacity to awaken, inspire and motivate others in order to light the spark that, sometimes, is lacking in the accomplishment of their project. However, when the negative aspect is predominant, these people become, in certain occasions, sectarian, resisting the least change, then becoming infatuated with the slogan "if you do not think like me, then you are against me."

Contrary to what people may believe, the individual ruled by ray 6 is not necessarily a follower. Indeed, he seeks to serve, to dedicate himself to a cause or to an individual he admires, but he remains fundamentally independant in his actions. No one will make him do what he does not wish to do, unless, of course, he is subjugated by the influence of an individual with more cunning than himself, who will take advantage of his naivety.

Ray 6 influence on the initiation level

The individual whose initiation level fluctuates between 0.8 and 1.2 **is under the apprenticeship of devotion.** He seeks, unconsciously or not, to devote himself, body and soul, to a person or a cause he holds in high esteem. He idealizes this person or this cause and whoever disagrees with his vision will be in trouble! He then becomes a merciless warrior, ready to destroy anything that can potentially harm "his" cause or "his" universe, be it a husband, spouse, children or boss. This ray makes young souls very "family oriented", very "patriotic" and ready to defend everyone who is part of this "family," extended or not. One has to add that these souls demonstrate warmth and are welcoming when they think that their beliefs are shared, but often demonstrate harshness and vindictiveness when they feel betrayed or victim of others.

The individual whose initiation level fluctuates between 1.3 and 2.2 **undertakes the apprenticeship of altruistic dedication.** He begins to discover this unidirectional and divisive side that is often linked to dedication. He then attempts to change and enlarge his vision in order to include in his field of interest a diversity of opinions. This apprenticeship is difficult and includes multiple setbacks and suffering, because he will have to face opinions different from his own. He must diminish his need to control his environment and others, even if he thinks he is acting for their good. A great insecurity may then emerge that will provoke in him various fears he will have to learn to manage well. However, he is starting to gradually include other ways of seeing things and to develop a devotion tinged with sincerity and compassion. He understands others better and tries, to the best of his knowledge, to help and support them.

The individual whose initiation level fluctuates between 2.3 and 3.4 **begins to relentlessly dedicate himself to his Ideal,** which gradually translates itself as a merging with his Soul. He begins to feel its presence and to let himself be guided by it. He becomes a sincere being devoted to others and he forgets himself easily without necessarily demanding payback on the part of his peers. If betrayed, he forgives more easily, which was not the case previously, and tries to see beyond appearances. He suffers a lot from not understanding others or being understood. He sees the Universe as more of a Whole of which he is part and in which everyone has his place. He gradually loses the sectarian aspect, characteristic of an immature ray 6, in order to become "inclusive" and tolerant towards everything around him.

When an individual reaches an initiation level higher than 3.4, **his Ideal becomes the leitmotiv of his life and dedication, the way to achieve it**. He devotes himself entirely to his work focused on humanity, forgetting his needs. If he suffers, he remains centered and avoids complaining needlessly, knowing that others suffer as much as he, even more. Not being preoccupied anymore by a unique and narrow vision, he works toward the realization of his goal while encouraging others to pursue theirs. Inspired and guided by the Soul, he reveals himself to be faithful, jovial and caring, a pleasant person to mix with, a reliable person. He often becomes a leader who helps his peers liberate themselves from the chains of servitude, whether visible or not.

Ray 6 influence on the different bodies

Here is a brief overview of ray 6 influence on the five bodies that compose the human being in its entirety.

The physical body under Ray 6 influence

Previously, the physical bodies influenced by ray 6 were rather rare, which is not the case today.

Characteristics:
- Possesses an active and fiery physical body, if of a 'Martian' type.
- Is endowed with a soft muscular tone; tends to accumulate a lot of water, if 'Neptunian' in nature.
- Likes to be touched, but rapidly feels pain if the touch is too deep (due to the accumulation of toxins).
- Has a strong tendancy to be overweight.
- Feels a lot through the solar plexus, which provokes an enhancement of the emotions characteristic of this ray and the pathologies that touch the organs of the abdominal area, thus creating an interference with intellectual and rational energies.
- Literally eats his emotions, and prefers rich food.
- Generally perspires profusely.

- Manifests a tendency to be melancholic.
- Is not very inclined towards exercise.
- Is very sensitive to the streams of the astral world; their brain has the capacity to remember their dreams.
- Is predisposed to astral voyages and mediumship.
- Easily yields to the attraction of dependancies (food, alcohol, etc,)`
- Has a tendency to speak a lot, thus vampirizing other people's energy.
- Hates to be alone.

Here are some examples of people whose physical body was or is under the ray 6 influence: Penor Rinpoche; and as a sub-ray, Alice A. Bailey, Helena Petrovna Blavatsky, Winston Churchill, Benjamin Creme, Master Eckhart, Justin Moreward Haig, Christopher Hills, Ron Howard, Nelson Mandala, Roy Orbison, Ramakrishna, Steven Seagal, Jules Verne, Oprah Winfrey.

THE ASTRAL BODY UNDER THE RAY 6 INFLUENCE

Ray 6 is presently the most used ray to experiment with at the level of the astral body. It is therefore often influential in this configuration.

Characteristics:
- Manifests devotion and an emotional dependence.
- Lacks emotional control, reacts rapidly.
- Becomes easily susceptible.
- Tends to get attached, to become possessive.
- Does not appreciate solitude and constantly seeks other people's company.
- Is inclined to be led by his desires.
- Demonstrates strong emotional intensity that can lead to fanaticism.
- Manifests an exclusive attachment to the object of his desire and shuts himself off, sometimes to the rest, thus breeding possessiveness and jealousy.
- Has a tendency towards emotional mirages that stimulate distortion and an altered perspective.

In its positive aspect:

- forgets himself for the cause and for others;
- demonstrates warmth and friendliness;
- has a good listening ability;
- demonstrates reliability;
- is endowed with a good sense of humour, not susceptible;
- wants to be a good motivator;
- likes to work in a team and exchange ideas;
- is interested in everything.

Here are some examples of people whose astral body was or is under the ray 6 influence: Ashoka, Ludwig van Beethoven, George W. Bush, Jim Carrey, Fidel Castro, Agatha Christie, Winston Churchill, Benjamin Creme, Tom Cruise, Albert Einstein, Olivier Föllmi, Gampopa, Bill Gates, Michael Jackson, George Lucas, Michelangelo.

THE MENTAL BODY UNDER THE RAY 6 INFLUENCE

This type of body is very rare in the front line. It exists more frequently as a sub-ray.

Characteristics:

- Has mental concentration directed towards a unique point of interest.
- Manifests a great attachment to thought.
- Uses a repetitive thought process, sometimes producing a closed mind.
- Deploys continuous effort of the mind that almost never gives up.
- Is rigid and inflexible.
- Demonstrates a receptivity towards idealized thought, therefore is endowed with great intuition.
- Does not let go easily.
- Proves to be a good leader.

Here are some examples of people who were or are under the ray 6 influence: Gurumayi, Elvis Presley.

THE PERSONALITY UNDER THE RAY 6 INFLUENCE

It is not rare nowadays to meet individuals experimenting with a ray 6 in their personality configuration.

Characteristics:

- Proves to be faithful, devoted.
- Does not let go; perseveres.
- Aligns his entire life with a cause.
- Inspires, communicates enthusiasm, promotes faith.
- Is warm, affectionate, may become possessive.
- Has a propensity to become rigid, to resist change.
- Sometimes too emphatic, too extremist, unreasonable.

Here are some examples of people who acted or act under the ray 6 influence: George W. Bush, Tom Cruise, Marie Curie, Alexandra David-Neel, Walt Disney, Wayne Dyer, Mikhaïl Gorbatchev, Hazrat Inayat Khan, Rene Levesque, Michael Newton, Theodore Roosevelt, David Spangler, Robin Williams, Oprah Winfrey.

THE SOUL UNDER THE RAY 6 INFLUENCE

It is not very frequent to meet individuals possessing a ray 6 in their Soul.

Characteristics:

- Ardently desires to find someone to devote himself to or something to which he can dedicate himself.
- Wishes to perfectly express the most noble ideals.
- Inspires by his courage or his example.
- Can forget himself and even sacrifice himself for his ideal.
- Rejects any compromise related to his ideal.
- Manifests extreme loyalty.
- Has a tendency to regard as sacred the object of his ideal or his vision.

Here are some examples of people whose Soul was or is under the ray 6 influence: Rene Levesque, Paul of Tarsus, Theodore Roosevelt.

In short the general characteristics of individuals under the ray 6 influence express:

In their positive aspects:

- idealism;
- power of abstraction (to be in the world but not of this world);
- intense devotion;
- unshakeable faith, optimism;
- loyalty, sincerity;
- great humility;
- unidirectional vision;
- self-sacrifice;
- receptivity to spiritual guidance;
- persistance;
- power to awaken, inspire and persuade;
- purety, kindness, saintliness.

In their negative aspects:

- rigidity regarding their idealism;
- unreasonable devotion;
- blind faith;
- excessiveness, extremism;
- fanaticism, militarism;
- emotionalism, possessiveness, jealousy;
- tendency to rely too much on others;
- superstition and gullibility;
- martyr complex and self-denial;
- insufficient practical sense;
- absence of realism;
- lack of harmony in the face of instinctual nature.

What distinguishes the individual under the influence of Ray 6

Master of Ray 6: Jesus.
Associated Colour: purple.
Symbolism: horse.
Strong points: warmth, empathy, devotion.
Weak point: tendency to be divisive.
What he likes: loyalty.
What he dislikes: detachment.
Gait: vigorous and ardent or, on the contrary, obviously prostrated when in self-denial.

Clothes: comfortable and according to the mood of the moment; a tendency to wear ample clothes to conceal his excess weight.

Profession: relentless worker; he is a devoted individual to whom one can entrust multiple tasks. He rarely occupies a management position, preferring to work for a boss or a company that is close to his heart. He likes to make himself useful and, in order to be loved, he sometimes undertakes unrewarding tasks that no one wants. Sincere and honest, he can be trusted as long as the expansion of the company does not provoke very speedy changes.

Teamwork: sometimes has difficulty integrating within a team. Generally, he likes to work for one person or for a reduced group that he idealizes, which will bring him the desired attention. He likes to feel indispensible. As long as he knows that his work is valued and appreciated, he will prove to be indefatigable, dynamic and will give of himself one hundred and fifty percent. On the other hand, he may withdraw and jeopardize the whole project if he is not sufficiently consulted or appreciated by his peers.

Verbal expression: he can be very expressive and perseverant. Often, he tends to laugh and speak loudly, liking to be noticed. However, if he decides to become more discreet, he may be silent and manage to go unnoticed.

Qualities: loyalty, unity of intention, love, tenderness, devotion, intuition.

Faults: jealousy, possessiveness and sectarianism. He has a tendency to feel personally targeted, which leads him to have violent fits of anger. The more he evolves, the more he learns to radiate love with a growing unselfishness.

Qualities to acquire: strength, self-sacrifice, truth, tolerance, serenity, balance and common sense.

Mirages: blind and idealistic devotion, savior complex, fanaticism, meddling, sentimentality, narrow vision.

Ray 7

The "Leader" incarnating Ceremonial Order or Magic

The key word incarnating the main ray 7 influence is undoubtedly "perfection." The person mainly influenced by this ray seeks perfection in everything. He is demanding towards himself and towards others. He likes the established order to be respected and shows himself to be very organized and respectful of laws, rules and social conventions. Disliking risk, he is always seeking a better process to accomplish something, and once this process is found and approved, he keeps it without desiring to change it.

He reveals himself to be very "practical" and full of common sense, a bit like ray 5. But he differentiates himself from the latter because of a concern for details that often borders on obsession. He neglects nothing and nothing escapes him. He allows himself no faux pas. Thus to avoid any failure, he develops a particular routine, a ritual he respects judiciously.

He adores working with matter that gives shape. Possessing magnetic hands, he will excel in professions using them (therapist, architect, carpenter, artist and … magician), particularly if he can play, experiment and inprove the "shape." When he evolves, he will become more and more conscious of the link binding matter to spirit, a matter that is animated under his fingers and through his guidance.

THE RAY 7 INFLUENCE ON THE INITIATION LEVEL

An individual whose initiation level fluctuates between 0.8 and 1.4 **undertakes the apprenticeship of perfection through Order and Magic.** Often obsessed by order, he can prove to be a real tyrant to his entourage. He reveals himself to be a conservative who detests chaos; he likes to restrict himself to established values in order to avoid the anguish and the uncertainty of novelty. He often trips over details that prevent him from rapidly moving forward on the path. He loves perfection in everything and takes whatever time is necessary to succeed in what he does, what may sometimes aggravate those working with him. He is not shy to criticize since, according to his vision (limited at this stage), he thinks he is an expert in everything and the only one to know the perfect way to carry out certain things. Beware of those who do not listen to him or do not perform the work his way, because his anger will often show itself to be devastating to others, sometimes creating wounds that are difficult to heal.

When his evolution fluctuates between 1.5 and 2.2, the individual **starts to integrate in a more conscious fashion, the importance of perfection in everything he does.** He is more and more aware of his desire to make everything perfect, and often to the detriment of others' whose feelings can be hurt by his remarks or his actions. Not having yet acquired the wisdom allowing him to act with finesse and sensitivity, he is still believed, in the eyes of his entourage, to be a very demanding perfectionist. Acquiring more power, his demands may seem high-handed if he does not show vigilance towards himself. He has to acquire a broader vision and learn real communication with his entourage. As he succeeds generally in everything, he may delay changing his behaviour in fear of not "perfectly succeeding" in his projects, because for him, imperfection is synonymous with failure which he strongly detests.

When his initiation level fluctuates between 2.3 and 3.4, the individual **learns the mastery of perfection in the world of form.** He gradually perceives magic in everything, which helps him to trust destiny and the power of the energy guiding him, as he begins to perceive this guidance that reassures him and makes him more "human." Little by little he becomes more gentle and conscious of his influence on his environmnent. He appreciates the work of others and is less fearful of chaos in his life. He even learns to play with disorder in order to find some order but in a more harmonious way, which attracts the admiration of all those watching him act. Becoming increasingly magnetic, he often is looked upon by the others as a magician who can easily play with the world of matter. The reaching of perfection in everything becomes easier because he gives it less importance, discovering that nothing can be completely perfect in a world of illusions, particularly the much sought after perfection.

When his initiation level exceeds 3.5, the individual **gradually becomes the perfect Leader in a world of perfection and magic in form**. He plays with matter, working it, changing and creating it. He seems to have no limits. He is successful in everything and, if he accidentally encounters imperfection, he learns to accept it and to cherish it, becoming aware that it could add an essential note to the game of his life. Having acquired the sense of refinement, he sows this refined beauty everywhere creating a healthy and harmonious environment for all. No longer seeking perfection because now it is part of him, he may act with the *devas* of the world of matter without risking falling under their power. He cooperates with them, which was almost previously impossible, to help humanity to grow in an environment more appropriate to human life, which implies comfort and peace.

RAY 7 INFLUENCE ON THE DIFFERENT BODIES

Here is a brief overview of ray 7 influence on the five bodies comprising the human being in its entirety.

THE PHYSICAL BODY UNDER THE RAY 7 INFLUENCE

It is not rare to find ray 7 physical bodies. They will be more and more present in the future.

Characteristics:

- Refined and delicate while being strong and resistant.
- Endowed with a natural and overall elegance.
- Sensitive to the etheric world and energies.

- Ritualistic.
- Functions with a sense of rythme to preserve its energy.
- Easily trainable; enjoys discipline.
- Shows proof of finesse and an economy of movement.
- Well adapted to live on earth.
- Has strong energy in the hands as a means to manifest; is an excellent healer or builder.
- Reveals himself to be a good magician, because his refined body may receive and transmit energies without distortion.

Here are some examples of people whose physical bodies were or are under the ray 7 influence: Gampopa, Charles de Gaulle, Carl Gustav Jung, Elvis Presley, Rudolf Steiner, Susan Sarandon, Ken Wilber.

THE ASTRAL BODY UNDER THE RAY 7 INFLUENCE

It is to be noted that this type of body is extremely rare, even non-existent.

Characteristics:

- Possesses a disciplined emotional body.
- Demonstrates a predictable sequence with regards to emotional reactions.
- Lives emotions subjected to the body's rhythm.
- Shows desires directed towards physical objects.
- Has a talent for mediumship.

THE MENTAL BODY UNDER THE RAY 7 INFLUENCE

It is very frequent nowadays to meet individuals having such a ray in their mental body.

Characteristics:

- Synthesizes.
- Graced with an excellent memory thanks to his capacity to organize and create order.

- Has the capacity to coordinate and synthesize.
- Produces clear and precise thoughts.
- Is a meticulous mentalist who likes routine and details.
- Expresses a tendancy to standardize and conform to rules.
- Demonstrates a lack of adaptability and spontaneity.
- Proves to be mentally inflexible and rigid, someone who does not like to change his way of thinking.
- Likes to come up with abstract or intangible ideas.

Here are some examples of people whose mental bodies were or are under ray 7 influence: Ashoka, Anton Bruckner, Deepak Chopra, Walt Disney, Epictetus, Huineng, Nelson Mandela, Jules Verne.

The Personality under the Ray 7 influence

It is more and more frequent to meet individuals whose personality is under ray 7 influence.

Characteristics:

- Has a high level of organization.
- Disciplined and methodical.
- Meticulously follows his daily agenda, holds to his routine.
- Knows how to recognize priorities (everything at the right moment).
- May become too rigid and resist change.
- Preoccupied by appearances and conventions (sometimes excessively).
- Tendancy to judge according to appearances.
- Believes his method is the best.
- Gives importance to the social status.
- Likes order and cleanliness.

Here are some examples of people whose personality acted or acts under the ray 7 influence: Benjamin Creme, Justin Moreward Haig, Abraham Lincoln, Helena Roerich, Pierre Elliot Trudeau.

THE SOUL UNDER THE RAY 7 INFLUENCE

It is rare to meet individuals possessing such a ray in their Soul.

Characteristics:

- Manifests divine ideas into form.
- Helps human beings to organize their lives, and adequately and efficiently accomplish their destiny.
- Brings a rhythm, puts order in chaos.
- Cultivates the sacred and expresses it in the form.

Here are some examples of people whose Soul was or is under the ray 7 influence: Jim Carrey, Tom Cruise, Marie Curie, Barack Hussein Obama.

In short, the general characteristics of individuals under the ray 7 influence express:

In their positive aspects:

- power to create order;
- tendancy to have rigid habits;
- power to demonstrate, transform and concretize on the material plane;
- power to plan and organize;
- tendancy to perform in rituals and ceremonies;
- power to manipulate energies and work with the devas and elementals: magicians;
- sense of rhythm and synchronization;
- power to coordinate groups;
- power to understand and apply the law;
- power to build;
- power to synthetize.

In their negative aspects:

- tendancy to have rigid habits and submit to them;
- conservatism, likes to apply the rules and the laws;
- excessive ritualism;
- materialistic;
- lacks originality;
- fears the unpredictable;
- excessive conformity;
- excessive perfectionism;
- easy judgement based on appearances;
- sectarianism;
- could be inclined to participate in black magic;
- emphatic exaggeration of sexuality;
- distinct taste for occult and spiritualistic phenomena.

What distinguishes the individual under the Ray 7 influence

Master of Ray 7: Saint Germain.
Related colour: indigo blue.
Symbolism: the alchemist.
Strong point: organization.
Weak points: conformism, rigidity.
What he likes: order.
What he dislikes: the unpredictable.
Gait: harmonious and elegant.

Clothes: quality and style. Well groomed, he has to appear perfect. He does not like flashy colours and loves the small details that increase the refined and "distinguished" effects.

Profession: skillful in perfecting the form to make it the most perfect possible; also likes to preserve the environment and participate in organizational expertise. Demonstrates patience and does not try to force the completion of a project, but mainly to manage the different energies and resources in a manner to deploy them at the appropriate moment. He excels in legal professions such as lawyer or crown prosecutor, because he never forgets to read the small characters attached to the different laws and codes. He likes to "build" and "create" which makes him a good business executive or a good conductor, an excellent architect and a fearsome businessman.

Teamwork: has a great capacity to organize, coordinate and possesses courteous behaviour; excels in a well-organized group that demands respect for the laws. When more evolved, he is very respectful of peoples' differences and is an excellent collaborator to the well-being and integrity of the whole group. For him, the team is more important than the individual. In this field, he is a precursor because, in the future, the group's creative work will definitely replace the individual's.

Verbal expression: polite, courteous and respectful of rules and customs.

Qualities: strength, perseverance, courage.

Faults: formalism, narrow-mindedness, superficial judgements, too much indulgence in personal opinion, pride, bigotry.

Qualities to acquire: achievement of unity, broad-mindedness, tolerance, humility, kindness and love.

Mirages: magical work, what unites, the physical body, the mysterious and secret, sexual magic, the manifestation of forces.

The Circle of initiates – Volume II
Partial List of 108 Initiates to come

1. Aïvanhov, Michaël Omraam
2. Atatürk, Mustafa Kemal
3. Balsekar, Ramesh
4. Bambi, Baaba
5. Bellucci, Monica
6. Bernard de Montréal
7. Bethune, Henry Norman
8. Boone, J. Allen
9. Bouchard, Lucien
10. Boucher, Vincent
11. Brinkley, Dannion
12. Burroughs, Catherine
13. Clooney, George
14. Cohen, Leonard
15. Court (Master of Matt Guest)
16. Dadaji
17. Da Free John
18. Das, Krishna
19. Deunov, Peter
20. Dickens, Charles
21. Dolma, Ani Choying
22. Francis of Assisi, Saint
23. Gere, Richard
24. Gibran, Khalil
25. Gross, Darwin

26. Guest, Matt
27. Hamid (Sufi Master of Reshad Feild)
28. Hughes, Howard Robard
29. Jacques de Zebedee
30. John, Saint
31. Jesus the Nazarene
32. Jnaneshwar
33. Jolie, Angelina
34. Keller, Helen
35. Kepler, Johannes
36. Khamtrul Rinpoché
37. Kemp, Daniel
38. Kennedy, John F.
39. Klemp, Harold
40. Krishnamurti, Jiddu
41. Kunley, Drukpa
42. La Fontaine, Jean de
43. Lao Tsu
44. Mâ Ananda Moyî
45. Maharshi, Ramana
46. Mao Tse-Toung
47. Mares, Theun
48. Mary Magdalene
49. Mary, Mother of Jesus
50. Marpa
51. Matus, Don Juan
52. Mother Meera
53. Mother Teresa
54. Milarepa

55. Muktananda, Swami
56. Nagarjuna
57. Nanak, Guru
58. Ngawang, Geshe Thubten
59. Nisargadatta
60. Nityananda
61. Oppenheimer, Julius Robert
62. Orgyen Trinley Dorje (17th Karmapa)
63. Patrul Rinpoche
64. Perry, Diane
65. Peterson, Wayne
66. Pythagore
67. Ramakrishna
68. Redford, Robert
69. Ricard, Matthieu
70. Rûmî, Djalâl ad-Dîn
71. Sahib, Bhai
72. Samwar Singh, Baba
73. Sanchez, Oscar
74. Sangye Padampa
75. Schwarzenegger, Arnold
76. Shakespeare, William
77. Shantideva
78. Shaw, Idries
79. Shriver, Maria
80. Singh, Kirpal
81. Sivananda, Swami
82. Sogyal Rinpoche
83. Spielberg, Steven

84. Surya Das, Lama
85. Tabrizi, Shams Al-din
86. Thich Nhat Hanh
87. Tilopa
88. Tolle, Eckhart
89. Travolta, John
90. Tweedie, Irina
91. Twitchell, Paul
92. Vimalananda
93. Vivekananda, Swami
94. Whitman, Walt
95. Yogananda, Paramahansa
96. Yongey Mingyour Rinpoche

... and 12 new people to be added and discovered!

Books by the same author:

- *Tantric Training in the Age of Ray 7*
- *New Tantrism*
- *New Tantrism, Introductory Themes*
- *Conclave of the Cryptic 7*
- *The Lion's Roar – The Master from Montreal*

Books by The Group of 5

- *The Eight Crystal Alliances – The Influence of Stones on the Personality*
- *Crystals & Stones: A Complete Guide to their Healing Properties*
- *A Parent's Guide to Crystals*

Upcoming book releases (translated from original French to English)

- *The Benefits of Stone and Crystal Elixirs: A User's Guide*
- *The Divine Arcana and the Stones of Destiny*
- *Quartztherapy — The Medicine of the Future*
- *The Teachings of Simhananda*
- *The Crystal Skull of Compassion — Daikomyo-zo Chenrezi*

Orange Palm Publications[©]
1206 Saint-Luc Boulevard, Suite 110
Saint-Jean-sur-Richelieu, Quebec, J2Y 1A5, Canada
info@palmpublications.com
www.palmpublications.com

_____

_____

_____

_____

Orange Palm Publications©
1206 Saint-Luc Boulevard, Suite 110
Saint-Jean-sur-Richelieu, Quebec, J2Y 1A5, Canada

Please complete and send us this card if you would like to be informed of our upcoming publications.

Name: _____

Address: _____

City: _____ Province/State: _____

Country: _____ Postal/Zip Code: _____

Email: _____

In which book did you find this card?

_____

Would you like to receive our catalogue? __ yes __ no

Would you like to be notified of new publications? __ yes __ no

Visit our website at www.PalmPublications.com